Zen and the Art of Solitude

Finding mindfulness, peace, and inner mastery in seclusion

By Carl E Conti

Dedication

I dedicate this to my wonderfully mindful and beautiful daughters, Lola Jay and Arabella.

Acknowledgments

I'd like to acknowledge the inspiration from: Robert Pirsig's wonderful book; bodhisattva, Jack Kerouac's mad-ramble scrolls; and my daughters, Lola and Bella, who always inspire me to creativity and introspection; and lastly my constant, 4-legged source of satorial bliss – Bruno.

Foreword

I wrote this book as a guide to using the methods and practices of Zen Buddhism and controlled isolation to assist in unlocking human potential.

Part I explores the nature of Zen Buddhism and the challenges of isolation in seeking peace and solitude in our noisy, reactive, and demanding lives.

In **Part II,** I develop practical ways in which you can implement these practices in an orderly and coherent manner to achieve peace and find solitude in your everyday routine. I also explore the Zen-like duality of the power of the ego as a fountainhead of human achievement, while at the same time, how its controlled abandonment removes hurdles to release and unfold potential.

I wrote it in a manner that it can be a continuing reference for the reader. Each chapter can stand alone, covering a relevant topic in building this mindset and weaving it into your daily lives. I hope you are able to benefit in some small way or even start a dramatic shift in your routine and mindset that benefits you immensely. Each chapter helps to stimulate thought and exploration into the material presented and ultimately, mindfulness in each minute within the hours of our everyday lives.

I've interwoven a young local artist Brenda Diamond's sketches into the fabric of the book, which I think adds a bit of texture and dimensional quality to it.

Each chapter stands alone with useful and, I hope, inspiring content that will elicit thought and introspection and a drive to delve deeper into the material that resonates with you. I feel that each time you pick up this book, if just to peruse one chapter, you will be rewarded with new knowledge and inspiration in digestible/actionable steps, which will aid you in your mindful journey.

Contents

Introduction

What essence of Zen might you uncover in a single breath, where the dance of fleeting thoughts dissolves into the boundless serenity of the present moment?

In the aspiring and tenacious, light of human ambition, where the eternal soul grapples with its own frail, temporal, bodily-stricken desires, one who seeks to find peace in our noisy, demanding world, or to master any endeavor—be it to achieve that peace and find joy in the humble toil of daily labor or the labyrinthine pursuits of an intricate craft—soon discovers a disquieting truth: the structure of their existence must shift.

It is not enough to labor blindly, to heap effort upon effort in the hope of triumph. No, a deeper alchemy is required. A map to guide the spirit through the shadowed valleys of mastery. Yet, in this fevered rush of aspiration, a subtle truth eludes the seeker: the change demanded is not merely of habit or method, muscle-memory or rote re-trace of what came before, but transforming of the very self—an inward voyage, perilous and uncharted.

Many, in their nescience, believe they can skirt this inner transformation, as if mastery were a mere garment to don without cost. They cling to the monotony of their days, their lives a procession of unexamined hours, while secretly yearning for the power that comes with true understanding. They gaze upon their own faculties as fixed stars, immutable and distant, incapable of being shaped by will or wisdom. And yet, in the quiet recesses of their hearts, there stirs a longing for that elusive spark—a push, a whisper of insight—that might set them free to achieve. This is the path we wish to explore here.

Before one can tread the path from solitude to the serene clarity of Zen, from Zen to the tranquil harbor of peace, and from peace to the hard-won shores of wisdom and mastery, it becomes apparent that the expectation of what mastery entails must be unmade and forged anew. It is not the cold perfection of the divine, for we are but men, frail and faltering, forever bound to err. Mastery is rather the marriage of a tempered mind and a deep well of knowledge- an eternal striving toward betterment, where each step forward is both triumph and torment. To seek mastery is to embrace the journey itself, to find passion in the pursuit of a horizon that ever recedes. In this, one may weave a rare and precious thing, a treasure coveted by the common heart yet rarely grasped: the power to craft one's own peace, not as a fleeting guest, but as a steadfast companion, born of the soul's quiet labor and sustained through the endless unfolding of the self. Solitude as meditation, total focus while at the same time total relaxation. Thus, our title.

It emanates first from Eugen Herrigel's *Zen in the Art of Archery*. A chronicle of a man's pilgrimage into the veiled heart of the mysterious world that is Japanese archery, known as **Kyūdō**. Published in 1948, it stands as a beacon for those wishing to explore a Zen approach to mastery of a spiritual communion and silent interplay between Zen Buddhism's austere grace and methodology through an aesthetic discipline such as archery.

Such is the voyage we now seek to undertake together, our minds unshod, novices before the vastness, yearning for some ineffable mastery that lies, perhaps, beyond the horizon of our knowing. I, a scribe of mechanisms and designs, shall chart this course with the stark clarity of 'first principles', tracing the shadowed paths of history's truths. My companion, a weaver of aesthetic visions, shall lend the hues of beauty to our endeavor, and together we aspire to render this journey a thing of reward, a tapestry unfurled. For, as I have learned in wanderings both corporeal and cerebral, the truest odysseys are those from which no man returns unchanged—where the soul, touched by some obscure alchemy, emerges transfigured, bearing the weight of revelations unuttered.

The best journeys are ones you do not return from. – Carl E. Conti

My aim is to forge a compass for this bewildering epoch, a framework of purpose, mindfulness, and the quiet resolve to seize achievement from the chaos, to navigate the heart's desire, the mind's will, and the soul's uncharted seas to unlock potential. Any task that renders all of one's inner ego to be demolished and a requirement of devotion to the things they have yet to learn can be transferred throughout all actions and pursuits throughout the course of one's life and missions. Such is my purpose in this labor, amid an age where the soul is besieged by a tempest of voices—information, falsehoods, comparison, diversions, a ceaseless clamor of distractions that swirl like leaves in a gale, yet where, too, the wonders of all human striving lie open, shimmering at the touch of a finger.

I would be remiss if I did not contrast this with one of my inspirations decades ago where conversely, Author Ayn Rand viewed the ego as the very core of individual identity and rational self-interest, central to her philosophy of Objectivism. She saw the ego as the source of personal motivation, driving individuals to pursue their own happiness and flourish through reason, purpose, and self-esteem. In her view, the ego is not a selfish, destructive force but a rational faculty that enables individuals to act in accordance with their own values and long-term interests, rejecting altruism's demand to sacrifice oneself for others. She argued that embracing one's ego leads to authentic, productive lives and mutually beneficial relationships based on voluntary exchange, not coercion or self-denial. This is evident in her works like The Fountainhead, where characters like Howard Roark embody ego-driven integrity and independence. Conversely, she criticized suppressing the ego as leading to dependency and moral compromise. We will also explore this zen-like duality; ego, as both an essential driving force and its ultimate barrier.

Herrigel's book and its importance arise not merely from its subject matter—archery—but from its attempt to show how any art form, practiced with dedication, can become a gateway to deeper self-realization. This is our goal in writing this book—in a time where we are immersed in a massive daily barrage of information; mis-information; amusements; attractions; distractions; curiosities of all types and in all manner and form of media, noise, and nonsense, while at the same time, having unprecedented access to all of life's wonders and human creations. So, we must prioritize the human experience of growth and humility that encourages higher levels of self-discovery. A journey that requires personal experience and practice; a journey that must be started somewhere; quite literally at our fingertips.

All minds alike desire a peek behind the curtain of humanity. My goal is to establish a framework to navigate this amazing era with inner purpose, mindfulness, focus, and achievement of goals that may not have been made yet.

Any art form, practiced with dedication, can become a gateway to deeper self-realization.

One of the most discussed elements in *Zen in the Art of Archery* is the phrase "It shoots." Herrigel's struggle revolved around the notion that the archer must not be the one releasing the arrow; rather, the release must happen on its own.

"It shoots."

This is tied to the broader Zen concept of **wu-wei** in Chinese or **mushin** in Japanese: <u>effortless action arising from a state of flow</u>. It implies that the ultimate mastery occurs only when the subject-object duality dissolves. In simpler terms, once one becomes unattached to the idea of succeeding, becoming so immersed in the process that it consumes their action, better results are seen.

Mastery occurs only when the subject-object duality dissolves

Zen Buddhism is often associated with the concept of emptiness, or **śūnyatā**. In the context of Kyūdō, emptiness refers to a state in which the self is not imposing willful control. The archer, the bow, and the target exist in a relationship free of ego-driven manipulation. Herrigel's narrative vividly shows how this emptiness is not a barren void but rather an openness that allows a higher intelligence, or "life force," to animate the body.

non-duality: *the dissolution of subject-object separation*

Although Herrigel focuses on archery, his insights resonate with other Japanese "Ways" such as swordsmanship (**Kendō**), flower arrangement (**Kadō**), tea ceremony (**Chadō**), and calligraphy (**Shodō**). Each of these arts shares the core Zen principles of form, mindfulness, and transcendence of ego. Mastery involves rigorous training in technique, yet the end goal is not simply technical perfection. Rather, it is the refinement of the practitioner's character, culminating in an artful expression that arises from a place of deep intuition.

Form, mindfulness, and transcendence of ego.

One of the most profound and core tensions in *Zen in the Art of Archery* lies in Herrigel's wrestling with his Western intellectual heritage. As a philosophy professor, he was accustomed to seeking logical explanations for phenomena. Yet in archery practice, reason often proved inadequate. While not dismissive of rational thought, Herrigel realized that Zen demanded a different mode of learning. It's a mode in which the mind's clinging to conceptual frameworks must relax to allow direct, pre-rational experience to come through. As Herrigel puts it: *"Man is a thinking reed, but his great works are done when he is not calculating and thinking. 'Childlikeness' has to be restored with long years of training in the art of self-forgetfulness."*

"Man is a thinking reed, but his great works are done when he is not calculating and thinking. 'Childlikeness' has to be restored with long years of training in the art of self-forgetfulness." – Zen and the Art of Archery

This tension is not entirely resolved by the book's end. Rather, Herrigel shows that he had to integrate his philosophical training with the experiential wisdom of Zen. This synthesis is not about jettisoning the intellect, abandoning reason and logic, but about recognizing its limits in the realm of spiritual or artistic practice. The importance of balance between logic and "supreme freedom" is found when one acknowledges their beginning and allows their humbleness to lead them to a larger grasp on their topic; *"I had realized, therefore, that there is and can be no other way to mysticism than the way of personal experience and suffering, and that, if this premise is lacking, all talk about it is so much empty chatter," – Zen and the Art of Archery*

By the final chapters, Herrigel acknowledges that Zen cannot be fully dissected or explained by the mind—it must be lived. The interplay between faith (or trust in the master, the process, and the intuitive faculties) and reason becomes the fuel that propels Herrigel's transformation. It is a dynamic interplay that many modern seekers grapple with, making Herrigel's account timeless and relevant.

Zen cannot be fully dissected or explained by the mind—it must be lived.

Although Herrigel's text focuses on a specific martial art, it contains seeds of Zen philosophy that illuminate the broader tradition. Zen, derived from the Chinese

Chan (and ultimately Indian **Dhyana**), emphasizes direct experience of reality, unmediated by conceptual thought. Key principles include **impermanence** (everything is in constant flux), **non-attachment** (freedom from clinging to desires or aversions), and **non-duality** (the dissolution of subject-object separation).

Herrigel's archery practice becomes a microcosm for understanding these concepts. The ephemeral nature of each shot illustrates impermanence. The repeated exhortations to "let go" point to non-attachment, and the merging of archer, bow, and target represents non-duality. By consistently folding these themes into his narrative, for me, Herrigel's book offers a vital functional primer on Zen for Western audiences who might have found the more abstract aspects of Buddhist philosophy difficult to grasp. Archery provides a concrete application of Zen principles: mind and action converge seamlessly in a single, unselfconscious motion, although these parameters and concepts can be extended to any endeavor.

Archery provides a concrete illustration: mind and action converge seamlessly in a single, unselfconscious motion

One of the most poetic images in Herrigel's account is the phenomenon of **stillness in motion**. When the arrow releases effortlessly, it seems as though time stands still. There is action—an arrow traveling through space—yet there is also a profound stillness in the archer's mind. This duality captures a core Zen paradox: dynamic activity and meditative stillness are not opposite; they can coexist in a single moment. Some current and more widely relatable examples of this stillness in motion can be found when exercising or training the body through the practice of yoga; as our physical bodies stay in organized and methodical motion, our minds are focused on the connection of breath, muscle to mind connection, and underneath these variables, calmness and lack of other thought processes.

Zen paradox: dynamic activity and meditative stillness are not opposites; they can coexist in a single moment

In many Zen arts, practitioners cultivate an inner calm that persists even under pressure or rapid movement. Samurai warriors, for example, were trained to maintain mental clarity and composure in the heat of battle. For Herrigel, archery became a safe container for experimenting with this principle. His success in embodying stillness in motion later informed us how he handled other challenges, reflecting the Zen idea that true calm originates within and accompanies us wherever we go, rather than being dictated solely by external circumstances. I've experienced this state profoundly in several motorcycle trips across the country. The mental state is one of profound and intense focus, while at the same time a deep calm, a stillness within, processing everything around you as you are immersed in the scene. Unlike driving in a car, where the scenery can be more of a movie/screen viewing. Just as reading a book demands 90% of your conscious attention, watching a movie really requires you to do it with a 10-15% commitment.

Many times you become very meditative, conscious of your own breath, while processing everything your senses bring.

Breathing emerges as a subtle but crucial component of Herrigel's training. Zen practices often emphasize **proper breathing** as the key to harmonizing mind and body. In archery, the breath sets the rhythm for drawing the bow and releasing the arrow. When breath is calm and centered, movements are fluid and intuitive. When breath is erratic—perhaps due to nervousness or frustration—technique suffers. This applies in many aspects, for instance, when I am in the process of executing a detailed painting, not only am I required to reject all outward thoughts that may distract my steady hand and focus, but I must keep my breathing organized for crisp, steady lines and for the experience to stay peaceful, rather than frustrating and tedious.

Herrigel's teacher often focused on the breath rather than providing elaborate instructions on stance or aim. From a Zen perspective, the breath is the bridge between the conscious and subconscious, the voluntary and involuntary. Observing the breath can reveal hidden tensions, anxieties, or mental wandering. Mastery of the breath thus becomes mastery of the mind. In the modern era, many mindfulness-based therapies incorporate breath awareness for similar reasons: it grounds attention in the present moment and fosters emotional regulation.

From a Zen perspective, the breath is the bridge between the conscious and subconscious, the voluntary and involuntary.

While most archers fixate on hitting the bullseye, in Herrigel's journey, the target assumes a more symbolic dimension. It becomes an object that helps reveal the archer's interior landscape. In Zen, the target is both literal and metaphorical. Literally, it is the straw-wrapped disc that receives the arrow. Metaphorically, it is the "goal" or the "ultimate truth" that one seeks in practice. Yet ironically, the Zen archer must release the desire to hit the target perfectly in order to *truly* hit it.

This paradox speaks to the heart of Zen: letting go of the desire for results can paradoxically lead to better results, because one's mind is no longer fragmented by expectation. Herrigel's moments of greatest success come when he transcends the usual subject-object dynamic, merging with the bow so completely that the shot is an expression of unity rather than a means to an end. In daily life, the "target" could be our aspirations or dreams, and the same principle applies; sometimes, relinquishing rigid control is what allows grace to enter.

In fact, the phrase "It shoots" resonates with modern concepts of **flow state**, as popularized by psychologist Mihaly Csikszentmihalyi. A flow state involves complete absorption in an activity to the point that the sense of self-consciousness vanishes. Herrigel's descriptions align strikingly with these contemporary psychological frameworks, indicating that his personal encounter with Zen archery tapped into universal human experiences now recognized in Western scientific research.

"It shoots."

Zen does not encourage moralizing or preaching; instead, it fosters character growth through direct encounter with one's limitations. Each frustration, every missed shot, becomes an invitation to examine the ego, let go of reactivity, and recommit to the present. Over time, this approach can reshape not only how one practices an art but also how one lives day to day. In a broader sense, Herrigel's narrative serves as a case study for the **transformative power of dedicated practice**—a principle applicable across various disciplines, from martial arts to creative writing and beyond.

If one were to distill *Zen in the Art of Archery* to a single key lesson, it might be **letting go**. Letting go of conscious control, letting go of ego, and letting go of outcomes. This letting go does not imply passivity or sloppiness; it is instead a focused surrender that arises from deep trust in the process. Paradoxically, when the student truly lets go, the shot is most accurate, the movement is most graceful, and the experience is most fulfilling.

Focused surrender

Each new challenge, whether tension in the bow, impatience with progress, or confusion about the master's guidance, carries the hidden instruction to release. In modern self-help terminology, we might call this "getting out of your own way." In Zen parlance, it is the dissolution of the small self into a larger awareness. Herrigel's emphasis on letting go resonates with spiritual seekers across traditions, affirming a universal principle: that true creativity and clarity often emerge when we relinquish the need to micromanage reality.

⑥ The Interplay of Discipline and Freedom

Another salient theme is the **interplay of discipline and freedom**. At first glance, the strict forms and repetitive drills of Kyūdō seem antithetical to creative freedom. Yet Herrigel's eventual discovery was that discipline fosters true freedom. By internalizing the form to a point where it becomes second nature, one transcends conscious effort, moving with an unimpeded spontaneity.

Discipline fosters true freedom

This stands in contrast to the misunderstanding that freedom means "doing whatever one wants." In Zen, freedom arises when the practitioner merges so completely with the practice that the boundaries between self and action dissolve. This phenomenon is observed in martial arts, music, and other disciplines where countless hours of practice pave the way for a seemingly effortless, expressive performance. Structured discipline can open the doors to spontaneous creativity and liberated movement.

Zen in the Art of Archery raises the question of **enlightenment,** but does not explicitly answer: Is Herrigel's moment of effortless release the same as spiritual enlightenment, or is it merely a glimpse? Zen tradition differentiates between partial insights (**kenshō**) and the more profound, sustained realization of **satori,** an **"**awakening" or "enlightenment". Herrigel's experience appears more like a kenshō—a valuable glimpse into the deeper reality of non-duality.

From a Freudian perspective, the passage from *Zen in the Art of Archery* illustrates a profound intrapsychic conflict within Herrigel, rooted in the dynamics between the ego, the id, and the superego. Freud's structural model of the psyche presents the ego as the rational mediator between the impulsive id (driven by primal instincts and unconscious desires) and the moralistic superego (internalized societal norms and ideals). Herrigel's *"wrestling with his Western intellectual heritage"* can be seen as an ego-dominated struggle, where his role as a philosophy professor embodies the ego's reliance on logic, reason, and conceptual frameworks to maintain control and order in the face of reality. This Western mindset, steeped in Enlightenment rationality, functions as a defensive fortress against the chaotic, pre-rational forces of the id—much like how the ego employs repression or intellectualization as defense mechanisms to ward off anxiety from unconscious impulses.

The core tension arises when archery practice exposes the inadequacy of this rational approach. In Freudian terms, Zen's demand for a "different mode of learning" represents a call to loosen the ego's grip, allowing the id's instinctual, non-verbal energies to emerge unfiltered. The "direct, pre-rational experience" Herrigel must embrace mirrors the id's raw, pleasure-seeking drives, which operate beyond logic and language—similar to the dream work or primary process thinking in Freud's theory, where symbols and intuitions bypass secondary (rational) processes. Herrigel's initial resistance to this shift could be interpreted as ego anxiety: the fear of regression to a more primitive, id-dominated state, evoking the dread of losing one's civilized self (a concept Freud explored in *Civilization and Its Discontents*, where cultural progress demands suppression of instincts). By "relaxing" the mind's "clinging to conceptual frameworks," Herrigel is essentially undergoing a form of psychoanalytic surrender, akin to free association, where the ego steps aside to let repressed unconscious material surface.

Furthermore, the superego plays a subtle role here as the internalized voice of Western academia and philosophy, which Herrigel is "not dismissive of" but must transcend. This creates a superego-ego alliance that initially hinders progress, enforcing ideals of intellectual mastery and control. The archery practice, then, acts as a therapeutic arena, much like the analytic couch, compelling Herrigel to confront and integrate these conflicting psychic forces. Ultimately, the passage suggests a path toward psychic wholeness: not the annihilation of the ego, but its humbling, allowing for a healthier balance where the id's vitality infuses conscious experience without overwhelming it. This aligns with Freud's later ideas on ego integration, where true maturity involves accessing the unconscious without defensive barriers, leading to a more authentic self—echoing Herrigel's journey from intellectual rigidity to Zen enlightenment.

Herrigel's book concludes without claiming any ultimate attainment. Herrigel acknowledges his continuing path, suggesting that one lifetime might not suffice to plumb the depths of Zen. This humility aligns with Zen's perspective that there is always more to learn, more layers to shed. Readers are thus encouraged to see the book not as a definitive statement on enlightenment but as an honest account of one man's journey and the insights he gleaned along the way. We offer a Koan as one approach to this insight.

A young archer, eager to hit the target, drew his bow with force and focus. His arrows flew, yet none struck true. Frustrated, he sought the master.

"Master," he said, *"I aim with all my might, yet the target eludes me. What must I do?"*

The master took the bow, closed his eyes, and released an arrow. It pierced the target's heart.

"Did you aim?" the archer asked.

"I did not aim," the master replied. *"The bow, the arrow, the target—they are one. When you cease to strive, the arrow finds its way."*

The archer pondered this. Years passed. One day, he drew his bow, forgot himself, and let go. The arrow flew, and the target was no more.

Whether one is seeking to master a profession, a martial artist, a musician, an artist in another medium, or simply a curious soul seeking balance in a hectic world, these insights offer guidance. The essence of his teaching is universal: through consistent, mindful practice, we can break free of our self-imposed constraints and experience a deeper harmony with life itself. While the book has sparked debates over its authenticity and interpretations, its core message remains powerfully relevant: the true target lies within, and the arrow that finds it is guided by an intelligence beyond the calculating mind. In that timeless moment of release—"It shoots"—we glimpse the possibility that life, too, can unfold with the same grace and effortless precision.

You have to know everything, then you have to forget it all. The most difficult thing, I think, in being a musician is to get out of the way." – John McLaughlin (virtuoso guitarist)

It was more than a decade ago, amid the shadowed recesses of a painful personal event—an abrupt failing tore the fabric of my being and plunged me into abysmal depths of self-scrutiny—that I first was pulled into the cleansing call of solitude, whence, I now surmise, this volume took its first stir. In those days, the flickering apparition of television ("the lightbox" as I referred to it) loomed as a still monstrous invader upon the human psyche, a spectral intruder that preyed upon the unguarded soul; and no sooner had the hush of isolation descended, enveloping me in its inexorable embrace, than I discerned the true nature of that luminous casket, that "light box,"—a contrivance, in the mordant words of Fred Allen, *"devised to enable those who can do nothing, are viewed vacuously by those with nothing to do."*

And through that epoch, extending into the eighteen months that followed, a voyage into uncharted seas, I immersed myself in reading, in contemplation, and in the austere discipline of meditation, with an intensity unknown to my wandering spirit. My reading became voracious, and upon concluding each work, I would hurl it against the vast expanse of a wall, tracing the scar of its impact and inscribing therein the title. A scar of a healed psyche, perhaps? One revelation emerged from this ritual with crystalline force: a book demands the devotion of nine-tenths of one's vigilance and intellect, a surrender to its depths as profound as the ocean's claim upon the mariner; whereas television, that insidious counterpart, exacts but a tenth—or less—of the mind's faculties, absorbing them in a shallow, listless drift. How arduous it proves, indeed, to forge the architecture of one's inner self when the idle hours of existence are squandered upon pursuits that summon so meager a portion of our essence, leaving the soul adrift in the fog of triviality.

In the intervening years and decades, so came the internet, *mosaic* query of academic papers then Mozilla and Netscape that helped navigate the ever increasing content that was available to today where we live in a world saturated with noise, but also calls, digital alerts, podcasts, social media comments and implied commitments, and a constant pull away from self and toward a quality of being a node on a neural network. Your phone is constantly intervening in your psyche unannounced. This great information source can sometimes provide knowledge if properly guided with parameters and discipline.

Yet, in the quiet moments when we stand apart from the commotion, we can hear the gentle whisper of solitude calling us home. This book explores how Zen principles can guide us to find peace, clarity, and self-understanding in the stillness of aloneness.

The best journey, is one that you do not return from. – Carl E. Conti

It is my hope and goal to take you on a journey that you will not return from, that at the end, you will not be the person that started the journey. A lofty goal with heavy responsibility.

My self-study and meditation evolved, then came *Zen and the Art of Motorcycle Maintenance: An Inquiry into Values* by Robert M. Pirsig, a philosophical novel that intertwines a cross-country motorcycle journey with deep reflections on life, technology, and the pursuit of what the author refers to as "quality".

I rode cross country several times on my Roadking in this decade and often reflected on this brilliant novel that was: a narrative; an autobiography; and ultimately a philosophical discourse—exploring the tension between rational thought and intuitive understanding.

The book follows an unnamed narrator, later revealed to be the author himself, on a motorcycle trip from Minnesota to California with his young son, Chris, and two friends, John and Sylvia Sutherland. The physical journey serves as a framework for a deeper intellectual and emotional exploration. The narrator, a former philosophy scholar, reflects on his past self, referred to as "Phaedrus," a brilliant but troubled figure whose obsession with defining "Quality" led to a mental breakdown and institutionalization. The narrative alternates between the present-day trip, memories of Phaedrus's life, and philosophical "Chautauquas"— extended reflections on life's big questions.

"Chautauquas"—extended reflections on life's big questions

The motorcycle is both a literal vehicle and a metaphor for the narrator's approach to life. He contrasts his own meticulous, analytical maintenance of his bike with John and Sylvia's romantic, intuitive avoidance of mechanical details. This sets the stage for the book's central inquiry: reconciling the "classical" (rational, analytical) and "romantic" (intuitive, aesthetic) ways of understanding the world. As the trip progresses, the narrator grapples with his fractured relationship with Chris, haunted by Phaedrus's legacy and his own fear of slipping back into madness. The journey becomes a quest for self-reconciliation and a deeper connection with his son.

"classical" (rational, analytical) and "romantic" (intuitive, aesthetic) ways of understanding the world

Phaedrus, a university instructor, became consumed with understanding Quality—a concept he saw as fundamental yet undefinable by traditional philosophy. His relentless inquiry alienated colleagues, strained his family, and ultimately led to his psychological collapse. The narrator, now rebuilt after electroshock therapy, seeks to make sense of Phaedrus's ideas while protecting himself and Chris from their destructive potential.

At the heart of the book is Pirsig's exploration of Quality, a concept he argues underlies both rational and intuitive experiences. Quality, for Pirsig, is not merely subjective or objective but a pre-intellectual reality that exists before categorization. It is the "knife-edge" of experience, the moment of pure perception before thought divides the world into subject and object. What makes this journey so compelling is Phaedrus's academic pursuit of Quality leads him to challenge Western philosophy's dualistic frameworks, drawing upon thinkers like Plato, Aristotle, and Eastern philosophies such as Zen and Taoism.

Pirsig uses the metaphor of motorcycle maintenance to illustrate Quality in action. A well-maintained bike reflects care, attention, and an intuitive grasp of the machine's needs, blending technical precision with aesthetic satisfaction. The narrator critiques modern society's alienation from technology, arguing that understanding and caring for machines fosters a sense of unity with the world. This contrasts with the Sutherlands' romantic rejection of technology, which the narrator sees as a refusal to engage with reality's complexity.

Pirsig's "Metaphysics of Quality" proposes that Quality is the source of all existence, preceding both mind and matter. He rejects the subject-object dichotomy, suggesting that reality is a dynamic interplay of values. This philosophy draws heavily on Zen Buddhism's emphasis on direct experience and non-dualistic thinking. For example, the narrator describes moments of "just being" on the motorcycle, where rider, machine, and landscape merge into a single, Quality-filled experience. These insights are not merely abstract; they guide the narrator's efforts to live authentically.

Quality is the source of all existence, preceding both mind and matter

⑥ Emotional and Personal Resolution

The book's emotional core lies in the narrator's struggle to reconnect with Chris, who senses his father's emotional distance and carries unspoken grief over their fractured past. The narrator's fear of Phaedrus's return—symbolized by recurring dreams and moments of intellectual intensity—creates a barrier between them. As the journey nears its end in California, the narrator confronts these fears, realizing that Phaedrus's ideas, while dangerous in their extremes, hold truths worth embracing.

A pivotal moment occurs when Chris, frustrated and tearful, demands his father's attention. The narrator, prompted by this raw emotional plea, begins to integrate Phaedrus's insights with his present self. He acknowledges Quality as a lived experience, not just an intellectual construct, and finds peace in small, authentic moments with Chris, like sharing a quiet conversation or fixing the bike together. The book closes with a sense of cautious hope: the narrator and Chris ride off, their relationship strengthened, and the narrator is more at peace with his past.

The book's blend of narrative and philosophy makes it accessible yet profound, inviting readers to reflect on their own values. The book's cultural impact is significant, selling millions of copies and influencing thinkers, educators, and artists for decades, myself included. Its exploration of mental health, particularly through Phaedrus' breakdown, offers a compassionate portrayal of intellectual obsession and recovery.

In closing, we offer a Zen Koan on the duality of ego when exploring human potential.

A monk asked the master, *"The ego's virtues—rationality, pride, and independence—as the path to a fulfilled life. Yet Zen teaches us to abandon the ego to find wisdom. How can these truths coexist?"*

The master replied, *"A proud tree stands tall, its roots gripping the earth, yet it sways with the wind. Is it the tree's strength or it's yielding that keeps it whole?"*

Part I

Chapter 1: The Call of Solitude

Solitude *[sol-i-tood, -tyood]*

noun

1. *the state of being or living alone; seclusion.*

Synonyms: *privacy, retirement*

2. *remoteness from habitations, as of a place; absence of human activity.*

Synonyms: *loneliness*

3. *a lonely, unfrequented place.*

Solitude is not an escape; it is a return—return to the self that is usually drowned out by the cacophony of life. Where noise ceases, wisdom begins to speak.

⑥ The Whispers Beneath the Noise

We live in a society that seems to grow louder by the day—relentless notifications from our electronic devices, the hum of 24/7 and 365 daily news cycle, the pull of podcasts, the constant pressure to stay visible on social media, and stay responsive to our personal text threads. Rarely does our environment, let alone our minds, experience a moment of genuine quiet. We are encouraged to perform, to produce, to socialize, and to fill every gap in our schedules. During periods where we fail to do so, we are conditioned to feel as if we are falling behind.

Yet, beneath the surface of all this commotion, something gentler and more profound is trying to get our attention. There comes a time—often in the middle of a busy city street or during a sleepless night—when we hear a subtle call, a faint invitation to step away from the noise and discover what lies within. This is the call to solitude, a stirring that might feel both comforting and unsettling. It is comforting because a part of us knows we long for rest and reflection, and it is unsettling because we fear what we might find if we sit quietly with ourselves.

Solitude offers a chance to reconnect with the present moment. It provides room for honest self-dialogue and the unfiltered expression of our deepest thoughts and emotions. However, the path toward solitude can be intimidating. More often than not, we avoid time uninterrupted with our thoughts because of our own unanswered questions, insecurities, and flaws that we don't easily give room to breathe without spiraling.

Our culture often labels aloneness as "loneliness," suggesting that isolation is undesirable. We might worry that time spent alone signals antisocial tendencies or emotional problems. In reality, solitude can be a source of immense strength, clarity, and joy. It is in this serene space, free from external expectations, that we learn who we really are. It is the one place we can be honest with ourselves, free of judgement, if we let go of the judgement ourselves.

⑥ Differentiating Loneliness from Solitude

Before delving into the depths of solitude, it is crucial to acknowledge the difference between solitude and loneliness. While both states involve a physical separation from others, they diverge dramatically in emotional tone and psychological impact.

Loneliness is often characterized by a sense of disconnection or a longing for companionship. It arises when we desire intimacy or validation from others and find ourselves lacking it. Loneliness can make us feel unworthy, invisible, or unloved.

Solitude, on the other hand, is a conscious choice to be alone for a period of time. Rather than feeling like a burden, solitude can be a wellspring of creative energy and insight. It is a deliberate retreat into oneself—a chance to cultivate mindfulness, self-care, and perspective.

One of the first steps in heeding the call to solitude is understanding that time alone does not inherently mean feeling lonely. Solitude can become a sacred space for healing and rejuvenation. When we carry this mindset forward, we transform isolation into an opportunity rather than a punishment.

⑥ Why We Resist the Call

Despite the potential benefits, many of us instinctively resist the call to solitude. Contemporary life conditions us to remain perpetually busy and connected. Each moment we spend in quiet reflection can feel like time *wasted*—when we could be checking our emails, scrolling through social media, or responding to someone's message. There is also the possibility of encountering uncomfortable emotions once the external distractions fade away.

Some common reasons we might resist solitude:

1. **Fear of Facing Ourselves:** When we remove the usual noise and chatter, unresolved issues and repressed emotions can surface. The fear of confronting old wounds or insecurities can keep us running from silence.
2. **Social Conditioning:** People often believe that having a large social network or being constantly "on the go" is a sign of success. Taking time alone may be perceived as laziness, selfishness, or antisocial behavior.

3. **Pressure to be Productive:** Modern culture equates busyness with importance. We tend to measure our worth by what we accomplish in a day. Solitude, perceived as "doing nothing," challenges this paradigm.
4. **Habitual Distraction:** Many of us have developed habits of immediate gratification, filling every spare second with music, videos, podcasts, or messages. These habits can become so ingrained that silence feels unnatural at first.

Understanding these hurdles helps normalize the struggle. Acknowledging them is an essential step. Once we see these obstacles clearly, we can choose to move through them with understanding, resolve, and courage.

⑤ The Zen Perspective on Solitude

Zen, a school of Mahayana Buddhism, often emphasizes direct experience over conceptual knowledge. At its core, Zen invites practitioners to cultivate *mindfulness*—a state of open, non-judgmental awareness of the present moment. It also highlights the benefits of silent meditation, or *zazen*, as a tool for self-discovery. I will devote an entire chapter in Part II to Zazen.

In Zen tradition, solitude is not meant to be a permanent withdrawal from life but rather a crucible for insight. Historically, many Zen monks and nuns have spent prolonged periods in hermitages or remote temples, dedicating themselves to meditation and introspection. This is not done out of misanthropy or avoidance; it is a deliberate way to cut through mental clutter and cultivate a clear mind. Paradoxically, stepping away from society for a while allows deeper, more empathetic engagement with it when one returns. This practice can be done repeatedly, used as a tool we can pick up when needed and put down once rejuvenated.

At its heart, Zen teaches us that stillness and silence are gateways to wisdom. As we sit in solitude, we become aware of our internal workings—our fleeting thoughts, shifting moods, and habitual patterns. This heightened awareness, free from external input, can reveal profound truths about the nature of our own mind and reality.

A time to "defragment" our mind if you will as we did hard drives in the early days of computers. The analogy seems cold and impersonal, yet it does have merit in the sense that it organizes like thoughts, discards garbage and makes room for what is important going forward.

⑤ Nature's Role in the Call

A compelling aspect of solitude is the natural world's capacity to host and nurture it. Throughout history, countless sages, philosophers, and poets have sought hermitage in forests, deserts, and mountains. The rhythmic sounds of nature—

the wind rustling leaves, the distant call of birds, the gentle flow of a stream—have a soothing effect on the mind.

In these natural settings, silence is not an absence but a rich tapestry of subtle sounds and sensations. Here, solitude effortlessly mingles with *connection*: connection to the earth, to animals and plants, and ultimately to ourselves. The call to solitude can often feel strongest when we are surrounded by nature's grandeur. The connection to nature, whether knowingly or unknowingly, reminds us of the vast existence and creation around us, both grounding our minds and bodies.

If you find it challenging to carve out alone time in a busy city, consider making periodic excursions to a local park, garden, or nature reserve. Allow the sights and sounds of the natural environment to guide you into a slower pace. Notice how your breath synchronizes with the ebb and flow of wind through the trees. It is no accident that the path to solitude feels easier when you leave behind concrete walls and artificial or mechanized noise.

⑥ Answering the Call in Everyday Life

Solitude need not mean a month-long retreat in a mountain cabin. While extended periods of seclusion can be transformative, day-to-day life also offers micro-opportunities for stepping into quiet spaces. We explore both here and all points in between.

⑥ The Emotional Landscape of Solitude

When we finally settle into solitude, we may be surprised by the emotional terrain that unfolds. Sometimes it feels like a gentle haven, a warm embrace of peace and contentment. Other times, we encounter sharp pangs of loneliness or the re-emergence of old regrets and fears.

- **Moments of Peace:** Solitude can bring a sense of relief, like sinking into a soft armchair at the end of a long day. There is a sweetness in knowing that you have permission to just *be*, with no one making demands or judging you.
- **Resurfacing Wounds:** The mind may wander to painful memories, unresolved conflicts, or longings we have yet to fulfill. Rather than seeing this as a failure of solitude, view it as an invitation to observe these wounds kindly. Journaling, meditating, or simply breathing through these emotions can help them transform.
- **Fresh Insights and Creativity:** Many people report bursts of inspiration or clarity when they spend time alone. With no external noise, the mind can tap into its deeper layers, generating new ideas or connecting old dots.
- **Ego and Identity Shifts:** Extended solitude can challenge our self-image. Without the usual feedback from others, you may begin to question who

you are beyond your job title, social role, or reputation. This questioning can be unsettling yet liberating—it opens the door to a truer sense of self.

Emotions are part of the journey, not obstacles to it. Each feeling that arises—whether pleasant, painful, or neutral—has something to teach us and should be analyzed as such for personal growth. Solitude gives us the space and patience to listen to these internal messages and respond with understanding. It creates a safe space for all truths to exist.

I will explore this in some detail in Part II.

⑥ Practical Preparations

If you feel a strong pull toward solitude—maybe a weekend away, a daily meditation regimen, or a more extended retreat—there are practical steps to prepare:

1. **Set Clear Intentions:** Why do you want to spend time in solitude? Is it for rest, creative work, spiritual insight, or emotional healing? Having a clear intention can guide your choices and help you stay committed.
2. **Communicate with Others:** If you live with family, friends, or a partner, let them know about your plan. Explain that your need for alone time is not a rejection of them but a personal practice for renewal. Setting boundaries in a kind and open way can prevent misunderstandings and help protect the goal you are striving for without feelings of guilt.
3. **Curate Your Environment:** Decide where you will practice solitude. If you cannot travel, create a quiet corner in your home. Add elements that invite calm—soft lighting, cushions, a journal or sketchbook, perhaps some plants or natural objects that soothe your senses.
4. **Leave Technology Behind (Set Limits):** If your goal is a deeper inward journey, consider turning off your phone or placing it in another room. Let loved ones know how to contact you in an emergency, but otherwise give yourself the gift of being "off-grid."
5. **Gather Supplies for Comfort:** If you are going on a longer retreat, pack wholesome snacks, plenty of water, and perhaps some reading materials that foster reflection rather than distraction. Comfort items like a cozy blanket or a favorite tea can also encourage you to settle in.

Nurture the journey of building trust in yourself through the motions of self-care, inevitably involving the call to solitude. Treat this preparation as a ritual that signals to both your mind and body: *"I am choosing to answer the call. I am choosing to slow down and listen"*.

⑥ Overcoming Common Myths and Misconceptions

Despite the growing cultural acceptance of mindfulness and meditation, misconceptions about solitude abound. Tackling these misunderstandings can help you confidently move forward.

Myth 1: Solitude is for Introverts Only.

> Although introverts may naturally gravitate toward solitude, extroverts can find it equally transformative. In fact, those who recharge through social interaction might discover how periodic alone time balances their energy and sharpens their interpersonal skills.

Myth 2: Solitude is Wasting Time.

> Solitude can be one of the most productive uses of your time—albeit in a less conventional sense. Emotional processing, creative insight, and personal growth all flourish in the space of quiet. The benefits extend into your work and relationships, making solitude an investment as well as a luxury.

Myth 3: Wanting Solitude Means You Don't Value Relationships.

> On the contrary, people who cultivate regular alone time often develop healthier connections because they know themselves better. Self-awareness fosters compassion and authenticity, qualities that enrich all relationships. This time also allows empathy and a direction of thoughts that is harder to reach with distraction and/or the presence of others.

Myth 4: Solitude Must Be Strict Isolation.

> True solitude is more about an internal state than physical separation. You can feel deeply connected to yourself even in a bustling environment if you practice mindfulness. Conversely, you can be physically alone yet mentally scattered by electronic distractions. Genuine solitude involves intentional presence, not just an empty room.

By dispelling these myths, you free yourself from societal or self-imposed stigmas and step into solitude as a conscious, life-affirming practice.

⑥ Embracing the Invitation

The call to solitude is not a demand; it is an invitation. You are not forced into stillness but rather *invited* to explore what lies beyond the noise. Accepting this invitation can be as simple as sitting quietly on your balcony at dawn, letting your thoughts float by like clouds in the sky. Over time, you may find yourself longing for these moments of peace more and more, ultimately integrating them into a lifelong practice.

When we answer solitude's call, we discover parts of ourselves that might remain hidden amid constant company. We also fall prey to internal battles we avoid through distraction that, while underlying, affect our everyday reactions without us realizing. In stillness, we realize that our worth is not contingent on what we do but on who we *are*. We begin to see that the hustle and bustle can mask a deep inner reservoir of calm and wisdom just waiting to be fed.

⊚ To embark on this journey:

1. **Listen Inwardly:** Pay attention to the subtle cues in your body and mind that tell you it's time to rest and reflect.
2. **Welcome Discomfort:** Understand that unresolved feelings may surface, and that's okay. Welcome them in a safe, gentle way.
3. **Stay Curious:** Approach your alone time with an open, child-like curiosity—ready to learn, to observe, and to grow.
4. **Return to the World Renewed:** Once you leave the stillness, notice how your sense of presence carries over into conversations, decisions, and daily responsibilities. You might find that you have more patience, clarity, and empathy.

The call to solitude is timeless; it has echoed through centuries of spiritual traditions, philosophical musings, and artistic expressions. From a small daily practice to an extended retreat, solitude remains one of humanity's most potent tools for self-discovery. It reconnects us with ourselves and, paradoxically, deepens our ability to connect with others.

Ultimately, solitude does not sever us from life. It is not an escape but a *return*— a return to the quiet center from which we can see the world and ourselves more clearly. A center we all have in common. When you feel that gentle pull to step away from the noise, trust that call. Within the stillness, you might just hear the voice of your own deepest wisdom speaking softly, guiding you toward greater peace, insight, compassion, and your deepest desires.

If you have felt even the slightest yearning for solitude, take it as a sign that part of you is ready to grow through silence. Recognize that every step you take—be it a few minutes of daily meditation or a weekend spent off-grid—empowers you to explore the vast landscape of your inner world. Responding to the call to solitude is a gift that only you can grant yourself. In that serene space, you may find answers to questions you never thought to ask and discover a tranquility that endures well beyond your time alone.

In the final chapter of Part I, I present examples of a few individuals that chose extended isolation in order to achieve focus and uninterrupted solitude, in order to achieve great works of art.

Chapter 2: What is Zen? Foundations and Philosophy

While Zen is often associated with temples and monks, it also offers universal lessons for the modern seeker: simplicity, attentiveness, and a compassionate heart.

☀ First Principles

When exploring a new field of knowledge, one should take a "first principles" approach that involves breaking down complex topics or problems into their most fundamental truths and reasoning from there, rather than relying on assumptions or conventional wisdom.

One of the greatest inventors of our day, Elon Musk, often refers to this, and a concise description of the method of first principles thinking: *(1) Identify and Challenge Assumptions:* Identify the source of the knowledge, its foundations, and early history. Proceed from a good structural foundation, then *(2) Break it down to Fundamental Truths:* Reduce the topic/problem to its core components—basic facts or truths that are indisputable. These are the "first principles" that cannot be simplified further, often rooted in physics, economics, or other foundational disciplines. Once these are established, *(3) Reason Up from Scratch:* Build a solution using only these fundamental truths, free from preconceived notions or traditional methods. This involves asking, "What do we *know* to be true, and what can we logically build from that?" From there *(4) Innovate Without Constraints:* By ignoring how things are "usually done," first principles thinking encourages creative solutions that may disrupt established norms.

With that, I shall define the Foundations of Zen so we can build from there.

☀ What Is Zen? Foundations and Philosophy

Zen, at its core, defies simple definitions. It is a living tradition rooted in the Buddhist teachings that arrived in China from India and eventually flourished in Japan, Korea, Vietnam, and beyond. Yet, to say Zen is purely a sect of Buddhism does not capture the full breadth of its philosophy, practice, and cultural influence. Zen transcends dogmatic boundaries and encourages direct insight into the nature of reality, often through simple daily activities.

In exploring the foundations and philosophy of Zen, we embark on a journey that is both historical and personal, as it challenges our assumptions and invites us to engage with everyday existence in a radical, mindful way. Over the course of these pages, we will delve into the origins of Zen, examine its philosophical underpinnings, and explore how Zen practice has shaped—and continues to shape—spirituality and cultural life around the world.

❋ Historical Roots of Zen

Zen originates from the Sanskrit word **dhyāna**, meaning "meditation," and traces its beginnings to the historical Buddha, Siddhartha Gautama, who lived and taught in India approximately 2,500 years ago. The Buddha emphasized the importance of meditation, mindfulness, and ethical conduct as a means to end suffering and achieve liberation. Over the centuries, Buddhism spread from India to other parts of Asia. In China, it encountered Daoism, Confucianism, and local cultural expressions, which influenced how Buddhist teachings were interpreted and practiced.

*Zen originates from the Sanskrit word **dhyāna**, meaning "meditation,"*

By the 6th century CE, the Indian monk Bodhidharma is traditionally credited with bringing this meditative form of Buddhism to China. It was called **Chan** in Chinese—a transliteration of the Sanskrit term *dhyāna*—and focused on direct insight into one's nature rather than reliance on doctrinal study or scriptural knowledge alone. Chan masters in China often lived in monastic communities that were somewhat austere, emphasizing simplicity and the rigorous practice of **zazen** (sitting meditation). Over time, the Chan tradition developed distinctive features, such as the use of **kung'an** or **gōng'àn** (known in Japanese as *koans*), which are paradoxical anecdotes or questions meant to break through ordinary patterns of thinking.

Eventually, several distinct schools formed within Chan. Some emphasized sudden awakening (as in the **Linji** or **Rinzai** lineage), while others emphasized gradual cultivation (as in the **Caodong** or **Sōtō** lineage). As Chan Buddhism migrated to Korea (where it became **Seon**) and later to Japan (where it became **Zen**), it further adapted to local cultures. The Japanese Zen masters reinterpreted Chan texts and incorporated aesthetic, artistic, and cultural elements into their spiritual practice. The result was a unique blend of ascetic discipline, minimalist aesthetics, and poetic expression.

❋ Key Figures and the Spread of Zen

While Bodhidharma is widely considered the "first patriarch" of Chan in China, other significant figures contributed to the spread of Zen philosophy and practice. In China, the Sixth Patriarch **Huineng** (638–713) wrote (or inspired) the famous *Platform Sutra*, which articulated a perspective of "sudden enlightenment." Huineng's teaching emphasized that one's original nature is inherently pure and that genuine insight can occur spontaneously, without gradual stages of progress. This notion contrasted with other schools that emphasized methodical cultivation over time.

Later, as Chan took shape in China, iconic masters like **Linji Yixuan** (d. 866) used energetic and sometimes shocking teaching methods—shouts, slaps, paradoxical statements—to jolt students out of conceptual thinking. This approach would later heavily influence the Rinzai school of Zen in Japan. Meanwhile, in Japan itself, Zen found fertile ground in the Kamakura period (1185–1333), a time of political upheaval when samurai warriors were ascendant. Monks such as **Eisai** (1141–1215) and **Dōgen** (1200–1253) brought Chan teachings from China to Japan and established the Rinzai and Sōtō schools, respectively. Eisai introduced the Rinzai school, known for its dynamic approach and koan practice. Dōgen, on the other hand, focused on "just sitting" (shikantaza) as the core of Sōtō Zen.

By the 13th century, Zen was well established in Japan, influencing everything from martial arts (kendo, kyūdō) to art forms like calligraphy, painting, tea ceremony (chanoyu), and flower arrangement (ikebana). The aesthetic of **wabi-sabi**—which values simplicity, imperfection, and impermanence—came to be intertwined with Zen ideals. Over time, Zen spread to the West, where it attracted attention from intellectuals, writers, and artists. Figures like **Suzuki Daisetsu Teitarō (D.T. Suzuki)** (1870–1966) were instrumental in interpreting Zen for Western audiences, shaping a global understanding of its essential teachings.

⁑ Core Philosophical Foundations

Despite Zen's varied expressions, several philosophical tenets remain central throughout its history:

1. **Emptiness (Śūnyatā)**: A fundamental Buddhist concept emphasizing that all phenomena are without independent, permanent essence. In Zen, this doesn't imply nihilism or non-existence but points to the interdependence and flux of reality.
2. **Buddha-Nature**: In many Mahayana traditions, including Zen, it is taught that all sentient beings possess an innate potential to realize enlightenment. This is sometimes referred to as the "bright pearl," "original face," or "true self." The mission of Zen practice is to awaken to this inherent nature.
3. **Non-Duality**: Zen teachings frequently challenge dualistic thinking—self vs. other, subject vs. object, mind vs. body. In Zen, such categories are seen as provisional tools of language rather than ultimate realities. Direct experience transcends conceptual distinctions.
4. **Impermanence**: All conditioned phenomena arise and pass away. This insight, central to Buddhism, underscores the futility of clinging to fixed forms or identities. Zen encourages practitioners to navigate the flow of change with ease and composure.
5. **Prajñā (Wisdom)**: Prajñā, or intuitive wisdom, is different from intellectual knowledge (vijñāna). Zen emphasizes an immediate, intuitive apprehension of reality that arises from deep meditative insight. Koan practice, for example, is aimed at activating this kind of wisdom.
6. **Compassion**: While Zen is sometimes portrayed as austere or self-focused, genuine realization includes compassion for all beings. This stems from

the recognition that the self is not separate from others, so caring for others becomes an expression of one's awakened nature.

The insistence on direct awareness, stripped of conceptual overlays, marks Zen's distinctive flavor within the broader Buddhist tradition. Together, these philosophical pillars form the backbone of Zen. They steer practice away from mere intellectual speculation and ground it in lived experience.

The Practice of Zazen

While I dedicate a chapter to this later, Zazen is an important first principle of Zen to be established here. **Zazen**, or seated meditation, is often seen as the heart of Zen practice. While various lineages and teachers may approach zazen differently, they generally share certain commonalities. A practitioner typically sits on a **zafu** (round cushion) with legs crossed—commonly in the half-lotus or full-lotus position—and the spine held upright. The hands rest in the **cosmic mudra** position, with the left hand over the right and thumbs gently touching.

In the Sōtō tradition, as expounded by Dōgen, the primary instruction is **shikantaza**, meaning "just sitting." Rather than focusing on a particular mantra, image, or koan, the practitioner simply remains aware of whatever arises in the present moment. Thoughts, sensations, and emotions come and go. One neither clings to them nor actively pushes them away; the goal is to cultivate a **stable**, open presence.

*Zazen is an important first principle of Zen. **Zazen**, or seated meditation, is often seen as the heart of Zen practice.*

In the Rinzai tradition, zazen is often coupled with **koan** practice. A koan is a paradoxical phrase, question, or anecdote—such as "What is the sound of one hand clapping?"—meant to confound logical thinking and trigger an intuitive leap. Students may bring their responses to a teacher (roshi) in private interviews (dokusan or sanzen). The teacher guides the student, often pushing them with probing questions, to break through intellectual habits and directly experience insight.

Regardless of the school, zazen is not simply about relaxation or stress relief—although it may yield those benefits. Rather, it is intended as a direct confrontation with the nature of mind and its innate process. Through diligent practice, Zen practitioners aim to recognize the emptiness of thoughts, the conditioned nature of emotions, and the fluidity of "self." Over time, practitioners may experience shifts in their perception, leading them to embody the wisdom and compassion that Zen teaches. Embracing the nature of change through this process helps to welcome a new perspective that is forever forming.

The Role of Koans

A hallmark first principle of Zen, particularly in the Rinzai school, is **koans.** The word "koan" comes from the Chinese **gōng'àn**, originally meaning "public case"—akin to a legal precedent. They serve as gateways into deeper levels of insight. Over time, these "cases" became teaching stories or riddles that demonstrate a Zen principle. Iconic koans include:

- **Mu (無)**: When a monk asked Master Zhaozhou, *"Does a dog have Buddha-nature?"* Zhaozhou famously replied, "Mu," typically translated as *"No"* or *"Not."*
- **The Sound of One Hand**: This koan asks, *"You know the sound of two hands clapping. What is the sound of one hand?"*

A koan cannot be solved by rational analysis. Instead, the practitioner must inhabit the koan, letting it permeate their consciousness. They may wrestle with it in the zendo (meditation hall) and carry it through daily life, seeking an answer that resonates with the deeper truth. When the mind surrenders its habitual logic, a breakthrough (sometimes called **kensho** or "seeing one's true nature") may occur, characterized by a sudden, intuitive grasp.

Though koans can appear bizarre, comedic, or even harsh (some stories involve sudden slaps or unexpected shouts), their function is to disrupt the mind's reliance on linear thinking. Koan study is systematic in many Zen monasteries: a student progresses through a specific curriculum, presenting their understanding to a teacher who verifies its authenticity. While the process can be demanding, those who undertake it often report profound shifts in understanding and the quality of the living experience.

Daily Life Practice and Mindfulness

One of Zen's most distinctive features is its emphasis on integrating meditative awareness into all activities. In Zen monasteries, daily life is structured around communal tasks—cooking, cleaning, gardening—that are carried out with mindful attention. This approach is sometimes summarized by the famous saying, *"Before enlightenment: chop wood, carry water. After enlightenment: chop wood, carry water."* The mundane tasks of life are no longer separated from spiritual practice; they become the vehicle for continuous presence and self-inquiry. The way we condition ourselves to view these opportunities for further enlightenment changes our reality; the circumstances may stay the same, but we are seeing through a different lens that entirely alters our position.

One of Zen's most distinctive features is its emphasis on integrating meditative awareness into all activities

Zen teachings encourage practitioners to fully participate in the present moment. Whether one is washing dishes, walking to the store, or engaging in conversation, there is an invitation to remain grounded in the sensations, thoughts, and awareness as they arise. This attitude of continuous mindfulness allows the practitioner to see that the distinction between "practice" and "daily life" is artificial. Every moment—joyful, neutral, or difficult—becomes an opportunity for awakening. Living under these pretenses also helps to avoid regretful actions and missed opportunities.

Every moment—joyful, neutral, or difficult—becomes an opportunity for awakening. Living under these pretenses also helps to avoid regretful actions and missed opportunities.

Over centuries, these Zen-inspired modes of everyday attention also informed cultural expressions. The **tea ceremony** (chanoyu), for instance, is not merely about drinking tea. It is a carefully choreographed ritual that underscores beauty in simplicity, attentiveness to subtle details, and the transience of each moment. Similarly, **Zen calligraphy** (shodō) requires a unified body-mind state, as the stroke of the brush reveals one's state of consciousness in that very instant. These arts exemplify how Zen transforms ordinary actions into profound expressions of presence and insight, along with trust in one's abilities and potential.

Ethics and Social Dimensions

Although Zen is frequently portrayed as an inward-focused path, ethics and social awareness also have their places. Zen, like all Buddhist traditions, upholds fundamental precepts such as *not killing, not stealing, not lying, and not harming others*. At the heart of these ethical principles lies compassion and the recognition of interdependence. When one deeply understands the interconnected nature of all beings, unethical or harmful actions lose their appeal because they are seen as harming oneself as much as others.

In addition, Zen communities, especially in traditional monastic settings, often operate under rigorous communal rules that foster harmony and respect. The principle of **samu**, or work practice, cultivates humility and service. You practice working as one moving part in a larger whole outside of yourself. Senior monks guide novices through the nuances of daily practice, creating a supportive environment for spiritual growth.

In the modern era, some Zen practitioners engage with pressing social and environmental issues. Figures like **Thich Nhat Hanh**—though not strictly Zen in the Japanese sense, but in the Vietnamese Thiền tradition—embodied socially engaged Buddhism, emphasizing peaceful activism, community building, and mindfulness as means to address global challenges. Likewise, **Rōshi Bernie Glassman** in the United States promoted Zen-based social enterprises to help marginalized communities. These initiatives illustrate how Zen's insights into non-separation and compassion can be applied beyond the meditation hall.

The Aesthetics of Zen

Beyond the internal experiences of meditation, Zen's philosophy finds expression in various aesthetic forms, each reflecting the values of simplicity, impermanence, and unity. **Wabi-sabi**, a Japanese aesthetic principle closely related to Zen, prizes the beauty of imperfection and impermanence. It sees value in weathered wood, cracked tea bowls, and fleeting moments of natural beauty. It finds beauty in imperfection, impermanence, and simplicity, emphasizing acceptance of transience and the natural cycle of growth and decay. It encourages appreciating what is modest, weathered, and unique, rather than striving for perfection or newness, and is deeply rooted in Zen Buddhism and the Japanese tea ceremony. This stands in contrast to Western ideals of perfection or everlasting youth. In a Zen-influenced culture, the marks of time are not flaws but reminders of life's transient nature.

Zen finds beauty in imperfection, impermanence, and simplicity, emphasizing acceptance of transience and the natural cycle of growth and decay. It encourages appreciating what is modest, weathered, and unique, rather than striving for perfection or newness

Zen in the Modern World

Zen took root in the West in the mid-20th century, primarily through scholarly works and the efforts of Japanese teachers who established Zen centers across North America and Europe. Thinkers like **Alan Watts** drew from Zen to critique materialistic culture and encourage a more holistic, present-oriented perspective. Beat Generation writers like **Jack Kerouac** and **Gary Snyder** popularized Zen ideals in literature, seeing them as catalysts for creativity and social change. As Zen spread, it adapted to new cultural contexts, leading to novel interpretations and practices.

Today, Zen-inspired mindfulness techniques are found in therapy, corporate leadership programs, and stress management workshops. The language of Zen has become part of mainstream discourse, though sometimes diluted or commercialized. Nevertheless, there remains a genuine interest in formal Zen practice. Many Zen centers outside Asia maintain traditional customs such as sesshin (intensive meditation retreats) and dokusan (private interviews with a teacher). Western Zen communities often reflect democratic values, with men and women practicing side by side and lay practitioners taking on leadership roles.

Debates arise around how much Zen can adapt without losing its authenticity. Some argue that stripping away rituals and historical contexts might reduce Zen to merely a relaxation technique, ignoring deeper ethical and spiritual dimensions. Others see adaptation as inevitable, pointing out that Zen has always been shaped by the cultures in which it takes root. Despite these debates, the core of Zen—the emphasis on direct insight, compassionate action, and the integration of practice and daily life—continues to resonate in contemporary society. Unknowingly, we reflect these values in areas that require a moral compass.

Critiques, Challenges, and the Ongoing Evolution of Zen

Zen, like any spiritual tradition, is not without its critiques. Scholars and practitioners alike sometimes question whether Zen's famed spontaneity and rejection of dualistic concepts can be misused to justify unethical behavior or social indifference. In certain historical periods, Zen institutions in Japan aligned with militaristic governments, raising ethical questions. Critics also point out that the ideal of "sudden enlightenment" can be romanticized, leading some to chase mystical experiences rather than engage in consistent, grounded practice. This interpretation, along with the impatience that is prevalent in our modern society, can cause many to stray away from Zen.

Another challenge lies in the idealization of the teacher-student relationship, which can become imbalanced. In the West and Asia, there have been controversies surrounding certain Zen teachers accused of misconduct or abuse of power. Such incidents illustrate the importance of transparent structures, ethical guidelines, and checks and balances within Zen communities. Zen teachers are humans on the same journey, and this must be something we remind ourselves of. They do not possess the power to start our enlightenment; they possess wisdom and experience that we can pull from and find inspiring. By idealizing them and romanticizing our expectations, we are pulled farther away from the true mission we wish to succeed through Zen.

Despite these challenges, Zen continues to evolve. Lay practitioners are taking on greater roles, and new dialogues are emerging between Zen and fields like psychology, neuroscience, and environmental activism. Contemporary teachers are re-articulating timeless principles to address the modern human condition—stress, digital overload, social fragmentation—while maintaining the essence of Zen: seeing reality "as it is," beyond the veil of conceptual thought.

Thus, the idea of a first principle of Zen: *"seeing reality as it is"* is a starting point. A jumping-off point from which creativity can be released and developed on a firm footing.

Ultimately, Zen remains an invitation to look deeply into the nature of mind, self, and world. It calls us to fully engage with life—whether we are sitting in silent meditation, sipping tea, or grappling with ethical dilemmas. It is a tradition that spans centuries and continents, yet it is also immediate and personal, challenging us to awaken to each moment. By learning from its foundations and living its philosophy in our own contexts, we carry forward the living flame of Zen's insight into whatever future awaits.

Zen is simultaneously timeless and ever-changing. Born from ancient Buddhist roots, shaped by Chinese, Japanese, Korean, and Vietnamese cultures, and further refracted through Western perspectives, Zen stands as a testament to the universal human quest for meaning and peace. Its foundational philosophy rests on the insight that every moment—no matter how ordinary—contains the seeds of enlightenment. Through the disciplined practice of zazen, the puzzling wisdom of koans, and the integration of mindfulness into daily tasks, Zen invites each individual to realize their inherent Buddha-nature.

Though often misunderstood as aloof or inscrutable, the idea of Zen is deeply concerned with ethical responsibility and compassionate action. Its monastic roots include communal living and service, while modern adaptations emphasize social engagement and personal transformation. Like a clear mirror, Zen offers a reflection of our true nature if we dare to look directly. In a world frequently marred by distraction and division, the Zen path remains a quietly radiant option, guiding practitioners toward a life of insight, authenticity, and heartfelt connection with all beings. For those who may view the methods present in Zen to be too simplistic and aged, consider that as we become more advanced as a society, the methods become more critical than ever.

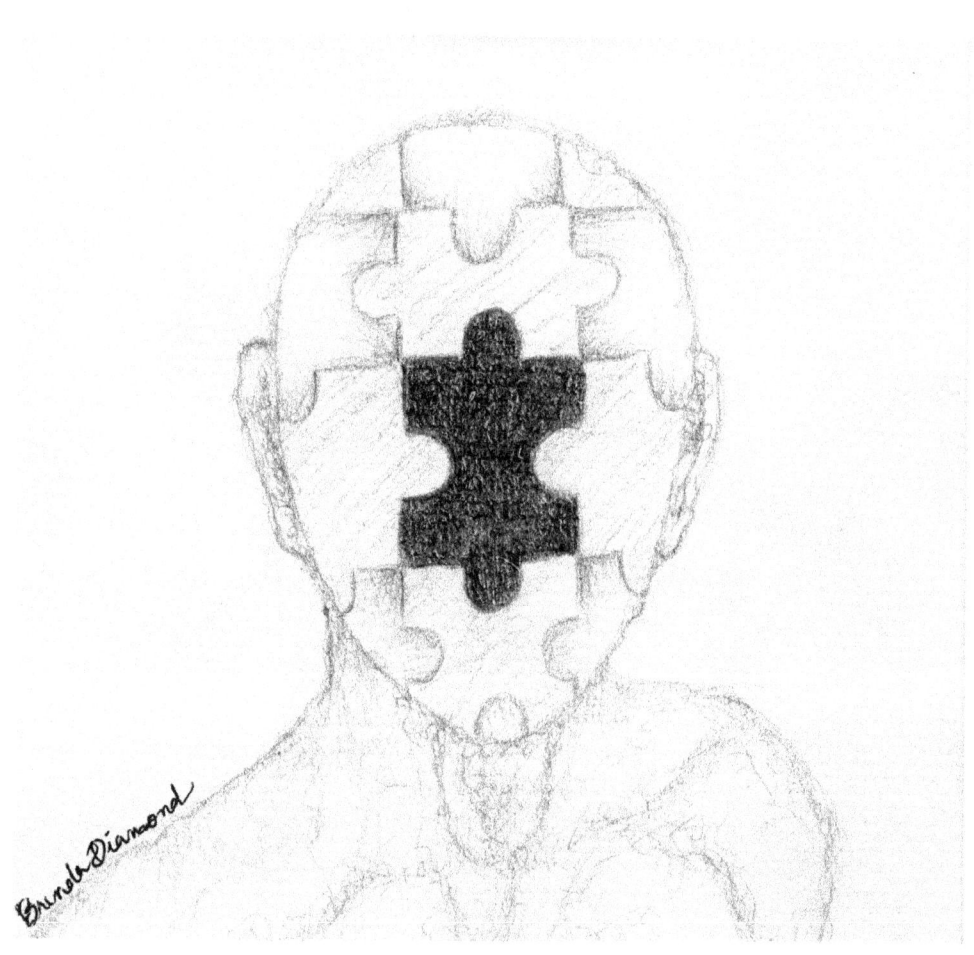

Chapter 3: The Art of Being Alone vs. Loneliness

Loneliness is the mind clinging to what is not. Solitude, in aloneness, is the heart resting in what is.

The concepts of solitude and loneliness are often conflated, yet they differ significantly in both emotional and psychological impact. Many people struggle with distinguishing between the positive aspects of spending time alone—which can be fulfilling, restorative, and creative—and the more harmful state of loneliness, marked by feelings of isolation and despair. In a world that values constant connectivity and busyness, it can be challenging to make sense of these two experiences and understand how they shape one's mental and emotional well-being. To truly master the art of being alone, one must first learn to embrace solitude as a worthwhile pursuit rather than as a punishment and disconnection from productivity.

Solitude often gets a bad reputation in modern society. From a young age, people are encouraged to be social, to make friends, and to engage in communal activities. While there is nothing wrong with valuing social skills and community ties, this emphasis can inadvertently create a stigma around spending time alone. We learn to associate solitude with antisocial tendencies, sadness, or eccentricity. On the other hand, loneliness is a genuine emotional experience characterized by a perceived gap between one's desired social connections and one's actual level of interaction. Even if surrounded by people, a person can still feel lonely if they do not feel connected or understood.

This distinction between choosing solitude and suffering from loneliness is critical to navigating the psychological terrain of aloneness. Solitude is often a voluntary act, rooted in a desire to reflect, recharge, or engage in solitary tasks. Loneliness, however, usually arises involuntarily, triggered by a lack of satisfying relationships or a sense of not belonging. What is difficult to see in these moments of loneliness is that we can turn it into an intentional break for solitude and spend that time navigating ways to connect deeper to ourselves and others. As we dive deeper into this topic, it becomes clear that learning to be alone, to cultivate solitude in healthy ways, can be a powerful antidote to the negative aspects of loneliness. Embracing solitude fosters creativity, emotional resilience, and self-awareness, while loneliness can lead to a variety of mental health struggles if left unaddressed. Understanding the nuances between these two states of being is a vital step in developing the art of being alone.

Embracing solitude fosters creativity, emotional resilience, and self-awareness, while loneliness can lead to a variety of mental health struggles if left unaddressed.

Throughout history, solitude has held a special place in various cultures and intellectual traditions. Philosophers, artists, and religious figures have often touted the importance of being alone for clarity of thought, spiritual growth, and creative innovation. For instance, Henry David Thoreau famously withdrew to Walden Pond to live simply and reflect deeply on society and self-reliance. His writings illustrate how voluntary withdrawal from the bustle of daily life can yield profound insights and personal growth.

In the monastic traditions of Christianity, Buddhism, and other religions, solitude serves as a cornerstone for spiritual practice. Monks and nuns often reside in monasteries far removed from worldly distractions so they can focus on prayer, meditation, and the contemplation of sacred texts. This approach recognizes the transformative power of uninterrupted reflection, which can only be cultivated through extended periods of solitude. A common theme in each religion that uses solitude is this: quiet makes it easier to hear the divine word clearly. Regardless of where one believes this divine word stems from, it is easy to decipher that it is less likely to be heard during busyness and constant motion. By stepping away from the noise of everyday life, the individual can look inward, confront personal limitations, and strive toward enlightenment or a closer connection to the divine.

In the monastic traditions of Christianity, Buddhism, and other religions, solitude serves as a cornerstone for spiritual practice.

Despite these strong endorsements of solitude, not all historical perspectives viewed it in a positive light. In many societies, social belonging was, and often still is, paramount. Individuals who chose or were forced to live in isolation could be regarded with suspicion or pity. The tension between admiration for the wisdom gained in solitude and fear of ostracism underscores the complexity of this topic. Historically, solitude could either be a privileged choice—reserved for monks, philosophers, and artists—or a forced condition of outcasts and exiles.

Understanding how solitude has been perceived over time helps clarify why, in some instances, being alone is celebrated as a source of strength, and in others, it is dreaded as a sign of social or personal failure. These historical insights set the stage for exploring how solitude, when harnessed wisely, can be a constructive force, allowing one to differentiate it clearly from the often debilitating experience of loneliness. Differentiating the two can even help exile loneliness altogether.

Psychological Underpinnings of Solitude vs. Loneliness

From a psychological perspective, being alone can serve as both a balm and a burden. Solitude can offer the mental space necessary for self-reflection and emotional processing. During these quiet moments, people can examine their anxieties, aspirations, and personal beliefs free from external judgment or interference. This internal dialogue fosters a deeper understanding of oneself, leading to heightened emotional maturity and resilience. Moreover, solitude can stimulate creativity and problem-solving. Without the constant barrage of opinions, an individual has the freedom to brainstorm, experiment, and play with ideas. Solitude becomes a form of training wheels; fail as one may, there will be little consequence, just lessons learned and experience gained. When I was first teaching myself to play guitar, I had to evaluate the elements of multitasking separately. The first few weeks of practice were done in pure solitude, my teenage bedroom door closed with towels stuffed in the cracks so as to be "soundproofed" so no one would hear my mistakes. I had to build a tolerance for allowing myself to learn and grow without anxiety of others' opinions.

On the other hand, loneliness often triggers emotional distress. Psychologist John Cacioppo's groundbreaking research on loneliness highlights its detrimental effects on both mental and physical health. Chronic loneliness can lead to increased stress levels, disrupted sleep, and a weakened immune system. In a psychological sense, loneliness is a perceived discrepancy between desired and actual social connections. It is as much about one's subjective feelings as it is about objective reality. Someone can have many acquaintances yet still feel profoundly lonely if they do not experience meaningful emotional bonds.

Neural-brain studies further confirm the impact of loneliness: increased activity in the regions associated with social pain can mirror the experience of physical pain. The lack of human connection triggers an alarm system in our bodies, shaped by evolution to perceive isolation as a threat. Unlike solitude, which can be chosen and beneficial, loneliness often feels imposed and harmful. Recognizing this difference is crucial: a physically solitary individual may be perfectly content if they choose solitude and feel they have enough supportive relationships in their life, whereas someone who appears socially active may silently battle loneliness. This emphasizes the point that healthy and clear communication should be given to one's closest relations when choosing solitude.

By identifying these fundamental psychological underpinnings, we begin to see how one's internal perception plays a critical role in distinguishing the art of being alone from the anguish of feeling lonely. The difference lies not just in external circumstances but in the mindset and emotional framework that shapes how one experiences aloneness, along with what circumstances and choices have granted them that place.

The Role of Technology in Modern Aloneness

The digital age has introduced new complexities to the concepts of solitude and loneliness. With smartphones, social media platforms, and round-the-clock internet access, many people are never truly "alone." Even when physically isolated, one can remain virtually connected to a vast network of friends, family, and strangers. This phenomenon blurs the boundaries between solitude and social interaction. On one hand, technology allows people to find community regardless of geographical distance. Video calls, online forums, and social media groups can mitigate loneliness for those who lack a robust local social circle.

However, the flip side is that technology can also exacerbate feelings of isolation. The constant pressure to present a curated image of one's life online can create a sense of disconnection from reality. People may measure their self-worth by the number of likes, comments, or followers, which can foster deep-seated insecurity and a fear of missing out (FOMO). Moreover, online interactions are often superficial, lacking the depth and nuance of face-to-face relationships, which is reflected in the lifestyles of the younger generation; the façade of our presence to others (on social media or in public) dictates our value. This digital veneer can intensify loneliness because, despite constant chatter and updates, a person might not experience the genuine emotional support or understanding they crave.

Paradoxically, technology can also impede the ability to cultivate solitude in its healthy sense. True solitude often involves disconnecting from external stimuli to focus inwardly. Constant phone notifications, email alerts, and social feeds can fragment attention and disrupt the reflective process. When we desire to use solitude to our benefit, whether the purpose is for self-discovery or improvement of a craft, comparison cannot coexist. Individuals who wish to practice solitude must now make a conscious effort to step away from their devices, setting boundaries that preserve pockets of undisturbed time. Only by balancing the benefits of virtual connectivity with the necessity of real-world introspection can one fully experience the art of being alone without slipping into loneliness.

Embracing Solitude for Self-Discovery

One of the most profound benefits of solitude is the opportunity for self-discovery and personal growth. In the quiet moments when external distractions are minimized, individuals can delve into their inner worlds—exploring their emotions, motivations, and life goals. This process of introspection is central to developing self-awareness, a key component of emotional intelligence and well-being. By understanding one's triggers, values, and aspirations, a person becomes more equipped to make conscious decisions that align with their authentic self and goals.

This self-discovery often involves grappling with uncomfortable truths. Without the noise of constant social engagement, insecurities and unresolved emotional wounds can surface. While confronting these aspects of oneself can be challenging, it is also liberating. Recognizing and addressing personal weaknesses is the first step toward growth and self-improvement. This difficult step aids in building trust and honesty in oneself. In solitude, people can work through difficult emotions at their own pace, without feeling judged or hurried by external pressures.

Moreover, time spent alone can spark creative breakthroughs. Many artists, writers, and innovators cite solitude as a critical ingredient in their creative process. With fewer distractions and external obligations, the mind is free to wander, experiment, and visualize new possibilities. Whether it's brainstorming a new business idea or writing a poem, solitude can be the fertile ground where seeds of inspiration take root.

During my several weeklong motorcycle tours, the solitude and meditative state achieved almost instantly as you move out of the city and onto the open road is very liberating. One's senses are sharpened and honed in order to assure safety, and the residual effect is that you take in and process sounds, smells, heat, humidity, and even barometric pressure on an unprecedented level. And yet at the same time, you must be calm, processing all of this massively unusual input in a logical, almost emotionless manner, again for safety, but also the awareness that your every movement/input to the controls is crucial and cannot be overly reactive.

In embracing solitude for self-discovery, it is essential to do so with intention and mindfulness. This is not about escaping from the world indefinitely but about creating deliberate moments of quiet reflection. Journaling, meditative practices, or even solo walks in nature can serve as gateways to self-awareness. By integrating such practices into daily life, one gradually strengthens the sense of self, enabling one to bring clarity and purpose back into their relationships and social engagements.

Loneliness, Mental Health, and Community Support

While solitude can be enriching, loneliness is often a symptom of unmet social or emotional needs. Persistent loneliness has been linked to depression, anxiety, and other mental health concerns. Humans are inherently social creatures, shaped by evolution to depend on group cohesion and mutual support. When this need for connection is not met, the impact can be profound and long-lasting. Chronic loneliness can distort how one perceives social interactions, leading to a vicious cycle wherein isolation begets more isolation. Over time, a lonely individual might withdraw further, either due to fear of rejection or a belief that meaningful connections are out of reach.

Addressing loneliness requires both personal initiative and communal support. On a personal level, therapy, support groups, and self-help resources can help individuals examine the root causes of their isolation and develop strategies to build healthier social networks. Cultivating emotional resilience and communication skills are key components in breaking down barriers to connection. It may involve learning how to set boundaries in unhealthy relationships, how to initiate conversations, or how to nurture trust with new acquaintances.

On a broader societal level, community programs, social clubs, religious congregations, and volunteer organizations can provide a structured environment for people to form genuine bonds. These institutions often serve as a buffer against the social fragmentation of modern life. Technology can complement these efforts by allowing people to find niche communities online, but it should not replace the tangible sense of belonging that comes from face-to-face interactions. Whether one is attending a local meetup, joining a sports league, or participating in a charitable cause, engaging in shared activities fosters a sense of community and mutual support.

Ultimately, recognizing loneliness as a public health concern underscores the importance of empathy and collective responsibility. Combating loneliness is not solely the individual's job; it's also a community endeavor where society at large benefits from stronger social ties, happier citizens, and a more vibrant social fabric.

Balancing Social Connection and Solitude

One of the most significant challenges in modern life is finding the right balance between social connection and solitude. An imbalance on either side of the spectrum can lead to emotional distress or missed opportunities for growth. Individuals who fear being alone often fill their schedules to the brim with social engagements, never giving themselves the room to reflect or recuperate. This non-stop socializing can lead to burnout, superficial relationships, and a loss of personal identity.

Conversely, those who struggle to engage socially may retreat into prolonged isolation, leading to feelings of alienation and despair. In such cases, solitude stops being a conscious choice and morphs into a state of enforced loneliness. The key to navigating these extremes lies in intentional self-awareness. Periodically evaluating one's social and emotional needs can help identify whether more connection or more alone time is needed at any given point.

Striving for a healthy balance involves active self-regulation. For instance, if you recognize that prolonged solitude is causing you to feel disconnected, it might be time to seek out shared experiences—whether that's meeting a friend for coffee, taking a group fitness class, or joining a local club. Conversely, if constant social obligations leave you feeling drained, scheduling blocks of solitude—turning off your phone, reading a book, or simply daydreaming—can provide the necessary mental rest and personal reflection.

Mindful communication with friends and family can also help. Letting people know you need time alone can prevent misunderstandings or hurt feelings. Similarly, expressing a desire for social interaction when loneliness strikes invites others to include you in their activities. By advocating for your own needs, you not only take responsibility for your emotional well-being but also foster healthier, more authentic relationships with those around you.

Practical Strategies to Cultivate Healthy Solitude

Many people struggle with how to implement healthy solitude in their day-to-day lives, especially in a culture that often equates constant activity with success. However, even small steps toward intentional alone time can yield tangible benefits. Below are a few practical strategies:

1. *Designate "Solitude Spaces":* Whether it's a corner of your home, a local park, or a quiet café, select physical environments where you feel comfortable and safe being alone. Consistency in the environment can help ease into reflective states.
2. *Set Boundaries with Technology:* Plan specific intervals during which you're disconnected—no checking emails, no social media, no phone calls. Use this time to focus on a creative project, read, meditate, or simply sit quietly with your thoughts.
3. *Engage in Mindful Activities:* Solitude can be more fulfilling when paired with practices that encourage presence, such as journaling, yoga, or nature walks. These activities turn solitude into a constructive exercise rather than a passive state of avoidance.
4. *Schedule It:* Just as you would set appointments or social events, pencil in "alone time" on your calendar. Honor this commitment to yourself the same way you would any other important engagement.
5. *Develop a Solitude Ritual:* Create a short routine—like making tea, lighting a candle, or stretching—that signals to your mind and body it's time to shift into a reflective mode.
6. *Seek Inspiration from Solitary Role Models:* Read books or watch documentaries about individuals who have found meaning in solitude. Their experiences can serve as a guide or motivation, dispelling misconceptions that alone time is inherently lonely.

By practicing these techniques, individuals can slowly reshape their relationship with solitude, viewing it as a nourishing part of life rather than an undesirable state. As these habits become ingrained, the lines between solitude and loneliness become clearer, making it easier to recognize when healthy alone time transitions into unwanted isolation.

Navigating Transitions and Life Changes

Life transitions—such as moving to a new city, changing jobs, or undergoing a personal loss—can dramatically alter one's social landscape. In these moments of uncertainty, the distinction between solitude and loneliness can become blurred. For example, someone relocating to a new city for work may find themselves without their usual support system. Initially, this period of aloneness might feel lonely, as old friendships are far away and new connections have not yet formed. However, approaching this transitional solitude as an opportunity for self-discovery can transform what might otherwise be a painfully isolating experience.

Similarly, major life changes such as divorce, retirement, or children leaving home can leave individuals feeling unmoored. In such times, practicing the art of being alone becomes particularly valuable. By intentionally cultivating solitude, one can process emotions, grieve losses, and chart a path forward. This approach shifts the focus from victimhood to empowerment. Rather than succumbing to loneliness, one might explore new hobbies, volunteer opportunities, or educational pursuits that not only fill time but also stimulate personal growth.

Nevertheless, it's important to recognize when loneliness persists and becomes a barrier to well-being. If negative emotions dominate, seeking professional help from counselors or therapists may be essential. Support groups can also be invaluable, especially for specific life challenges (e.g., bereavement groups, divorce support groups). These safe spaces allow individuals to share experiences and coping strategies, reminding them they are not alone in their struggles. Ultimately, navigating transitions successfully involves a dance between reaching out for support and turning inward for self-reflection—a balancing act that underscores the art of being alone vs. the anguish of loneliness.

Cultivating the art of being alone is an ongoing journey that requires mindful engagement with oneself and one's community. It demands that we shed cultural stigmas around solitude and recognize it as a fertile ground for creativity, emotional resilience, and profound self-awareness. While loneliness can be a painful reality, particularly in a world where technology and social fragmentation can exacerbate disconnection, understanding the distinction between solitude and loneliness is the first step toward healthy aloneness.

By tracing historical perspectives, exploring psychological research, and examining the role of technology, we gain clarity on why people often struggle to be alone and how loneliness can arise even amidst crowds. Yet we also discover that intentional solitude can be deeply rewarding. The practices and strategies outlined—ranging from setting boundaries with technology to designing solitude rituals—offer a roadmap to harness the power of alone time constructively.

As life ebbs and flows, personal and societal circumstances can shift, requiring us to continually adapt our approach to solitude and social engagement. Sometimes, the scales will tip toward more time alone; at others, reaching out to loved ones or community is essential. What remains constant is the need for self-awareness and genuine intention. In this way, the art of being alone becomes not a static skill but a lifelong practice—an evolving relationship with oneself and the world. Embraced wisely, solitude can become a cornerstone of a rich, purposeful life, a sanctuary from which genuine connections can flourish, and a shield against the ravages of loneliness.

A monk sat alone in a mountain hut, the wind whispering through the pines. A traveler, weary and heavy-hearted, arrived and said, "I am lonely, though I walk among many. You are alone, yet you seem at peace. What is the difference?"

The monk smiled and placed a single pebble on the floor. "This is loneliness," he said. Then he swept the floor clean and sat in silence. "This is being alone."

The traveler frowned. "The pebble is gone, but the hut is still empty. How is this an answer?"

The monk replied, "Loneliness is the pebble you carry, seeking others to fill the void. Being alone is the empty hut, complete in its stillness."

The traveler sat, gazing at the bare floor. The wind sang, and the hut was no longer empty.

Chapter 4: Challenges of Solitude

✵ Challenges of Living in Solitude

Living in solitude, whether by choice or circumstance, presents a unique set of challenges that test an individual's emotional, psychological, and practical resilience. While solitude can offer opportunities for self-reflection and personal growth, it also demands a level of self-sufficiency and mental fortitude that can be difficult to sustain. This essay explores the multifaceted challenges of living in solitude, focusing on emotional isolation, practical self-reliance, and the psychological toll of limited social interaction.

Married people, or people with enormous professional commitments, or people with hourly wage jobs, all of the demands of their lives that mount, accumulate to the level that each day is a consecutive execution of tasks/commitments/obligations. Divorce statistics suggest that the current state of relationships in the world and trends are not encouraging. Each person needs to retain and develop the self while fulfilling obligations and commitments. A balance of these two is not a goal; it is essential.

✵ Emotional Isolation

One of the most profound challenges of living in solitude is the emotional isolation that often accompanies it. Humans are inherently social creatures, wired to seek connection, validation, and companionship. In solitude, the absence of regular interpersonal interaction can lead to feelings of loneliness, which, over time, may erode emotional well-being. Without others to share joys, sorrows, or even mundane daily experiences, individuals may struggle to find meaning or purpose in their routines.

Loneliness in solitude is not merely a fleeting emotion but can evolve into a chronic state that impacts mental health. Studies have shown that prolonged isolation is associated with increased risks of depression, anxiety, and even cognitive decline. For instance, the lack of external perspectives can cause individuals to ruminate excessively, amplifying negative thoughts or self-doubt. Furthermore, the absence of emotional support networks—friends, family, or colleagues—means that solitary individuals must navigate life's challenges without the buffer of communal encouragement or advice, making setbacks feel more insurmountable.

✵ Practical Self-Reliance

Beyond emotional hurdles, living in solitude demands a high degree of practical self-reliance. Solitary individuals must often handle all aspects of daily life without assistance, from household maintenance to financial management. This can be particularly daunting in remote or rural settings, where access to services or resources may be limited. For example, a solitary individual living off-grid might need to master skills like repairing equipment, growing food, or managing energy resources—tasks that require both knowledge and physical effort.

The pressure to be entirely self-sufficient can be overwhelming, especially when unexpected problems arise. A single illness, for instance, can become a significant ordeal without someone providing care or assistance. Similarly, financial instability or logistical challenges, such as transportation or supply shortages, can feel amplified when there is no one to share the burden. While some may find empowerment in mastering these tasks, they may find that they have little validation without others to share the experience with. Others may feel trapped by the relentless demands of self-reliance, particularly if they lack the skills or resources to cope effectively.

🕷 Psychological Toll of Limited Social Interaction

The psychological impact of limited social interaction is another critical challenge of solitude. Social engagement provides mental stimulation, helping individuals process ideas, challenge assumptions, and maintain cognitive sharpness. In solitude, the lack of diverse perspectives can lead to intellectual stagnation or a narrowing of thought. Over time, this may manifest as difficulty concentrating, reduced creativity, or a sense of detachment from the broader world.

Moreover, solitude can distort one's sense of time and reality. Without regular social cues or shared routines, days may blend together, creating a sense of temporal disorientation. This can exacerbate feelings of purposelessness, as individuals struggle to anchor their lives in meaningful milestones or interactions. In extreme cases, prolonged solitude has been linked to perceptual distortions or heightened sensitivity to stimuli, as the mind seeks to fill the void left by external engagement.

The psychological toll is particularly acute for those who did not choose solitude but were thrust into it by circumstances, such as geographic isolation, loss of loved ones, or social ostracism. For these individuals, solitude may feel like a punishment rather than a choice, intensifying feelings of abandonment or unworthiness. Even for those who embrace solitude, maintaining mental equilibrium requires deliberate effort, such as engaging in creative pursuits, journaling, or cultivating a strong sense of self-discipline.

🕷 Balancing Solitude with Connection

While the challenges of solitude are significant, they are not insurmountable. Many individuals develop strategies to cope, such as establishing routines, pursuing hobbies, or leveraging technology to maintain limited but meaningful connections. For instance, online communities or periodic visits to social hubs can provide a sense of belonging without compromising the independence of solitary living. Others find solace in nature, spirituality, or intellectual pursuits, which can fill the emotional and psychological gaps left by human interaction.

However, these strategies require intentionality and resilience. The solitary individual must be proactive in addressing their emotional, practical, and psychological needs, as there is no one else to rely on. This self-directed approach can be both a burden and an opportunity, forcing individuals to confront their vulnerabilities while discovering untapped strengths. It is true in most cases that we don't know if we can successfully complete something until we try, regardless of the knowledge at hand; experience is always necessary on the path to growth and mastery.

Living in solitude is a complex experience that challenges individuals on multiple fronts. The emotional weight of isolation, the practical demands of self-reliance, and the psychological toll of limited social interaction create a unique set of obstacles that require resilience and adaptability. While solitude can foster introspection and independence, it also tests the limits of human endurance. By acknowledging these challenges and developing strategies to address them, individuals can navigate the solitary path with greater confidence, finding a balance between the freedom of independence and the universal need for connection.

🦟 Ralph Waldo Emerson's 'Self-Reliance'

Ralph Waldo Emerson's *Self-Reliance*, published in 1841 as part of his collection *Essays: First Series*, is a cornerstone of American transcendentalism and one of the most influential works in American literature. The essay articulates Emerson's philosophy of individualism, urging readers to trust their own instincts, reject conformity, and cultivate personal authenticity. Written during a period of rapid social and intellectual change in the United States, *Self-Reliance* reflects Emerson's response to the pressures of societal expectations and the emerging American identity. The essay is both a call to action and a meditation on the human spirit, advocating for self-trust as the foundation for a meaningful and liberated life.

The essay articulates Emerson's philosophy of individualism, urging readers to trust their own instincts, reject conformity, and cultivate personal authenticity.

Emerson, a former Unitarian minister turned essayist and lecturer, was a leading figure in the transcendentalist movement, which emphasized the inherent goodness of individuals and nature, as well as the supremacy of intuition over institutionalized knowledge. *Self-Reliance* encapsulates these ideals, challenging readers to break free from the constraints of tradition, conformity, and external authority. Over the course of the essay, Emerson weaves together philosophical arguments, aphorisms, and vivid metaphors to inspire a radical reimagining of personal and societal values.

At its heart, *Self-Reliance* is an impassioned defense of individualism. Emerson begins by asserting that each person possesses a unique genius, a divine spark that can only be realized through self-trust. "To believe your own thought, to believe that what is true for you in your private heart is true for all men—that is genius," he writes. This opening sets the tone for the essay, emphasizing the importance of inner conviction over external validation. Emerson argues that society often stifles this individuality by rewarding conformity and punishing originality. He critiques the tendency to defer to the opinions of others—whether through tradition, religion, or social norms—calling it a form of intellectual cowardice.

> *Emerson begins by asserting that each person possesses a unique genius, a divine spark that can only be realized through self-trust. "To believe your own thought, to believe that what is true for you in your private heart is true for all men—that is genius,"*

One of the essay's central arguments is that self-reliance requires courage to stand alone. Emerson warns against the seductive pull of consistency, which he famously dubs "the hobgoblin of little minds." He encourages readers to embrace contradiction and change, arguing that true growth comes from following one's evolving truths rather than clinging to past beliefs for the sake of appearances. This rejection of rigid consistency is radical, as it challenges the societal expectation that individuals should present a predictable, uniform persona. Instead, Emerson celebrates the dynamic, ever-unfolding nature of the self.

Emerson also critiques the ways in which society enforces conformity through institutions such as religion, education, and commerce. He views these as mechanisms that diminish personal agency by prioritizing collective dogma over individual insight. For example, he argues that organized religion often substitutes ritual for genuine spiritual experience, while education can dull creativity by emphasizing rote learning. Similarly, he sees economic systems as fostering dependency, urging individuals to prioritize self-sufficiency over material accumulation. This critique is not merely a rejection of institutions but a call to reform them by grounding them in personal authenticity.

Another key theme is the relationship between self-reliance and universal truth. Emerson, influenced by transcendentalist ideas, believes that individual intuition is a gateway to divine or universal wisdom. By trusting one's own thoughts, a person aligns with the "Over-Soul," a spiritual unity that connects all beings. This metaphysical dimension elevates Self-Reliance beyond a practical guide to independence, positioning it as a spiritual manifesto. Emerson suggests that self-reliance is not selfish but rather a means of contributing to the greater good, as authentic individuals inspire and uplift others.

Emerson suggests that self-reliance is not selfish but rather a means of contributing to the greater good, as authentic individuals inspire and uplift others.

✺ Self-Reliance - Historical and Cultural Context

Self-Reliance emerged during a transformative period in American history. The early 19th century saw the rise of industrialization, westward expansion, and debates over slavery, all of which shaped the national character. The United States was grappling with its identity as a young nation, seeking to define itself apart from European traditions. Emerson's emphasis on individualism resonated with this quest for self-definition, offering a philosophical framework for American independence—not just politically, but intellectually and spiritually.

The essay also reflects the influence of transcendentalism, which drew from European romanticism, Eastern philosophies, and American idealism. Emerson was inspired by thinkers like Immanuel Kant, who emphasized the role of individual perception in shaping reality, and by Hindu texts like the *Bhagavad Gita*, which celebrated inner divinity. At the same time, *Self-Reliance* critiques the materialism and conformity of Jacksonian America, where economic ambition often overshadowed moral and intellectual pursuits.

Emerson's ideas were not without controversy. His rejection of traditional authority, particularly in religion, alienated conservative readers, while his emphasis on self-reliance was sometimes misinterpreted as endorsing selfishness. Nevertheless, the essay's bold vision of human potential struck a chord, influencing later American thinkers like Henry David Thoreau, Walt Whitman, and the pragmatists.

✺ Self-Reliance - Relevance and Legacy

Self-Reliance remains profoundly relevant in the modern world, where individuals navigate competing pressures from social media, consumerism, and ideological polarization. Emerson's call to trust one's own voice resonates in an era of information overload, where external opinions can drown out personal conviction. His critique of conformity speaks to contemporary debates about authenticity, as people grapple with curated identities and societal expectations.

The essay's emphasis on courage and nonconformity has inspired countless movements, from civil rights to countercultural revolutions. Figures like Martin Luther King Jr. and Steve Jobs have cited Emerson as an influence, drawn to his belief in the power of individual vision to effect change. However, *Self-Reliance* is not without its critics. Some argue that Emerson's focus on individualism overlooks the importance of community and collective action, particularly in addressing systemic injustices. Others contend that his idealism can seem impractical in a world of economic and social constraints.

Despite these critiques, *Self-Reliance* endures as a testament to the human spirit's capacity for self-discovery and resilience. Its message—that true fulfillment comes from within, not from external validation—continues to inspire readers to question, create, and live authentically.

Ralph Waldo Emerson's *Self-Reliance* (1841) is a timeless exploration of individualism, authenticity, and the courage to live according to one's own truth. Through its passionate prose and profound insights, the essay challenges readers to reject conformity, embrace their unique potential, and align with universal wisdom. While rooted in the intellectual and cultural currents of 19th-century America, its themes of self-trust and nonconformity remain universal, offering guidance in an increasingly complex world. As both a philosophical treatise and a call to action, *Self-Reliance* invites each generation to rediscover the power of the self, making it a foundational text in the canon of human thought.

🦟 Self-Reliance – Eight (8) Timeless Truths

Emerson's strategies for timeless exploration of individualism, authenticity, and the courage to live according to one's own truth:

1. *Trust Your Own Intuition:* Emerson emphasizes believing in your own thoughts and instincts as the foundation of self-reliance. He urges individuals to recognize their unique genius and trust their inner voice over external opinions, asserting that what is true for you is universally valid.

Trusting your intuition is like leaning on an inner compass for decision-making when logic alone isn't enough. It's your subconscious piecing together patterns from past experiences, emotions, and subtle cues that your conscious mind might miss. Studies suggest intuition is most reliable in areas where you have expertise—think of a seasoned doctor sensing something off in a patient despite normal test results. In high-stakes or ambiguous situations, like choosing a career path or sensing danger, intuition can cut through overthinking and align you with your deeper values.

But it's not infallible. Intuition can be skewed by biases, stress, or wishful thinking—say, ignoring red flags in a bad relationship because you "feel" it's right. The wisdom lies in balancing it: use intuition as a guide, not a dictator. Cross-check it with facts and reflection. People who trust their gut while staying open to evidence tend to make faster, more confident decisions without sacrificing accuracy. It's about knowing when to listen to that quiet voice and when to question it.

2. *Reject Conformity:* He advocates resisting societal pressures to conform, criticizing the tendency to adopt others' beliefs or traditions blindly.

Emerson encourages nonconformity, urging readers to prioritize personal conviction over the expectations of society, religion, or institutions.

Rejecting conformity involves embracing individuality and critical thinking over blindly following societal norms or expectations. Its wisdom lies in fostering authenticity, innovation, and personal growth. Here's a concise breakdown:

- *Authenticity:* Non-conformity allows you to live true to your values, desires, and identity, rather than suppressing them to fit in. This leads to greater self-awareness and fulfillment.
- *Innovation:* History shows that breakthroughs—scientific, artistic, or social—often come from those who challenge the status quo (e.g., Galileo, Rosa Parks, or Steve Jobs). Rejecting conformity fuels creativity and progress.
- *Critical Thinking:* Conformity can stifle independent thought, encouraging groupthink. Questioning norms sharpens your ability to evaluate ideas and make informed decisions.
- *Resilience:* Standing apart requires courage and builds inner strength, as you learn to navigate criticism or isolation while staying true to your convictions.
- *Diversity of Perspective:* Non-conformity enriches society by promoting diverse ideas and lifestyles, preventing stagnation, and fostering inclusivity.
- *Caveats:* Blind rebellion without purpose can be counterproductive. The wisdom lies in discerning when to reject norms thoughtfully, balancing individuality with respect for constructive traditions.

Ultimately, rejecting conformity wisely empowers you to live authentically, think boldly, and contribute uniquely to the world.

3. *Embrace Individuality and Contradiction:* Emerson advises embracing your unique identity, even if it leads to inconsistency. He famously calls consistency "the hobgoblin of little minds," encouraging people to evolve and adapt their beliefs without fear of appearing contradictory.

Embracing Individuality and contradiction is a path to authentic self-discovery and growth. Individuality means honoring your unique perspective, values, and quirks, even when they clash with societal norms. It's the courage to carve your own path, recognizing that conformity often dilutes truth. Contradiction, meanwhile, is the messy reality of being human—holding conflicting beliefs, emotions, or desires. Accepting these tensions, rather than forcing resolution, fosters depth and resilience.

Philosophically, Whitman's "I contain multitudes" captures this: we are vast, inconsistent, and ever-evolving. Psychologically, embracing contradiction aligns with cognitive flexibility, allowing us to adapt and learn from complexity. Socially, it challenges groupthink, sparking innovation and dialogue. Yet, it's not without pitfalls—unrestrained individuality can breed isolation, and unresolved contradictions can paralyze decision-making.

The wisdom lies in balance: celebrate your distinctiveness, but stay open to connection; embrace your contradictions, but seek clarity when needed. It's a dynamic dance, not a destination.

4. *Cultivate Courage to Stand Alone:* Self-reliance requires the bravery to act independently, even in the face of criticism or isolation. Emerson urges readers to have the fortitude to pursue their own path, regardless of societal disapproval.
5. *Avoid Dependence on External Validation*: He warns against relying on others' approval or material wealth for self-worth. Instead, Emerson promotes self-sufficiency, encouraging individuals to find fulfillment within themselves rather than through external achievements or possessions.
6. *Engage with the Present Moment:* Emerson advises living authentically in the present, free from the burdens of past mistakes or future anxieties. He believes that self-reliant individuals focus on their current actions and insights.
7. *Connect with Universal Truth through Self-Trust:* Influenced by transcendentalism, Emerson suggests that trusting your own thoughts aligns you with the "Over-Soul," a universal spirit. This spiritual dimension frames self-reliance as a means to access divine wisdom.
8. *Challenge Institutional Authority:* He critiques institutions like religion, education, and commerce for fostering dependency and stifling individuality. Emerson encourages reforming or bypassing these systems by grounding decisions in personal insight.

By practicing these strategies, Emerson believes individuals can achieve true self-reliance, living authentically and contributing to the world through their unique perspectives.

In the quiet valley, a monk sat alone, the wind his only companion.
Day after day, solitude pressed heavy, whispering doubts into his stillness.
One evening, a single leaf fell before him, dancing in the breeze.
"Why do you dance alone?" the monk asked.
The leaf replied, "I am not alone; I move with the wind, the earth, the sky."
The monk smiled, and in his silence, solitude became vast, embracing all things.

Chapter 5: Self-Compassion in Isolation

An In-Depth Exploration

Isolation, whether physical, emotional, or social, can be a challenging experience that evokes a spectrum of feelings—from loneliness and anxiety to guilt and self-criticism. In times of isolation, we often lack the comforting presence of friends, family, or colleagues, which can make it more difficult to maintain a sense of well-being. With fewer external distractions, we may become more intensely aware of our own inner dialogue. This heightened self-awareness can be a double-edged sword: while it can lead to insightful reflection, it can also amplify negative patterns of thinking if we are not careful.

One potent antidote to these difficult emotions is self-compassion. Broadly defined by psychologist Kristin Neff, self-compassion involves treating ourselves with the same kindness, concern, and understanding that we would show a dear friend. It counteracts harmful self-criticism by offering a gentle, supportive voice in our heads—one that acknowledges pain and difficulty without judgment. It also promotes the recognition that our struggles are part of the shared human experience, rather than a personal failing.

In an era where remote work and physical distancing measures have become more prevalent, isolation might not always be a choice; sometimes, it is imposed by circumstances. Regardless of the reason, periods of isolation can trigger or intensify mental health challenges. Learning to practice self-compassion in these moments can be transformative. By turning our attention inward with acceptance and empathy, we cultivate resilience and emotional balance.

This portion explores how isolation intensifies our internal dialogue, the role self-compassion plays in countering negative thinking, and various practical strategies to integrate self-compassion into daily life. We will delve into the psychological, emotional, and even physiological benefits of self-compassion, and we will examine the barriers that can prevent us from treating ourselves kindly when it is most needed. By understanding both the theory and practice of self-compassion, we can better support ourselves—and even those around us—during periods of isolation.

Understanding Isolation

Isolation can manifest in many ways. Physical isolation refers to being physically separated from others, as in remote living situations, quarantine, or extended hospital stays. Social isolation is characterized by a limited network of interpersonal relationships, which can happen even in a crowd if one feels disconnected from the people around them. Emotional isolation, meanwhile, takes root when individuals feel unable to share their feelings or find solace in others. These forms of isolation can overlap, leading to an even greater sense of loneliness and vulnerability.

Historically, isolation has been used as a punishment (consider solitary confinement in prisons), underscoring its psychological impact. Still, there are instances where short-term isolation can be beneficial—for instance, in the form of mindful solitude or meditation retreats. The difference between beneficial solitude and harmful isolation often hinges on whether the individual feels it is a chosen and empowering experience or a forced and distressing one.

Periods of isolation, whatever their origin, tend to shift a person's focus inward. Without the usual social cues and interactions, self-talk can become the loudest voice we hear. If we lack a practice of self-compassion, this inner voice might default to criticism and judgment. Even for individuals generally skilled at self-regulation, isolation can erode emotional resilience over time. Moments of self-doubt can spiral more easily when there is no external feedback or support.

The Stress Response in Isolation

When we experience isolation, our brains can perceive this as a threat. Social connectedness is integral to human survival—thus, any threat to belonging can trigger a "fight-flight-freeze" response. Under stress, our sympathetic nervous system may become overactive, leading to increased anxiety, shallow breathing, and a racing heart. Over time, chronic stress in isolation can manifest as fatigue, irritability, or depressive symptoms. Without healthy coping strategies or positive self-talk, we risk deepening the impact of the stress response.

It is within this context that self-compassion serves as a particularly powerful tool. By bringing a gentle awareness to our struggles, we can mitigate the stress response, coaxing ourselves back into a state of calm. A self-compassionate mindset reduces reactivity, shifts our perception, and allows us to approach our predicament with understanding rather than panic.

Defining Self-Compassion

Self-compassion, as conceptualized by Kristin Neff, has three core components:

1. *Self-kindness vs. self-judgment*

   Self-kindness involves offering warmth and understanding toward oneself during moments of pain or failure rather than judgment or criticism. It means recognizing that imperfection is a natural part of the human experience and extending the same empathy to ourselves that we would to a loved one.

2. *Common humanity vs. isolation*

   Instead of interpreting suffering as something that separates us from others, common humanity reminds us that everyone experiences hardship. This perspective combats the sense of alienation often accompanying emotional or social pain, thus preventing us from feeling uniquely flawed.

3. *Mindfulness vs. over-identification*

   Mindfulness here involves being aware of present-moment experiences—particularly pain or emotional discomfort—without becoming overwhelmed or swept away by them. It means acknowledging difficult emotions as they arise, neither suppressing nor exaggerating them.

These pillars work together to create an internal environment of warmth, understanding, and balanced awareness. Even in isolation, where external compassion may be scarce, self-compassion can bring stability and comfort.

Why Self-Compassion is Vital in Isolation

When we lack external support or company, negative self-talk can escalate. We might ruminate on past mistakes or future anxieties, fueling cycles of self-doubt and even self-loathing. In such scenarios, self-compassion is crucial. It reassures us that moments of failure, fear, or loneliness are part of being human.

In the absence of social connection, self-compassion steps in as a supportive ally. It says: "This is difficult. You are not alone in these feelings. Let's handle this moment with kindness." Such an inner dialogue can counterbalance the harshness of isolation. While it does not eliminate the reality of being physically or emotionally alone, it reorients us to an inner reservoir of empathy and understanding.

The Psychological Benefits of Self-Compassion

1. *Reduced Anxiety and Depression*

   Multiple studies have shown a correlation between high levels of self-compassion and lower levels of anxiety and depression. In isolation, where fear and loneliness can exacerbate anxiety or depressive symptoms, self-compassion provides a buffer. It allows individuals to approach their emotional states with curiosity rather than judgment, diffusing their intensity.

2. *Greater Emotional Resilience*

   Emotional resilience refers to the ability to recover from or adapt to challenging life events. Self-compassion fosters resilience by encouraging positive self-talk and reducing self-critical rumination. When setbacks occur, a self-compassionate individual is more likely to view them as surmountable and less likely to spiral into despair.

3. *Improved Self-Worth*

   Self-compassion is distinct from self-esteem, but it can indirectly bolster a healthy sense of self-worth. Unlike self-esteem, which often hinges on external validation or achievements, self-compassion remains steady regardless of success or failure. In isolation—where validation may be scarce—self-compassion offers an inherent sense of worth that does not depend on outside opinions or accomplishments.

4. *Enhanced Motivation*

   Contrary to the concern that being kind to oneself leads to complacency, research suggests that self-compassion can actually enhance motivation. When we treat ourselves with understanding rather than condemnation, we are less afraid of failure. Discipline plays a key part in motivation; the more often one pushes past the lack of desire to do something and executes it anyway, one builds an endurance for doing so in all areas. This encourages us to persevere in our goals—even when isolated and lacking external support.

The Emotional Paradox of Isolation

Isolation can create a paradoxical emotional state: on one hand, we have more time to reflect and potentially grow; on the other hand, we might feel cut off from sources of meaning and love. In these circumstances, self-compassion is not just helpful—it can be life-changing. It prevents us from turning our solitude into emotional self-punishment. By guiding us to approach our fears and loneliness with acceptance, it paves the way for deeper introspection and inner healing through mental honesty.

Practical Techniques for Cultivating Self-Compassion in Isolation

1. *Mindful Breathing Exercises*

   Setting aside a few minutes each day to engage in mindful breathing can anchor you in the present moment. When anxious thoughts arise, focus on the sensation of your breath entering and leaving your body. If self-critical or fearful thoughts emerge, gently label them as "thoughts" or "feelings" without judgment and return to the breath. Over time, this practice strengthens the mindfulness component of self-compassion.

2. *Loving-Kindness Meditation*

Often called "meta" meditation, loving-kindness practices involve silently repeating phrases such as "May I be happy. May I be well. May I be safe. May I be peaceful." This practice directs warmth and goodwill toward oneself, and then extends those feelings to loved ones, strangers, and even adversaries. Particularly in isolation, loving-kindness meditation serves as a reminder that we remain connected to humanity in our shared desires for well-being.

3. *Self-Compassion Breaks*

When stress flares or negative self-talk spirals, a self-compassion break can interrupt the cycle. Speak gently to yourself:

- "This is a moment of suffering." (Mindfulness)
- "Suffering is part of life." (Common humanity)
- "May I be kind to myself?" (Self-kindness)

This short script can be adapted to your own words, but it captures the three pillars of self-compassion. Even 30 seconds spent repeating this can diffuse heightened stress.

4. *Journaling*

Writing out your experiences can help you gain clarity about your emotions. An effective self-compassion journal might include prompts such as:

- What am I feeling right now?
- How might these feelings be understandable given my circumstances?
- If a friend were in my situation, how would I respond to them?

By putting feelings into words, you not only gain perspective but also practice the art of kind, non-judgmental self-awareness.

5. *Creative Expression*

Sometimes words are not enough to capture or process complex emotions. Engaging in creative pursuits—painting, music, dance, or crafting—can be profoundly therapeutic. Isolation presents a unique opportunity to explore creative outlets without the pressure of an audience. Approach these endeavors with self-kindness, allowing for mistakes and unpredictability. The goal is expression, not perfection.

6. *Guided Visualizations*

    Guided meditations or visualizations can be especially soothing in isolation. Whether you listen to an audio recording or simply imagine a calm, safe space in your mind, these practices help shift attention away from worry and self-criticism. Visualizations that emphasize warmth, light, or compassion can reinforce a sense of inner safety and connection, even when physical contact with others is limited.

7. *Daily Check-Ins*

    Make it a habit to check in with yourself at least once a day. Ask: "How am I feeling—physically, mentally, emotionally?" This simple practice can be enhanced by rating your well-being on a scale from 1 to 10 and noting any patterns in a journal. Following each check-in, offer yourself a phrase of kindness: "Whatever I am feeling right now is okay. May I offer myself understanding and compassion."

Overcoming Resistance to Self-Compassion

For some, the concept of self-compassion may seem foreign or even uncomfortable. Common objections include the belief that self-compassion is self-indulgent or that criticism is necessary for self-improvement. However, research indicates that self-compassion actually improves both emotional well-being and personal accountability. When confronted by internal resistance, it can help to remind yourself of how you would treat a friend in a similar situation. This practice additionally hones our ability to look at situations as a big picture, rather than getting stuck on small details and difficulties. Often, the qualities of patience and empathy feel perfectly natural when directed toward others—self-compassion calls us to extend that same kindness inward.

Barriers to Self-Compassion in Isolation

1. *Perfectionism*

    Perfectionistic tendencies often make self-compassion a significant challenge, particularly in isolation. If an individual believes they must perform flawlessly at all times, they may see compassion as an excuse to slack off. Paradoxically, embracing self-compassion can help perfectionists cope more effectively when mistakes inevitably occur, fostering healthier achievement and perseverance. In most creative outlets, allowing room for mistakes aids in one's finding their style and keeps the hobby enjoyable and liberating.

2. *Social Stigma and Shame*

In certain cultures or family dynamics, self-compassion might be perceived as weakness. This societal or familial stigma can create shame around self-kindness. When isolated, without external affirmation, individuals with these beliefs may double down on self-criticism, mistakenly viewing harshness as "strength." Recognizing that vulnerability and kindness are not signs of weakness, but marks of emotional maturity, can help dismantle this barrier. Embracing moments of weakness and using them to benefit one's personal growth is a mental strength.

3. *Lack of Self-Worth*

Isolation can exacerbate feelings of worthlessness, especially if one is already prone to low self-esteem. If a person feels fundamentally unworthy of kindness—whether from others or themselves—self-compassion will not come naturally. Consistent small acts of kindness toward oneself, repeated over time, can gradually shift these deep-rooted beliefs.

4. *Fear of Emotions*

Isolation offers fewer distractions, which can make intense emotions feel overwhelming. Rather than confronting painful thoughts or feelings, some may prefer to stay busy, numb out, or deny their experiences. Self-compassion requires a willingness to face discomfort with gentleness. While challenging, learning to do so can be profoundly healing. The fear of uncomfortable thoughts naturally starts to dissipate when one addresses them frequently and honestly.

Strategies for Sustained Practice

1. *Set Realistic Goals*

If you are new to self-compassion, avoid setting unrealistic expectations like meditating for an hour every day. Aim for manageable goals, such as five minutes of breathing exercises or a quick daily journal entry. Consistency over time is far more beneficial than sporadic bursts of effort. Easing your way into your goals not only heightens your success rate but also slowly helps you build trust in your own word.

2. *Incorporate Technology Wisely*

In an age of virtual connectivity, technology can be both a blessing and a curse during isolation. Apps dedicated to mindfulness, meditation, or positive psychology can provide structure and guidance. However, excessive social media use might trigger comparisons and negatively impact mental health. Aim to balance your screen time so it serves as a tool for growth rather than a source of stress.

3. *Community Support (Even from Afar)*

   While the term "isolation" implies a lack of connection, virtual communities, online support groups, or phone calls with trusted friends can offer encouragement. Sharing your self-compassion journey with others—even digitally—can reinforce accountability and reduce feelings of loneliness. A quick check-in with a friend or mentor can bolster your efforts and remind you that you are not alone.

4. *Professional Help*

   If isolation is taking a severe toll on your mental health, seeking professional help is a sign of strength, not weakness. Therapists, counselors, and psychologists can offer specialized tools for coping with isolation and practicing self-compassion. Teletherapy platforms have become more accessible, enabling individuals in remote settings to receive professional care.

The Interplay of Self-Compassion and Spirituality

For some, spiritual or religious beliefs can complement self-compassion practices. Traditions that emphasize forgiveness, interconnectedness, or divine love can reinforce the idea that compassion for oneself is a moral and spiritual imperative. Prayers or spiritual readings that promote compassion can be integrated into a daily routine, offering comfort in solitude.

However, self-compassion is not inherently tied to religion or spirituality. It is equally effective for those who identify as secular. A humanistic perspective on shared experience and universal suffering can be just as potent in cultivating a sense of connection and empathy.

Physical Health and Self-Compassion

Isolation can also disrupt healthy routines, such as balanced eating, regular exercise, or sufficient sleep. Lack of structure might lead to neglecting physical health, which then impacts mental well-being. A self-compassionate approach to physical health acknowledges that maintaining healthy habits is not about rigid discipline or punishment but about caring for your body and mind. Your body requires fuel, such as rest, food, and moments of stillness, to continue to function at its highest capacity. For example, gentle movement—like stretching or walking indoors—can be viewed as a gift of well-being rather than a chore.

In this way, self-compassion invites a holistic understanding of health, recognizing that the mind and body are intricately connected. Tuning into physical signals—such as tension or fatigue—allows us to respond with kindness, whether that means taking a short nap, drinking water, or going for a calming walk.

The Transformational Power of Self-Compassion in Isolation

Self-compassion is not a quick fix or an escape from the realities of isolation. Rather, it is a courageous choice to face our struggles head-on with empathy and understanding. By treating ourselves the way we would treat a beloved friend, we become our own source of comfort. This gentle, caring stance creates internal safety—an inner sanctuary to which we can return when external circumstances are beyond our control.

The effects of self-compassion can ripple outward, even when we feel physically or emotionally cut off from the world. We might notice improved moods, a more balanced perspective on our challenges, and an increased capacity to offer compassion to others—when and if we do connect. Our expectations, both in others' actions and the outcomes of current situations, will drastically change and become less prominent. Over time, self-compassion can change the narrative we carry about ourselves, replacing harsh judgments with a gentler, more realistic understanding of what it means to be human.

In a society that often prizes self-sufficiency, admitting that we need kindness—even from ourselves—can feel vulnerable. Yet it is precisely this vulnerability that fosters genuine growth, healing, and resilience. Isolation may remove us from our usual supports, but it also provides a unique opportunity to cultivate a profound inner resource: the ability to meet ourselves with empathy, no matter what.

Ultimately, self-compassion in isolation paves the way for deeper self-awareness and emotional stability. It helps us navigate the treacherous waters of loneliness, stress, and doubt with greater poise and understanding. By embracing our own humanity, flaws and all, we discover that we are never truly alone. We carry within us the capacity to be our own ally, healer, and friend, regardless of the external circumstances. This inner resource becomes a wellspring of hope and resilience, proving that isolation, while challenging, can also be a stepping stone to profound personal growth and deeper self-acceptance.

Chapter 6: Embracing Emotional Vulnerability

Behind closed doors, be fully yourself—raw, unguarded, and real. This is the crucible where the true self is tempered.

Emotional openness and vulnerability are qualities that are often undervalued or misunderstood in modern society. We grow up in cultures that stress the importance of self-reliance, stoicism, and the appearance of invulnerability. We often learn, early on, that showing too much emotion or expressing any form of vulnerability might be seen as a weakness or a liability, something that may be used against us or later regretted. Yet, recent research in psychology, coupled with centuries of philosophical reflection, underscores that emotional openness and vulnerability are cornerstones of human connection, empathy, authenticity, and personal growth. To embrace vulnerability is to allow ourselves to be seen as we truly are—a challenging but profoundly rewarding endeavor. We will explore the significance of emotional openness and vulnerability, dissect the personal and social barriers that keep us from embracing these qualities, and offer practical steps for cultivating them in our daily lives.

Defining Emotional Openness and Vulnerability

Emotional openness is the willingness to acknowledge and share genuine feelings, thoughts, and experiences without filtering, denying, or suppressing their authenticity. It involves recognizing our emotional states—be they joy, sadness, fear, anger, or confusion—and choosing to open up about them to ourselves and potentially to others. Vulnerability, while closely related, refers to the state of being exposed to the possibility of emotional harm, rejection, or misunderstanding when we reveal our inner selves. It is both a cognitive and an emotional stance, in which we accept that we do not have full control over how others might respond to or perceive us.

When we choose to be emotionally open, we allow ourselves to access a broader range of human experiences. Vulnerability, in this context, is not an occasional status—it is a baseline in which we exist as complex, feeling beings. Without vulnerability, our emotional landscape can become stunted, restricted by fear of rejection or judgment. Lack of vulnerability can also lead to a feeling of not being understood, or even convince us that we are entirely alone in our experiences and emotions. When we are truly honest with ourselves and others, new pathways to deeper empathy, connection, and self-understanding emerge.

Although many may mistakenly believe that emotional openness involves dumping raw emotion indiscriminately, genuine emotional openness is more nuanced. It is about thoughtfully sharing our emotions in a safe environment and in ways that enrich relationships. Vulnerability is not about drama but about authenticity. It is revealing honest feelings with the full recognition that people could respond in various ways—support, understanding, or sometimes discomfort or judgment. The intention of vulnerability should not stem from the listeners' reaction.

The Importance of Emotional Openness in Relationships

Human beings are inherently social creatures. We form relationships—romantic, familial, platonic, professional, and communal—that shape our identities and experiences. Emotional openness fosters trust and intimacy in these relationships, offering a gateway to deeper emotional bonds.

1. *Trust and Authenticity:* Trust emerges more organically when people see each other's genuine thoughts, struggles, and joys. When we withhold our true selves, the foundation of a relationship may become shaky. Relationships thrive on honesty, and emotional openness serves as proof that we are not hiding or wearing masks. By embracing vulnerability, we assure others we trust them enough to share our inner world, thus encouraging mutual authenticity.

2. *Conflict Resolution:* Emotional openness can play a pivotal role in resolving conflicts. When people communicate clearly about their feelings, they reduce the chance of misunderstandings and resentments. Instead of passive-aggressively hinting at dissatisfaction or suppressing it until it bursts, honest emotional expression enables us to address concerns directly. Vulnerability in this sense can foster empathy, allowing each party to understand that conflicts are often rooted in unmet needs or unexpressed anxieties.

3. *Deeper Intimacy:* Romantic relationships in particular rely on emotional intimacy—knowing each other's fears, dreams, and insecurities. While physical intimacy is one form of closeness, emotional intimacy requires that both partners be open about their vulnerabilities. Emotional openness can thus heighten the sense of closeness, reinforcing a relationship's foundation and providing a stronger incentive to overcome hurdles together.

4. *Group Cohesion:* Even in group settings—at work or in communal projects—vulnerability can result in a sense of unity and shared purpose. When team members feel safe to express not only ideas but also concerns or apprehensions, the group can address underlying tensions preemptively, ensuring that relationships remain healthy. This emotional honesty within groups fosters a sense of belonging and empathy among team members; bonds that cannot be achieved at a surface level, resulting in both better output and better spirits.

Overcoming Societal and Cultural Barriers

Despite its many advantages, emotional openness is often discouraged. From early childhood, many of us learn certain "rules" about which emotions are acceptable to display and which are not. Boys may be told not to cry or show weakness; girls may be taught not to express anger or assert themselves. Our cultural narratives often elevate the "strong," stoic individual, implying that showing emotion signals inadequacy. These ingrained beliefs can make the path to vulnerability steep.

1. *Gender Norms:* Gender expectations can hamper the ability to be vulnerable. Men may be conditioned to believe that tears or open displays of pain or fear are signs of emasculation. Women, on the other hand, may be criticized for being "too emotional," which can lead them to repress feelings of anger or frustration. Cultural scripts, therefore, affect all genders, though in different ways. Overcoming these requires recognizing that emotional expression is a fundamental human need, not a gendered liability.
2. *Fear of Rejection or Judgment:* One of the most prevalent barriers is the fear that others will judge, ridicule, or reject us if we reveal our deeper feelings or insecurities. This fear can lead to a protective strategy: never let anyone see your vulnerability. By doing so, we might avoid certain forms of judgment, but we also miss out on the opportunity to bond more deeply with others who might relate to our struggles.
3. *Social Media and Cultural Pressure:* The rise of social media has created an environment where people frequently curate an image of perpetual success, happiness, and resilience. We rarely see snapshots of failure or raw vulnerability. This can perpetuate the illusion that everyone else is coping effortlessly with life's challenges. Consequently, individuals may feel pressured to conform to these unrealistic narratives, suppressing genuine emotion to maintain a facade.
4. *Power Dynamics:* In certain professional or hierarchical contexts, showing vulnerability might be perceived as a professional risk. People worry about how superiors, subordinates, or colleagues might interpret their emotional openness. In these situations, the pressure to project competence and confidence can leave little room for admitting weaknesses or insecurities. While these concerns are sometimes valid, an increasing number of organizations and leaders now recognize that healthy vulnerability fosters creativity, trust, and productivity.

Psychological Underpinnings and Benefits

From a psychological standpoint, emotional openness and vulnerability have profound impacts on our mental and emotional well-being. According to humanistic psychology, people are driven by the desire for authenticity, self-discovery, and meaningful relationships. By opening ourselves up, we lean into these core needs.

1. *Self-Awareness:* The act of self-disclosure—acknowledging and sharing our feelings—helps us better understand ourselves, even if this communication is only internal initially. Emotions serve as indicators, pointing us to areas in our lives that require attention or change. Emotional openness compels us to recognize patterns, motivations, and triggers we might otherwise overlook.

2. *Emotional Resilience:* Contrary to popular belief, sharing our vulnerabilities does not necessarily make us fragile. In fact, acknowledging and expressing difficult emotions like guilt, shame, or fear can build resilience. By confronting these feelings head-on, we learn to cope with them rather than let them fester in hidden recesses. This practice strengthens our emotional muscles and equips us with healthier coping strategies.

3. *Reduction of Shame:* Research by Dr. Brené Brown highlights that shame thrives on secrecy. When people hide their shameful feelings or experiences, the shame grows deeper. In contrast, speaking openly about shame can dismantle its power, leading to a sense of acceptance and self-compassion. Emotional openness counters shame by offering a path to empathy and understanding from others.

4. *Health Benefits:* Studies in psychoneuroimmunology show that chronic emotional suppression can manifest in physical health issues, including higher stress levels and weaker immune response. Conversely, expressing emotions in healthy ways correlates with improved mental and physical health. By openly processing what we feel, we minimize stress and create conditions for better overall wellness. Confronting our mental struggles and developing habits to address them before they become crippling is a large part of self-care.

Common Misconceptions About Vulnerability

Despite mounting evidence about the benefits of emotional openness, several misconceptions persist:

1. *"Vulnerability is a Sign of Weakness":* Many people believe that revealing doubts or fear undermines their strength or competence. In reality, vulnerability is an act of courage—it means taking an emotional risk despite uncertain outcomes. True strength lies in being honest about who we are rather than pretending to be invulnerable.

2. *"Always Be Positive":* Some self-help narratives push a relentless positivity that leaves no room for negative emotions like sadness, anger, or frustration. However, authentic emotional experience includes the entire spectrum of emotions. Denying or invalidating certain feelings leads to

emotional dishonesty, which can stifle growth and deepen our pain over time.

3. *"Sharing Emotions Means Oversharing Everything":* Vulnerability does not mean publicly broadcasting every aspect of our inner world. A careful discernment of context, audience, and boundaries is crucial. Healthy vulnerability is about truthful self-expression where it matters most, not about turning every personal experience into a public confession. The intention of sharing also plays a part in balancing when to be vulnerable and open; if one seeks pity or intends to manipulate the future reactions of those they share with, this form of communication can become counterproductive.

4. *"Only Certain People Should Be Vulnerable":* It's a common mistake to believe that vulnerability suits only certain "emotional" or "sensitive" individuals. In truth, everyone has the capacity—and, arguably, the need—to be emotionally open. The capacity for vulnerability is not restricted by one's personality type, cultural background, or professional role. The difference lies in those we choose to be vulnerable with and how often that is needed for mental stability and close relationships.

Strategies for Cultivating Emotional Openness

Embracing emotional openness is neither automatic nor instantaneous. It often requires proactive strategies, self-reflection, and repeated practice to overcome the internal and external barriers.

1. *Self-Reflection and Mindfulness*

   Start by identifying your emotional states without judgment. A daily journal or a few minutes of mindfulness practice can help you tune into how you really feel. By acknowledging and labeling your emotions ("I am anxious," "I am feeling hopeful," "I am overwhelmed"), you create the mental space necessary to address them honestly.

2. *Gradual Exposure*

   If you are unused to sharing your feelings, begin with small steps. Confide in a close friend or family member about a minor concern. Over time, as you gain confidence and see that supportive responses are possible, you can tackle deeper or more challenging disclosures.

3. *Therapeutic Support*

   For many people, especially those dealing with trauma or long-standing emotional suppression, professional support is invaluable. Therapists provide a structured, confidential environment in which vulnerability is welcomed. Group therapy, too, can help you see that you are not alone in experiencing struggles. Therapy can teach you communication skills and coping mechanisms to handle the discomfort that comes with letting down emotional defenses.

4. *Practice Empathy*

When we learn to see the humanity in others' vulnerabilities, it becomes easier to accept our own. By listening actively and suspending judgment when others share, we create a cycle of healthy disclosure and mutual support. We also gain perspective that is vital for empathy towards others and ourselves at times. When we are able to view situations we are affected by from the other side, we hold onto less resentment and accept others' actions easily without being deeply hurt or confused. Empathy is transformative not only for relationships but also for our ability to be open about our own challenges.

Overcoming Personal Fears Around Vulnerability

Fear is one of the greatest barriers to embracing emotional openness. Whether it's fear of judgment, rejection, or a deep-seated worry about losing control, it can be paralyzing. However, there are techniques to confront and navigate these fears:

1. *Recognize the Inner Critic*

Many of our worries stem from negative self-talk: "They'll think I'm weak" or "I'll embarrass myself." The first step is to identify these internal criticisms. Once recognized, you can challenge their validity. Often, these thoughts are irrational or exaggerated. By reframing them—"It's brave to share how I feel"—you open a path to growth.

2. *Establish Boundaries*

Part of the fear around vulnerability may stem from past experiences of betrayal or exposure. Setting appropriate boundaries can provide a sense of safety. Decide when and with whom you'll share personal information. This approach ensures that you are not exposing yourself to people who are not prepared or trustworthy enough to hold space for your vulnerability.

3. *Celebrate Small Victories*

Each time you share an honest feeling, and it is met with understanding or even simple acknowledgement, it's a step forward. Reflect on these positive experiences and store them as proof that vulnerability can lead to deeper connections. Over time, these small successes build confidence, making vulnerability more comfortable. Celebrating even small steps forms motivation to continue on the path of growth.

4. *Self-Compassion*

Treat yourself with kindness and understanding as you experiment with vulnerability. Being open might be messy or uncomfortable. You might occasionally share too much or with the wrong person, and that's part of the learning process. Compassion toward yourself fosters resilience and prevents you from shutting down after missteps. These occasional missteps are critical in the process, sometimes offering more insight than successful outcomes.

The Interplay Between Vulnerability and Leadership

Contrary to the stereotypical image of the leader as unflappable and always composed, vulnerability can be a powerful tool in leadership roles. When a leader admits they do not have all the answers or owns up to a mistake, they demonstrate accountability and authenticity. This openness sets a tone for an entire organization or team, encouraging honesty and creativity.

1. *Building Trust Within Teams*

Teams led by individuals who demonstrate emotional openness tend to report higher levels of trust. Employees feel they can safely voice concerns, share innovative ideas, or admit to mistakes without fear of harsh judgment. This mutual trust fosters a more dynamic and supportive work environment.

2. *Inspiring Loyalty and Engagement*

Leaders who balance confidence with vulnerability humanize themselves, making them more relatable. Employees or followers often feel a stronger sense of belonging and loyalty to a leader who can say, "I need help" or "I was wrong." That level of humility and reality encourages a collaborative spirit and deeper engagement. Respect is given when a leader is conscious of acknowledging their mistakes and aiming for the best results, even if it requires the help of others.

3. *Fostering Adaptability*

In fast-changing environments, a leader's ability to be flexible and transparent about challenges can pivot organizations more effectively. When leaders openly communicate the obstacles or uncertainties they face, teams can rally around finding collective solutions. The leader's vulnerability invites the combined intelligence of the team rather than dictating solutions from a place of unquestionable authority.

4. *Empowering Others*

By modeling vulnerability, leaders empower others to take thoughtful risks and grow. When people see that failure or imperfection will not result in ridicule or punitive measures, they become more willing to step out of their comfort zones. Vulnerability thus fosters a learning culture that fuels innovation and continuous improvement.

Societal Shifts and the Future of Vulnerability

In recent years, there has been a cultural shift toward valuing authenticity over superficial appearances. Social movements around mental health awareness, body positivity, and open discourse about personal struggles have put vulnerability at the forefront of public conversation. Many public figures—from athletes to actors to corporate CEOs—have begun speaking openly about their emotional challenges and mental health journeys, contributing to a broader acceptance of vulnerability as a strength.

1. *Evolving Work Cultures*

Forward-thinking companies are incorporating emotional intelligence and psychological safety into their core values. Some organizations now offer mental health days, counseling services, and workshops on effective communication. These initiatives validate the fact that emotional openness can elevate productivity, retention, and innovation.

2. *Changing Gender Narratives*

There is a growing pushback against rigid gender roles that constrict emotional expression. Movements encouraging men to talk about mental health and women to assert their needs equally contribute to dismantling the barriers to vulnerability. This shift, while still ongoing, points to a future where emotional expression is considered a universal right, not a sign of weakness.

3. *Public Discourse and Media*

Social media influencers, podcasts, and TED Talks by thought leaders like Brené Brown are spreading awareness about the power of vulnerability. While the curated world of social media can still perpetuate unrealistic images, an increasing number of voices challenge these norms, encouraging more honest depictions of life's trials and triumphs.

4. *Educational Initiatives*

    Some schools and universities incorporate emotional literacy into curricula, teaching students to identify, express, and manage their feelings from an early age. If this trend continues, future generations may find it more natural to embrace vulnerability and empathy in personal and professional contexts.

Embracing emotional openness and vulnerability is a journey that requires patience, courage, and consistent practice. Below are practical tips and final reflections on how to integrate vulnerability into one's life:

1. *Create Safe Spaces for Sharing*

    Whether it's a trusted friend, family member, or a support group, find environments where you feel comfortable being yourself. Nurture these relationships by reciprocating the openness others show you.

2. *Develop Emotional Vocabulary*

    Enhance your ability to identify and label your emotions. Instead of resorting to general descriptors like "good" or "bad," explore precise words (e.g., "anxious," "excited," "disappointed," "hopeful"). A broad emotional vocabulary can help you express yourself more accurately and avoid misunderstandings.

3. *Practice Self-Disclosure Gradually*

    If vulnerability is new to you, start with less personal topics and build up to sharing more intimate concerns. This approach allows you to gauge your comfort level and the other person's reactions before revealing deeper aspects of yourself.

4. *Engage in Active Listening*

    Part of embracing vulnerability is being open to what others share with you. Active listening—making eye contact, reflecting back what someone has said, and refraining from judgment—creates an environment in which vulnerability can flourish on both sides.

5. *Adopt a Growth Mindset*

    Understand that emotional openness is a skill to be refined. Mistakes, misunderstandings, or even negative reactions from others are opportunities to learn. Embrace these outcomes as part of the process rather than as indicators that you should retreat into old habits of emotional silence.

6. *Seek Ongoing Support*

    Whether it's therapy, coaching, or mentorship, tapping into professional or peer support can ease the challenges of vulnerability. Workshops and group discussions on emotional intelligence can also provide fresh perspectives and strategies.

Emotional openness and vulnerability are pathways to more authentic living, deeper relationships, and greater emotional well-being. While societal norms, personal fears, and misunderstandings can deter us from embracing these qualities, the transformative power they carry is evident. By stepping into the realm of vulnerability, we unlock empathy, resilience, and genuine connection—both with ourselves and with others. Embracing our emotional truths is not only an act of courage but also a profound investment in our collective humanity and peace. In a world that often pushes us to put up walls and barriers, choosing to remain open and honest enables us to connect with each other in ways that truly matter.

A young monk asked the master, "How do I forge a heart that does not waver?"

The master pointed to a bamboo stalk bending in the storm. "See how it yields, yet never breaks? Its roots grip the earth, unseen, unmoved."

The monk sat by the bamboo, watching it sway through days and nights. At last, he smiled, for he saw: true strength is not in resisting the wind, but in rooting deeply within.

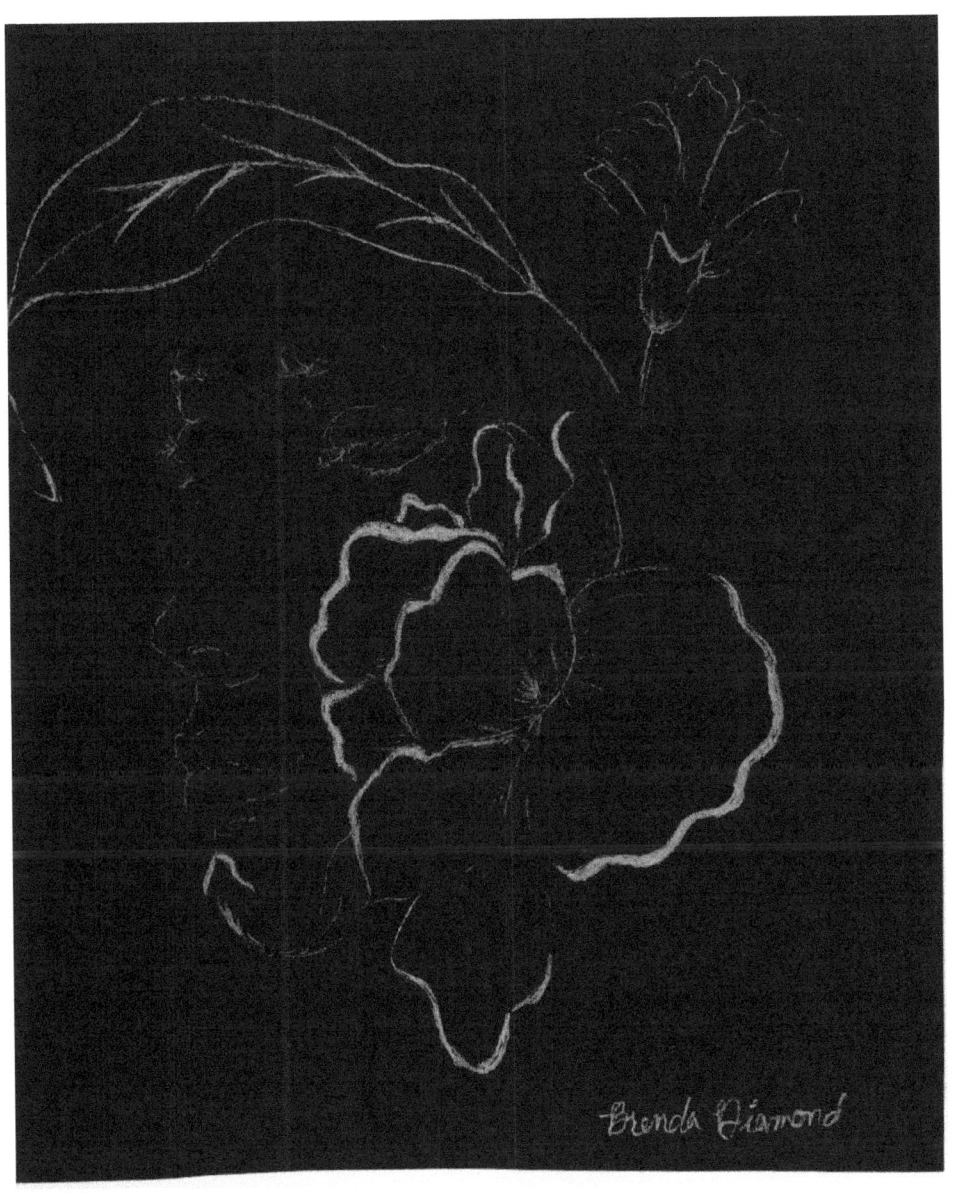

Brenda Diamond

Chapter 7: Seeking Balance and Harmony

Balance arises when we honor each aspect of ourselves: the doer, the dreamer, and the divine observer within.

In a world characterized by rapid technological advances, constant connectivity, and an influx of information, the concept of seeking balance and harmony has taken on renewed significance. While each era in human history has had its own set of challenges, our current globalized environment presents unique complexities that test our well-being at individual, communal, and planetary levels. Never before has humanity possessed such vast technological power to shape realities—nor have we experienced such widespread environmental, social, and psychological repercussions of our collective choices. The pursuit of balance and harmony, therefore, involves reconciling our ever-accelerating lifestyles with the human need for connection, meaning, and sustainability.

Increasingly, we find ourselves in a paradox of abundance and scarcity. We live in a time of unprecedented access to knowledge, entertainment, and opportunities. Yet simultaneously, people face deep social isolation, heightened stress levels, and ecological crises. The tension between progress and preservation has led many to ask: *How can we thrive in an age of excess?* The call for a more integrated, harmonious way of living is not new. Philosophical and spiritual traditions, from ancient Stoicism to Eastern wisdom practices like Zen Buddhism, have long championed the value of equilibrium. However, integrating these timeless lessons into modern life demands practical strategies that speak to contemporary concerns—from managing screen time to fostering community cohesion in diverse, interconnected societies.

Finding balance can seem an elusive quest, especially when it entails navigating a complex interplay of physical, mental, emotional, and spiritual needs. It requires a concerted effort to understand ourselves, examine our habits, and question systems that shape our daily experiences. It also necessitates an awareness of the planet's limits, recognizing that genuine harmony must encompass more than just the personal sphere—it must extend to our relationships, our communities, and our environment. This essay delves into various facets of balance and harmony, exploring their importance across different domains of modern life. By highlighting challenges and opportunities, we can illuminate paths forward that not only serve individual fulfillment but also reinforce the social and ecological fabric upon which all life depends.

Historical Perspectives on Balance and Harmony

Humans have long wrestled with the challenges of living in relative equilibrium. Ancient cultures, despite lacking modern technologies, developed rich philosophical and religious traditions around moderation and harmony. For instance, the Confucian concept of the "Doctrine of the Mean" promotes a nuanced approach to moral virtue and social harmony, urging individuals to avoid extremes and seek balance in thought and deed. Ancient Greek philosophy, likewise, extolled virtues such as *sophrosyne*—temperance or moderation—and *eudaimonia*, often translated as human flourishing or well-being. Greek thinkers like Aristotle argued that the virtues integral to a balanced life are cultivated through habitual practice, demonstrating that balance is not a static state, but rather an ongoing journey requiring mindful effort.

In parallel, indigenous cultures across the globe have traditionally emphasized living in harmony with nature. Their practices often involved rituals, communal decision-making, and ecological stewardship rooted in an understanding of the interconnectedness of all life. Such perspectives recognized that the environment is not merely a resource to be exploited, but a delicate system in which humans play a participatory role. This ecological awareness laid a foundation for what modern sustainability movements strive to recover: that genuine well-being is inseparable from the health of the planet.

Though these historical traditions varied by geography and worldview, they shared a central premise: Excess or imbalance leads to personal and social discord. Whether through the allegories of the Buddha's "Middle Way," the balanced path between indulgence and asceticism, or the symbiotic worldview of Native American tribes that integrated spiritual reverence for the land, diverse cultures underlined the importance of harmonious living. These lessons are neither outdated nor irrelevant. As we revisit these traditional insights, we can glean lessons that inform our strategies for coping with 21st-century dilemmas, blending time-honored wisdom with contemporary innovation.

⑥ The Modern Landscape: Overstimulation and Overload

The phenomenon of "digital overload" refers to the stress and cognitive burden brought on by relentless streams of notifications and updates. The average person checks their phone dozens, if not hundreds, of times per day, often interrupting tasks that require deep focus. This fragmented attention can erode productivity, hamper creativity, and elevate anxiety. Even when we do aim to unwind, the sheer array of options on our screens can leave us feeling restless rather than rejuvenated. Consequently, "unplugging" has emerged as both a catchphrase and a necessity, as people recognize the importance of setting boundaries around technology usage to regain a sense of inner calm.

A related concern stems from the social dimensions of digital life. Although online networks can forge connections that transcend geography, they can also foster comparison, envy, and a constant quest for external validation. The curated nature of social media often presents an idealized snapshot of others' lives, leading users to feel inadequate or "behind" in their own life trajectories. This perceived pressure to keep up—financially, socially, and even spiritually—adds yet another layer of complexity to modern life. It may be beneficial to consider what you want to gain from technology, and then find ways to avoid from the negative impacts that you don't want to partake in. In pursuit of genuine balance and harmony, it becomes crucial not only to moderate the volume of digital content we consume but also to cultivate a more intentional, mindful approach to how we engage with technology.

⑥ The Importance of Mental and Emotional Well-Being

Amidst the flurry of modern distractions, achieving balance hinges significantly on tending to mental and emotional health. Stress, anxiety, and burnout have become increasingly prevalent in societies that prize productivity and perpetual activity. Workloads expand, demands intensify, and the lines between professional and personal life blur, especially with remote work becoming more commonplace. At the same time, many communities lack robust support systems or safe spaces for discussing mental health, making it challenging for individuals to seek or receive the help they need.

One of the central pillars of emotional well-being is self-awareness. Understanding our own triggers, energy cycles, and emotional responses allows us to tailor our daily habits and relationships in ways that promote balance. Self-awareness additionally lessens the pressure and expectations we put on those we communicate with, which makes us more cautious about putting unnecessary baggage or blame on them. For some, this self-awareness comes through formal psychotherapy; for others, it might develop via mindfulness practices like meditation and yoga, or contemplative pursuits such as journaling or reflective nature walks. The key is recognizing the necessity of taking stock of our internal landscapes in a world that often encourages external achievement above all else.

Emotional intelligence extends beyond personal introspection—it has clear implications for our social ties, workplace dynamics, and broader societal interactions. When we nurture empathy, kindness, and authentic communication, we lay the groundwork for communities that care for one another's well-being. In practical terms, this might involve implementing mental health initiatives in schools and workplaces, providing resources for stress management, or simply fostering open conversations about emotional struggles. By acknowledging that mental and emotional harmony is an essential facet of overall balance, we shift societal norms away from a purely competitive ethos to one that values compassion and mutual support. The ripple effects of this shift can be profound, influencing how we design organizational policies, plan urban spaces, and even frame legal structures to uphold the mental well-being of diverse populations.

⑥ Physical Health and Lifestyle

While modern societies grapple with digital overload and mental health challenges, the pursuit of physical well-being remains a foundational aspect of seeking balance and harmony. Paradoxically, advances in medicine and public health have extended average life expectancies in many parts of the world, yet lifestyle-related conditions such as obesity, heart disease, and diabetes have become increasingly widespread. The ease of accessing convenient, highly processed food and the sedentary nature of contemporary work contribute to these trends. Balancing nutritional and exercise needs in a fast-paced environment can feel daunting, but doing so is key to overall vitality.

Regular physical activity serves not only to maintain a healthy weight and cardiovascular function, but also to alleviate stress and improve mood. Even moderate forms of exercise—like brisk walking or gentle yoga—boost endorphins, promote better sleep, and foster resilience. Just as the skills of mindfulness are practiced and continue to advance through time and effort, outlets of physical activity can be the same. There is an endurance that must be built, but the journey to getting there should not be shied away from because it may not be immediately rewarding. Likewise, the food choices we make can either support or undermine the pursuit of harmony. Mindful eating—paying attention to flavors, textures, and hunger cues—encourages a more harmonious relationship with nourishment. Reducing intake of refined sugars and prioritizing whole, nutrient-rich foods can lead to higher energy levels and improved mental clarity, enhancing our capacity to meet life's demands with equilibrium.

Nonetheless, physical health is not solely about individual behavior; it's also shaped by social and environmental factors. Urban design that prioritizes walkability, green spaces, and recreational facilities can foster healthier lifestyles at the community level. Workplace policies that encourage breaks, fitness initiatives, and flexible hours help employees maintain a healthier work-life balance. Beyond policy, a collective shift in cultural attitudes—from glorifying overwork and busyness to celebrating balance and rest—is essential. When societies value overall wellness and intentionally promote it, individuals are better equipped to integrate healthy behaviors into their daily lives, making the pursuit of physical harmony more attainable.

⑥ Technology and the Search for Equilibrium

Considering the digital revolution's ubiquity, it is essential to examine how technology can be harnessed to serve balance and harmony rather than erode it. On the one hand, there are myriad apps and online platforms designed to support mindfulness, meditation, and fitness tracking, offering personalized guidance toward healthier habits. Telehealth services and mental health apps have proven transformative, especially in areas where access to in-person care is limited.

⇔ For example, *www.enalign.com* helps with energy alignment so you experience more clarity, balance, harmony, focus, fulfillment, love, happiness, and abundance in your life.

On the other hand, the very same technology can contribute to chronic distraction and eroding attention spans if not used judiciously. Push notifications, autoplay algorithms, and targeted advertisements capitalize on cognitive biases, keeping us hooked in a cycle of consumption that leaves little room for introspection or calm. Little room for thoughts that we conceive all on our own. Moreover, social media "echo chambers" can polarize public discourse, making it more difficult to find common ground in addressing collective challenges. Navigating these digital pitfalls requires both structural changes—like ethical design principles in software development—and personal discipline, including mindful usage of devices and setting firm boundaries around screen time.

⇔ A balanced approach to technology acknowledges its dual nature. Rather than romanticizing a return to a pre-digital era (which had its own limitations), we can advocate for "tech wisdom," a concept encompassing both responsible use and technological innovation geared toward well-being. Tech companies are increasingly exploring design philosophies centered on user flourishing, an encouraging trend that aligns corporate interests with the social good. On an individual level, regular "digital detoxes," curated content consumption, and purposeful use of technology can help us harness its benefits without succumbing to its more toxic attributes. The future of balance in a digital world ultimately depends on collective efforts to cultivate a healthier relationship with our devices, ensuring that technology remains a tool to enhance (rather than overshadow) our pursuit of harmony.

⑥ Environmental Harmony

Harmony cannot be fully addressed without considering humanity's relationship with the natural environment. Our modern way of life—fueled by mass production, overconsumption, and fossil fuel dependency—has led to climate change, resource depletion, and biodiversity loss. The planetary crisis we face underscores that real balance is not solely personal or societal; it is also ecological. The concept of sustainability, then, is at the heart of environmental harmony. It involves using resources at a rate that does not compromise future generations' abilities to meet their own needs, as articulated in the Brundtland Report of 1987. Yet sustainability is more than a technical blueprint for resource management; it reflects a deeper ethical and spiritual orientation to life that values respect, responsibility, and reciprocity.

In practical terms, seeking environmental harmony involves a broad range of actions—from adopting renewable energy solutions to supporting regenerative agriculture that enriches soil rather than depleting it. It also includes reimagining urban design to prioritize green spaces and public transportation, thereby reducing carbon emissions and encouraging human-nature interaction. On a more personal level, choices like reducing plastic waste, conserving water, and engaging in community cleanup efforts can strengthen our sense of connectedness to the planet. When each person or household takes steps toward more sustainable living, the cumulative impact can be substantial. Moreover, when entire industries, guided by public demand and regulatory frameworks, shift toward circular economies and eco-friendly practices, the impact is transformative.

Perhaps just as important as these tangible actions is the cultivation of an environmental consciousness—a recognition that we are part of, not separate from, the natural world. This outlook fosters humility, gratitude, and a willingness to cooperate across cultural and national boundaries, acknowledging that the challenges we face are global in scope. Caring for the environment thus becomes not only a matter of responsibility but also an expression of harmony itself: living in tune with the rhythms and limitations of the Earth, mindful of the delicate balance upon which all life depends.

⑥ Social and Community Dimensions

No discussion of balance and harmony is complete without considering the social dimension—how our interactions, relationships, and communities shape (and are shaped by) our quest for equilibrium. In many modern societies, individualism and competition are deeply ingrained, encouraging us to focus on personal success sometimes at the expense of collective well-being. Yet humans are inherently social creatures, and isolation can have detrimental effects on mental, emotional, and even physical health. The modern environment, with its sprawling cities and online networks, offers a paradox: we are more connected virtually than ever before, but many still report feeling lonely and disconnected in their immediate surroundings.

Communities that embrace cooperation, inclusivity, and shared responsibility for each other's well-being often fare better in fostering harmony. For instance, neighborhoods that organize community gardens, communal childcare, or cooperative living arrangements allow individuals to share resources and emotional support. This collective approach can lighten the load of modern demands, creating more bandwidth for personal growth and stronger interpersonal bonds. When institutions—be they schools, religious centers, or civic organizations—adopt inclusive, participatory models, they also contribute to a social climate that values empathy, fairness, and mutual upliftment. In turn, this diminishes stress and division, allowing individuals to focus on thriving in tandem with their communities.

Moreover, diversity and multiculturalism play pivotal roles in modern societies, offering both challenges and opportunities. Navigating different cultural norms and perspectives can be a source of conflict, but it can also expand our capacity for empathy and global awareness. By acknowledging that harmony does not require uniformity but rather a respectful acceptance of differences, communities can harness the strengths that arise from varied backgrounds. This inclusive ethos has broader implications for addressing social injustices, such as racial or gender discrimination, ensuring that the benefits of modern progress are equitably shared. Ultimately, a socially harmonious environment flourishes when collective structures and individual mindsets prioritize compassion, collaboration, and mutual respect.

⑥ Approaches to Personal Growth and Spirituality

For many people, the path toward balance and harmony is intimately tied to personal growth and, often, a sense of spirituality or life purpose. Spirituality, in this context, need not refer solely to religion; it can encompass any practice or worldview that connects individuals to a sense of something larger than themselves, be it a higher power, the universe, or simply the mystery of life. This inward journey can provide a counterbalance to the frantic pace of external demands, offering refuge, wisdom, and clarity.

Meditation and mindfulness are common gateways to this deeper perspective. By focusing on the breath or practicing non-judgmental awareness, individuals can cultivate an inner stillness that recalibrates the mind and emotions. Over time, such practices can encourage more thoughtful responses to life's challenges rather than reflexive reactions. In a broader sense, personal development might involve studying philosophies and moral frameworks that align with one's values, or engaging in creative endeavors—art, music, writing—that nurture self-expression and heightened consciousness. These pursuits remind us that human existence is not purely transactional, tied to consumerism or professional milestones, but also includes aesthetic, spiritual, and ethical dimensions.

Additionally, various traditions—from yoga and Tai Chi to Sufism and Christian contemplative prayer—offer structured approaches to cultivating inner harmony. Common to these systems is the idea that personal transformation and broader harmony are interlinked. By refining our character, resolving internal conflicts, and attuning ourselves to a sense of deeper purpose, we become more capable of extending empathy and love to others. This ripple effect can influence families, workplaces, and communities, sowing seeds of balance at multiple levels. Whether through formal spiritual discipline or simple self-reflection, aligning our inner lives with our outer actions can be a powerful cornerstone in the quest for harmony in the modern world.

ⓖ Leadership and Collective Responsibility

The quest for balance and harmony is not solely an individual journey; it also demands visionary leadership and collective responsibility. Leaders in government, corporations, education, and nonprofits hold considerable sway over how systems are structured—whether they prioritize short-term gains or invest in long-term well-being. Policies that support workers' rights, fair wages, environmental protection, and educational equity can cultivate broader societal balance, but they require leaders who view success through a holistic lens rather than just economic metrics.

Likewise, corporate entities can play a crucial role by adopting sustainable and socially responsible practices. A growing number of businesses now recognize that balancing the profit motive with social and environmental stewardship is vital both to brand reputation and to meeting consumer expectations. B Corp certifications, corporate social responsibility (CSR) initiatives, and green business models offer pathways for companies to contribute to collective harmony. Such leadership, however, needs to be genuine rather than tokenistic, grounded in real accountability and transparent metrics. Stakeholders at all levels—employees, shareholders, and customers—must push for consistent commitments that align with the values of balance and fairness.

Grassroots movements and civic engagement are equally significant. Individuals can unite around local causes—such as improving public transportation or establishing urban gardens—and thereby influence policy and culture from the ground up. Collaborative efforts, whether at the neighborhood or global scale, exemplify the idea that balance is a shared project: when a critical mass of people demand and work toward harmony, systemic changes become possible. The media also plays a role, shaping narratives around what constitutes well-being and success. Journalists, filmmakers, and influencers can amplify stories that showcase positive models of community, sustainability, and ethical innovation, inspiring others to follow suit. Through such collective endeavors, the pursuit of balance and harmony transcends personal aspiration to become a driving force for societal transformation.

ⓖ Charting a Path Forward

Seeking balance and harmony in the modern world is a multifaceted endeavor, touching upon every dimension of human life: mental and emotional well-being, physical health, technological engagement, environmental stewardship, social connectedness, personal growth, and leadership. While each domain presents its own set of challenges, they are all interlinked, reflecting the holistic nature of genuine harmony. The rapid pace of change, the incessant digital chatter, and the scale of global issues can sometimes seem overwhelming, but they also present opportunities to forge new paradigms of living—ones that prioritize depth over speed, cooperation over competition, and sustainability over short-term exploitation and greed.

It is easy to be swept away by the currents of modern life, but we retain agency in how we respond. On an individual level, cultivating self-awareness, setting healthy boundaries, and nurturing physical, emotional, and spiritual practices can restore a sense of equilibrium. Collectively, supporting just and forward-thinking policies, championing ethical business practices, and fostering inclusive communities can anchor us in shared values that uplift rather than drain. Philosophical and spiritual wisdom traditions from around the globe offer roadmaps for inner and outer harmony, reminding us that moderation, empathy, and reverence for life are timeless virtues, as necessary today as in any other era.

In charting a path forward, it is essential to remember that balance and harmony are not destinations but processes—a constant dance between effort and rest, commitment and openness, focus and letting go. This dynamic quality invites us to remain adaptive, humble, and open to learning. Regardless of the upheavals and pressures of the modern era, we can choose to orient ourselves toward harmony at each step, incrementally transforming our personal routines, our social structures, and our relationship with the planet. By doing so, we honor the interconnected web of existence that sustains us, and we build a future in which human flourishing is intimately woven with ecological care, social equity, and a deep sense of shared purpose. Ultimately, seeking balance and harmony in the modern world is more than a noble aspiration—it is a vital imperative for ensuring that both current and future generations can lead lives of meaning and resonance with the greater tapestry of life.

A seeker asked the Zen master, "My ego fuels creations that shape the world, yet the true path calls me to release it. How do I honor both?"

The master tossed a stone into the river. It sank, guiding the current's dance, while the water flowed free, embracing the stone's gift.

The seeker smiled, seeing both paths as one.

Brenda Diamond

Chapter 8: Mindfulness and Solitary Reflection

The purpose of solitude is not merely to be away from others but to witness each moment with clarity. In that clarity, the essence of Zen emerges.

In a world characterized by rapid technological advances, constant connectivity, and the pressure to multitask, individuals often find themselves searching for greater peace, self-understanding, and emotional balance. Amid this ongoing quest, the practices of **mindfulness** and **solitary reflection** have emerged as powerful methods to cultivate a sense of calm and clarity. Mindfulness, derived from ancient Buddhist traditions, involves remaining present and fully engaged with one's moment-to-moment experiences, whether they are external or internal. Solitary reflection, by contrast, emphasizes the power of spending time alone for introspection, personal growth, and creative inspiration.

Together, mindfulness and solitary reflection can serve as complementary disciplines that guide individuals toward greater self-awareness, improved stress management, and an enhanced understanding of their place in the world. This paper delves into the fundamental principles of mindfulness, explores the concept of solitary reflection, and articulates the ways in which these practices intersect and reinforce each other. We will examine the historical roots of mindfulness, its key components, and how it is applied in modern therapeutic settings. Furthermore, we will discuss the inherent value of intentional solitude, spotlighting the potential hazards of social isolation versus the benefits of thoughtful solitude. Finally, we will highlight how integrating mindfulness into periods of solitary reflection can lead to transformative, lasting changes in one's life.

✵ Defining Mindfulness

At its core, **mindfulness** is the practice of paying attention to the present moment with an attitude of nonjudgmental curiosity. Originating from contemplative Buddhist traditions—most notably from the teachings of Siddhartha Gautama (the Buddha)—mindfulness found its way into contemporary Western discourse largely through the work of Jon Kabat-Zinn and his colleagues in the late 1970s. Kabat-Zinn integrated Buddhist wisdom with modern science to create Mindfulness-Based Stress Reduction (MBSR), a structured program aimed at alleviating stress, anxiety, and various physical ailments.

The defining characteristic of mindfulness is **intentional awareness**. Rather than allowing the mind to wander aimlessly through memories and daydreams, mindfulness brings conscious, gentle attention back to the breath, bodily sensations, or any other anchor one chooses. This act of redirecting attention, repeated many times over, fosters an acceptance of the present moment while cutting through habitual patterns of judging thoughts and emotions as inherently "good" or "bad." This practice also desensitizes us to what we view as detrimental thoughts. Mindfulness practitioners learn to become more neutral observers, developing a sense of emotional balance and increased tolerance for discomfort.

Central to mindfulness is the idea that **thoughts are not facts**—they are fleeting mental events that need not dictate one's behavior or dominate one's emotional landscape. By practicing mindfulness, individuals gain the capacity to pause before reacting, creating the mental space to respond with greater clarity and compassion.

Historical and Cultural Roots of Mindfulness

Though mindfulness has garnered widespread popularity in the modern West, the concept has deep roots in **Buddhist philosophy**. In the Pāli language, the term for mindfulness is "sati," which means to remember or to bear in mind. According to Buddhist teaching, mindfulness is one of the core elements of the Noble Eightfold Path, pointing practitioners toward heightened awareness of their thoughts, words, and actions. Early Buddhist practitioners used mindfulness in meditation to observe the impermanent nature of reality, let go of attachment, and cultivate wisdom.

Mindfulness practices were traditionally passed down through monastic lineages, but in modern times, they have become accessible to secular audiences. The Eastern cultural contexts in which mindfulness developed emphasize an integrated view of physical, mental, and spiritual well-being. Asian cultures often used mindfulness principles for ethical self-discipline, focusing on compassionate action and emotional regulation as pathways to personal liberation.

Over the centuries, variations of mindful practice appeared in Taoism, Confucianism, and Hindu traditions, typically emphasizing self-cultivation, harmony with nature, and awareness of the subtle interplay between body and mind. Today, mindfulness has spread across healthcare, education, corporate environments, and even military training programs, reflecting its versatile and universally relevant nature.

✩ The Key Components of Mindfulness

Although mindfulness is often described as a simple concept—"paying attention, on purpose, in the present moment, non-judgmentally"—it is underpinned by several critical components:

1. *Focused Attention:* One of the foundational practices in mindfulness is the focus on a single point of reference, often the breath. By returning repeatedly to this anchor, practitioners strengthen their ability to sustain attention.

2. *Open Monitoring:* Beyond focusing on a specific object, mindfulness also involves cultivating a receptive, non-elaborative awareness of thoughts, sensations, and emotions **as they arise.** Rather than pushing away uncomfortable thoughts or clinging to pleasurable ones, individuals note these experiences and then gently let them go.
3. *Non-Judgmental Attitude:* Practitioners work to suspend categorizing or evaluating experiences as good, bad, or neutral. This aspect is vital to reduce reactivity and to develop greater acceptance and compassion for oneself and others.
4. *Self-Compassion:* As mindfulness practice deepens, there is a growing emphasis on nurturing kindness and compassion toward all experiences. A self-compassionate stance fosters emotional resilience and counters perfectionistic or self-critical thought patterns.
5. *Present-Moment Awareness:* Mindfulness is characterized by a deliberate immersion in the now. This negates the anxiety-provoking nature of future worries and guilt-ridden flashbacks into the past, enabling a grounding presence in reality.

In combination, these elements help individuals transform repetitive or negative patterns, improve self-regulation, and deepen interpersonal connections. Each of these core facets is strengthened through consistent practice—sitting meditation, walking meditation, mindful breathing, mindful eating, or even brief pauses of awareness during daily routines.

✧ Practical Applications of Mindfulness

The growing popularity of mindfulness in clinical and nonclinical settings reflects a widespread recognition of its practical benefits. Research in psychology and neuroscience underscores mindfulness's positive effects on stress, anxiety, depression, and emotional regulation. Several widely-known programs employ mindfulness as a primary or complementary method of intervention:

- *Mindfulness-Based Stress Reduction (MBSR):* Developed by Jon Kabat-Zinn, this 8-week program addresses chronic pain, stress, and various medical conditions. Through guided meditation, gentle yoga, and group discussions, participants learn to relate differently to their physical and psychological suffering.
- *Mindfulness-Based Cognitive Therapy (MBCT):* This adaptation of MBSR, developed by Zindel Segal, Mark Williams, and John Teasdale, was designed specifically to prevent relapse in individuals with recurrent depression. MBCT combines traditional cognitive-behavioral techniques with mindfulness practices to interrupt negative thought spirals.
- *Mindfulness in Schools:* Educators increasingly adopt mindfulness techniques to help students reduce test anxiety, improve focus, and develop self-awareness. Simple exercises, like mindful breathing or body

scans, can be integrated into the classroom to foster emotional intelligence.

- *Corporate Mindfulness Programs:* Many businesses introduce mindfulness training to promote employee well-being, reduce burnout, and enhance creativity and productivity. Examples include short guided meditations in the workplace, workshops on mindful communication, and the establishment of wellness spaces.

Moreover, the essence of mindfulness extends beyond formal programs—people can practice mindfulness informally in daily life. Being attentive during a walk, savoring each bite of a meal, or taking a few deep breaths before responding to an email are all examples of mindful micro-practices that, over time, enrich personal resilience and insight.

☆ Understanding Solitary Reflection

While mindfulness is primarily about cultivating present-moment awareness, **solitary reflection** involves intentionally stepping away from social and digital stimuli to engage in introspective thought. It is an ancient practice observed in many spiritual and philosophical traditions—from Christian hermits and Buddhist monks to transcendentalist writers like Henry David Thoreau. Despite cultural differences, the underlying purpose remains consistent: **alone time** devoted to self-examination, personal growth, and inner alignment.

Solitary reflection can be practiced in various ways: journaling, walking in nature, or simply sitting in silence. The common thread is a purposeful disconnection from external input, providing the mental space for ideas to percolate and for emotions to be processed. This solitude is not the same as social isolation or loneliness. Indeed, **solitude** and **loneliness** differ fundamentally:

- **Solitude** is a chosen, healthy withdrawal aimed at self-discovery and mental clarity.
- **Loneliness** often involves feelings of sadness, disconnectedness, and social pain.

When solitude is framed as a conscious and positive decision rather than an imposed or distressing condition, it fosters **reflection, restoration, and creativity**. Many renowned thinkers and artists emphasize that breakthroughs in literature, science, and art often occur during quiet, solitary moments. The unhurried, undistracted mental state allows for deep rumination and original insights.

☆ The Value of Solitude in a Hyperconnected World

The modern world is increasingly hyperconnected, with social media, instant messaging, and digital tools weaving themselves into nearly every aspect of life. Paradoxically, despite these constant digital interactions, many people feel more isolated and anxious than ever. With a barrage of notifications and the perpetual pressure to be "always on," it can be challenging to find genuine space for self-reflection.

In this context, deliberately cultivating solitude becomes a powerful counterbalance. The benefits of solitary reflection include:

1. *Mental Clarity:* Solitude reduces external distractions and obligations, allowing one's mental processes to settle and expand. Unfiltered by social expectations, individuals can think more comprehensively about their goals, values, and passions.
2. *Emotional Processing:* With fewer outside stimuli, one can more effectively tune into inner emotional states, identify unresolved pain points, and work through them in a controlled, private environment.
3. *Creativity and Problem-Solving:* Alone time encourages introspection and daydreaming, proven to enhance creativity. By stepping back from immediate tasks, the subconscious mind processes problems in novel ways—often leading to fresh perspectives.
4. *Self-Discovery and Independence:* Spending time alone encourages greater self-reliance, helping individuals form a clearer identity separate from group norms or peer influence.
5. *Stress Relief and Restoration:* Solitude provides a break from the demands of constant communication, helping restore energy and mental balance.

Nonetheless, it is crucial to distinguish solitude as a purposeful choice from social isolation driven by fear, anxiety, or inability to connect. Healthy solitude is empowering and regenerative; involuntary isolation, in contrast, can exacerbate mental distress and hinder personal growth.

☆ Integrating Mindfulness into Solitary Reflection

Mindfulness and **solitary reflection** are complementary practices that can powerfully reinforce each other. By infusing solitude with mindful awareness, individuals can ground their reflections in the present moment, preventing the mind from drifting into rumination or worry. Conversely, solitary reflection offers the quiet setting necessary to deepen one's mindfulness practice.

1. *Mindful Journaling:* One way to combine mindfulness and solitary reflection is through journal writing. Begin by centering the mind with a brief meditation—focus on the breath or perform a body scan—and then allow thoughts and observations to flow onto the page. This process captures spontaneous mental and emotional states while retaining the clarity and nonjudgmental spirit cultivated by mindfulness. Over time, reviewing these journal entries can illuminate patterns, deepen self-knowledge, and track personal evolution.

2. *Nature Walks and Sitting Meditations:* Another tactic is to merge the solitude of nature with mindful awareness. By walking slowly, feeling each step, and taking in the surrounding environment—sights, sounds, scents—one can experience heightened vitality and presence. For those who prefer sitting still, finding a quiet spot in a park or under a tree can offer profound mental clarity, as nature's rhythms remind practitioners to let go of racing thoughts and focus on the simplicity of the here and now.

3. *Intentional Mindful Retreats:* Individuals may choose to participate in structured mindfulness retreats or self-imposed "digital detoxes." These experiences remove external distractions—smartphones, laptops, social obligations—and create a protected space dedicated to introspection. Sustained silence encourages deep reflection and allows mindfulness to bloom in an immersive environment. Such retreats can be done over a weekend, or even a day, creating a mini "cocoon" of solitude.

4. *Guided Meditation in Private Spaces:* Modern technology, while often the source of distraction, can also be harnessed to support mindful solitude. Guided meditation apps or recorded sessions provide structure for those unaccustomed to silent sitting. However, it is essential that these resources not detract from the essence of solitude; setting a device on "Do Not Disturb" can ensure outside notifications do not interfere with reflective space.

By purposefully weaving mindfulness into moments of solitude, individuals may find they achieve more profound insights and a sense of tranquility that is difficult to access in the hustle of everyday life. This synergy can significantly enhance mental health, creativity, and overall life satisfaction.

✩ Psychological and Physiological Benefits

Empirical research supports the notion that mindfulness practice—and by extension mindful solitary reflection—yields both psychological and physiological benefits. Let us examine some key findings:

1. *Reduced Stress and Anxiety:* Numerous studies demonstrate that mindfulness interventions lower cortisol levels, the hormone associated with stress. By remaining present instead of obsessing over future or past concerns, practitioners often report less chronic anxiety.

2. *Enhanced Emotional Regulation:* Mindfulness fosters the ability to observe emotions without immediately reacting. In turn, solitary reflection provides a calm space to process feelings, leading to improved mood regulation and reduced reactivity in challenging situations.

3. *Improved Cognitive Function:* Mindfulness training has been associated with better attentional control, working memory, and executive functioning. Individuals who engage in regular mindfulness meditation—even for short daily sessions—tend to maintain sharper focus and greater mental clarity, essential skills for productive solitary reflection.

4. *Better Sleep Quality:* Solitary reflection, when paired with mindfulness, can help settle the mind before bedtime, reducing insomnia and improving overall sleep quality. A calm and reflective state before rest mitigates the mental overstimulation that many experience from digital devices late into the evening.
5. *Boosted Immune System:* Some research suggests a correlation between consistent mindfulness practice and improved immune function. Lower stress levels, better emotional management, and increased self-awareness contribute to a body that is more resilient against infections and illnesses.
6. *Increased Empathy and Compassion:* While it may seem paradoxical that spending time alone enhances empathy, solitary reflection can provide the mental rest and self-understanding necessary to be fully present for others. Mindfulness helps dissolve barriers of judgment and fosters a genuine concern for the well-being of self and others.

These benefits highlight why mindfulness and solitude have become such popular tools in mental health counseling, workplace wellness, and personal development frameworks. When practiced consistently and with intention, they can significantly bolster one's control over their physical and emotional well-being.

Overcoming Obstacles to Mindfulness and Solitary Reflection

Despite the documented advantages of mindfulness and solitary reflection, many individuals face obstacles that prevent them from fully embracing these practices:

1. *Fear of Being Alone:* Modern culture often associates being alone with social rejection or personal failure. The stigma around solitude makes people reluctant to prioritize alone time, fearing it will be perceived as antisocial or indicative of loneliness.
2. *Impatience and Distraction:* In an era of instant gratification and social media scrolling, sustained focus can feel challenging. Beginning meditators frequently give up when they discover how quickly their attention wanders, mistaking this normal phenomenon for failure.
3. *Excessive Busyness:* Work schedules, family responsibilities, and social engagements leave little time for reflection. Incorporating mindfulness into a busy life may require deliberate scheduling and negotiation of priorities. Avoid guilt when your schedule needs to be prioritized differently for the sake of your emotional well-being and productivity. Without these breaks from noise, burnout becomes more frequent, inevitably becoming more of an obstacle than creating time for personal reflection and rest.
4. *Emotional Discomfort:* Sitting quietly often brings unresolved emotions and painful memories to the surface. Without proper guidance or coping strategies, individuals may resist solitude to avoid confronting their internal realities.

5. *Unrealistic Expectations:* Some newcomers to mindfulness expect an immediate sense of tranquility or dramatic insight. When these rapid changes do not occur, frustration ensues, undermining motivation to continue practicing.

Overcoming these barriers often involves reframing solitude from an act of withdrawal to one of **self-care**. Techniques such as setting small, achievable goals, building supportive communities (e.g., mindfulness groups or retreats), and using guided meditations can help novices navigate the early stages. Furthermore, professional counselors and therapists trained in mindfulness-based interventions can provide the necessary support for those dealing with trauma or acute mental health challenges that arise during periods of reflection.

⍣ Strategies for Sustained Practice

1. *Small Steps and Consistency:* Commit to a few minutes of mindfulness practice daily rather than sporadic, lengthy sessions. Even short practices, if done consistently, create the neural groundwork for lasting habit change.
2. *Set Boundaries with Technology:* Consider designating "technology-free" zones or times in your schedule to foster genuine solitude. Silence notifications, reduce screen time, and be intentional about engaging in digital detox sessions.
3. *Create a Sacred Space:* If possible, designate a corner in your home or a quiet park bench as a space for mindfulness and reflection. Over time, this space becomes a psychological trigger for calm and introspection.
4. *Experiment with Different Modalities:* Not all forms of meditation or reflective practices will resonate with every individual. Experiment with sitting meditation, walking meditation, journaling, yoga, or creative activities like painting or music to find the right fit.
5. *Seek Guidance and Community:* Consider attending workshops, retreats, or local mindfulness groups to find guidance and accountability. Sharing experiences and challenges with like-minded individuals can sustain motivation.
6. *Practice Self-Compassion:* Above all, approach mindfulness and solitude with patience and kindness toward yourself. When the mind wanders or self-criticism arises, gently redirect focus. The path of mindfulness is iterative and non-linear.

Mindfulness and solitary reflection hold enduring value in a fast-paced, overstimulated world. Together, they form a potent antidote to the chronic stress, fragmented attention, and superficial engagements so prevalent in modern life. By turning inward—through disciplined attentiveness to the present moment and purposeful solitude—individuals can cultivate greater self-awareness, emotional balance, and creative insight.

While obstacles to sustained practice—such as fear of loneliness, impatience, and emotional discomfort—are real, they can be overcome through consistent effort, reframing solitude as nourishment, and seeking social support when needed. Ultimately, mindfulness and solitary reflection are not about escaping the world but engaging more fully with it—recognizing that true fulfillment often arises from understanding oneself deeply and relating to others with genuine compassion.

In this age of perpetual connectivity that will only increase as the user interfaces are advanced and blurred, the deliberate cultivation of mindful solitude stands as a vital counterbalance. By integrating both practices into daily life—starting small, setting clear boundaries with technology, and practicing self-compassion—the benefits inevitably blossom. Stepping back from the chaos, one can gain clarity on personal values, uncover creative spark, and reconnect with the simple, potent realities of being alive. Through mindfulness and solitary reflection, we find that our capacity for insight, empathy, and authentic presence grows, ultimately enriching both individual lives and the wider communities we inhabit.

A student, distracted by endless notifications, asked the master, "How do I stay mindful amidst these insidious alerts?"

The master replied, "Your phone buzzes, but who decides to look?"

The student paused, then silenced the device and sat still. In the quiet, her breath spoke louder than any alert.

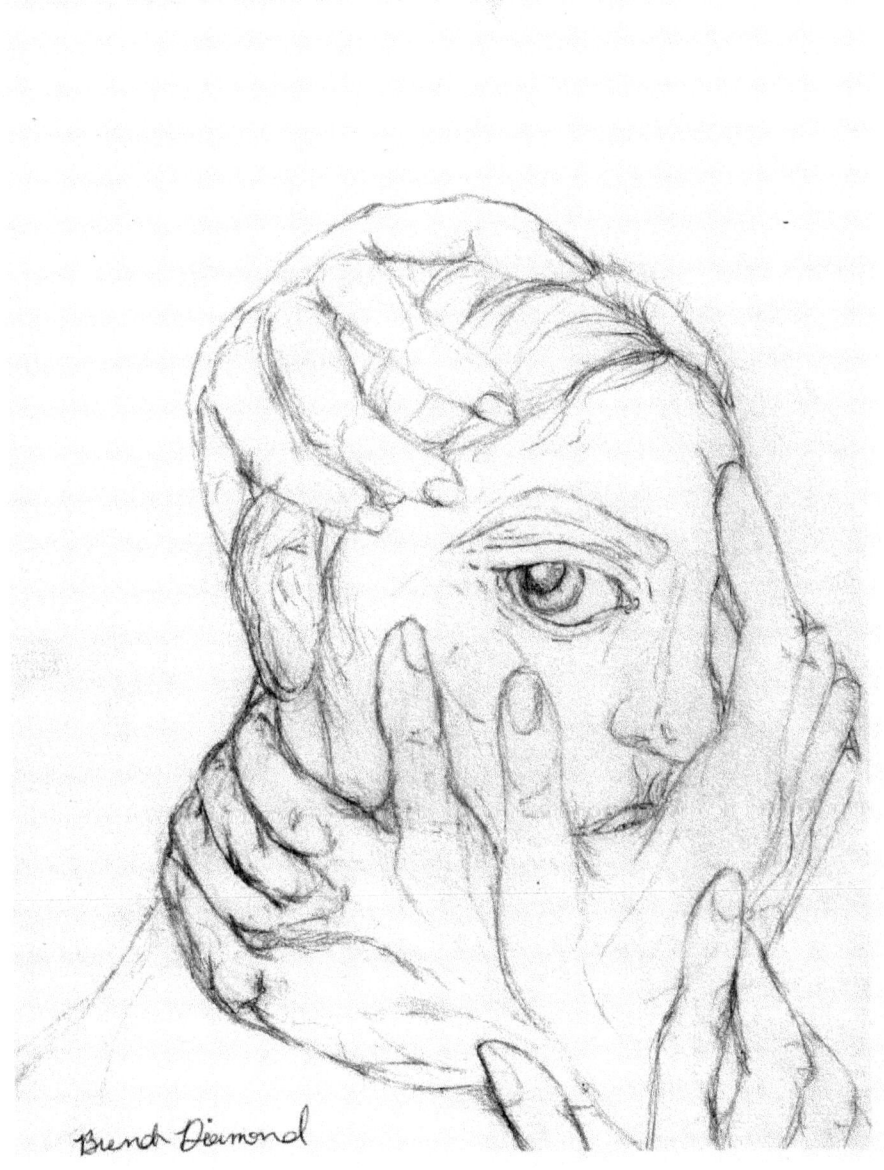

Brenda Diamond

Chapter 9: Overcoming Fears and Shadows

Solitude is the space in which the unspoken can finally speak. Our fears, resentments, and old wounds become visible, inviting transformation rather than avoidance.

Fear is a universal human experience, an emotion that has ensured our survival by alerting us to potential dangers and pushing us to take precautionary measures. Yet in the modern world, many of the threats that once were life-or-death challenges have transformed into subtler, more psychologically oriented anxieties. We fear failure, rejection, loneliness, the unknown, and even success. Often, these fears are not readily visible on the surface; instead, they hide in the shadows of our subconscious, influencing our actions and reactions in ways we might not immediately recognize. When left unchecked, these shadows of fear can grow and restrict our growth, creativity, and ability to connect with our deeper selves.

Zen practice, combined with the broader spectrum of meditation techniques, offers powerful tools to help us navigate and transform these deep-seated fears. Rooted in centuries-old traditions, Zen emphasizes direct experience and awareness, cutting through our mental chatter to help us recognize the nature of our minds. By sitting with ourselves—by observing the breath, noticing our thoughts, and gently returning to the present moment—Zen practice invites us to peel back layers of conditioning and uncover the luminous awareness that underlies our habitual patterns.

This journey is not about eradicating fear entirely, for fear itself holds important lessons. Rather, it is about seeing fear for what it is—an emotion that arises and passes away, a mental event that does not need to define our identity. Meditation and Zen encourage us to accept every aspect of our being, including the shadows we often try to suppress. In that acceptance, we find a path toward greater harmony and wisdom. Over the following pages, we will explore how fear arises, how to work skillfully with it through a dedicated meditation and Zen practice, and how to integrate these insights into daily life. Through courage, patience, and compassionate self-inquiry, we can learn to embrace our inner shadows and reclaim the wholeness of our being.

ⓖ Understanding the Nature of Fear

Before we can address fear directly, it is crucial to understand its nature. Fear typically has two components: the physiological (e.g., increased heart rate, sweating palms, shallow breathing) and the psychological (e.g., catastrophic thinking, negative self-talk, or anticipating worst-case scenarios). Taken together, these symptoms can easily spin out of control, creating a self-reinforcing cycle of anxiety. In other words, once fear takes root, it can perpetuate itself by causing us to scan obsessively for potential threats, magnifying our distress.

From a Zen perspective, fear arises when we become attached to a certain outcome or vision of ourselves. We might fear failing at work because we are attached to the identity of being "successful." Alternatively, we might fear intimacy because we are deeply attached to the notion of self-protection or not exposing our vulnerabilities. In this sense, fear and attachment go hand in hand. Recognizing this relationship is the first step toward freeing ourselves from the grip of fear.

Another significant aspect of fear is its temporal dimension. Fear often resides either in the past, where it reminds us of old traumas, or in the future, where it projects dire possibilities. Rarely does fear exist in the present moment, when we are simply aware. In Zen teachings, the present moment is seen as the gateway to clarity. When we bring our minds into the "now," fear—deprived of its temporal anchors—has less ground upon which to sustain itself.

Though fear can feel overwhelming, it also holds potential for growth. By leaning into discomfort and recognizing that all emotions are transient, we gain insights into the nature of the mind. Fear becomes a teacher, revealing the places where we still cling, resist, or harbor illusions. With each moment of mindful attention and acceptance, fear loosens its hold on us and evolves from a limiting force into a powerful catalyst for self-discovery.

⑥ The Shadow Within

The concept of the "shadow" has roots in both psychology and spiritual traditions. Psychologist Carl Jung famously spoke about the shadow as the collection of rejected or disowned parts of ourselves—traits or tendencies we have cast aside because we consider them unacceptable, shameful, or undesirable. Yet what we deny in ourselves does not vanish; it simply goes underground, influencing our behavior from behind the scenes. Fears often dwell in these shadowy corners, growing in potency the more we try to ignore or suppress them.

In Zen, there is a parallel notion: all phenomena, including our darker emotions and impulses, have a place in the wholeness of reality. The light cannot exist without the dark, and vice versa. Our task, as practitioners, is to notice and embrace these seeming opposites without getting trapped by them or identifying too strongly with them. When we see fear—along with anger, doubt, or desire— as just another part of the human experience, we begin to loosen its power to define us.

Unacknowledged shadows can manifest in numerous ways. We might find ourselves reacting disproportionately to small triggers, or we might engage in habitual patterns such as procrastination, conflict-avoidance, or people-pleasing.

At other times, we internalize fear as a pervasive sense of low self-worth, convincing ourselves that we are "not good enough" or unworthy of love. Over time, these mental patterns become deeply ingrained, shaping our reality and influencing our life choices.

What Zen and meditation reveal is that by gently turning toward these hidden aspects—by inviting them into conscious awareness—we can begin a process of real transformation. Rather than viewing our shadows as enemies to be conquered, we can begin relating to them with compassion and curiosity. This approach diminishes their power, allowing us to integrate these once-disowned parts into a more holistic sense of self. Far from a sign of weakness, the willingness to face our fears and shadows becomes a profoundly courageous act, one that opens the door to authentic growth and liberation.

⑥ Foundations of Zen Practice

Zen practice is as diverse as the individuals who undertake it, but its core elements revolve around meditation (zazen), mindfulness, and the cultivation of a direct, unfiltered experience of reality. One of the hallmark instructions in Zen is to "just sit," meaning to settle into a stable posture—often on a cushion or chair—while gently holding the spine upright. In zazen, the eyes are typically partially open, resting comfortably on a spot a few feet in front of you. Place the hands in a mudra, with palms up, one hand resting on the other, thumbs lightly touching.

As you sit, you allow thoughts, sensations, and emotions to arise and pass. You do not try to suppress them, nor do you chase after them; you simply witness them with a nonjudgmental awareness. When you notice that you have become lost in a train of thought, you gently bring your attention back to the breath or to the simple state of "just sitting." This act of returning again and again to the present moment is the crucible in which mindfulness is forged.

In working with fear, Zen practitioners often learn that the mind's tendency to spin stories—about the past, the future, or hypothetical scenarios—is one of the main contributors to anxiety. Zazen provides a practice ground to observe this storytelling faculty firsthand. As you become more attuned to your inner landscape, you can notice fear-based thoughts forming, watch how they summon physical tension, and then see them dissolve as your attention returns to the simplicity of each breath.

Zen also includes kōan practice in certain lineages—short paradoxical anecdotes or riddles that defy logical explanation. While kōans are not explicitly designed to target fear, they serve as potent tools for unraveling the habitual mind, revealing hidden assumptions, and opening pathways to deeper insight. By loosening the grip of rational thought, kōans can indirectly release the stranglehold of anxiety and open the heart to a more spacious way of being.

⑥ Mindfulness Meditation and Its Role in Facing Fear

While Zen is a distinct school of Buddhism, it shares much with other mindfulness-based practices. Mindfulness, often defined as "paying attention on purpose, in the present moment, and nonjudgmentally," is a universal tool that can be cultivated through various forms of seated, walking, or movement-based meditation. In facing fear, mindfulness can be especially powerful because it trains the mind to observe rather than react. Instead of being hijacked by fearful thoughts or sensations, you develop the capacity to witness them objectively.

One common mindfulness practice is the "body scan," where you systematically move your attention through different regions of the body. This practice not only relaxes the body but also develops the capacity to notice how fear might manifest physically—as tightness in the chest, a clenched jaw, or a churning stomach. By becoming intimately familiar with these signals, you learn to recognize fear at its earliest stages rather than allowing it to escalate uncontrollably.

Another beneficial practice for working with fear is "labeling." When a strong emotion arises, you silently label it—"fear," "anxiety," or "worry"—and then observe how it shifts and morphs. This labeling interrupts the automatic identification with the emotion: instead of saying "I am afraid," you move toward "fear is arising." That subtle shift in language and perspective creates mental space, enabling you to see fear as a passing phenomenon rather than a fixed identity.

Mindfulness also allows for greater emotional intelligence. As your practice matures, you develop a nuanced understanding of the causes and conditions that give rise to fear. You may notice certain triggers—a conversation topic, a memory, or an upcoming event—that inflame anxious thoughts. Equipped with this knowledge, you can approach these situations more skillfully, either by proactively soothing the mind or by reframing the narrative that fuels your fears. Over time, mindfulness fosters resilience: fear may still arise, but it no longer reigns as an unchallenged ruler of your inner world.

⑥ Embracing the Shadow—Techniques and Attitudes

Confronting our shadows involves more than a single technique; it requires a shift in attitude from aversion to acceptance. In many spiritual traditions, there is an emphasis on "spiritual bypassing," where practitioners try to stay in a perpetual state of positivity or calmness and avoid the messy realities of their inner world. True transformation, however, comes from integrating the full range of human experience, including our darkness and fear.

A potent technique for embracing the shadow is "metta" or loving-kindness meditation, which is used across various Buddhist traditions. Although metta is often directed toward others—sending wishes of well-being, happiness, and peace—it can also be turned inward to those parts of ourselves we find difficult or frightening. By systematically offering loving-kindness to our fears and to the aspects of ourselves we wish were different, we begin to dissolve the barriers of judgment and shame.

Another approach is inquiry-based meditation, where instead of focusing on the breath or a mantra, you hold a question—such as "What is this fear?"—in your awareness. This question is not to be answered intellectually but rather to be lived with curiosity. As you sit quietly, let images, memories, or sensations arise naturally. Perhaps you will recall childhood incidents, or maybe you will see mental images of an internal critic. By staying with the question, you create a contemplative space where the deeper roots of fear can surface into consciousness.

It is essential to balance this investigative work with gentleness. Facing one's shadows can be emotionally charged, and harsh self-criticism or impatience may only deepen the wounds. A supportive environment—a community of practitioners, a teacher or mentor, or even a trusted friend—can provide the psychological safety necessary for genuine exploration. Over time, the very process of bringing compassion and mindfulness to our shadows transforms them from menacing figures into allies on our journey toward wholeness.

Overcoming Fear Through Insight and Wisdom

In Zen practice, insight (prajna in Sanskrit) is not merely an intellectual understanding but an experiential, transformative realization of the nature of self, mind, and reality. As you deepen your meditation, you begin to sense that your thoughts and emotions, including fear, are phenomena that arise and disappear within awareness. This realization can be liberating because it loosens the identification with any single state. You are not your fear; you are the space in which fear unfolds.

One classic insight in Buddhism is the concept of impermanence (anicca). All things—material objects, thoughts, emotions—are in a constant state of flux. Fear might visit you today, but it will inevitably change form or vanish. Recognizing impermanence on an experiential level helps you relax your grip on the stories that fear tells. It becomes easier to accept that fear is a temporary visitor rather than a permanent resident in your psyche.

Another important insight is "nonself" (anatta), the idea that there is no unchanging, permanent "I" at the center of experience. While this teaching can be perplexing at first, it points to a liberating truth: the self is a process, not a static entity. When fear arises, it is often tied to a particular self-narrative—"I must protect myself," "I am not worthy," or "I cannot handle this." But as you see through the illusion of a fixed identity, you start to perceive these narratives as ephemeral movements of the mind. This perspective undercuts the roots of fear, revealing a vast, open awareness that is inherently free.

Wisdom also extends to our understanding of cause and effect (karma). Every action, whether mental, verbal, or physical, has a consequence. If we continually react to fear with avoidance or aggression, we reinforce those patterns. If, however, we meet fear with mindfulness and compassion, we plant seeds for a different future—one characterized by openness, courage, and love. In this sense, the work of overcoming fear is never just about oneself; it is an offering to the greater tapestry of life, generating ripples of transformation that extend far beyond our personal sphere.

⑥ Integrating Practice into Daily Life

Meditation does not happen in a vacuum; its benefits and insights are meant to flow seamlessly into everyday activities. Daily life offers countless opportunities to apply the skills cultivated on the cushion. For instance, if you notice yourself tensing up before a difficult conversation at work, you can take a brief mindful pause: feel your feet on the ground, observe your breath, and remind yourself that sensations of anxiety are transient. Approaching each moment with this wakeful presence helps break the cycle of habitual reactions.

Zen teachings often emphasize everyday activities—such as washing dishes, drinking tea, or walking—as an integral part of practice. When you wash dishes mindfully, you attend to the temperature of the water, the sensation of the soap, and the shape of each dish. This humble act becomes a meditation in motion. Fear can show up even in simple tasks (e.g., worrying about the next day's responsibilities), so using routine activities as mindfulness practice grounds you in the present and curtails the proliferation of anxious thoughts.

Establishing a consistent schedule can also bolster the integration of practice. Setting aside a regular time for meditation each day—whether it is 5 minutes or 30 minutes—builds a foundation of stability and discipline. If possible, attending a Zen center or joining a virtual sangha (community) can provide structure and support. Group practice allows you to learn from others, share experiences, and feel less isolated in your journey.

Finally, self-reflection and journaling can help bridge the gap between formal practice and daily life. After each meditation session, or at the end of the day, spend a few moments noting what arose. Did fear visit you? How did you respond? Reflecting in this way helps you track patterns and measure growth over time. The insights gained can further inspire your commitment to transform fear into a stepping stone for deeper awareness and compassion.

Here are some simple ways to heed the call without fully withdrawing from your usual responsibilities:

1. *Early Mornings or Late Evenings:* Carve out half an hour in the early morning or late at night when everyone else is asleep. Use this time to meditate, journal, or simply sit in silence.

2. *Mindful Commutes:* If you use public transportation, consider putting away your phone and resting in a reflective, observant state. Notice the world passing by outside the window, listen to the hum of the bus or train, and ground yourself in the present.

3. *Device-Free Intervals:* Create small windows during the day where you set aside your phone and any other devices. Use these mini-breaks to breathe, stretch, or simply be.

4. *Nature Walks:* Find a local park or garden for a slow, mindful walk. Let your senses open to the environment—listen to birds, feel the sunlight, inhale the fresh air.

5. *Dedicated Creative Time:* If you enjoy drawing, painting, or playing an instrument, schedule an hour of uninterrupted creative solitude. Let your imagination flow without external interference.

6. *Reading for Enjoyment: Pick up something that allows you to float away from internal worries and anxieties.* Regardless of the content, reading can help extend the attention span and hone your focus to one area.

By integrating these practices into daily life, you demonstrate to yourself that solitude is not an elusive luxury but a basic need—much like food, water, and rest. Each small step is a way of answering the call, forging a relationship with quiet that can deepen over time.

⑥ Transforming Fear into Compassion and Connection

One of the most beautiful aspects of confronting fear is that it can open the heart to greater compassion—for both yourself and others. When you intimately understand how limiting and painful fear can be, you become more attuned to the struggles of those around you. This empathy is a cornerstone of Buddhist teachings, where the cultivation of compassion (karuna) is viewed as integral to wisdom. Fear and suffering are universal human experiences, and by facing your own shadows, you become better equipped to support others on their path.

Engaging in compassionate actions can also help loosen the grip of fear. When you offer kindness or generosity to another person—especially if you do so without expecting anything in return—you expand your sense of self. Rather than being wrapped up in your personal concerns, you see that you are part of a greater interconnected web of relationships. This perspective can counteract the isolating effect of fear, which often convinces us that we are alone and vulnerable.

In Zen monasteries and communities, there is often an emphasis on service (samu), whether it is cleaning the temple, preparing meals, or helping maintain the grounds. These activities are seen not as distractions but as integral parts of practice. By serving others, practitioners learn to let go of ego-centered fear and self-interest, replacing them with a spirit of shared responsibility and care. The resulting sense of connection fosters resilience; you realize you are not facing life's uncertainties alone but in concert with a supportive community.

As fear transforms into compassion, you may also experience a shift in how you view adversity. Challenges and hardships become occasions to deepen empathy rather than reinforce walls around your heart. By choosing to remain open in the face of discomfort, you not only heal your own fears but also create a ripple effect that can touch countless others. In this way, the personal work of overcoming fear through Zen practice becomes an act of collective healing, uniting personal growth with universal well-being.

Overcoming fears and illuminating the shadows of our psyche is not a quick fix or a one-time event; it is a lifelong journey that calls us to return, again and again, to the present moment. Meditation and Zen practice provide us with the tools and the framework to engage this journey with courage and honesty. By cultivating mindfulness, insight, and compassion, we learn to regard fear not as an enemy but as a messenger pointing us to areas in need of attention and care.

Each time you sit on the meditation cushion, you rehearse the art of being with whatever arises: joy, restlessness, boredom, or fear. You learn that you have the capacity to stay steady, to breathe through difficult moments, and to watch them dissolve into the ever-shifting stream of experience. Through sustained practice, you become familiar with the gaps between thoughts, the stillness between the inhale and the exhale—a space where fear momentarily pauses and reveals its empty nature. In that space, you glimpse the radiant awareness that is your birthright.

The insights gained on the cushion do not remain confined to formal practice. They flow into your relationships, your work, and your moments of solitude. By integrating meditation and Zen principles into everyday life, you create a seamless tapestry of awareness, weaving calm and clarity into the fabric of each day. As you learn to embrace your fears and the shadows they cast, you free up enormous amounts of energy once locked in self-doubt and avoidance. This energy can be redirected toward creative pursuits, deeper connections, and a more profound exploration of life itself.

Finally, it is important to remember that the path of awakening is both deeply personal and profoundly universal. Your struggles and triumphs, fears and insights, echo across the spectrum of humanity. By dedicating yourself to transforming fear into wisdom, you contribute to a collective evolution of consciousness—one that may very well hold the key to healing not just individuals, but our global community. May your practice be a refuge in times of darkness and a beacon of light for all those seeking peace and wholeness.

A monk sat alone by the quiet stream, its waters whispering softly.

A traveler passed and said, "Why sit here in loneliness, far from others?"

The monk smiled and replied, "The stream is my companion, yet I am alone. Loneliness seeks what is missing; being alone finds what is here."

The traveler pondered, then sat beside the stream, listening.

Chapter 10: The Wisdom of Non-Attachment

As we sit in solitude, we see that we are both the wave and the ocean. We rise, we fall, and ultimately return to the vastness of being.

Introduction and Context

Non-attachment is a concept that has resonated throughout human history, particularly within spiritual and philosophical traditions. From the teachings of Buddhism, Taoism, and Stoicism to contemporary self-help frameworks, non-attachment is repeatedly cited as a cornerstone of emotional freedom and inner peace. But what precisely does it mean to practice non-attachment? Often, people conflate non-attachment with indifference or lack of caring; they envision a state in which one is entirely apathetic or disconnected from the world. However, this interpretation is incomplete. Rather, non-attachment is about finding freedom from the destructive clutches of obsession, ego, and an overactive mind that constantly fixates on external outcomes. It acknowledges that while we inhabit a world brimming with experiences, responsibilities, and relationships, a peaceful heart does not need to cling to them with rigid intensity.

Non-attachment teaches us to remain engaged in life's endeavors while maintaining a healthy emotional boundary—a middle path where we care deeply but are not undone if our expectations go unmet. Non-attachment is as relevant to a parent worried about their children's future as it is to a young professional seeking success in a competitive field. Its wisdom is not limited to monastic life or extreme asceticism; on the contrary, non-attachment is a skillful way of relating to oneself and the world. In relinquishing the chains of clinging, we build a sanctuary of calm within. This essay explores the multifaceted dimensions of non-attachment, clarifies misconceptions, delves into its philosophical roots, and offers practical methods for cultivating it in everyday life.

By exploring non-attachment, we do not seek to become cold or unfeeling. Instead, we cultivate resilience, openness, and a deep sense of compassion that is unburdened by rigid expectations. The wisdom of non-attachment can fundamentally transform how we approach challenges, relationships, and our own sense of purpose.

Historical and Philosophical Roots

Non-attachment has broad historical roots, finding expression across numerous traditions. In **Buddhism**, the idea of non-attachment is central to the notion of freedom from suffering, or *dukkha*. The Buddha taught that clinging—whether it be to objects, relationships, ideas, or even one's identity—is at the core of human dissatisfaction. By understanding the ephemeral nature of all things (the doctrine of impermanence), one realizes that clinging ultimately results in frustration and suffering. Thus, practicing non-attachment becomes a practical approach to reduce suffering and foster equanimity.

In **Hindu philosophy**, the *Bhagavad Gita* emphasizes the importance of performing one's duty (dharma) without attachment to the outcomes. Lord Krishna advises Arjuna to act righteously but to surrender the fruits of his actions to a higher truth. This is a form of non-attachment that supports righteous action while freeing the individual from the anxieties of success or failure.

Stoicism, in the Western tradition, also contains a parallel notion. The Stoic philosophers—most notably Epictetus, Marcus Aurelius, and Seneca—believed that external events lie beyond our control, and that real peace is found by focusing on what we can control: our own perceptions, judgments, and reactions. By practicing a form of non-attachment to external circumstances, the Stoics argued that we can maintain tranquility of mind even amid life's most tumultuous events.

Christians are called to live in the world but not be of it, resisting the temptations of worldly desires that lead us astray from God's truth. Scripture warns us in 1 John 2:15-17:

"Do not love the world or anything in the world. If anyone loves the world, love for the Father is not in them. For everything in the world—the lust of the flesh, the lust of the eyes, and the pride of life—comes not from the Father but from the world. The world and its desires pass away, but whoever does the will of God lives forever."

This passage reminds us to guard our hearts against fleeting pleasures and to seek a life rooted in God's eternal purpose.

While the nuances differ, these traditions converge in their view that deep-seated clinging—be it to outcomes, possessions, or even a sense of self—can become a breeding ground for suffering. Non-attachment, however, is not a synonym for aloofness or disengagement. Instead, it is a skillful stance that allows us to experience life fully, yet remain flexible in the face of change.

Common Misconceptions

One of the primary obstacles to understanding non-attachment is the confusion between caring less and caring *differently*. A frequent misconception is that non-attachment equals detachment. Detachment often carries the connotation of emotional withdrawal, numbness, or disinterest. It is reminiscent of someone who has "checked out" of life's responsibilities and relationships. While detachment can be a psychological defense mechanism to avoid pain or vulnerability, non-attachment goes deeper. It recognizes that caring deeply and loving wholeheartedly are not inherently opposed to letting go of rigid expectations.

Another misconception is the belief that non-attachment means renouncing all material possessions or worldly ambitions. Historically, some ascetic traditions did encourage monastic living and the renunciation of personal property. However, a person practicing non-attachment in a modern context does not have to abandon a comfortable home or professional pursuits. Instead, they approach these with a lighter grip: they recognize that possessions, success, and external validation are transient. When these things inevitably change, diminish, or disappear, a non-attached individual can navigate the shift with greater ease and resilience.

Similarly, non-attachment should not be confused with fatalism or passivity. It is not an excuse to avoid effort under the assumption that "nothing really matters." Rather, it inspires us to engage in meaningful actions with clarity and grace. We still set goals, nurture relationships, and care for others. The difference is how we respond when life unfolds unpredictably. Instead of falling into despair or incessant worry, we remain anchored in an understanding of impermanence, thereby cultivating emotional balance.

The Psychology of Clinging

From a psychological perspective, clinging often arises as a response to uncertainty and fear. Human beings naturally seek stability and consistency, so we cling to relationships for fear of abandonment, to personal achievements for fear of failure, or to material security for fear of scarcity. While these motivations stem from fundamental survival instincts, they can morph into disproportionate anxieties that overshadow the present moment.

Cognitive-behavioral psychology has explored how negative thought patterns, such as catastrophizing or black-and-white thinking, intensify clinging behaviors. For instance, one might believe that losing a job or being rejected by a loved one constitutes an irreparable catastrophe, leading to frantic efforts at control. This focus on controlling external circumstances overlooks the transformative power of reframing one's internal experiences.

The mind's tendency to chase after pleasures and avoid discomfort can fuel cycles of attachment. When pleasures become less satisfying or fade entirely, dissatisfaction arises, prompting a search for the next pleasurable experience. Thus, the cycle of pursuit and aversion ensues, trapping us in a perpetual treadmill of psychological neediness. Non-attachment shifts the paradigm: instead of reacting automatically to desires and aversions, we observe them, acknowledge their impermanence, and choose more skillful responses.

On a deeper level, clinging often intertwines with self-identity. We become attached to roles, labels, and stories about "who we are." When circumstances threaten these self-concepts—such as a significant career change or a shift in a primary relationship—we feel our very sense of self is under siege. The practice of non-attachment can gradually dismantle these rigid self-narratives, allowing for a more fluid and authentic identity.

The Fruits of Non-Attachment

When one consistently practices non-attachment, several transformative changes begin to surface:

1. *Inner Peace and Equanimity:* By releasing the white-knuckle grip on expectations, we gain a sense of inner calm. This does not mean that challenges vanish; it means that our capacity to navigate them grows. Unforeseen hurdles, disappointments, or changes in fortune become more manageable because our sense of well-being no longer hinges solely on external certainties.

2. *Enhanced Relationships:* Ironically, non-attachment can foster deeper connections with others. When we abandon the need to control outcomes or manipulate others to validate our sense of self, our interactions become more genuine. We can love and support the people in our lives without imposing unrealistic expectations or succumbing to codependent behaviors.

3. *Greater Resilience:* When we recognize the impermanent nature of things, we become more adaptable. Life is characterized by constant flux, and clinging to any one state can create friction. Non-attachment equips us with emotional elasticity, allowing us to pivot gracefully when life asks us to shift course.

4. *Decreased Anxiety and Stress:* Much of our stress originates from worrying about future outcomes or regretting past events. The practice of non-attachment can reduce this mental clutter, drawing our attention more fully into the present. Consequently, we develop a more balanced nervous system and a healthier psychological baseline.

5. *Clarity of Purpose:* With the fear of loss diminished, our motivations shift away from ego-based desires and toward more meaningful pursuits. We become less distracted by fleeting accolades or superficial benchmarks of success, tuning instead into pursuits that resonate with our core values.

Practical Strategies—Mindfulness and Meditation

One of the most direct methods to cultivate non-attachment is through **mindfulness and meditation**. By consciously observing thoughts and emotions without judgment, we develop a more spacious perspective. For instance, a daily mindfulness practice might involve simply sitting for 10 to 20 minutes, focusing on the breath, and acknowledging any intrusive thoughts as they arise—then gently letting them go. This exercise mirrors the central principle of non-attachment: observe, acknowledge, and release.

Loving-Kindness Meditation (Metta) can also support non-attachment. By sending goodwill and compassion to oneself and others, we lessen the grip of ego-driven desire. Paradoxically, cultivating genuine love for others often liberates us from the fear of not being loved in return. Over time, this compassionate mindset evolves into a stable foundation from which we can practice non-attachment more naturally.

Additionally, many find it helpful to engage in short, daily reflections on impermanence. A simple exercise might be to observe a fresh flower in one's home each day and note how it changes over time, eventually wilting. This observation, repeated consistently, reminds us that all things—no matter how beautiful—are subject to change.

✴ Practical Strategies—Cultivating Gratitude and Letting Go

Gratitude is another cornerstone of non-attachment. When we consciously appreciate the good things we have—be they relationships, talents, or experiences—we recognize their value without taking them for granted. This realization can paradoxically make it easier to let go when changes occur, because our gratitude does not morph into a desperate need to cling. By acknowledging that everything is a gift of sorts, we reduce the sense of entitlement that feeds attachment.

One tangible way to practice non-attachment through gratitude is by maintaining a **gratitude journal**. Each day, note a few moments, events, or individuals for whom you feel grateful. As you make these notes, remind yourself that these blessings are not permanent, but rather fleeting gifts of life. This gentle reminder subtly infuses daily life with the awareness that change is constant, and that each experience—joyful or challenging—has its season.

Letting go often involves ritual. Symbolic gestures can be surprisingly powerful. For example, writing down worries or unfulfilled desires on a piece of paper and then shredding or burning it offers a tangible release. While such an act does not magically erase problems, it can signal to your mind that it's time to move forward.

In relationships, letting go of attachment might involve granting others the space to grow and evolve without demanding they remain a static source of comfort. This can be challenging, especially if one's identity is intertwined with a specific role or outcome. However, stepping back to allow someone else's autonomy can deepen mutual respect, even if it means confronting your own insecurities.

Non-Attachment in Daily Life—Work, Relationships, and Goals

Work and Career: In a competitive environment, one might feel compelled to stay late, network vigorously, or chase promotions. These are not inherently negative behaviors; ambition can foster creativity and innovation. Problems arise when one becomes so attached to a particular outcome—like a promotion—that its absence or delay results in emotional turmoil. By practicing non-attachment, we learn to do our jobs diligently and passionately while accepting that outcomes might not always align with expectations. This frees us to explore growth opportunities without the crippling fear of failure.

Relationships: Whether in friendships, romantic partnerships, or family dynamics, non-attachment can foster mutual respect and emotional well-being. For instance, codependent patterns often involve one person clinging to another for validation, purpose, or security. Non-attachment helps dissolve such patterns, allowing each individual to stand on their own while remaining connected through genuine affection. This does not suggest emotional distance, but rather a transformation from needy attachment to a healthy interdependence rooted in respect and acceptance.

Personal Goals: Ambitious personal goals—running a marathon, writing a book, or mastering a musical instrument—can be approached with non-attachment. Set your intentions, create a plan, and work diligently, but remain open to the journey's twists and turns. Unexpected obstacles or changes of heart need not be treated as failures. Instead, see them as opportunities to learn, adapt, and grow. By focusing on the process rather than the product, you retain your joy and resilience even if the final outcome differs from your initial vision.

Navigating Challenges and Setbacks

Even with consistent practice, life will present circumstances that test our commitment to non-attachment. Perhaps a sudden job loss, a health crisis, or the end of an important relationship blindsides us. In such moments, it can be tempting to revert to old habits of clinging, panicking, or blaming external forces. Yet these periods of upheaval can be fertile ground for deepening our understanding of non-attachment.

1. **Accepting Reality**: A critical first step in responding to challenges is recognizing what is happening without denial. Acceptance is often misconstrued as passive resignation, but it is in fact the bedrock of wise action. By accepting reality—however painful—we can respond more constructively.

2. **Observing Emotions**: When faced with hardship, intense emotions such as grief, anger, or fear may arise. A practice of mindfulness can create space around these emotions, allowing us to observe them without being consumed. In so doing, we free ourselves from the reflexive impulse to react out of anger or despair.

3. **Revisiting Core Values**: Hard times offer a chance to reevaluate what truly matters. Sometimes, loss reveals attachments we didn't know we had—attachments to status, comfort, or an idealized vision of ourselves. By looking squarely at these attachments, we can realign our actions with our authentic values, even if that means reshaping our life path.

4. **Seeking Support**: Non-attachment does not mean journeying through difficulties alone. Leaning on a supportive community—friends, family, counselors, or spiritual mentors—can offer new perspectives and emotional solace. The key is to seek help not from a place of desperate dependence, but from a willingness to learn, grow, and stand on one's own over time.

☀ Toward a Liberated Life

The wisdom of non-attachment is not just a lofty spiritual ideal reserved for monks on distant mountaintops; it is an accessible, transformative practice that any individual can integrate into daily life. Although we live in a world that often glorifies acquisition, ambition, and unwavering certainty, the reality is that change is inevitable. Nothing remains static—neither our bodies, our relationships, nor our achievements. By embracing non-attachment, we come into closer harmony with life's inherent dynamism.

This does not imply cynicism or an abdication of responsibility. On the contrary, a non-attached person is often fully present and profoundly caring. They recognize that "attachment" and "love" are not synonymous; rather, it is possible to love without gripping so tightly that one crushes the very essence of what is loved. Such an approach to life can enliven our sense of wonder and gratitude, help us respond more resourcefully to challenges, and deepen our connections to ourselves and others.

Ultimately, non-attachment is a journey rather than a destination. It invites us to continually examine our habits, assumptions, and emotional patterns. Each time we notice ourselves clinging—whether to an idea, an expectation, or a relationship—we have a fresh opportunity to choose. Will we tighten our grip, risking inner distress and conflict? Or will we release, trusting the flow of life, and cultivating a spacious heart? In choosing the latter, we discover that non-attachment is not a loss, but a profound gain: the freedom to engage with life more wholeheartedly and compassionately than ever before.

Through its philosophical underpinnings, practical exercises, and real-life applications, non-attachment offers a roadmap to a more peaceful, liberated existence. Far from being cold detachment or apathetic withdrawal, non-attachment is an embrace of life with a light yet genuine touch. In letting go, we truly learn how to hold on—to peace, to love, and to a life infused with wisdom.

A monk asked the master, "How do I let go of my desires?"

The master pointed to a leaf falling from a tree. "Does the leaf cling to the branch, or does the branch cling to the leaf?"

The monk sat in silence, watching the leaf drift away on the wind. After much reflection, he asked, "But does not the leaf bring needed energy to the tree in the summer, and is not useful in winter?"

The master smiled and said, "True, the leaf serves the tree in summer, yet when winter comes, it falls without regret. Does the tree mourn its loss, or does it trust the spring to bring new leaves?"

The monk gazed at the bare branches, and in their stillness, he understood.

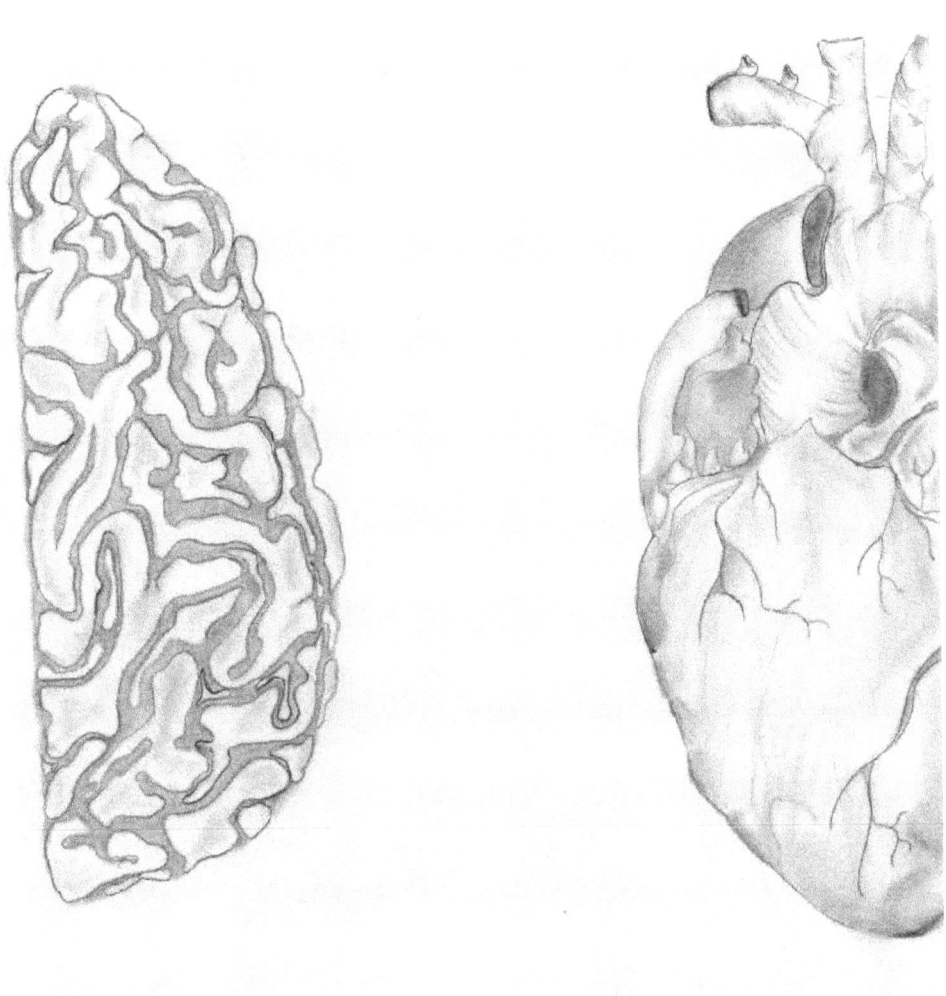

Brenda Diamond

Chapter 11: Quality

Robert M. Pirsig's books, Zen and the Art of Motorcycle Maintenance: An Inquiry into Values (1974) and Lila: An Inquiry into Morals (1991), explore the concept of Quality as a central metaphysical principle. Quality, as Pirsig defines it, is a profound and elusive idea that transcends traditional Western dualisms such as subject and object, mind and matter, and science and art. This chapter delves into Pirsig's exploration of Quality across both works, tracing its evolution from an intuitive insight in Zen to a structured metaphysical framework in Lila. The discussion spans its philosophical underpinnings, its implications for understanding reality, and its practical applications, while also addressing critiques and Pirsig's responses to them.

Quality in Zen and the Art of Motorcycle Maintenance

⑥ The Genesis of Quality

In *Zen and the Art of Motorcycle Maintenance*, Pirsig introduces Quality through a narrative that intertwines a cross-country motorcycle journey with a philosophical "Chautauqua." The book begins with the narrator, a former academic named Phaedrus, reflecting on his past obsession with defining Quality, which led to a mental breakdown. Quality emerges as a concept that defies conventional categorization. It is neither purely subjective (existing only in the mind) nor purely objective (existing independently of perception). Instead, Pirsig posits Quality as a pre-intellectual reality, the fundamental "stuff" of experience that precedes and informs both subject and object.

Pirsig illustrates this through the metaphor of motorcycle maintenance. A well-maintained motorcycle embodies Quality, evident in its smooth operation and aesthetic appeal, which cannot be fully reduced to mechanical specifications or personal taste. Quality is the "knife-edge" of experience, the immediate moment of perception where value is realized before analytical thought splits it into categories.

⑥ Quality as a Bridge Between Romantic and Classical Understanding

Pirsig frames the tension between romantic and classical modes of thought as a central problem. The romantic perspective values intuition, emotion, and aesthetics, while the classical perspective prioritizes reason, logic, and structure. Quality serves as a unifying force that reconciles these dichotomies. For example, a mechanic who approaches motorcycle repair with care and attention to detail (a romantic sensibility) while applying technical knowledge (a classical approach) achieves Quality. This synthesis suggests that Quality is not just an attribute but a dynamic process that integrates feeling and intellect.

⑥ The Philosophical Inquiry into Quality

Phaedrus's academic pursuit of Quality in the book leads him to challenge the subject-object metaphysics of Western philosophy. He argues that Quality is not a property of objects or a subjective judgment but a third entity that exists prior to both. This leads to a radical rethinking of reality: Quality is the source of both subjects and objects, the event at which they meet. Phaedrus's realization that Quality cannot be defined without losing its essence drives him to a mental crisis, as he struggles to articulate this insight within the constraints of academic philosophy.

Pirsig uses the example of grading student papers to illustrate Quality's elusiveness. When Phaedrus experiments by withholding grades and asking students to evaluate their own work, he finds that students intuitively recognize Quality in writing, even without formal criteria. This suggests that Quality is a universal, pre-rational awareness inherent in all human experience.

⑥ Practical Implications

In *Zen*, Quality is not just a philosophical concept but a way of living. Pirsig advocates for "care" and "attention" in everyday activities, whether maintaining a motorcycle or engaging in relationships. This mindfulness—being fully present in the moment—allows one to experience Quality directly. The book's narrative structure, blending personal reflection, philosophical inquiry, and practical advice, mirrors this holistic approach, encouraging readers to seek Quality in their own lives.

Quality in Lila: An Inquiry into Morals

⑥ The Metaphysics of Quality

In *Lila*, Pirsig expands his exploration of Quality into a full-fledged metaphysical system, which he calls the Metaphysics of Quality (MoQ). Here, Quality is explicitly defined as the fundamental reality, replacing traditional metaphysical categories like substance or mind. Pirsig divides Quality into two types: **Static Quality** and **Dynamic Quality**.

- *Dynamic Quality:* This is the immediate, undefined, and ever-changing force of creation and evolution. It is the source of innovation, spontaneity, and progress, akin to the pre-intellectual awareness described in *Zen*. Dynamic Quality is experienced in moments of insight, creativity, or breakthrough, such as when a scientist discovers a new theory or an artist creates a groundbreaking work.
- *Static Quality:* This represents the patterns and structures that emerge from Dynamic Quality and provide stability and order. Static Quality includes social norms, scientific laws, and cultural values. While necessary

for continuity, Static Quality can become rigid, stifling further evolution if it resists Dynamic Quality.

The interplay between Static and Dynamic Quality drives reality forward. For instance, a scientific paradigm (Static Quality) may dominate until a revolutionary discovery (Dynamic Quality) disrupts it, leading to a new paradigm.

⑥ The Levels of Static Quality

Pirsig further refines his metaphysics by categorizing Static Quality into four evolutionary levels, each governed by its own moral framework:

1. *Inorganic Level:* The realm of physical matter and natural laws, such as gravity or chemical bonds. This is the most basic level of Static Quality, providing the foundation for all higher levels.
2. *Biological Level:* The domain of life, characterized by the drive for survival and reproduction. Biological Quality includes instincts and behaviors that sustain living organisms.
3. *Social Level:* The patterns of human society, including laws, customs, and institutions. Social Quality ensures collective stability and cooperation but can conflict with individual freedom.
4. *Intellectual Level:* The realm of ideas, reason, and abstract thought. Intellectual Quality includes science, philosophy, and democratic principles, which prioritize truth and individual rights over social conformity.

Each level evolves from the one below it, and higher levels depend on lower ones but are not reducible to them. Conflicts between levels (e.g., social norms versus intellectual freedom) are resolved by prioritizing the higher level, as it represents a more evolved form of Quality.

⑥ Moral Implications of the Metaphysics of Quality

In *Lila*, Pirsig frames morality as the alignment with Quality. Actions that promote Dynamic Quality or strengthen higher-level Static patterns are morally superior. For example, intellectual freedom (Intellectual Level) is morally superior to oppressive social structures (Social Level), which in turn are superior to mere biological survival. This hierarchy provides a framework for resolving ethical dilemmas, such as the conflict between individual rights and societal demands.

Pirsig illustrates this through the character of Lila, a woman whose chaotic, instinct-driven life represents a struggle between biological and social Quality. The narrator, a continuation of Phaedrus, grapples with understanding Lila's value within the MoQ, ultimately concluding that her pursuit of Dynamic Quality, however flawed, is a valid expression of life's evolutionary drive.

⑥ Quality as a Universal Principle

Unlike *Zen*, which focuses on Quality as a personal and philosophical insight, *Lila* positions Quality as a universal principle that underlies all existence. Pirsig argues that Quality is not just a human experience but the force that shapes the cosmos, from subatomic particles to human societies. This makes the MoQ a monistic metaphysics, where Quality is the singular reality from which all else derives.

Comparing Quality in Zen and Lila

⑥ Evolution of the Concept

In *Zen*, Quality is an intuitive, almost mystical concept, explored through personal narrative and philosophical reflection. It is felt more than defined, serving as a bridge between romantic and classical worldviews. In *Lila*, Pirsig formalizes Quality into a systematic metaphysics, providing a structured framework to explain its role in reality. While *Zen* emphasizes the experiential and practical aspects of Quality, *Lila* extends it to a cosmological and moral theory.

⑥ Narrative vs. Systematic Approach

Zen uses a narrative-driven approach, blending autobiography, travelogue, and philosophy to convey Quality's immediacy. The motorcycle journey serves as a metaphor for living with Quality, emphasizing mindfulness and care. *Lila*, by contrast, is more analytical, using the boat journey and Lila's story to explore the MoQ's implications. The shift from a motorcycle to a sailboat reflects a move from individual exploration to a broader, more contemplative inquiry into society and morality.

⑥ Practical vs. Theoretical Focus

In *Zen*, Quality is practical, tied to everyday actions like maintaining a motorcycle or teaching students. In *Lila*, it becomes a theoretical tool for understanding evolution, morality, and reality itself. However, both books maintain that Quality is accessible through direct experience, whether through mindfulness (*Zen*) or aligning with evolutionary progress (*Lila*).

⑥ Critiques and Pirsig's Responses

Pirsig's concept of Quality has faced criticism for its ambiguity and perceived subjectivity. Critics argue that Quality, especially in *Zen*, is too vague to serve as a rigorous philosophical concept. Pirsig counters this in *Lila* by formalizing the MoQ, providing a structured framework that grounds Quality in observable patterns of evolution and morality. However, some philosophers contend that the MoQ still lacks empirical testability, as Quality remains a metaphysical rather than scientific principle.

Another critique is that Pirsig's rejection of subject-object dualism oversimplifies complex philosophical problems. Pirsig responds by arguing that traditional dualisms create artificial divisions that obscure the unity of experience, which Quality reveals. He also addresses accusations of relativism by asserting that Quality, while experiential, is universal and hierarchical, providing objective criteria for moral and intellectual judgments.

⑥ Practical Applications of Quality

Pirsig's exploration of Quality has practical implications across various domains:

- *Education:* In *Zen*, Pirsig suggests that recognizing Quality in student work fosters creativity and intrinsic motivation. Teachers can cultivate Quality by encouraging students to engage deeply with their subjects rather than focusing on grades.
- *Technology and Craftsmanship:* Both books emphasize the importance of care in technical work. Quality in motorcycle or boat maintenance reflects a broader ethic of attentiveness that can apply to any craft or profession.
- *Ethics and Society:* The MoQ in *Lila* provides a framework for resolving moral conflicts by prioritizing higher levels of Quality. For example, intellectual freedom should take precedence over social conformity, guiding decisions in politics, law, and social policy.
- *Personal Growth:* Pirsig's emphasis on mindfulness and alignment with Dynamic Quality encourages individuals to seek meaning and value in their actions, fostering a sense of purpose and connection to the world.

⑥ Cultural and Philosophical Impact

Pirsig's concept of Quality has influenced fields ranging from philosophy to management theory. In philosophy, the MoQ challenges traditional Western metaphysics, offering an alternative to materialist and idealist frameworks. In business, concepts like Total Quality Management (TQM) echo Pirsig's emphasis on care and excellence, though Pirsig himself distanced his work from such applications. Culturally, *Zen* resonated with the counterculture of the 1970s, blending Eastern mysticism with Western rationalism, while *Lila* appealed to readers seeking a more systematic ethical framework.

Robert Pirsig's exploration of Quality in *Zen and the Art of Motorcycle Maintenance* and *Lila* offers a profound and multifaceted understanding of value, reality, and morality. In *Zen*, Quality is an intuitive, unifying force that bridges romantic and classical perspectives, encouraging mindfulness and care in everyday life. In *Lila*, it evolves into the Metaphysics of Quality, a comprehensive system that explains the evolution of reality through the interplay of Static and Dynamic Quality. Together, these works challenge readers to reconsider their assumptions about reality, urging them to seek Quality in both the mundane and the profound. Pirsig's legacy lies in his ability to make philosophy accessible and relevant, inviting readers to engage with Quality as both a personal practice and a universal principle.

Chapter 12: Natural Law

While a book on Quality is an inspiration for the title of this book, as I thought, researched, and meditated on the concept of quality, something always bothered me about the term. It is similar to the term often used, "integrity". Both are characteristics of a thing, with linear scales from less to more. Yet they are used to imply goodness or morality. It is my hope that this book stimulates similar inquiry.

I feel a better, more first principles approach may have been to explore the concept of **Natural Law.** It has deep historical roots, with contributions from various thinkers across cultures and eras. The original thinkers who shaped the concept, focusing on those who laid foundational ideas, were ancient Greek philosophers Heraclitus (c. 535–475 BCE), Socrates (c. 470–399 BCE), Plato (c. 427–347 BCE), and **Aristotle (c. 384–322 BCE)**.

Heraclitus is one of the earliest figures associated with natural law ideas. He proposed a universal logos (reason or order) governing the cosmos, suggesting an inherent rational order that humans can discern and align with through reason. The cosmos operates under a universal law that transcends human laws, accessible through rational thought.

Socrates, as depicted in Plato's dialogues, emphasized moral truths discoverable through reason, laying groundwork for the idea that *just laws align with a higher moral order*. And that ethical principles exist independently of human conventions and can be uncovered through philosophical inquiry. As they are innate in our being.

Plato, in works like *The Republic* and *Laws*, explored the idea of an ideal justice rooted in a universal order. He suggested that true justice reflects eternal forms or ideals, which human laws should emulate, and that laws should align with the eternal, rational principles of justice and the good.

Aristotle is often considered a pivotal figure in natural law theory. In *Nicomachean Ethics* and *Politics*, he distinguished between "natural justice" (universal principles inherent in nature) and "conventional justice" (human-made laws). He argued that natural law is based on reason and the natural telos (purpose) of human beings. Natural law is universal, rational, and rooted in human nature's purpose, guiding just human laws.

© Stoic Philosophers-

Zeno of Citium (c. 334–262 BCE) and Later Stoics (e.g., Cicero, Seneca):

- o The Stoics developed the idea of a universal law governing the cosmos, accessible through human reason. They believed humans, as rational beings, should live "according to nature," aligning personal conduct with cosmic order.
- o *Cicero (106–43 BCE),* a Roman Stoic, explicitly articulated natural law in *De Legibus* and *De Re Publica,* describing it as a universal, eternal law rooted in divine reason that binds all humans.
- o Key Idea: Natural law is a universal moral code, derived from divine or cosmic reason, obligating all rational beings.

© Roman Jurists-

Roman Legal Tradition (e.g., Gaius, Ulpian, c. 1st–3rd Century CE):

- o Roman jurists, particularly in the *Corpus Juris Civilis* (compiled later under Justinian), incorporated Stoic ideas into Roman law. Ulpian, for instance, defined natural law as what "nature has taught all animals," including universal principles like self-preservation and procreation, though human natural law was tied to reason.
- o Key Idea: Natural law underpins legal systems, providing universal principles that inform positive law.

© Later Contributions-

While not "original" in the sense of being the earliest, these thinkers built on Greek and Roman foundations, further shaping natural law:

Thomas Aquinas (1225–1274):

- o Aquinas synthesized Aristotelian and Christian thought in *Summa Theologica,* defining natural law as the participation of rational creatures in God's eternal law. He argued humans discern natural law through reason, reflecting divine order.
- o Key Idea: Natural law is God-given, accessible through reason, and serves as a moral foundation for human laws.

John Locke (1632–1704):

- o Locke, in *Two Treatises of Government,* described natural law as a God-given moral framework guaranteeing natural rights (life, liberty, property), which human laws must respect.

- Key Idea: Natural law underpins individual rights and limits governmental authority.

⑥ Cross-Cultural Perspectives

Ancient Chinese Philosophy:

- In Confucianism (e.g., Confucius, Mencius, c. 5th–3rd century BCE), concepts like the "Mandate of Heaven" and moral order (li) resemble natural law, suggesting a cosmic moral framework governing human conduct.
- Key Idea: Human laws should align with a universal moral order inherent in the cosmos.

Indian Philosophy:

- In Vedic traditions and later Hindu texts (e.g., *Manusmriti*, c. 2nd century BCE–3rd century CE), *dharma* represents a universal moral law governing human and cosmic order, akin to natural law.
- Key Idea: Dharma provides a natural, universal code for ethical living.

The **original thinkers** on natural law were primarily **Ancient Greek philosophers** (Heraclitus, Socrates, Plato, Aristotle) who established the concept of a universal, rational order governing human morality and law. The **Stoics** (Zeno, Cicero) systematized these ideas, emphasizing cosmic reason, while **Roman jurists** integrated them into legal frameworks.

Later, **Aquinas** and **Locke** refined natural law within Christian and Enlightenment contexts, respectively. Parallel concepts in Chinese and Indian thought (Confucianism, dharma) also contributed to a broader understanding of universal moral principles.

Our nation unleashed the capacity of the average man and woman, and it did so by asserting the self-evidence and truth of Natural Law. The American Founders heavily relied on the legal principle of **Natural Law** when crafting the philosophical and legal foundations of the United States. Natural Law, rooted in the belief that certain rights and moral principles are inherent to human nature and discoverable through reason, was a guiding force in shaping the Declaration of Independence, the Constitution, and the broader framework of American governance.

Key Aspects of Natural Law in the Founders' Thinking:

1. *Inherent Rights:* The Founders, influenced by philosophers like John Locke, believed that individuals possess inalienable rights—life, liberty, and property (or the pursuit of happiness)—granted by a higher authority,

often understood as God or nature, rather than by governments. This is evident in the Declaration of Independence (1776), where Thomas Jefferson wrote, "We hold these truths to be self-evident, that all men are created equal, that they are endowed by their Creator with certain unalienable Rights."

2. *Moral Foundation for Law:* Natural Law provided a moral basis for challenging unjust laws. The Founders argued that laws contradicting natural rights, such as those imposed by British rule, were illegitimate. This justified their rebellion against the Crown, as they saw themselves defending universal principles rather than merely defying authority.

3. *Influence on Governance:* The Constitution and Bill of Rights reflect Natural Law principles by prioritizing individual liberty and limiting government power. For instance, the First Amendment's protections of speech and religion align with the idea that these freedoms are inherent, not government granted. James Madison and others drew on Natural Law to design a system balancing order with liberty.

4. *Philosophical Roots:* The Founders were inspired by Enlightenment thinkers like Locke, Montesquieu, and Cicero, who emphasized reason, justice, and the natural order. They also drew from English common law traditions, which incorporated Natural Law concepts, ensuring that American legal principles were grounded in universal truths rather than arbitrary rule.

5. *Practical Application:* Natural Law-informed debates on slavery, property rights, and governance. While some Founders, like Jefferson, acknowledged the tension between slavery and Natural Law's emphasis on equality, others used these principles to advocate for gradual emancipation or to frame the Constitution as a flexible document capable of evolving toward justice.

Impact and Legacy:

The reliance on Natural Law gave the American experiment a universal appeal, framing the United States as a nation founded on timeless principles rather than transient political whims. It provided a moral and intellectual justification for independence and a framework for constitutional governance. However, contradictions, such as the initial toleration of slavery, highlight the challenges of applying Natural Law consistently in a complex society.

Natural Law was a cornerstone of the Founders' vision, shaping the ideological and legal foundations of the United States by grounding its core documents and principles in the belief that human rights and justice are universal and inherent.

Chapter 13: Historic figures who sought Solitude in Extreme Isolation

∀ **Solitude's Triumphs:** *A Narrative of Greatness Forged in Isolation*

While this is not the thrust of this book, I wanted to include a chapter in honor of epic souls who chose more extreme isolation in order to chase their visions *and sought* wisdom in focused, longer-term isolation. Exploring these people's lives and art is a treasure trove of insight and inspiration. In the more raw, unyielding grip of solitude, where the world's clamor fades to a whisper, certain souls found their truest strength.

For sure, they are the outliers, the ones who turn from the herd, seeking not the applause of crowds but the quiet pulse of their own hearts. We weave a short tapestry of those unflinching souls, whose tales of rugged individualism and primal struggle echo through the ages, who carved greatness from the stone of solitude. From the forests of Walden to the deserts of Egypt, from the Siberian taiga to the Alaskan wilds, these figures—historical, religious, and contemporary—stand as monuments to the power of the solitary path.

∀ **Henry David Thoreau:** *The Sage of Walden Pond*

From within the heart of Massachusetts, where the Concord River murmurs secrets to the pines, Henry David Thoreau built a cabin on the shores of Walden Pond. It was 1845, and for two years, two months, and two days, he lived alone, a deliberate castaway from society's clamor. His hands shaped the timbers, his mind shaped Walden, a book that would echo like a wolf's howl across generations. Thoreau sought not escape but truth, stripping life to its essentials—food, shelter, thought.

Astonishingly, Thoreau's cabin at Walden Pond was approximately 10 feet wide by 15 feet long, with a total floor area of about 150 square feet. It had a simple design with a pitched roof, one door, two windows, and a small fireplace. The cabin was built in 1845 for around $28, using mostly salvaged and hand-hewn materials, reflecting Thoreau's minimalist philosophy described in Walden.

The woods were his cathedral, the seasons his scripture. In solitude, he found the rhythm of existence, a pulse untainted by the marketplace's din. His days were labor—chopping wood, planting beans—and his nights were contemplation, pen scratching paper under candlelight. Thoreau's solitude was no retreat but a confrontation, a wrestle with the self that birthed a philosophy of simplicity and defiance. He emerged not softened but sharpened, his words a blade cutting through the fog of conformity.

∀ Diogenes of Sinope: *The Cynic in the Barrel*

Centuries before, in the sun-scorched markets of ancient Greece, Diogenes of Sinope spat on the trappings of civilization. A philosopher with a beggar's cloak and a madman's fire, he made his home in a clay tub, scorning wealth, power, and propriety. Diogenes, the cynic, lived as a stray dog, free from society's leash. He wandered Athens' streets, lantern in hand, seeking an honest man in a world of liars. His solitude was a rebellion, a middle finger to the gods of status and convention. When Alexander the Great offered him any boon, Diogenes, basking in the sun, growled, "Stand out of my light." In his tub, with only a bowl he later discarded, he found freedom in want, wisdom in simplicity. His life was a shout into the void, proving that greatness needs no palace, only a soul fierce enough to stand alone.

∀ Thomas Merton: *The Monk's Silent Song*

In the rolling hills of Kentucky, Thomas Merton entered the Trappist monastery of Gethsemani in 1941, trading the world's noise for a vow of silence. A poet, a scholar, a man of restless intellect, he sought God in the stillness of his cell. His solitude was not empty but brimming—with prayer, with words that poured into books like The Seven Storey Mountain. Merton's pen was his axe, hewing meaning from the raw timber of existence. The monastery's rhythm—chants at dawn, labor in the fields—framed his inner journey. Yet even in seclusion, he wrestled with the world's pain, his writings bridging the cloister and the chaos beyond. Merton's solitude was a crucible, forging a voice that spoke to millions, a beacon for those lost in the fog of modernity.

∀ Emily Dickinson: *The Poet in the Attic*

In Amherst, Massachusetts, Emily Dickinson lived as a ghost in her own home, a recluse weaving worlds from words. By her thirties, she rarely left her room, her white dress a shroud against the world's intrusion. Yet her mind roamed free, her poems—sharp, slant, electric—capturing the infinite in a stanza's span. Solitude was her forge, where she hammered thoughts into lines that cut like frost. Her letters, her verses, were sent out like messages in bottles; few answered in her lifetime. She wrote of death, love, eternity, her words a pulse beneath the floorboards of a sleeping world. Dickinson's isolation was no cage but a chrysalis, her poetry proof that a single soul, alone, could shake the heavens.

∀ J.D. Salinger: *The Recluse of Cornish*

J.D. Salinger, whose Catcher in the Rye caught the raw ache of youth, fled fame's glare for a cabin in Cornish, New Hampshire. After the book's roar in 1951, he turned his back on the world, seeking silence in the woods. His days were simple—writing, meditation, solitude—his nights a vigil over stories he rarely shared. Salinger's retreat was no coward's flight but a hunter's stalk, chasing truth in the quiet. Rumors swirled of manuscripts locked away, tales too pure for a world he distrusted. His solitude was a shield, guarding a spark that burned bright in his work. Like a wolf in winter, Salinger thrived in isolation, his legacy a howl that still echoes.

∀ Grigori Rasputin: *The Mystic's Lone Path*

In the vast, frozen reaches of Siberia, Grigori Rasputin wandered as a pilgrim, a self-styled holy man with eyes like storm clouds. Before his name became a legend, he roamed alone, fasting, praying, seeking God in the wilderness. His solitude was a forge of fire and ice, shaping a mystic who would sway a dynasty. Rasputin's visions, born in lonely vigils, drew followers and foes alike. He carried the weight of his solitude into the palaces of St. Petersburg, where his strange power shook the Russian empire. Yet it was in those early, solitary years—wandering, starving, praying—that Rasputin found the spark that made him both savior and demon in the eyes of history.

∀ Jack Kerouac: *The Road's Lonesome Dharma Bum*

In honor of JK himself, I will try to capture his prosaic tone in this summary: Man, up there on Desolation Peak, Jack's lonesome soul was a wild thing, howling with the wind, naked under the big ol' Cascades sky, where the stars winked like they knew his secrets. For Sixty-three days, it was just him and that battered typewriter, clacking out truths rawer than the jagged granite biting the horizon.

Desolation Angels poured out, man, like whiskey from a busted flask, all hot and rumbling, burning, a restless hymn to America's open road, but born in solitude's fierce grip. His novels—*On the Road*, *Dharma Bums*—are in my mind, complex jazz riffs over an endless American melody of freedom; raw, no varnish. And those quiet moments, Jack alone with his typewriter and 120 ft of scroll paper, tapped ink into paper like a coyote's cry, a sound that carved his name deep into the stone of forever. His voice, lonesome and true, still echoes, sharp as moonlight on a desert night. Take that, Jack!

∀ **Gautama Buddha:** *The Enlightened One*

Beneath a bodhi tree in ancient India, Siddhartha Gautama sat alone, the world falling away like leaves in autumn. For years, he wandered as an ascetic, starving his body to feed his soul. In solitude, he faced the tempests of desire, fear, and illusion, until enlightenment broke like dawn. His solitude was no retreat but a battlefield, where he wrestled the self and emerged as the Buddha. From that lone vigil, a philosophy bloomed, its roots sinking deep into the earth, its branches shading millions. The Buddha's solitude was a forge, hammering a prince into a teacher whose words still light the dark.

∀ **Saint Anthony the Great:** *The Desert's Anchor*

In the scorched wastes of Egypt's desert, Saint Anthony the Great built a fortress of solitude. Around 270 CE, he fled the world for a cave, then a mountain, living on bread and prayer. The desert was his crucible, demons his sparring partners. For decades, he wrestled with visions—temptations, terrors—emerging as the father of monasticism. His solitude was a fire, burning away the dross of the world, leaving only faith. Others followed, drawn to his example, but Anthony's greatness was born alone, in the silence where God's whisper drowned out the world's roar.

∀ **Julian of Norwich:** *The Anchoress's Vision*

In a stone cell tethered to a Norwich church, Julian of Norwich lived as an anchoress, her world no larger than a room. Born in 1343, she chose solitude, sealing herself from society to seek God. In that confinement, visions came—sixteen revelations of divine love, scribbled in a book that would outlive her. Her solitude was a lens, focusing the infinite into words of hope: "All shall be well." Julian's cell was no prison but an observatory, her writings a star chart for souls lost in the dark. In isolation, she found a voice that still sings across centuries.

∀ **The Hermit Fathers:** *Voices of the Wilderness*

In the deserts of Egypt and Syria, the Hermit Fathers—nameless save for their deeds—fled the world's clamor for the silence of sand and stone. From the 3rd century, they lived alone in caves, their days a rhythm of prayer and labor. Solitude was their anvil, faith their hammer, forging lives of stark purity. They sought God in the emptiness, their souls tempered by hunger and silence. Their legacy, woven into the fabric of monasticism, proves that solitude can birth not just peace but power, a quiet that shakes the world.

∀ **Christopher McCandless:** *The Wanderer's Last Trail*

In 1992, Christopher McCandless, a young man with fire in his veins, walked into the Alaskan wilderness, seeking truth in solitude. Chronicled in Into the Wild, his journey was a rebellion against the world's chains. He lived in a rusted bus, the Stampede Trail his only road, the wild his only companion. For months, he hunted, foraged, and dreamed, his heart beating with the pulse of the land. His solitude was a gamble, a dance with death that ended in tragedy. Yet McCandless's quest, reckless and raw, lit a spark in those who heard his tale, a reminder that greatness often walks alone.

∀ **Agafya Lykova:** *The Siberian Recluse*

Deep in the Siberian taiga, Agafya Lykova lives as the last of her kind, an Old Believer born in 1944. Her family fled Stalin's grasp, carving a life from the wilderness. Alone since her father's death, Agafya tends her garden, prays her prayers, her world a speck in the vastness. Her solitude is no choice but a legacy, a thread of faith unbroken by time. In her cabin, surrounded by snow and silence, she embodies endurance, a solitary flame burning against the cold.

∀ **Richard Proenneke:** *The Alaskan Craftsman*

In 1968, Richard Proenneke, a man of iron will, built a cabin in Alaska's Twin Lakes with his own hands. For over thirty years, he lived alone, his days a hymn to self-reliance. His journals, later One Man's Wilderness, tell of crafting tools, hunting game, and watching seasons turn. Proenneke's solitude was a masterpiece, each log hewn with a stroke of purpose. In the wild, he found not loneliness but completeness, his life a testament to the strength found in standing alone.

∀ **Christopher Knight:** *The Shadow in the Woods*

Christopher Knight, the North Pond Hermit, vanished into Maine's forests in 1986, a young man seeking silence. For twenty-seven years, he lived alone, surviving by stealth, pilfering supplies from cabins. He spoke to no one, his only companions the trees and stars. Discovered in 2013, Knight's solitude was a mystery, a life stripped to its bones. His story, raw and strange, speaks of a man who found not just survival but a kind of peace in the wild's embrace, a greatness born in the shadows.

These souls, scattered across time and place, prove that solitude is no void but a forge. In the quiet, where the world's noise fades, they found strength, wisdom, and a fire that burns still. Like London's wolves, they howled their truths, their lives a challenge to the tame and the timid. Solitude was their wilderness, and in its depths, they became legends.

And last but not least:

∀ **Miles Davis:** *Resurrection in rural seclusion to Jazz greatness*

In the winter of 1953, Miles Davis, then 27 years old and spiraling from a severe heroin addiction that had begun eroding his jazz career around 1950, made a desperate bid for recovery by retreating to his father's farm in Millstadt, Illinois— a rural property near East St. Louis owned by his father, Miles Davis Sr., a successful dentist and cattle rancher. By this point, the trumpeter's habit had become all-consuming; he described in his autobiography how it stripped him of discipline, leaving him emaciated, unreliable in performances, and reliant on hustling—pimping, borrowing from friends, and scraping by in New York's underworld—to fund daily fixes that cost him up to $100 a day.

The seclusion began in December 1953, amid the biting chill of a Midwest winter, when Davis locked himself inside a small guest room or two-room apartment on the farm, determined to quit cold turkey without rehab, methadone, or medical intervention. For roughly two weeks, he endured the brutal physical and psychological torment of heroin withdrawal: chills, sweats, nausea, insomnia, muscle cramps, and waves of excruciating pain that he later likened to "dying" or being "tortured." Isolated from the city's drug scene and supportive yet stern family environment, Davis had no distractions beyond the farm's quiet desolation—perhaps the occasional sight of snow-covered fields or the distant lowing of cattle, but mostly just his own suffering. He emerged around late December or early January 1954, clean but weakened, having successfully purged the drug from his system through sheer willpower.

This harrowing episode marked a turning point. Physically and mentally revitalized, Davis returned to New York City by January or February 1954, where he quickly reassembled his musical life, forming influential quintets and recording seminal works like Walkin' and Blue Haze. The farm's seclusion, set against the stark winter landscape, symbolized his raw confrontation with addiction, paving the way for the creative resurgence that would define his legacy in the mid-1950s.

PART II

Chapter 14: The 7 Spiritual Principles of Ralph Waldo Emerson

While this chapter may be more suited to Part I, I felt the 7 spiritual principles of Ralph Waldo Emerson are very prescriptive to developing and adapting methods to integrate Zen practices into our daily lives. Thus, for me, our journey would not be complete, it seems, if I did not bring to you in the less-accessible recesses of the human spirit, where the eternal currents of the soul flow and swirl like some vast, uncharted river winding through what? ...primordial jungles of the mind. There lies my slim, wrinkled, and creased over time, yet mysteriously concise, treasure map to unfold. OK, I might point out that when fully inspired, yes, I tend to write long if somewhat ethereal sentences, mostly for fun but also ironic succinctness. This worn and softened scroll, or what's left of it, is: *"Living from the Soul: The 7 Spiritual Principles of Ralph Waldo Emerson"* by Sam Torolde, permeates the shelves of my mind. I hope my sharing it here, is appreciated.

Torode serves as a beacon through the fog of our close friend on this journey, Ralph Waldo Emerson's, transcendental musings. It is a stellar achievement in translating his labyrinthine prose penned in the distant and calmer recesses of the nineteenth century, into a sort of stark clarity for our own noisy, turbulent age.

I felt the best presentation of Emerson's work was via Torode, having journeyed through the mind of Emerson and publishing: *Everyday Emerson: The Wisdom of Ralph Waldo Emerson Paraphrased;* and *Secrets of the Mind: Ralph Waldo Emerson's Keys to Expansive Mental Powers,* culminating in his concise but sweeping work *The 7 Spiritual Principles.*

Having probed stoic emperors and Taoist sages, Torode plumbs the depths of Emerson's private journals, particularly those penned in 1833, a year fraught with the spectral echoes of loss RWE. For it was then, after the cruel hand of tuberculosis had snatched away his beloved Ellen Tucker in 1831, that Emerson set sail upon the stormy seas of Europe, encountering the colossal intellects of Coleridge, Carlyle, and Wordsworth—figures who loomed like ancient monoliths, challenging the rigid dogmas of creed and compelling him toward a revelation of the inner divine and eventually resolved into transcendentalism.

Instead of exploring these giants left for another time, let's detour just briefly to capture a resonant observation, zen-like, as if mindful and in the present, seems pertinent in our journey. Carlyle on Wordsworth:

Carlyle wrote, *"On that summer morning (in 1840) I was apprised by Taylor that Wordsworth had come to town, and would meet a small party of us at a certain tavern in St. James's Street, at breakfast, to which I was invited for the given day and hour. We had a pretty little room, quiet though looking streetward (the tavern's name is quite lost to me); the morning sun was pleasantly tinting the opposite houses, a balmy, calm and sunlight morning. Wordsworth, I think arrived just along with me; we had still five minutes of sauntering and miscellaneous talking before the whole were assembled. I do not positively remember any of them, except that James Spedding was there, and that the others, not above five or six in whole, were polite intelligent quiet persons, and, except Taylor and Wordsworth, not of any special distinction in the world. Breakfast was pleasant, fairly beyond the common of such things. Wordsworth seemed in good tone, and, much to Taylor's satisfaction, talked a great deal; about poetic correspondents of his own; then about ruralties and miscellanies. Finally, he spoke of literature, literary laws, practices, observances, at considerable length, and turning wholly on the mechanical part, including even a good deal of shallow enough etymology, which was well received. On all this Wordsworth enlarged with evident satisfaction, and was joyfully reverent of the wells of English undefiled; though stone dumb as to the deeper rules and wells of Eternal Truth and Harmony, which you were to try and set forth by said undefiled wells of English or what other speech you had. For the rest, he talked well in his way; with veracity, easy brevity and force, as a wise tradesman would of his tools and workshop--and as no unwise one could."*

Carlyle concluded with a remarkably vivid description of the Wordsworth, "His voice was good, frank and sonorous, though practically clear distinct and forcible rather than melodious; the tone of him businesslike, sedately confident; no discourtesy, yet no anxiety about being courteous. A fine wholesome rusticity, fresh as his mountain breezes, sat well on the stalwart veteran, and on all he said and did. You would have said he was a usually taciturn man; glad to unlock himself to audience sympathetic and intelligent, when such offered itself. His face bore marks of much, not always peaceful, meditation; the look of it not bland or benevolent so much as close impregnable and hard: a man multa tacere loquive paratus, (t: Be prepared to speak or remain silent) in a world where he had experienced no lack of contradictions as he strode along. He had a vivacious strength looking through him which might have suited one of those old steel-grey markgrafs whom Henry the Fowler set up to ward the marches and do battle with the intrusive heathen in a stalwart and judicious manner."

Again:

His face bore marks of much, not always peaceful, meditation; the look of it not bland or benevolent so much as close impregnable and hard: a man multa tacere loquive paratus, in a world where he had experienced no lack of contradictions as he strode along.

OK, where were we? Torode's book. Yes, it explores the idea of the soul as a powerful, eternal spark that connects humans to a divine, universal spirit flowing through everything. It's like a Zen saying: all that lives is holy. Torode shows that Emerson saw people not as lonely travelers in a harsh world, but as threads woven into a larger, universal fabric—a mystical idea similar to teachings in Taoism and Stoicism. These philosophies encourage connecting with a higher power while navigating life's challenges one day at a time.

The book acts as a guide for living authentically in a noisy, chaotic world. It urges readers to let go of ego—those inner fears, societal pressures, and desires for material things—and instead follow the soul's wisdom for peace and purpose. Torode sums up Emerson's insights into seven spiritual principles. These aren't just ideas; they're practical calls to listen to your inner voice, align with nature's rhythms, and embrace the present moment. By rooting yourself in the soul, life's true purpose unfolds naturally, bringing strength, gratitude, and a deep connection to the universe.

Despite being short, the book is profound and worth revisiting, like a wise, weathered sailor's unforgettable stories. Readers praise it for simplifying complex ideas without losing their depth, calling it a "clear gem of wisdom" or "mind-blowing." It's a beacon for anyone exploring spirituality, mindfulness, or the journey to understand themselves better. In a distracted, confusing world, Torode's work revives Emerson's belief: true fulfillment comes from within, where the soul meets the universal spirit.

One such soul described it as "a crystal clear gem of wisdom," another as "mind-blowing," a catalyst for delving into the murky depths of one's own conduct. Torode's labor resurrects Emerson's creed: that authentic fulfillment surges from the abyssal well within, affirming that *"the soul is the meeting point with the Universal Soul."*

Again, I felt the best presentation of Emerson's work was via Torode, as he draws from Emerson's writings that include: *"Self-Reliance"*; *"Compensation"*; *"Fate"*; *"Nature"*; *"The Over-Soul"*; and *"Experience"*.

Presented here through each principle Torode concisely developed, laden with elucidations, profound glimpses, pragmatic rites, and tendrils reaching back to Emerson's vast philosophical expanse and massive writings:

☑ **Principle 1: Trust Yourself** – *All that you need for growth and guidance is already present inside you*

Emerson's essay *"Self-Reliance"* (1841) urges you to trust yourself. He writes, *"Trust thyself: every heart vibrates to that iron string."* Your soul holds everything you need for life's journey. Outside influences—like churches, society's rules, or even friends' advice—lose their power compared to your inner voice.

Doubting yourself comes from relying too much on others' opinions, which cuts you off from your true self. Emerson's trip to Europe, as Torode describes, showed him this. After losing his wife and feeling let down by organized religion, he turned inward. He realized true guidance comes from your intuition, not loud doctrines. To follow this, practice daily habits like journaling or meditating to listen to your soul. When faced with choices, don't follow the crowd—listen to your inner pull.

This idea connects to modern mindfulness practices, which emphasize trusting your instincts to stay strong through challenges. One writer said this approach helped them solidify their beliefs by embracing their uniqueness, as Emerson encourages. By trusting yourself, you avoid conformity and grow from your inner potential.

☑ **Principle 2: As you sow, you will reap** – *Your Thoughts and Actions Shape Your Character, and Your Character Determines Your Destiny*

This principle builds on the first, showing that every action has consequences, like the saying "*what goes around, comes around.*" Torode drew it from Emerson's 1841 essay "Compensation," suggesting that our deeds shape our lives, much like seeds growing into plants. Your thoughts and actions matter: negative ones breed fear and limitation, while positive ones foster strength and clarity. Torode points to Emerson's life—how he moved from grief to insight by reflecting during his travels. To apply this, build mindful habits: replace self-criticism with positive affirmations or act kindly to create a cycle of goodness. As English poet and painter William Blake put it so powerfully:

"What is the price of Experience? Do men buy it for a song?

Or wisdom for a dance in the street? No, it is bought with the price

Of all that a man hath, his house, his wife, his children

Wisdom is sold in the desolate market where none come to buy

And in the wither'd field where the farmer ploughs for bread in vain

It is an easy thing to triumph in the summer's sun

And in the vintage and to sing on the waggon loaded with corn

It is an easy thing to talk of patience to the afflicted

To speak the laws of prudence to the homeless wanderer

To listen to the hungry raven's cry in wintry season

When the red blood is fill'd with wine and with the marrow of lambs"

It is an easy thing to laugh at wrathful elements,

To hear the dog howl at the wintry door, the ox in the slaughter house moan;

To see a god on every wind and a blessing on every blast;

To hear sounds of love in the thunder storm that destroys our enemies' house;

To rejoice in the blight that covers his field, and the sickness that cuts off his children,

While our olive and vine sing and laugh round our door, and our children bring fruits and flowers.

Then the groan and the dolor are quite forgotten, and the slave grinding at the mill,

And the captive in chains, and the poor in the prison, and the soldier in the field

When the shatter'd bone hath laid him groaning among the happier dead.

It is an easy thing to rejoice in the tents of prosperity:

Thus could I sing and thus rejoice: but it is not so with me.'

So too had Emerson traveled, and so too, his ethereal conclusion. Blake explores the cost of wisdom and experience, presenting a stark, almost bitter meditation on human suffering, spiritual insight, and the superficiality of easy optimism. The High Cost of Wisdom and Experience, thus the value of being mindful in the present experience to draw immediate conclusions and adjustments. And that true wisdom is born from profound loss, sacrifice, or suffering, not from fleeting pleasures or superficial achievements. That wisdom is often unrecognized or unwanted by society, existing in barren, overlooked places. And both authors suggest a rejection of facile happiness or prosperity in favor of a more authentic, albeit painful, engagement with life's complexities.

Blake's observation on wisdom in this passage is that it is a hard-earned, costly attribute, born from personal sacrifice and a deep engagement with life's darker realities. It stands in opposition to superficial optimism or societal indifference, requiring an individual to confront loss, empathy, and the desolate truths of existence to attain it.

☑ Principle 3: Nothing Outside You Can Harm You – *Circumstances and Events Don't Matter as Much as How You Deal with Them*

This idea, drawn from Emerson's *"Fate"* (1860), says that outside problems, like storms, can't truly harm your inner self. Torode explains that life's challenges only hurt when you react poorly, not because of the challenges themselves. Instead of fighting troubles, see them as lessons. Emerson, for example, turned his grief and career changes into spiritual growth. Torode suggests staying calm and detached, treating hardships as teachers, not enemies. Practically, this means finding peace inside yourself during tough times and avoiding resistance.

This approach rejects feeling like a victim and encourages choosing how to respond. It's like Thoreau's simple life at Walden, finding calm amid chaos. One person described this mindset as a "warm blanket" that comforts you through life's storms. By embracing this, you gain a steady, unshakable inner strength, like the deep ocean.

Personally, when I face a large setback, a profound loss, after a period of introspection and learning, I try to be inspired to do four or five things that I would not have otherwise done, to turn the experience into a net positive or at least to balance the loss.

☑ **Principle 4: The Universe Is Inside You** – *The World Around You Is a Reflection of the World Within You*

Torode explores the connection between the inner self and the outer world, drawing from Emerson's "Nature" (1836). The external world reflects our inner struggles—what we feel inside shapes how we see the world. Change your inner state, and the world around you shifts too.

Change your inner state, and the world around you shifts too.

Our mindset changes how we perceive things: a fearful mind sees threats, while a calm one finds harmony. Emerson said it well: exploring nature helps us understand ourselves. Every new experience or fact we learn expands our mind and spirit. The more we connect with nature, the better we know who we are.

To practice this, pay attention to how your inner feelings show up in the world around you, or spend time in nature to align with its rhythms. This builds compassion, seeing others as reflections of a shared human spirit. Writers praise this approach for sparking wonder and revealing deep truths within us.

☑ **Principle 5: Identify with the Infinite** – *Center Your Identity on the Soul and Your Life's Purpose Will Unfold*

Emerson's "The Over-Soul" (1841) argues that shifting focus from the fleeting ego to the eternal soul is key. Torode suggests that clinging to the ego leads to emptiness, while embracing the soul reveals your true calling with ease. Real breakthroughs come from letting go of attachments to identity or possessions, opening the door to divine inspiration. Emerson's own shift from preacher to philosopher shows this in action. To apply it, affirm your soul's nature: say, *"I am infinite spirit,"* to gain clarity on your purpose. This approach aligns with Campbell's idea of following your bliss, echoing modern mysticism and transcendental roots. Many who've tried it call it transformative, drawing them toward inner strength.

☑ Principle 6: Live in the Present – *The Present Moment Is Your Point of Power. Eternity Is Now*

Torode stresses staying alert, just like Emerson's disdain for dwelling on past regrets or future fears in his 1844 essay "Experience." Only the present moment lasts; eternity isn't out there in the distance—it's right here in your immediate reach.

Key insights are that distractions weaken your power, but being fully present strengthens it. Emerson's reflections after his European travels show this, even in times of grief. In practice: Focus on your breathing to anchor yourself in the now.

This fights against the rush of modern life, offering real calm. It's like Alcoholics Anonymous's daily slogan or Lao Tzu's call for peace. It helps you handle tough times with grace, as many people who've tried it can confirm.

☑ Principle 7: Seek God Within – *The Highest Revelation Is the Divinity of the Soul*

The core idea, inspired by Emerson, is that true spirituality comes from within, not from external gods or rituals. Torode sees the soul as a spark of the divine, making personal struggles a source of profound truth.

Forget ceremonies—real connection to the divine happens through direct experience. Emerson's transcendentalism says everyone can access the sacred without priests or intermediaries. To tap into this, try quiet reflection or walks in nature.

This approach fosters awe and gratitude, making life feel sacred. It connects to ideas of universal harmony. People who embrace it find it enlightening, a gateway to understanding Emerson's deeper mystery.

In my view, we are surrounded by miracles. While we have discovered some scientific laws, we've just scratched the surface of wonderment that is everyday life around us. From gravity to the interplay of the birds and the bees. We observe but have little core understanding of natures first principles, and thus much remains that is in**explicable** by natural or scientific laws and thus miraculous. The work of a divine agency.

mir·a·cle /ˈmirək(ə)l/ noun

a surprising and welcome event that is *not **explicable** by natural or scientific laws* and is therefore considered to be the work of a *divine agency*.

Chapter 15: Everyday Zen: Living with Intention

When done with full awareness, any action—no matter how mundane—becomes a door that opens to boundless presence.

Introduction

The concept of Zen, derived from the Buddhist tradition, is often associated with serene monasteries, robed monks, and hours of silent meditation. For many, Zen can appear removed from the hustle and bustle of modern life—something reserved for spiritual seekers on retreat or those who have renounced worldly concerns. Yet, at its heart, Zen is not necessarily about retreating from life but about engaging fully with it. Everyday Zen aims to bring the spirit of mindful awareness and deliberate intention to the mundane tasks and routines that make up most of our days. By integrating core Zen principles into day-to-day life, it becomes possible to experience clarity, peace, and deep fulfillment without abandoning our responsibilities or relationships.

Living with intention sits at the heart of Everyday Zen. Intention shapes our actions, guides our decisions, and helps us steer a course aligned with our deepest values. In Zen, the emphasis on awareness—often cultivated through meditation—merges seamlessly with a purposeful approach to life. Everyday Zen invites us to harness our natural capacity for awareness and direct it toward each moment, creating a sense of coherence, compassion, and joy.

In this chapter, we will explore how Everyday Zen can be cultivated, the centrality of living with intention, and the practical techniques that can help bring these insights into reality. We will discuss mindfulness, acceptance, non-judgment, and compassion as essential aspects of this practice. We will also look into the obstacles and misconceptions that often arise when attempting to maintain Zen in the midst of daily routines and responsibilities. Finally, we'll offer suggestions for integrating these lessons into the fabric of everyday life so that anyone—regardless of background or beliefs—can experience a greater sense of peace and presence in each passing moment.

The aim is not to demand perfection or unwavering equanimity at all times. Instead, it is to spark curiosity about how we use our minds, hearts, and energy in life's ordinary activities. With the right intention and a steady dedication to awareness, even washing dishes, commuting to work, or having a difficult conversation can transform into opportunities for deeper insight and growth. By exploring the essence of Everyday Zen, we glimpse the possibility that serenity and peace can be found in the most commonplace experiences.

❀ The Roots of Zen and Its Relevance Today

Zen's historical roots trace back to the teachings of Siddhartha Gautama, the historical Buddha, and the tradition that later evolved through China (as Chan Buddhism) and Japan (as Zen). Core Zen teachings emphasize direct experience over intellectual understanding, encouraging practitioners to cultivate "beginner's mind,"—an openness and receptivity to the raw reality of each moment.

In centuries past, Zen flourished in monastic settings, where practitioners could devote themselves entirely to meditation, study, and silent reflection. The rigors of monastic life were meant to strip away unnecessary distractions and guide practitioners to awaken to the true nature of reality. For contemporary society, which values productivity, achievement, and constant stimulation, the idea of retreating from the noise can seem both alluring and intimidating. Yet the principles of Zen need not be confined to temples or restricted to those who follow a specific religious tradition. Indeed, Zen's core message, often expressed through metaphors like "chopping wood and carrying water," underscores that awakening can happen in the midst of daily life.

Despite our fast-paced world, the relevance of Zen has never been clearer. Modern stressors—digital overload, work pressures, constant striving for success—frequently erode our sense of well-being. As we scramble from task to task, it's all too easy to lose sight of the present moment, falling prey to anxiety about the future or regret about the past. Everyday Zen is a response to this state of fragmentation. It teaches us that true peace and stability are not found by controlling external conditions but by cultivating awareness and intention, no matter the circumstances. Thus, Everyday Zen resonates with anyone looking for a simpler, more grounded approach to life—one that acknowledges our responsibilities but also allows us space to breathe, reflect, and respond instead of react.

In making Zen a part of daily life, what we are truly doing is rediscovering the extraordinary in the ordinary. The ringing of a phone, the taste of tea, the sound of rain—each of these can become a gateway to clarity when approached with a mindful, intentional perspective. Far from being esoteric or inaccessible, Zen can become a deeply personal and relevant practice for people of all ages, cultures, and belief systems.

In making Zen a part of daily life, what we are truly doing is rediscovering the extraordinary in the ordinary.

❀ Defining Intention in Everyday Zen

To live with intention means to engage each moment with a clear sense of purpose and attention. But what exactly is intention within the context of Zen?

First, it is crucial to differentiate intention from mere aspiration or wishful thinking. Intention in Everyday Zen is not about conjuring grandiose plans or hyper-focusing on outcomes. Instead, it arises from a deeper awareness of who we are and how we want to be in the world. It is grounded in presence, compassion, and a commitment to mindful engagement.

Intention in Zen is deeply tied to the principle of "right intention," one of the steps in the Buddha's Noble Eightfold Path. While "right intention" is often interpreted in different ways across various traditions, a unifying perspective is that it involves cultivating wholesome mental states such as kindness, non-harm, and detachment from destructive impulses. When we align our daily actions with these wholesome states, we gradually reshape our habits and perceptions. Living with "right intention" does not mean we ignore external goals—on the contrary, it means we pay close attention to our reasons for pursuing them, ensuring these reasons come from a compassionate, clear-sighted place.

To live with intention means to engage each moment with a clear sense of purpose and attention.

In everyday life, intention can manifest in simple ways: choosing to greet a coworker with genuine warmth, cooking a meal mindfully, or setting boundaries for our own well-being. The difference between an intentional action and an automatic one lies in the quality of awareness. When we act out of habit or societal conditioning, we might find ourselves mindlessly checking social media every few minutes, engaging in gossip that sows discord, or reacting to stress by lashing out at others. When we live intentionally, we pause, reconnect with our values and presence, and decide on a course of action that reflects who we truly want to be.

This intentional mindset does not make daily life rigid or stifled. Instead, it injects our actions with authenticity and creativity. We become clearer about our motivations and more transparent in our relationships. Even our frustrations— such as dealing with a messy house or confronting a stubborn coworker—can serve as doorways to deepen our practice. Each frustration becomes a reminder to pause, recall our intention to live mindfully, and respond with greater compassion for ourselves and others. Over time, these moments accumulate and transform our inner landscape, opening the door to a more peaceful and connected way of being.

☯ The Role of Mindfulness in Everyday Zen

Mindfulness is often described as the engine that powers Everyday Zen. It is the practice of bringing one's attention to the present moment without judgment, whether that moment is pleasant, unpleasant, or neutral. In an age of perpetual distraction, mindfulness can feel like swimming upstream, yet it is precisely because of this that it holds transformative power. By turning our attention back to the present, again and again, we begin to see the patterns of our minds: how we cling to certain desires, recoil from discomfort, or zone out when bored. A mindful approach shines light on these tendencies and gives us the space to choose a new response.

In the context of Everyday Zen, mindfulness goes beyond the meditation cushion. Yes, formal sitting meditation remains a powerful tool to sharpen focus and develop mental clarity, but mindfulness, once tasted, can be woven into almost any activity. We can practice mindful walking—paying attention to how the feet meet the ground, how the arms swing, how the air feels against our skin. We can practice mindful eating—tasting our food with full awareness instead of gulping it down in haste. We can even practice mindful conversation—truly listening to the other person instead of preparing our response prematurely.

When mindfulness meets intention, our perspective on ordinary tasks shifts profoundly. Taking out the trash, for example, may at first glance seem like a chore we want to rush through. But if we approach it mindfully, noticing the textures, smells, and effort required, we can transform it into a moment of presence. The intention might be to care for my living space and environment. Suddenly, this mundane task becomes an expression of responsibility, gratitude, and attention. It might sound simple, yet such subtle shifts in perspective often yield surprising serenity.

On a deeper level, mindfulness helps untangle the knots of old habits and knee-jerk reactions. Each time we pause and become fully conscious of what we're doing and why, we reclaim our agency. We begin to realize that we are not merely passengers on the ride of life, subject to every twist and turn of circumstance. Instead, we are active participants, capable of choosing a response that aligns with our aspirations to be clear-headed, kind, and awake to the world around us.

☯ Acceptance and Letting Go

Acceptance and letting go are foundational attitudes in Zen practice, and they are vital to living with intention. It's important to clarify what acceptance means in this context. Acceptance in Zen does not imply resignation or passivity in the face of injustice or hardship. Rather, it is a willingness to see reality for what it is, rather than what we wish it to be. When we accept a situation, a feeling, or a limitation without clinging to a desire that things be otherwise, we free ourselves from a great deal of mental anguish. This does not mean we won't attempt to make constructive changes; rather, we do so from a place of inner calm and clarity rather than from denial or frustration.

Letting go complements acceptance. In our daily life, many of us carry a burden of regrets, resentments, or fears. We might cling to certain outcomes or harbor illusions about permanence—believing that if we just work hard enough, we can freeze life into a static ideal. Zen encourages us to see that everything is in flux: our thoughts, our emotions, and our external circumstances. Letting go simply means not chaining ourselves to outcomes or illusions that keep us in a perpetual state of dissatisfaction.

In practical terms, acceptance and letting go can be practiced through awareness of when we're resisting. For instance, if we find ourselves stuck in traffic, do we rail against reality, honking and fuming internally, or do we notice our agitation and breathe into the moment? Acceptance means acknowledging the traffic jam, seeing our impatience, and letting go of the need for immediate control. This can transform an otherwise stressful situation into an opportunity to practice mindfulness and compassion—especially compassion for our own tension and for others caught in the same predicament.

Letting go also applies to how we view ourselves. Many people carry an internal narrative about who they "should" be, often shaped by societal expectations or past conditioning. By practicing Everyday Zen, we see these narratives as constructs, not immutable truths. This insight can be liberating, allowing us to shed self-imposed limitations or judgments. Over time, acceptance and letting go create an inner spaciousness that invites genuine transformation and intention-driven living.

💧 Cultivating Compassion and Gratitude

Compassion and gratitude often arise naturally from a consistent Everyday Zen practice. When we slow down, pay attention, and choose to live intentionally, we become more attuned to our interdependence with all beings. Recognizing this interdependence—how the food we eat, the clothes we wear, and the technology we use all come from countless other people's efforts—tends to soften the edges of our ego-centric concerns. We realize that our actions ripple outward and that the well-being of others is intimately tied to our own.

Compassion in Everyday Zen is not limited to warm feelings of sympathy. It manifests in small, daily acts: listening deeply to a friend who's struggling, offering help to a neighbor, or being patient with a coworker who's late on a deadline. Compassion also includes self-compassion, which is crucial in any practice aimed at growth. Living with intention doesn't mean we will never make mistakes or lose our temper; rather, it means learning to respond to our own missteps with kindness instead of harsh self-criticism. This gentle attitude toward ourselves helps break the cycle of shame and allows us to correct course more skillfully.

Gratitude likewise becomes more accessible when we open our eyes to the richness of each moment. By practicing mindful awareness, we can notice the breeze on our skin, the taste of fresh fruit, or the presence of supportive friends and family. Recognizing these simple gifts fosters an appreciation for life's fleeting wonders. A sense of gratitude can even accompany the more challenging moments, as they often serve as catalysts for growth and introspection. In this way, gratitude is not dependent solely on life's "good" circumstances but can arise from a deeper understanding of how every experience shapes us.

Gratitude is at the core of achievement. Cael Sanderson took over as head coach of the Penn State Nittany Lions wrestling program in 2009, transforming it into one of the most dominant forces in college sports. Prior to his arrival, PSU had won only one NCAA team title in its history (1953). PSU wrestling under Sanderson ranks among the elite, particularly in college athletics of all time, due to its 12 titles in 15 years—a level of consistency rivaling some of the greatest across all sports. And it is still getting better. Cael Sanderson **emphasizes gratitude** as a foundational principle for success in both sports and life. He believes gratitude fosters peace of mind, happiness, and the ability to maximize one's potential, viewing it as a core element that transcends outcomes like winning or losing. Sanderson teaches that true gratitude involves focusing less on oneself and more on others and the opportunities available, regardless of circumstances. He encourages a mindset shift from obligation ("I have to") to privilege ("I get to"), which builds resilience and mental toughness. This philosophy, rooted in his belief that wrestling mirrors life, is a cornerstone of his coaching, where he instills gratitude in his athletes to appreciate their opportunities and maintain humility.

Penn State wrestling coach, Cael Sanderson believes gratitude fosters peace of mind, happiness, and the ability to maximize one's potential, viewing it as a core element that transcends outcomes like winning or losing.

When compassion and gratitude weave into our everyday thoughts and actions, our overall intention becomes gentler and more inclusive. We no longer see ourselves as isolated units fighting for limited resources; instead, we perceive the interconnected web of life in which we all participate. This shift in perspective has profound implications: we may find ourselves drawn to more sustainable living choices, more ethical decisions, and more considerate interactions. In short, compassion and gratitude help guide us toward a more harmonious, purposeful existence, grounded in respect for ourselves, others, and the planet.

☯ Practical Techniques for Everyday Zen

While the philosophical underpinnings of Everyday Zen are important, putting them into practice calls for concrete techniques that can be integrated into daily life. Below are several tools that can help cultivate mindful intention:

1. **Micro-Meditations**: Throughout the day, pause for short bursts of mindful breathing or awareness. This can be as simple as taking three conscious breaths every time you switch tasks or stand up from your desk. These micro-meditations anchor your mind in the present moment and recalibrate your focus.

2. **Mindful Routines**: Choose one daily activity—like washing dishes, folding laundry, or brushing your teeth—and commit to doing it mindfully. Pay attention to every sensation: the temperature of the water, the scent of the soap, the movement of your hands. Over time, you can extend this sense of presence to other routines.

3. **Body Scan**: A quick body scan at the beginning or end of the day helps reconnect you with physical sensations. Lying down or sitting comfortably, move your attention from head to toe, observing areas of tension or ease. This scan not only promotes relaxation but also fosters a habit of self-awareness that will carry into daily life.

4. **Intention Setting**: Each morning, take a moment to set a clear intention for your day. It could be as general as "I will remain present and calm," or more specific, such as "I will offer patience and kindness to colleagues today." Revisit this intention periodically throughout the day.

5. **Reflective Journaling**: Writing down your observations of the day— moments of mindfulness, challenges, insights—helps you internalize your practice. You can note how often you drifted into autopilot or felt triggered by stress, and how you responded. This reflection boosts self-awareness and accountability.

6. **Loving-Kindness (Metta) Practice**: At least once a day, pause to generate feelings of goodwill toward yourself and others. Silently repeat phrases like, "May I be safe. May I be happy. May I be at peace." Then direct the same wishes toward loved ones, acquaintances, and eventually all beings. This practice nurtures compassion, a key element of Everyday Zen.

Each of these techniques serves as a gentle reminder to stay in the here and now, to observe thoughts and emotions without being swept away, and to perform actions with intention rather than habit. While none of these are complicated, sustaining them requires genuine commitment. Little by little, these everyday practices reshape our mental and emotional patterns, allowing for a more grounded, intentional approach to living.

❦ Overcoming Common Obstacles

Despite the simplicity of these techniques, practicing Everyday Zen can be surprisingly challenging. Modern life, with its constant stimuli and demands, pulls us in a myriad of directions. Below are some common obstacles and suggestions for overcoming them:

1. **Time Constraints**: Many people feel they don't have time to practice Zen or mindfulness. Yet even a few seconds of conscious breathing can make a difference. Instead of viewing Zen practice as an addition to your to-do list, weave it into what you already do—whether that's commuting, working, or taking care of family.

2. **Restlessness and Boredom**: People new to mindfulness often feel restless or bored when they try to stay present. Our minds are used to ceaseless activity, and slowing down can feel strange. A gentle approach is best: accept the restlessness or boredom without judgment. Over time, the mind grows more comfortable with stillness.

3. **Performance Pressure**: Some individuals come to Zen practice expecting immediate results: perfect calm, unwavering focus, or constant positivity. This "performance pressure" can create frustration when real-life practice doesn't match the ideal. Remember, Zen is not about achieving a fixed mental state. It's about noticing what's here, moment by moment, and responding with kindness and awareness—even when that moment includes messiness or discomfort.

4. **Distractions and Technology**: With smartphones, social media, and perpetual notifications, staying present can feel like an uphill battle. One strategy is to set boundaries around technology use: designate tech-free times or spaces, mute non-essential notifications, and consciously decide when to check your phone rather than responding to every buzz or ping.

5. **Misconceptions About "Zen"**: A popular misconception is that Zen is all about being perpetually calm and unflappable. In reality, Zen includes being fully present with whatever arises—anxiety, anger, or sorrow—without being swallowed by it. Accepting difficult emotions is a part of practice, and it doesn't negate our capacity for peace; it can even deepen it.

By recognizing these obstacles, practitioners can prepare strategies that align with their unique circumstances. Flexibility is important: if a particular approach to mindfulness feels forced or unsustainable, experiment with different methods until you find a rhythm that suits your lifestyle. The essence of Zen is experiential, so allowing yourself the freedom to explore and adapt fosters a resilient, long-lasting practice.

☯ Integrating Everyday Zen into Relationships and Community

While Zen is sometimes portrayed as an individual path, it's important to remember that our lives unfold within a network of relationships. Family, friends, colleagues, and community members all shape our experiences and influence how we respond to the world around us. Therefore, integrating Everyday Zen includes recognizing and nurturing the relational aspect of our existence.

Communication is a prime area for applying mindfulness and intention. In conversation, are we truly listening, or are we waiting for our turn to speak? Do we allow space for silence, or do we fill every pause with words? By bringing awareness to how we communicate, we can reduce misunderstandings, deepen empathy, and foster genuine connections. A mindful conversation also entails being aware of nonverbal cues—body language, tone of voice, eye contact—which often speak louder than words.

Conflict resolution offers another opportunity for Everyday Zen. Conflicts arise when differing needs, desires, or viewpoints collide. A Zen-based approach invites us to first observe our internal reactions—anger, defensiveness, fear—without immediately acting on them. By creating a pause between stimulus and response, we can bring intention to the table. Instead of escalating the conflict or withdrawing entirely, we can choose to communicate honestly yet compassionately.

In broader community contexts, such as workplaces or neighborhood groups, Everyday Zen can manifest as shared practices. Some offices have adopted "mindful breaks" or short group meditations to relieve stress and enhance focus. Others encourage respectful dialogue circles where each participant speaks in turn, promoting inclusive and attentive communication. When an entire group or community embraces these practices, the collective atmosphere shifts toward mutual respect, responsibility, and goodwill.

Finally, **service**—contributing to the welfare of others—is a natural extension of Everyday Zen. Whether through volunteering, mentoring, or simply offering a helping hand, service is a powerful way to express compassion in action. When guided by mindful intention, service is less about gaining recognition and more about genuinely caring for others. This reciprocity—a willingness to give and receive support—nurtures a sense of belonging and purpose that enriches everyone involved.

Everyday Zen is, at its core, an invitation to wake up to the present moment and live intentionally—no matter how ordinary or complex our lives may appear. It does not promise a life free from difficulties. Instead, it offers a pathway to engage those difficulties with clarity, acceptance, and a compassionate heart. By weaving mindfulness into daily routines, we transform seemingly mundane tasks into touchstones of awareness. By setting clear intentions rooted in kindness and wisdom, we align our actions with the values that matter most.

As we've explored, fundamental Zen principles such as acceptance, letting go, and compassion can be more than abstract spiritual ideals. They become daily living practices that enrich our relationships, sharpen our focus, and expand our capacity for gratitude. Although there are practical obstacles—time constraints, technology distractions, and misconceptions about the nature of Zen—these can be navigated with creativity, patience, and self-compassion.

Moving forward, the real test of Everyday Zen is lived experience. Reading or discussing these concepts can spark inspiration, but the true transformation occurs when we integrate them into the flow of life. Each moment—whether joyful, neutral, or painful—carries potential for awakening. With consistent practice, we develop a more grounded presence, an open heart, and a sense of spaciousness that allows us to respond to life's complexities with greater insight and equanimity.

Ultimately, the journey of Everyday Zen is both deeply personal and profoundly universal. It reminds us that beneath the chaos and clamor of modern existence, there is a still point of awareness accessible to everyone. When we choose to live from that still point—deliberately, kindly, and with a clear sense of purpose, compassion, and gratitude—we join a lineage of practitioners across generations who have discovered that true peace and wisdom need not lie in distant monasteries or future dreams. They can be found in the here and now, woven into the very fabric of our everyday lives.

A young monk approached the master and asked, "How can I harness the fire of my ego to inspire my path, yet cast away its shadows that lead me astray?"

The master replied, "Look into a clear mirror under the midday sun."

The monk gazed into the mirror and saw his own face, radiant and bold, yet marred by fleeting flickers of pride and fear. "What do I see, Master?" he asked.

The master said, "The mirror holds your flame—its light drives you to climb mountains, to create, to seek truth. But the shadows you see are the ego's whispers, craving praise and fearing loss. To harness the flame, let it burn brightly, but do not cling to the mirror. Walk forward, and let the shadows fall behind."

The monk pondered this. One day, while meditating by a stream, he saw his reflection ripple in the water. The face was there, then gone, yet the stream flowed on. He smiled and returned to his practice.

Brenda Diamond

Chapter 16: Building a Home Meditation Practice

A meditation cushion is more than a piece of fabric stuffed with cotton; it is a portal to your inner world. Take a seat, straighten your spine, and begin the journey inward.

⑥ Building a Home Meditation Space and Practice

Almost all rooms in most homes have a designated or implied function in that they serve as a space for certain activities. We have worked out our rooms for physical activity; why not one for mental development and refinement, working toward wholeness and balance? In the course of writing this book, I went from a mat in my bedroom to a room dedicated to meditation and Zen practice. While this may facilitate the development, it cannot sequester the fullness achieved in that space.

Recently, on a business trip, I attended a meeting on the top floor of one of the tallest buildings in Los Angeles, California. You could see the Hollywood Sign, Laurel Canyon, Hollywood Hills, and Dodger Stadium all at once. On a break, I took a little tour of the floor to take in the panorama. They had a "zen room." It was a small room with a little recirculating waterfall and a couple of cushions—a weak execution of a noble thought and yet profound in its simplicity. This inspires me to put one in my own office. More on that, later.

The main function of a Zen room is primarily quiet reflection or meditation. Meditation has woven itself into the tapestry of modern well-being, offering a refuge from the rush of daily life. With a dedicated place to practice, meditation can become a transformative and grounding ritual—an opportunity to shift from chaos to calm, even if only for a few moments each day. Whether you're new to meditation or a seasoned practitioner, creating a home meditation space can be an empowering step toward a more mindful lifestyle. Through thoughtful design, attention to detail, and a commitment to consistent practice, you can carve out a sanctuary in the comfort of your own home. In this guide, we will explore how to build a meditation space that resonates with your personal style, supports your unique goals, and nurtures a lasting practice.

⑥ The Value of a Home Meditation Space

Before diving into design ideas and logistics, it's helpful to understand why a designated meditation space can be so beneficial. **First**, having a physical area in your home devoted exclusively to meditation creates a sense of ritual and intention. It reminds you daily that there is a space waiting for you to retreat into stillness, removing some of the common mental hurdles that can prevent regular practice.

Second, crafting a space that aligns with your aesthetic preferences and needs can enhance the meditative experience itself. When you enter a place specifically curated for peace, your mind and body receive subtle cues to slow down, breathe, and become more present. The arrangement of elements—light, aroma, cushions, or even nature-inspired décor—can ground your senses and guide you more easily into a meditative state.

Third, a home meditation space is flexible and adaptable. You can tailor your setup to accommodate different forms of meditation—whether it's guided meditation, silent sitting, sound baths, or movement-based practices like yoga or qigong. This means you can refine and evolve the space as your needs change. Over time, the area might become more than just a place to sit quietly; it can transform into a microcosm of personal growth, reflective of your intentions and milestones in the practice.

⑥ Choosing the Right Location

One of the most critical decisions in establishing a home meditation space is selecting its location. If you have a spare room, that may be the obvious choice, but for many, it's a corner of the bedroom, living room, or an attic nook that becomes their peaceful retreat. Regardless of the size or shape of the space, the key is finding an area that fosters tranquility.

1. *Quietness:* Aim for a spot in your home that is relatively quiet. Minimizing external noise allows you to settle into stillness with fewer distractions. If absolute silence is impossible, do not worry—some practitioners prefer low-level ambient sounds or nature noise. However, for beginners, quieter areas can be more supportive.

2. *Natural Light:* Spaces with windows providing natural light can help you maintain a sense of warmth and openness. If your location lacks sunlight, gentle artificial lighting can work equally well, provided that it can be adjusted to create a calm ambiance.

3. *Privacy:* Whether you live alone or with others, having a bit of privacy can help you feel more at ease when you're meditating. Curtains, room dividers, or plants can serve as subtle partitions to carve out a personal zone.

4. *Space Constraints:* Meditation doesn't require significant square footage. Even a compact corner can work if arranged thoughtfully. The most important aspect is that you feel comfortable sitting or lying down in that space, free from feeling cramped.

5. *Proximity to Noise Sources:* Try to avoid setting up your meditation area near televisions, gaming consoles, or areas of heavy traffic in your home,

like the kitchen or front door. If you can't avoid it entirely, consider adding a small bookshelf, screen, or piece of furniture to buffer distractions.

Designing and Decorating the Space

When it comes to the aesthetic design of a meditation space, simplicity as discussed before, often reigns supreme. That said, there is no single correct approach—some people find minimalism soothing, while others draw comfort and inspiration from a space teeming with meaningful objects. The most important principle is that you genuinely feel relaxed and uplifted in the space you've created.

1. *Color Palette:* Neutral and soothing colors (think pale blues, soft greens, beige, or white) can provide a clean backdrop that promotes tranquility. However, if deep reds, purples, or earth tones feel more spiritually resonant, lean into your intuition. The color scheme can be subtle or bold, as long as it aligns with your personal style and intention for meditation.

2. *Textures and Fabrics:* Soft, natural fabrics can add a layer of comfort. Consider plush rugs, cotton or wool cushions, or even a soft blanket for those cooler days. Using organic materials can be grounding, connecting you with nature.

3. *Décor:* Decorations should be thoughtful rather than overwhelming. You might incorporate symbolic items such as a small statue, meaningful artwork, crystals, or personal photographs. Plants are another popular addition, as they bring a hint of nature indoors and can improve air quality.

4. *Scent:* Many meditators find that certain scents help them settle more easily. Essential oils, incense, or candles with fragrances like lavender, sandalwood, or frankincense can foster a calming environment. If you have allergies or sensitivities, opt for scent-free candles or choose an essential oil diffuser with mild, allergen-friendly oils.

5. *Organization:* Clutter can be a source of subtle stress. Make sure your chosen space remains tidy, storing any accessories or props neatly. Using baskets, shelves, or small cabinets allows you to keep your meditation tools accessible yet unobtrusive.

Ⓖ Incorporating Comfort and Function

A soothing environment is not just about visual appeal—it's equally about ensuring physical comfort and supporting function. Feeling at ease in your meditation posture can significantly influence the depth and length of your practice.

1. *Seating Options:* Many people use a meditation cushion (zafu) and mat (zabuton) for support, while others may prefer a meditation bench or a simple chair if sitting on the floor isn't comfortable. Experiment with different seating arrangements to find what works best for your body. Remember that your spine should be supported and relatively upright to facilitate easier breathing.

2. *Flooring and Mats:* If you plan to meditate on the floor, consider placing a soft rug or mat for comfort and insulation. Yoga mats can serve as a simple base if you already have one.

3. *Temperature Control:* Since meditation typically involves stillness, you may notice temperature fluctuations more easily. If possible, choose a room or corner where you can open a window to let in fresh air or where you can control the temperature so it's neither too hot nor too chilly.

4. *Supportive Props:* Beyond seating, props such as bolsters, rolled-up blankets, or yoga blocks can help maintain posture. For some forms of meditation that involve lying down, a soft cushion under the knees can relieve strain on the lower back.

5. *Cleaning and Maintenance:* Since you'll be sitting or lying down, keeping your space clean is paramount. Regularly vacuum or sweep the floors and wipe down surfaces to minimize dust accumulation. Regular upkeep fosters a clear and comfortable environment, free from distractions that might arise from a cluttered or dirty space.

Setting the Mood with Lighting and Sound

As you refine your meditation space, pay close attention to the elements of lighting and sound, as both significantly affect your ability to concentrate and unwind.

1. *Lighting:* If you have windows, consider installing curtains or blinds that can diffuse harsh sunlight. If you're relying on artificial light, opt for adjustable or soft lamps and bulbs. Some practitioners like using salt lamps or small LED candles that cast a gentle glow. Candlelight can be particularly conducive to relaxation, but always practice proper fire safety.

2. *Sound:* For many meditators, ambient noise can either help or hinder focus. Some prefer complete silence, while others may use nature sounds, white noise, or instrumental music to create a buffer against

disruptive household sounds. Consider placing a small speaker in your space if you enjoy listening to guided meditations or calming music. Conversely, if silence is your preference, invest in a set of comfortable noise-canceling headphones or earplugs, especially if your environment is frequently bustling.

3. *Sound Bowls and Chimes:* Some people like to incorporate Tibetan singing bowls, crystal bowls, or chimes into their practice. Gentle ringing or tonal sounds can help set the stage for a meditative session. If you incorporate these instruments, designate a small spot to store them so they're always within reach yet neatly tucked away.

4. *Aroma and Ambiance:* In addition to lighting and sound, consider how scents can shape the ambiance. Soothing aromas have the power to trigger the relaxation response in the body, enhancing the atmosphere of your meditation space. Whether you choose aromatic candles, essential oil diffusers, or incense, select high-quality products and scents that resonate with your personal preferences.

⑥ Stocking Your Meditation Space with Essentials

A well-stocked meditation space goes beyond just cushions and candles. The right selection of tools, accessories, and resources can enrich your practice and make meditation both enjoyable and sustainable.

1. *Meditation Cushion or Bench:* A dedicated seat is often the core feature of a meditation space. Whether it's a plush cushion, a low-profile bench, or a supportive chair, ensure it provides enough support for your lower back and hips.

2. *A Small Table or Altar:* If you're drawn to ritual or symbolic elements, you might place a small table or shelf to hold items such as a bell, your favorite book on mindfulness (this book of course), a small statue, or treasured objects that inspire feelings of peace.

3. *Journaling Supplies:* Many meditators like to reflect on their practice, noting any insights, emotions, or questions that arise. Keeping a journal and a pen nearby encourages introspection and helps track progress over time. You could even store affirmation cards or a favorite quote collection to provide motivation.

4. *Music Player or Smartphone:* If you use apps or guided meditations, having a device with a reliable speaker or headphones can be helpful. Consider storing it out of sight when not in use, as screens can be visually distracting.

5. *Blankets or Shawls:* Meditation sessions can be surprisingly chilly, especially if your body temperature drops while you're sitting still. Keeping a blanket or shawl in the room ensures you stay warm without interrupting your practice.

6. *Mindful Reminders*: Small reminders, such as a note on the wall or a favorite mantra, can anchor you to your intention for being in the space. You might place a short inspirational phrase somewhere visible to help set the tone for your practice each time you enter the space.

⑥ Creating a Regular Practice

A beautifully designed space can draw you in, but it's the discipline of consistent practice that yields the true benefits of meditation. Building a habit often requires thoughtful planning and gentle self-encouragement.

1. *Set Realistic Goals:* Especially for beginners, starting with five to ten minutes of meditation each day is more sustainable than aiming for an hour-long session. Over time, you can gradually increase the length or frequency of your sessions.

2. *Pick a Regular Time:* Consistency is key. Many people find it helpful to meditate first thing in the morning, setting a tone of calm for the rest of the day. Others prefer late evenings to unwind before sleep. Experiment to see which time works best for your schedule and energy levels.

3. *Create Rituals:* Ritual can transform routine into reverence. Something as simple as lighting a candle or striking a singing bowl before you sit can signal your mind that it's time to shift gears into stillness. Likewise, you might close with a short chant, a bow, or a silent moment of gratitude.

4. *Use Guidance and Tools:* If you're new or prefer structured sessions, guided meditation apps or recorded practices can be highly beneficial. You can also experiment with different techniques, such as mindfulness of breath, body scans, or loving-kindness meditation.

5. *Stay Flexible and Compassionate:* Not every session will feel serene. It's natural to have days where your mind seems especially restless. Practice patience and remember that meditation is a journey, not a destination. Each time you notice your mind wandering, gently bring it back to the present moment.

⑥ Common Obstacles and How to Overcome Them

Creating a soothing space and establishing a routine is essential, but obstacles are inevitable—both external and internal. Identifying them early on can help you develop strategies to stay on track.

1. *Lack of Time:* One of the biggest barriers to meditation practice is the feeling of having no time. To address this, consider waking up slightly earlier or carving out a short period during lunch breaks. Even brief three-minute pauses can be profoundly centering.

2. *External Distractions:* Family members, pets, or electronic devices can all intrude on your stillness. Communicate your needs with the people you live with—let them know when you plan to meditate. Put your phone on "Do Not Disturb" or place it in another room. If pets wander into your space, gently set boundaries or allow their quiet presence if it doesn't disrupt your practice.

3. *Physical Discomfort:* If you find yourself fidgeting or in pain, adjust your posture or consider adding more cushions. It might take a few attempts before you discover the perfect seating arrangement. Remember that lying down is also an option if upright sitting proves uncomfortable due to injury or chronic pain—just be mindful of potential drowsiness.

4. *Mental Restlessness:* The mind's chatter can seem especially loud once you decide to sit in silence. Techniques like focusing on the breath, chanting a mantra, or using a visualization can help anchor your thoughts. Over time, you'll likely become more adept at recognizing—and calmly releasing—intrusive thoughts.

5. *Expectations and Self-Judgment:* Meditation is sometimes romanticized as an instantly blissful experience. While tranquility can arise, it's equally important to acknowledge that frustration, boredom, and restlessness may surface. Embrace all experiences without labelling them as successes or failures.

⑥ Evolving Your Practice Over Time

Meditation is not just a one-off endeavor; it's a path of self-discovery that can shift with your changing life circumstances. Your home meditation space, while constant, can also evolve to match the arc of your personal growth.

1. *Adapting the Space:* As your preferences shift, you might add or remove décor items, change the color palette, or experiment with different

seating. The ongoing process of refinement can keep your meditation corner fresh and inviting.

2. *Exploring Different Techniques:* If your routine starts to feel stale, try different modalities. Delve into mindfulness-based stress reduction (MBSR), transcendental meditation, loving-kindness (metta) practice, or walking meditation. Variety can help you avoid plateaus in your spiritual or emotional development.

3. *Expanding the Practice:* Over time, your designated meditation area could also become a hub for journaling, light yoga, or breathwork exercises. Such integration can deepen your mind-body connection and solidify healthy habits. Likewise, you might invite friends or family to share the space occasionally for group meditation or a short, guided session together.

4. *Seeking Community and Support:* While a home meditation space is private, you don't have to practice in isolation. Many meditators find encouragement and inspiration through local or online meditation groups, classes, or retreats. Learning from teachers and peers can enhance your skills and maintain motivation.

5. *Celebrating Milestones:* Give yourself credit for sticking to your meditation practice. Whether it's reaching a certain number of consecutive days of practice or feeling a sense of inner calm during a stressful period, mark those moments. You might light a special candle or place a new plant in your meditation space to celebrate your progress.

Building a home meditation space goes beyond mere interior design—it's about establishing a dedicated realm for self-care, introspection, and growth. From selecting the right corner to choosing comforting textures, lighting, and scents, every decision shapes the ambience of your sanctuary. Equally crucial is how you engage with the space: forming a consistent routine, addressing obstacles with gentle awareness, and allowing your practice to evolve naturally over time.

What starts as a simple corner filled with cushions and soft lighting can blossom into a vital anchor for mental, emotional, and spiritual well-being. By integrating elements of comfort and personal significance, you create a haven that encourages you to sit quietly, breathe consciously, and, ultimately, discover the subtle layers of your own mind. The process of building a home meditation space—selecting décor, setting intentions, and establishing routines—becomes a metaphor for inner transformation: slow, intentional, and deeply rewarding. In an age where life can feel perpetually hurried, carving out a nook of peace in your home might be the most radical act of self-care you can offer yourself.

Brenda Diamond

Chapter 17: From Restlessness to Stillness

In the quiet, the mind can sound like a thunderstorm. Yet if we remain still, each rumble of thunder eventually dissolves into the open sky of awareness.

Introduction

In a modern world dominated by constant motion and an ever-growing stream of sensory input, many people find themselves swept up in a whirlwind of activity and distraction. The sense of restlessness—whether mental, emotional, or spiritual—can be overwhelming. It manifests in the seemingly endless to-do lists, the pressure to succeed, and the unrelenting flow of social media. Far from being a phenomenon unique to our current moment in history, restlessness has challenged human beings for centuries. Philosophers, spiritual teachers, and psychologists alike have struggled to pinpoint its causes and propose methods to navigate it. Across cultures and time, various wisdom traditions have emphasized the importance of cultivating stillness to counterbalance this restlessness. Yet, in a society that celebrates hustle and productivity, the concept of stillness is often misunderstood as laziness or a lack of ambition.

The journey from restlessness to stillness is not merely about slowing down one's pace; it is about transformation. It involves recognizing the nature of restlessness, examining its origins, and consciously nurturing states of peace and calm. In this essay, we will explore the roots of restlessness, discuss how it manifests in modern life, and offer pathways toward genuine stillness. By weaving together insights from philosophy, psychology, and spirituality, this work aims to provide a comprehensive look at one of humanity's most pervasive challenges.

Defining Restlessness

Restlessness can be understood as a persistent sense of dissatisfaction or unease that propels individuals to seek constant movement—whether physical, mental, or emotional. It is a complex phenomenon that can reveal itself in different ways: for some, restlessness is a literal inability to remain still, characterized by fidgeting or an incessant urge to move; for others, it appears as an internal racing of thoughts, an unceasing mental chatter that makes relaxation impossible.

Often, people associate restlessness with external circumstances. We believe that if we just change our job, relocate to a new city, or move on from a relationship, the underlying disquiet will fade. This assumption leads to a continuous cycle of searching for external solutions—like new hobbies, entertainment, and experiences—that may temporarily alleviate symptoms but rarely address the core issue.

To understand restlessness, we can look to ancient traditions and modern psychology for clues. In Buddhism, for example, the notion of *dukkha* (often translated as "suffering") pinpoints a pervasive sense of dissatisfaction intrinsic to human life. Psychological theories, on the other hand, highlight how heightened stress levels in contemporary society feed into chronic anxiety and restlessness. Both approaches point to the same underlying reality: a mind that is never fully at ease, always chasing after the next stimulation or distraction.

Modern Culture and the Cult of Busyness

The cultural landscape in which we live significantly influences our levels of restlessness. In many parts of the world, particularly in the West, a "cult of busyness" has taken hold. Productivity and constant activity have become synonymous with virtue. We are encouraged to "do more" and "work harder," often to the detriment of our mental and physical well-being. People wear their busyness like a badge of honor, equating the lack of downtime with success, or at least with an active life filled with meaning.

This social conditioning contributes to a chronic inability to be still. Smartphone notifications, social media feeds, and instant messaging foster an environment where silence and reflection become increasingly rare. We find ourselves multi-tasking—consuming news, responding to emails, and checking social media—even during brief moments of respite. As a result, the average attention span has diminished, and many people experience a nagging sense that they cannot "switch off" mentally.

Paradoxically, the more we fill our schedules, the more restless we may become. This can spiral into a cycle of anxiety, where the pressure to continually perform or stay connected diminishes the capacity to savor silence and stillness. While external demands are certainly part of the equation, it is the internal compulsion—the fear of missing out, the drive for validation—that truly fuels restlessness. Learning to break free from the "cult of busyness," therefore, becomes an essential step in any movement toward stillness.

The Psychology of Restlessness

From a psychological perspective, restlessness can be linked to several factors: anxiety, fear, boredom, lack of purpose, and unmet emotional needs. Individuals might feel stuck in a repetitive cycle of rumination or worry, particularly if they believe something crucial is missing from their lives. In many cases, childhood experiences or past traumas can also manifest as chronic restlessness in adulthood. A person who grew up in a chaotic household, for instance, might unconsciously equate calm with danger or boredom, constantly seeking external stimulation to avoid facing unresolved emotions.

European society has developed over time certain patterns and rituals that are innately healthy and wholesome. From which we in North America could learn. For example, **Communal Dining and Slow Food (Southern Europe, especially Italy, France, Spain),** where long, leisurely meals with fresh, local ingredients—think Mediterranean diet (olive oil, vegetables, fish, whole grains). Families and friends often eat together, prioritizing social connection over rushed meals. Emphasis on seasonal, locally sourced ingredients (e.g., Italian "zero-kilometer" restaurants) reduces environmental impact compared to the US's reliance on processed or imported foods. **Cycling as a Lifestyle (Netherlands, Denmark, Germany):** Daily bike commuting, supported by extensive urban bike infrastructure. **Sauna and Cold Exposure (Finland, Scandinavia)** Regular sauna use (often weekly) paired with cold plunges or outdoor cooling. Finns treat saunas as a social and spiritual ritual, with 90% of households having access (per Finnish Sauna Society). **Siesta or Rest Culture (Spain, Southern Europe)** Midday breaks for rest or naps, historically tied to agricultural life but still common in Spain. These methods and social habits are slowly weaving themselves into US culture in a positive way, which can help reduce restlessness.

Cognitive-behavioral theory examines how thought patterns contribute to emotional and behavioral outcomes. Restlessness often ties to negative thinking—someone might have an internal narrative that says, "I have to keep moving, or I will fall behind," or "If I take time to rest, I am being lazy." These beliefs drive behavior that continuously accelerates the pace of life, leaving little room for stillness.

Self-awareness is a critical starting point in psychological approaches to restlessness. By identifying the core beliefs or unresolved traumas that feed this perpetual motion, individuals gain a clearer understanding of why they are uneasy. Therapy, mindfulness-based interventions, and certain forms of meditation can help transform these patterns into healthier alternatives. Recognizing the role of the mind in generating restlessness empowers us to reclaim agency and gradually move toward a state of inner peace.

The Roots of Stillness in Spiritual Traditions

Despite the universal nature of restlessness, virtually all major spiritual traditions teach the practice of cultivating stillness or quietude. Christianity, for instance, offers the notion of *contemplation*—an interior, prayerful silence where one seeks communion with the divine. Islamic mystics, known as Sufis, speak of *dhikr*, a remembrance of God that involves deep concentration and repetition of sacred words, eventually leading to a tranquil heart. Similarly, Hinduism provides myriad paths—such as Raja Yoga—that involve disciplined breath control, meditation, and ethical living to quiet the mind and experience inner stillness.

Buddhism, particularly through its Zen and Theravada lineages, brings a laser-like focus to the importance of meditation. Practitioners are encouraged to sit quietly, observing the mind's fluctuations without judgment. Over time, this practice peels away layers of mental chatter, revealing an innate stillness that lies beneath the surface. The idea here is not to force the mind to stop thinking but to allow thoughts to settle, much like letting mud in water sink to the bottom, making the water clear. In Buddhist philosophy, stillness is closely tied to *equanimity*—an even-minded approach to life that neither clings to pleasure nor shrinks from pain.

Across these traditions, the cultivation of stillness is not a passive process; it requires dedication and discipline. Through prayer, meditation, or simply reflective silence, many have discovered a wellspring of peace that is independent of external events. Such practices help individuals ground themselves, offering respite from the unceasing demands of daily life and providing a stable platform for deeper introspection.

The Role of Mindfulness

Mindfulness, a concept deeply rooted in Buddhist teachings, has emerged in recent decades as a scientifically validated method to foster mental well-being and mitigate restlessness. At its core, mindfulness teaches individuals to become aware of the present moment without passing judgment or clinging to thoughts and emotions. Rather than attempting to halt the mind's incessant chatter, mindfulness involves gently returning one's focus to the present each time the mind drifts away.

Many mindfulness techniques emphasize the breath. By observing the natural flow of inhalation and exhalation, practitioners develop a stable anchor in the present. Over time, this constant returning to the breath strengthens the ability to notice restlessness before it escalates. Instead of getting lost in worries, plans, or regrets, one learns to witness these mental phenomena with curiosity and non-attachment.

Crucially, mindfulness extends beyond formal meditation sessions. It can be integrated into daily activities such as walking, eating, and even conversing. Each moment becomes an opportunity to remain fully present, thereby reducing the tendency to slip into autopilot. While restlessness often arises from the mind's projection into past regrets or future anxieties, mindfulness consistently calls us back to the "now." This return to the moment is the cornerstone of stillness, fostering a quieter interior landscape that provides relief from the ever-looming pressures of life.

The Art of Letting Go

One of the most challenging aspects of moving from restlessness to stillness is learning the art of letting go. Restlessness frequently stems from attachment—attachment to ideas, outcomes, or possessions. For instance, a person might feel restless because they want a particular job promotion, approval from peers, or a certain image of success. This attachment propels them to overwork, overthink, and overschedule to achieve their goals.

Letting go does not equate to giving up ambition or adopting a fatalistic worldview. Instead, it involves releasing the rigid clinging to specific results. You can still pursue career advancements, cherish close relationships, and maintain personal goals, but with an attitude that is more flexible and open. When we let go of the need to control every outcome, we create space for the natural flow of life. In that space, stillness can emerge.

Various strategies support the practice of letting go, journaling, therapy, self-inquiry, and spiritual exercises. Asking oneself, "What am I afraid of losing?" or "What truly matters in this situation?" can illuminate hidden attachments. Identifying and naming these attachments begins the process of loosening their grip. Over time, we can find a balance between taking constructive action and allowing events to unfold in their own time. This equilibrium helps break the cycle of perpetual doing and hurrying, guiding us toward a calm acceptance that is integral to stillness.

Physical Pathways to Stillness

Yoga

Although stillness is often understood as an internal state, the body plays a crucial role. Physical forms of movement such as yoga, tai chi, and qigong are specifically designed to harmonize body and mind, paving the way for greater inner tranquility. These practices incorporate slow, deliberate movements, synchronized with conscious breathing, to foster awareness of the present moment and reduce mental clutter.

Yoga, for example, includes *asana* (postures) and *pranayama* (breath control) practices that purify and energize the body, eventually preparing it for meditation. Through mindful movement, tension is released from the muscles, and the nervous system is soothed. In time, the practice shifts from merely physical to profoundly spiritual, as the practitioner becomes attuned to subtle sensations and energetic flows.

⚘ Tai Chi

Tai chi and *qigong* similarly involve flowing sequences that enhance bodily awareness and balance energy. The measured pace of these movements counters the frenetic tempo of modern life, inviting practitioners to engage fully in each motion. By shifting our focus to the body, we can alleviate the restless mind. In essence, when the body is at ease and in harmony, the mind often follows suit. These embodied disciplines remind us that stillness is not about rigid immobility but a dynamic alignment of the entire being.

Tai Chi, often described as "meditation in motion," embodies Zen-like qualities through its emphasis on mindfulness, fluidity, and inner stillness. Practitioners engage in slow, deliberate movements that flow seamlessly into one another, fostering a deep awareness of the present moment—a core principle of Zen philosophy. This mindful focus on breath and body alignment cultivates a state of calm, allowing individuals to release mental clutter and connect with their inner essence. The practice encourages a non-striving attitude, where the goal is not to achieve perfection but to embrace each movement with intention and grace, mirroring Zen's emphasis on being fully present without attachment to outcomes.

The Zen-like essence of Tai Chi also manifests in its harmony with natural rhythms and its cultivation of balance. Each posture, rooted in the principles of yin and yang, reflects the interplay of opposites—strength and softness, movement and stillness—creating a dynamic equilibrium that resonates with Zen's focus on interconnectedness. Practitioners often describe a sense of "flow," where the mind quiets, and the body moves effortlessly, as if guided by an inner wisdom. This state of effortless action, or *wu-wei*, aligns with Zen teachings of acting in harmony with the natural order, making Tai Chi a physical embodiment of Zen's serene, contemplative spirit.

Tai Chi offers profound benefits for older adults, promoting physical, mental, and emotional well-being. Its slow, flowing movements enhance balance and coordination, significantly reducing the risk of falling, a common concern with aging. Studies show that regular Tai Chi practice improves muscle strength, flexibility, and joint mobility, helping seniors maintain independence and ease discomfort from conditions like arthritis. Beyond physical health, Tai Chi fosters mental clarity and emotional resilience through mindful breathing and meditative focus, reducing stress, anxiety, and depression. It also boosts cognitive function, potentially delaying age-related decline. As a low-impact exercise, Tai Chi is accessible to most, requiring no special equipment and adaptable to various fitness levels. Socially, group classes build community, combating loneliness. By integrating body and mind, Tai Chi empowers older adults to age gracefully, with vitality and calm.

Cultivating Solitude and Silence

The outward bustle of daily life can be profoundly draining, and many people never allow themselves time to experience genuine solitude or silence. Yet, these states are pivotal in the transition from restlessness to stillness. Solitude is often misunderstood; it is not merely isolation or loneliness. Rather, it is a deliberate choice to spend time alone with oneself, free from external noise and demands.

Spending periods in solitude—be it a morning walk in nature, a silent retreat, or simply carving out time at home without screens—opens a doorway to deeper self-reflection. Silence, similarly, is not just the absence of sound but the cultivation of a receptive and spacious interior. When we allow silence to enfold us, unresolved thoughts and feelings may bubble up to the surface. This can be unsettling, but it is also an opportunity for transformation. In the quiet, we gain the chance to work through suppressed emotions, clarify our values, and regain a sense of balance.

Being comfortable with silence and solitude does not happen overnight. In a world where constant communication is the norm, moments of quiet can initially feel jarring or even uncomfortable. However, through consistent practice, these periods become immensely enriching. They act as oases of tranquility, allowing restlessness to dissipate and inner calm to deepen. The development of a regular routine that includes time for solitude and silence can thus serve as a powerful antidote to the frenetic pace of contemporary life.

Stillness in Daily Life

While formal practices like meditation, yoga, and silent retreats are invaluable, the true measure of stillness lies in how it manifests during our everyday routines. A mindful approach to work, relationships, and leisure activities can be transformative. For instance, a few minutes of quiet reflection before starting the day—perhaps during a morning cup of tea—sets a calm tone. Before you send an email or post on social media, you might pause, take a breath, and consider your intention.

Conscious breaks throughout the day can also mitigate restlessness. Short stretches of deep breathing or a brief walk outside can refocus the mind. Technology can be reshaped into a tool rather than a tyrant: turning off nonessential notifications, scheduling screen-free periods, or even using apps that remind us to take mindful pauses. Over time, these small changes yield significant benefits in cultivating stillness amid the storms of modern life.

Additionally, practicing gratitude and compassion can also lead to stillness. When we intentionally direct our awareness toward what we appreciate and how we can care for others, we shift from a self-centered perspective—often a source of restlessness—to a more expansive sense of connection. This attitude naturally calms the mind and fosters a grounded sense of well-being. By integrating stillness practices into the rhythms of daily life, we transform ordinary moments into catalysts for spiritual, emotional, and psychological growth.

Integration and Stillness

The movement from restlessness to stillness can be seen as a heroic journey of sorts—one that demands honesty, courage, and perseverance. At its core, this transformation involves recognizing the root causes of our restlessness, exploring how they intertwine with our cultural conditioning, psychological patterns, and spiritual longings, and then applying practices that gently realign us with our innate capacity for peace.

Ultimately, cultivating stillness does not mean eradicating restlessness entirely; rather, it means learning how to navigate life's ebbs and flows with equanimity. Periods of restlessness may still arise, but with consistent practice, we can recognize and address them before they balloon into full-blown anxiety. The tools we have discussed—mindfulness, meditation, letting go, physical discipline, solitude, and daily-life integration—work synergistically to foster a more balanced way of being.

Stillness is a universal human possibility. It transcends religious identities, cultural backgrounds, and personal histories. When we tap into stillness, we access a wellspring of clarity and stability that can guide us through the vicissitudes of life. Though modern society celebrates speed, multitasking, and productivity, embracing the power of stillness can be an act of liberation. It allows us to step off the hamster wheel of endless striving and rediscover the quiet riches of simply being.

The path from restlessness to stillness is both an inward and outward journey—a dance between the commitments we hold in the world and the deep interior spaces we sometimes neglect. By embracing the practices and principles outlined above, we gradually harmonize these dimensions of our lives. In that process, we discover a resonant peace that speaks to the deepest parts of our humanity and lights the way forward with grace, resilience, and an abiding sense of purpose.

Chapter 18: Maintaining zazen - Breathing and Meditation

Zazen is a meditative practice central to Zen Buddhism, involving seated meditation aimed at cultivating mindfulness, concentration, and insight. The term "zazen" translates to "seated meditation" (za = sitting, Zen = meditation). Practitioners typically sit in a specific posture—often the lotus or half-lotus position—on a cushion (zafu), with a straight spine, hands forming a mudra (hand gesture), and eyes half-open, gazing softly downward.

The goal of zazen is not to achieve a particular state but to observe the mind and body without attachment, letting thoughts pass without clinging to them. There are two main forms:

1. **Shikantaza** ("just sitting"): A formless meditation where one sits in open awareness, without focusing on a specific object or goal, simply being present with whatever arises.
2. **Koan-based zazen**: Involves contemplating a paradoxical question or story (koan) to transcend ordinary thinking and awaken insight.

Zazen is practiced in a quiet, distraction-free environment, often in a zendo (meditation hall), and is considered a direct path to experiencing one's true nature or Buddha-nature. It emphasizes direct experience over intellectual understanding, aligning with Zen's focus on immediacy and awakening.

Maintaining zazen, the core meditation practice of Zen Buddhism, requires consistent effort, proper posture, and a focused yet relaxed mind. Here's a concise guide based on traditional teachings and practical advice:

1. *Set Up a Consistent Practice:*

   o **Time and Place**: Choose a quiet, comfortable spot and practice at the same time daily, ideally early morning or evening when distractions are minimal. Even 10-20 minutes daily can be effective.
   o **Environment**: Keep the space clean and simple. A cushion (zafu) or chair, a mat, and minimal distractions help. Dim lighting or a blank wall can aid focus.

2. *Posture:*

   o **Seated Position**: Sit on a zafu or chair with your spine straight but not rigid. Common postures include full lotus, half lotus, Burmese, or seiza (kneeling). If using a chair, keep your feet flat on the ground.

- o **Alignment**: Tuck your chin slightly, align your ears over shoulders, and rest hands in the cosmic mudra (left hand on right, thumbs lightly touching). Eyes are half-open, gazing softly downward about 3 feet ahead.
- o **Stability**: Imagine your body as a triangle—stable at the base (knees and pelvis). Sway gently side-to-side when first sitting to find your center.

3. *Breathing:*

- o Breathe naturally through your nose, focusing on slow, deep abdominal breaths. Let the breath settle into a rhythm without forcing it.
- o Some traditions emphasize counting breaths (1-10, then repeat) to anchor attention, especially for beginners.

4. *Mindset (Shikantaza or "Just Sitting"):*

- o *Non-Attachment:* In zazen, particularly Soto Zen's shikantaza, the goal is to sit without striving for enlightenment or chasing thoughts. Simply be present.
- o *Handling Thoughts:* When thoughts arise, acknowledge them without judgment and gently return to your breath or posture. Don't suppress or engage with them.
- o *Open Awareness:* Maintain a state of alert relaxation, neither drowsy nor tense. If distracted, refocus on your breath or the sensation of sitting.

5. *Common Challenges and Solutions:*

- o *Physical Discomfort:* Minor aches are normal. Adjust posture slightly if needed, but avoid fidgeting. Over time, the body adapts. For persistent pain, consult a teacher or try a different posture.
- o *Restlessness or Drowsiness:* If restless, check posture or take a few deep breaths. If drowsy, open eyes wider, take a break to stretch, or sit at a cooler time of day.
- o *Wandering Mind:* Persistent distraction is normal. Gently return to the present moment. Counting breaths or focusing on a koan (in Rinzai Zen) can help.

6. *Deepening Practice:*

- o *Regularity:* Consistency builds discipline. Gradually increase session length (e.g., from 10 to 30 minutes) as you grow comfortable.

- *Study and Guidance:* Read texts like Dogen's *Fukanzazengi* or Suzuki Roshi's *Zen Mind, Beginner's Mind*. Joining a sangha (community) or working with a teacher provides support and corrects subtle errors.
- *Sesshin:* Participate in intensive retreats (sesshin) for immersive practice, if possible.

7. *Daily Life Integration:*

- Zazen isn't just sitting; carry mindfulness into daily tasks—eating, walking, or working. This reinforces the practice's benefits, like clarity and equanimity.
- Be patient. Zazen is a lifelong practice, not a goal to "master."

Today, in an era often marked by stress, anxiety, and digital overload, these techniques are seeing a resurgence. Meditation apps, breathing workshops, and mindfulness retreats are more popular than ever.

However, alongside this rise in popularity, misconceptions about these practices persist. Some regard meditation as an esoteric, purely spiritual endeavor inaccessible to the average person. Others believe breathing techniques are overly simplistic—"we all breathe anyway"—and thus underestimate how transformative conscious breathing can be. This text will dispel such misconceptions and provide a thorough, practical guide to various breathing and meditation practices. We will discuss their historical context, delve into scientific evidence supporting their benefits, and outline step-by-step methods, ensuring that anyone—even complete beginners—can safely explore the art and science of mindful breathing and meditation.

By the end of this exploration, readers will understand how breathing and meditation intertwine to support overall health, manage stress, and nurture emotional resilience. Whether you are a seasoned practitioner looking to refine your skills or a newcomer curious to try a meditation practice, these pages aim to guide you on a journey toward self-discovery, calm, and well-being.

Foundations of Breathing

 The Physiology of Breathing

Breathing is an automatic process driven by the respiratory system, primarily involving the lungs, diaphragm, and the respiratory center in the brainstem. With each inhale, oxygen enters the body and travels into the bloodstream, and with each exhale, carbon dioxide is expelled. While this fundamental rhythm of life occurs whether or not we pay attention, the act of breathing is also unique in that it can be consciously controlled. We can breathe faster or slower, shallower or deeper, holding our breath or letting it flow freely.

The Importance of Conscious Breathing

What sets human beings apart from many other creatures is our ability to bring awareness to breath. This conscious control of respiration allows us to influence physical functions like heart rate and blood pressure and regulate mental states such as stress and anxiety. When we become aware of the breath, we anchor ourselves in the present moment. This simple yet powerful shift supports mental clarity, emotional balance, and physiological stability. In many disciplines, from yoga to mindfulness-based stress reduction (MBSR), conscious breathing is the foundation upon which deeper meditative practices are built.

 ### Common Misconceptions

o *"I already breathe, so why do I need a technique?"* Breathing automatically does not necessarily mean we are breathing optimally. Stress, poor posture, and shallow breathing habits can reduce oxygen intake and create physical tension.

o *"Only people with anxiety need to practice breathing."* While conscious breathing is indeed beneficial for individuals struggling with anxiety or stress, it also boosts general health, resilience, and performance, making it useful for everyone.

Historical and Cultural Context

 ### Yogic Traditions

In yoga, breathwork—known as *pranayama*—is one of the eight limbs outlined by the sage Patanjali in the Yoga Sutras. Pranayama emphasizes the control and extension of one's vital energy through breathing exercises. Ancient yogis observed that controlling the rhythm and depth of breath had direct and profound effects on the mind, aiding in mental tranquility and preparing the student for deeper meditative states. Techniques such as *Nadi Shodhana* (alternate nostril breathing) and *Ujjayi* (victorious breath) have been passed down through centuries and are still widely practiced today.

 ### Buddhist and Taoist Perspectives

Buddhist mindfulness meditation often begins with simple breath observation, focusing on each inhale and exhale as a means to cultivate present-moment awareness. The breath becomes a tool for sharpening concentration and seeing the impermanence of each moment. In Taoist practice, breathwork is used to balance internal energies, or *qi*, supporting longevity and harmony of body, mind, and spirit.

Modern Approaches and Scientific Integrations

Contemporary approaches, such as the Wim Hof Method, use a combination of specific breathing patterns, cold exposure, and mindset techniques to demonstrate remarkable physical achievements. Meanwhile, mainstream medicine increasingly recognizes the role of guided breathing in managing stress-related disorders, improving cardiovascular health, and aiding in rehabilitation. Across various fields—psychology, neuroscience, sports performance—there is a growing appreciation for how conscious breathing and meditation synergize to produce tangible benefits.

Core Breathing Techniques

 ### Diaphragmatic Breathing

Also known as "belly breathing," diaphragmatic breathing emphasizes using the diaphragm muscle rather than the chest to draw air into the lungs. Many people, especially under stress, breathe shallowly, engaging the upper chest and shoulders. This contributes to tension and inefficient oxygen exchange. Diaphragmatic breathing counters these tendencies by promoting slow, deep, and relaxing breaths.

- *How to Practice:*

    1. Lie down or sit with your spine straight.
    2. Place one hand on your upper chest and the other on your abdomen.
    3. Inhale deeply through your nose for a count of four, feeling your abdomen rise while your chest remains relatively still.
    4. Exhale gently through your mouth or nose for a count of four, noticing your abdomen fall.

- *Benefits:* Reduces stress, lowers heart rate, improves oxygen exchange, and releases tension from the chest and shoulders.

 ### Box Breathing

This technique, also called "square breathing," is favored by Navy SEALs and high-performance individuals to promote focus and calm under pressure.

- *How to Practice:*
    - Inhale through the nose to a count of four.
    - Hold the breath for a count of four.
    - Exhale through the nose (or mouth) for a count of four.
    - Hold the breath again for a count of four.

o   Repeat the cycle, maintaining a steady rhythm.
o   *Benefits:* Enhances concentration, reduces stress, helps regulate the nervous system, and fosters mindfulness.

Pranayama Techniques

   ### Nadi Shodhana (Alternate Nostril Breathing)

A staple of yogic breathing, Nadi Shodhana is reputed to balance the left and right hemispheres of the brain and purify the energy channels of the body.

o   *How to Practice:*

1. Sit comfortably with a straight spine.
2. Use the right thumb to gently close the right nostril.
3. Inhale through the left nostril for a slow count of four or five.
4. Release the right nostril and use the ring finger to close the left nostril.
5. Exhale through the right nostril for the same count.
6. Inhale through the right nostril, then switch to exhale through the left.
7. Continue this pattern for several rounds.

o   *Benefits:* Improves mental clarity, reduces stress, balances energetic flow, and can aid in better sleep.

   ### Ujjayi (Victorious Breath)

Ujjayi breath involves creating a gentle "oceanic" sound in the back of the throat, often used during yoga asana practices.

- *How to Practice:*
  1. Inhale slowly through the nose, constricting the back of your throat slightly to create a soft hissing sound.
  2. Exhale through the nose with the same gentle constriction, maintaining the audible sound.
  3. Keep the breath slow, steady, and rhythmic.
- *Benefits:* Supports focus in yoga practice, warms the body, helps regulate energy, and calms the mind.

Meditation Fundamentals

 ### Defining Meditation

Meditation is a broad term encompassing various techniques designed to cultivate presence, awareness, and mental clarity. Common forms include mindfulness, concentration practices, mantra repetition, and loving-kindness (metta) meditation. Although these forms can differ in execution, they share a common goal: to help practitioners observe the workings of the mind without being swept away by them.

 ### The Role of Breath in Meditation

Breath-centered meditation is one of the simplest, most accessible methods. By placing attention on the natural rhythm of inhalation and exhalation, practitioners anchor themselves in the present moment. Thoughts inevitably arise, but the act of returning attention to the breath—gently, without judgment—trains the mind to remain aware, calm, and collected. This skill transfers into daily life, enabling practitioners to respond to stressors more calmly rather than reacting impulsively.

 ### Common Obstacles

○ **Restlessness and Wandering Mind:** It is normal for thoughts to wander during meditation. The key is to notice that you have wandered and gently come back to the breath.
○ *Physical Discomfort:* Finding a comfortable position and using props (cushions, chairs) can help alleviate discomfort so you can focus on your breath.
○ **Expectations:** Many newcomers expect immediate tranquility. Meditation is a practice that develops over time, and occasional frustration is part of the journey.

Establishing a Meditation Practice

 ### Choosing a Posture

While sitting on the floor in the classic lotus pose is traditional, it is not mandatory. You can meditate while seated in a chair, lying down (if you can stay awake), or even standing if necessary. The key element is a relaxed but upright posture that supports both alertness and ease. If you sit, try to keep your spine neutral, shoulders relaxed, and hands resting comfortably on your lap.

Setting a Timeframe and Environment

Begin with just five minutes daily and gradually extend to 15, 20, or even 30 minutes. Consistency is more important than duration. Select a quiet place where you are less likely to be interrupted. Turn off or silence electronic devices if possible, or use them only to track time or play soft ambient sounds if that aids your focus.

 ### Focal Points

- *Breath-Focused Meditation:* Concentrate on the physical sensations of breathing, such as the rise and fall of your abdomen or the air passing through your nostrils.
- *Mantra Meditation:* Repeat a chosen word or phrase silently or aloud. This can help break the cycle of distracting thoughts.
- *Guided Visualization:* Follow an audio or teacher-led script that guides you through imaginary landscapes or calming scenarios.

Mindfulness Meditation

 ### Mindfulness Defined

Mindfulness is the nonjudgmental awareness of the present moment. It stems from Buddhist teachings but has become immensely popular worldwide, supported by extensive scientific research. In mindfulness practice, one observes whatever arises—sensations, thoughts, emotions, sounds—without clinging or aversion. Over time, this nurtures a sense of acceptance and equanimity.

 ### Body Scan Practice

A foundational mindfulness technique is the body scan, typically done lying down or sitting comfortably:

1. Begin by focusing on the breath, then move your attention through the body step-by-step (from toes up to the head).
2. Notice sensations (tingling, warmth, tension) in each region without trying to change anything.
3. If the mind drifts, gently bring it back to the body region you intended to focus on.

Body scanning fosters relaxation and deeper awareness of what the body is holding onto—tension, pain, or stress—and teaches practitioners how to acknowledge and release these sensations.

Mindful Movement

Mindfulness can also be integrated into activities like walking, yoga, or tai chi. For instance, *mindful walking* involves walking slowly and noticing each step, the shifting of weight, and the contact between the feet and the ground. This practice helps expand the mindful attitude into everyday life, turning ordinary actions into opportunities for present-moment awareness.

Loving-Kindness Meditation

 ### The Essence of Metta

Loving-kindness meditation, or *metta bhavana*, focuses on nurturing compassion for oneself and others. It involves generating positive wishes for health, happiness, and well-being, first toward oneself and then expanding outward to loved ones, acquaintances, and even difficult individuals.

 ### Basic Method

1. Sit comfortably and begin with a few moments of breath awareness.
2. Silently repeat phrases such as "May I be well. May I be happy. May I be peaceful."
3. Extend these wishes to someone close: "May [Name] be well. May they be happy. May they be peaceful."
4. Gradually extend to neighbors, acquaintances, strangers, and eventually people with whom you have conflicts.
5. Conclude by extending the same wishes to all beings everywhere.

 ### Benefits

Research links loving-kindness meditation to increased empathy, better emotional regulation, and even improved vagal tone (a measure of how well the vagus nerve modulates heart rate). Practitioners often report feeling lighter, more open-hearted, and less reactive to stress.

Advanced Breathing Practices

 ### The Wim Hof Method

Founded by Dutch athlete Wim Hof, this method involves specific breathing exercises, cold exposure (e.g., ice baths), and focused mindset techniques. The breathing itself typically includes a series of deep inhalations followed by forced exhalations, culminating in retention phases. Advocates claim benefits for immune function, stress regulation, and resilience, though it should be practiced cautiously and with guidance, especially for beginners.

Holotropic Breathwork

Developed by psychiatrist Stanislav Grof, holotropic breathwork uses faster, deeper breathing patterns often accompanied by evocative music in a therapeutic group setting. The goal is to enter altered states of consciousness for psychological healing and self-exploration. Because these sessions can be intense, they are typically facilitated by trained professionals.

 ### Kumbhaka (Breath Retention)

A more advanced pranayama technique, *kumbhaka,* involves holding the breath at the end of an inhale or exhale. Retaining the breath consciously should be approached with caution and gradually increased. It is said to help still the mind, heighten concentration, and balance pranic energies.

The Science Behind Breathing and Meditation

 ### Stress Response and the Nervous System

Stress typically activates the sympathetic nervous system, increasing heart rate, releasing stress hormones like cortisol, and priming the body for "fight or flight." Conscious breathing and meditation activate the parasympathetic nervous system, or "rest and digest" mode, countering the stress response. This physiological shift reduces heart rate, lowers blood pressure, and mitigates tension.

 ### Brain Changes and Neuroplasticity

Studies using MRI and EEG scans have revealed that regular meditation can reshape the brain over time—a phenomenon known as neuroplasticity. Areas associated with emotional regulation, attention control, and self-awareness (such as the prefrontal cortex and the anterior cingulate cortex) tend to show increased activity or even structural changes, while the amygdala (involved in fear and anxiety) may show decreased reactivity.

 ### Immune Function and Inflammation

Recent research indicates that meditation and some breathwork techniques can lower markers of systemic inflammation and improve immune function. This suggests that stress-reducing practices may have wide-ranging effects on overall health, helping to protect against chronic diseases exacerbated by prolonged inflammation.

Tailoring Techniques for Different Needs

   Stress and Anxiety Management

- o *Recommendation:* Diaphragmatic breathing, Box Breathing, and basic mindfulness are especially effective for immediate stress relief. Practitioners can perform these techniques discretely at work or in public spaces.

   Sleep Support

- o *Recommendation:* Slow, deep breathing and body scan mindfulness can help calm the nervous system before bed. Counting breaths or practicing Nadi Shodhana for a few minutes often facilitates better sleep initiation.

   Athletic Performance and Recovery

- o *Recommendation:* Athletes may benefit from techniques that optimize oxygen uptake and focus, such as Ujjayi breathing or certain rhythmic breathing patterns. Post-exercise meditation or breathwork can promote faster recovery by enhancing relaxation.

   Chronic Pain Management

- o *Recommendation:* Mindfulness-based stress reduction (MBSR) often includes both breathwork and body scanning, helping individuals cope with chronic pain by changing their relationship to discomfort rather than trying to suppress it.

Integrating Technology

   Meditation Apps

Numerous apps—such as Headspace, Calm, and Insight Timer—offer guided meditations, reminder features, and breathing exercises. These resources can be particularly helpful for beginners, providing structure and support at any time of day.

   Biofeedback Devices

Wearable devices and apps can monitor heart rate variability (HRV), which reflects the balance between the sympathetic and parasympathetic nervous systems. By observing real-time feedback on HRV and other physiological markers, practitioners can refine their breathing and relaxation techniques for greater efficacy.

Virtual Reality (VR) Experiences

Emerging technologies offer immersive experiences designed to teach or enhance meditation. VR can guide users through serene landscapes or interactive breath exercises, potentially aiding in stress reduction and motivation. While it is not necessary for a fulfilling practice, these tools exemplify how ancient wisdom can merge with modern innovation.

Cultivating Consistency and Overcoming Challenges

Building Habits

Incorporating breathing and meditation into daily life requires consistent practice. Consider "habit stacking"—linking your meditation to an existing routine, like after brushing your teeth in the morning or during a lunch break. Scheduling practice at the same time every day can help establish a rhythm.

Dealing with Plateaus

At some point, practitioners might feel stuck or notice diminishing returns. When this happens, consider exploring new techniques, joining a meditation group, or working with a teacher to gain fresh insights. Sometimes, simply reinforcing foundational techniques with renewed intention is enough to reinvigorate one's practice.

Seeking Guidance

While many techniques can be self-taught, a qualified teacher or therapist may offer valuable feedback—correcting postural misalignments, customizing techniques for specific needs, and providing motivational support. Guidance is particularly important if you're exploring more advanced practices like holotropic breathwork, where emotional release can be intense.

Breath and Meditation in Daily Life

Micro-Practices

Small "mindful moments" sprinkled throughout the day can help maintain equilibrium:

- Take three deep breaths before opening your computer in the morning.
- Practice one minute of breath observation when transitioning between tasks.

- Perform a quick body scan in the bathroom mirror, noticing where you might be holding tension.

Mindful Communication

Before an important conversation or meeting, pause and take a few grounding breaths. This diminishes the likelihood of reacting out of stress, enabling more thoughtful, empathetic communication. Over time, mindful listening—focusing intently on the speaker without planning your next response—can build stronger, more compassionate relationships.

Everyday Mindfulness

Actions like washing dishes, eating a meal, or walking can become mindful practices if approached with full presence. Notice sensory details: water temperature, dish texture, flavors, footsteps. By grounding ordinary tasks in awareness, you transform them into opportunities for tranquility.

Meditation Retreats and Group Practices

Benefits of Retreats

Attending a meditation retreat—ranging from weekend workshops to extended silent retreats—allows for immersive practice removed from day-to-day distractions. A retreat setting can accelerate learning, deepen insights, and offer a supportive community of fellow practitioners.

Types of Retreats

- Multi-day silent retreats focusing on continuous mindfulness of breath and bodily sensations.
- *Yoga and Meditation Retreats:* Combining yoga practice with guided meditations, often in scenic, nature-rich locations.
- *Themed Workshops:* Specialized events, such as breathwork intensives, mindfulness for anxiety, or spiritual retreats focusing on compassion or gratitude.

Community and Accountability

Group meditation not only creates a supportive environment but also fosters accountability—knowing others share your goals can bolster motivation. Meditating in a group can also amplify the collective energy, making it easier to drop into deeper concentration.

Potential Risks and Precautions

 ### Physical Considerations

o   Certain advanced breathwork techniques can lead to dizziness or hyperventilation. People with heart conditions or high blood pressure should consult healthcare professionals before diving into intense methods like the Wim Hof Method or holotropic breathwork.
o   If you experience pain or discomfort during seated meditation, adjust your position. Long-term discomfort can distract from practice or even cause injury.

 ### Mental Health Factors

o   Individuals with severe psychiatric conditions (e.g., acute PTSD, psychosis) should approach intensive meditation retreats or breathwork cautiously and ideally under professional guidance.
o   Emotional releases can occur unexpectedly during practices like holotropic breathwork, so a supportive, informed environment is essential.

 ### Moderation and Mindful Exploration

Approach new techniques gradually, allowing your body and mind time to adapt. Consistency and gentle progression are more beneficial than pushing too hard too soon.

Integrating Philosophy and Ethics

 ### Non-violence and Compassion

Traditional meditation lineages often emphasize ethical precepts like *ahimsa* (non-violence). Cultivating inner peace through meditation can organically extend outward, encouraging practitioners to act more compassionately in their relationships and communities.

 ### The Power of Intention

When beginning a session, many practitioners set a personal intention, such as cultivating patience, gratitude, or equanimity. This framework can guide the mind and heart during practice, enhancing both concentration and meaningful growth.

Embodying Meditative Qualities

Meditation is not just something done on a cushion or mat; it's a way of being. By consistently returning to the breath and a mindful attitude, you can carry a sense of calm, clarity, and compassion into all areas of life.

Measuring Progress and Growth

 ### Subjective Indicators

- Reduced stress and anxiety levels.
- Greater emotional resilience and stability.
- Enhanced focus and creativity.

 ### Objective Indicators

- Improved HRV (heart rate variability).
- Lower blood pressure and resting heart rate.
- Better sleep quality, as tracked by wearables or personal notes.

 ### Lifelong Journey

Progress in meditation and breathwork is not always linear. It involves peaks, plateaus, and occasional setbacks. Over time, the practice becomes less about attainment and more about deepening awareness and presence in each moment.

Practical Tips for Busy Lives

 ### Time-Saving Techniques

- *Two-Minute Check-ins:* Whenever you feel overwhelmed, pause. Close your eyes if possible. Take slow, mindful breaths. Observe your body's sensations and your emotional state. Even two minutes can work wonders.
- *Commute Meditation:* If you commute via public transport, use that time to practice simple breath observation or repeat a calming mantra. Listening to a guided meditation on headphones can turn a mundane commute into a restorative practice.
- *Mindful Breaks at Work:* Instead of rushing to social media during short breaks, try a few rounds of Box Breathing. This can reset your focus for the next task.

Incorporating Family or Group Sessions

- o Share simple breathing exercises with children, teaching them to calm themselves and manage emotions.
- o Organize a short family or household "quiet time," where everyone practices mindful sitting or mindful reading.

 Recognizing and Celebrating Small Wins

Acknowledge when you successfully respond to stress more calmly or notice a negative thought pattern before reacting. These small moments of awareness are significant milestones in a meditation journey.

Breathing and meditation techniques have stood the test of time, evolving from ancient spiritual traditions into modern, scientifically supported practices with broad applications. Whether you are seeking stress relief, emotional healing, enhanced performance, or deeper insight into the nature of the mind, conscious breathing and meditation offer a powerful avenue for self-discovery.

From diaphragmatic breathing to advanced pranayama, from mindfulness to loving-kindness meditation, there is a wealth of practices suitable for every level and lifestyle. The key to reaping their benefits lies in consistency, patience, and a spirit of curiosity. By dedicating even a few minutes each day to mindful breath and reflection, you embark on a journey that can transform not just how you handle life's challenges, but how you experience each moment.

As you move forward, remember that these techniques are not quick fixes but ongoing practices. Accept that growth may be subtle and incremental. Find a balance between disciplined commitment and gentle self-compassion. And most importantly, trust your innate capacity to cultivate calm, clarity, and kindness— one breath at a time.

Chapter 19: Breath

Breathing, so crucial in meditation, is a much more complex and rewarding subject as you delve deeper. This book was a revelation to me in the subject of breathing, and I thought it was quite relevant to our journey inward.

☯ Introduction to the Importance of Breath

James Nestor's *Breath: The New Science of a Lost Art* opens with a fascinating premise: human beings have been breathing incorrectly for centuries, and this has led to a host of modern health problems. Rather than treating breath as an automatic bodily function, Nestor argues that we must cultivate it as a skill and an art to realize its full potential. The book is a deep exploration of the science, history, and cultural practices surrounding breathing, weaving together anthropological findings, personal experiments, and cutting-edge medical research.

Nestor himself was drawn to the subject after experiencing recurring respiratory issues and investigating the relationship between breathing and health. Starting with the observation that our modern lifestyles—characterized by processed foods, minimal physical exertion, and chronic stress—have reshaped our faces and airways, he unveils how these changes have contributed to poor breathing habits. He highlights a number of ailments tied to dysfunctional breathing: everything from snoring and sleep apnea to anxiety, asthma, and even autoimmune disorders.

At the core of his argument is the assertion that correct breathing techniques aren't simply new-age or esoteric practices but are instead backed by scientific evidence. The body's nervous, circulatory, and respiratory systems benefit from conscious, deliberate breath. With a focus on methods like nose breathing, specific breathing exercises, and biomechanical adjustments, Nestor shows how we inhale and exhale can alter our physical and mental well-being. Throughout the book, he offers both anecdotal and empirical proof, challenging the idea that breathing is just a "set it and forget it" process. Instead, *Breath* invites readers to rediscover an essential human skill that can profoundly change their lives.

☯ The Evolutionary Perspective

One of the most striking aspects of *Breath* is Nestor's discussion of how human evolution has influenced our ability—or inability—to breathe well. He introduces the work of researchers who have studied skull shapes across different historical periods. Through anthropological investigations, Nestor notes that early humans possessed wide jaws, robust facial structures, and large nasal openings. Over thousands of years, however, modern humans' facial shapes have narrowed, jaws have grown smaller, and sinus passages have constricted. These changes correlate with shifts in diet, such as transitioning from tough, fibrous foods to softer, processed diets.

Nestor points out that this facial narrowing has led to restricted airways, making us more susceptible to chronic mouth breathing. Mouth breathing, in turn, disrupts proper air filtration, affects oral health, and forces the body to compensate in ways that can trigger snoring and sleep apnea. By showing how these shifts occurred over millennia, he underscores that what we often dismiss as normal—like pervasive snoring or difficulty breathing—might be a modern abnormality.

Moreover, the author highlights the interplay between posture, muscle usage, and craniofacial development. When we stop chewing tough foods or using certain facial muscles, the body adapts by reshaping the jawline, which can further constrain our airways. Evolution, therefore, isn't just about survival-of-the-fittest in obvious ways but includes subtle influences from diet and environment. This evolutionary angle sets the stage for understanding the importance of nose breathing and the potential to reverse or mitigate many of these breathing complications through targeted exercises and conscious practice.

The Nose vs. Mouth Breathing Debate

Central to Nestor's message is the distinction between nose breathing and mouth breathing. Modern medical experts and ancient wisdom alike have championed nose breathing for multiple reasons: the nose filters air, traps pathogens, humidifies inhalation, and helps regulate airflow more effectively than the mouth. In stark contrast, mouth breathing bypasses these crucial processes. The unfiltered, dry air that rushes into the lungs can irritate the respiratory system and fail to trigger the natural production of nitric oxide, a critical molecule that helps sanitize incoming air and regulate blood pressure.

Nestor describes a personal experiment where he and a fellow researcher deliberately taped their mouths shut at night to encourage nasal breathing. The results were dramatic: improved sleep quality, reduced snoring, and overall better rest. Conversely, when they experimented with plugging their noses and forcing mouth breathing for several days, they experienced elevated stress, increased snoring, poor sleep, and a spike in various health markers like blood pressure.

This experiment underscores the profound physiological impact of simply changing how air enters the body. The data collected during these periods offer compelling evidence that mouth breathing can lead to a host of health issues, including elevated stress hormones, dental problems, and even lowered immune response. By shining a spotlight on the role of the nasal passages, Nestor gives readers a vivid understanding of why breathing through the nose is not just an aesthetic preference but a fundamental biological necessity.

🌑 The Role of Carbon Dioxide and the Bohr Effect

A significant revelation in *Breath* is the importance of carbon dioxide (CO_2) in maintaining optimal oxygen delivery. Many people believe that taking big, fast breaths to "get more oxygen" is inherently beneficial, but Nestor points to medical research indicating that hyperventilation and excessive blowing off of CO_2 can actually starve the body of essential oxygen. This is due to the Bohr Effect, a physiological principle where hemoglobin's ability to release oxygen to tissues is dependent on the presence of carbon dioxide. When CO_2 levels drop, hemoglobin clings to oxygen more tightly, depriving cells and organs of what they need.

Nestor recounts interviews with researchers and breathing specialists who emphasize that slow, controlled breathing—often through the nose—helps maintain a balanced level of CO_2. As a result, oxygen is more efficiently delivered throughout the body. This insight challenges the tendency many of us have to take quick, shallow mouth breaths during times of stress. In fact, a deliberate "slow and low" breathing pattern can mitigate anxiety by bolstering CO_2 retention, which aids in creating a calmer state of mind and a healthier physiological environment.

The book also examines various breathing exercises designed to intentionally manipulate CO_2 levels, such as the Buteyko method. These practices aren't new; ancient yogic and meditative traditions have advocated for slow, rhythmic breathing for centuries. However, it's the modern scientific backing that Nestor highlights, reinforcing that balancing oxygen and carbon dioxide is at the heart of healthy respiration and overall vitality.

🌑 Ancient Breathing Techniques and Modern Validation

In *Breath*, Nestor delves into the rich tapestry of historical practices that emphasize proper respiration, from yoga pranayama to Buddhist Tummo breathing and beyond. He details how different cultures have, for millennia, explored specialized breathing patterns to boost energy, sharpen focus, and maintain health. For instance, Tummo breathing, practiced by Tibetan monks, can generate warmth in frigid temperatures through a regulated pattern of inhalations and exhalations. Similarly, ancient Hindu yogis meticulously recorded various pranayama methods, believing that breath control was instrumental to spiritual progress and physical well-being.

What's particularly interesting is how modern science is beginning to corroborate these ancient insights. The book cites studies measuring practitioners' physiology during these breathing rituals: from reduced stress hormones to increased oxygen saturation, as well as the ability to modulate body temperature.

Researchers are documenting tangible benefits. In turn, these findings challenge Western skepticism that once dismissed such practices as mystical or unscientific.

Nestor argues that integrating these techniques into contemporary health approaches could yield profound benefits. Whether it's the navy using breathing exercises for mental clarity under pressure, or chronic disease patients employing them for symptom management, the evidence points toward a universal capacity for breath-based healing. This reconciliation of ancient wisdom and modern data underscores one of Nestor's key themes: humankind had an extraordinary knowledge of breath, lost much of it, and is now rediscovering how crucial breath is to health and resilience.

⚉ The Buteyko Method and Asthma Relief

Among the various modern breathing methods discussed, the Buteyko technique stands out for its efficacy in treating conditions like asthma. Developed by Ukrainian physician Konstantin Pavlovich Buteyko in the mid-20th century, this method involves deliberately reducing one's breathing volume through slow, nasal inhalation and exhalation. The goal is to recalibrate the body's relationship with CO_2. By training patients to breathe less and retain more carbon dioxide, Buteyko observed improvements in conditions related to constricted airways, including chronic asthma.

Nestor explores case studies showing children and adults who significantly reduced their reliance on inhalers and medications after a dedicated practice of Buteyko exercises. Critics of the method initially dismissed it as pseudoscience, yet a growing body of research now points to measurable physiological effects. For example, some studies have linked Buteyko to decreases in hyperventilation and improvements in airway function. Patients report fewer asthma attacks, better stress management, and enhanced overall respiratory efficiency.

Beyond asthma, Nestor suggests that the Buteyko approach can benefit anyone struggling with poor breathing habits. While skeptics may remain, the method's success stories, coupled with an emerging scientific foundation, make a compelling case for its inclusion in mainstream respiratory therapy. By centering on nasal breathing and controlled breath holds, Buteyko forces individuals to confront and correct the dysfunctional breathing patterns that exacerbate many modern health issues.

⚉ The Power of Chewing and Facial Development

An unexpected yet crucial theme in *Breath* revolves around the act of chewing. Nestor argues that our modern diet of soft, highly processed foods contributes to weakened jaw muscles and altered facial structures, which, in turn, lead to restricted airways. He draws on research that shows how a lack of robust chewing from an early age can shrink the jawline and misalign the teeth, creating less space for the tongue and nasal passages. The resultant narrowing can force more frequent mouth breathing and invite respiratory problems.

Throughout the book, Nestor highlights pioneering dentists and orthodontists—such as Dr. Kevin Boyd—who emphasize the importance of proper chewing for craniofacial growth in children. These experts suggest diets containing harder foods and gum-chewing regimens to encourage jaw muscle development. In some clinical cases, simply shifting a child's chewing habits can correct early signs of orthodontic issues and promote better breathing. Additionally, adult patients can also benefit from strengthening jaw muscles, although the skeletal changes are more challenging once growth plates have fused.

This focus on chewing illustrates how breathing is connected to broader aspects of physiology and lifestyle. While it may seem tangential at first glance, Nestor frames chewing as an integral part of a holistic approach to respiratory health. By reaffirming that form follows function—stronger jaws mean wider airways—the book offers a deeper understanding of the mechanical underpinnings of breath. The takeaway is that breathing better isn't only about exercise; it can involve rethinking our diet and daily habits.

🜸 Mewing, Posture, and Tongue Position

Closely connected to the discussion on chewing is the concept of "mewing," a technique popularized by the British orthodontist Dr. Mike Mew. Mewing encourages proper tongue posture—placing the tongue against the roof of the mouth—to foster optimal facial growth and breathing patterns. James Nestor explains how this practice can help train the oral cavity and muscles to remain in positions that promote nasal breathing over mouth breathing. It's a subtle yet constant form of exercise that can, over time, reshape aspects of the upper airway.

Nestor also explores broader posture issues, highlighting how the alignment of the head, neck, and spine can make or break healthy breathing. Slouching and forward head posture constrict the chest cavity and airways, reducing lung capacity. By contrast, maintaining an upright spine and a head position that aligns the ears with the shoulders can open the ribcage, facilitating deeper and more efficient inhales and exhales. Small shifts in posture can therefore have an outsized impact on respiratory function.

While Mewing and posture adjustments aren't the primary focus of *Breath*, they represent the multifaceted approach Nestor advocates. Breathing well, he argues, involves a confluence of factors—from how we hold our bodies and position our tongues to how we chew our food and manage stress. By addressing these pieces of the puzzle in tandem, individuals can unlock the fuller potential of their respiratory systems. In essence, the book promotes a holistic, lifestyle-based approach rather than any quick-fix solution.

The Experiment with Forced Mouth Breathing

One of the most talked-about sections of *Breath* is Nestor's self-imposed experiment: spending several days breathing solely through his mouth (with his nose taped shut) to measure the health consequences. He teams up with researchers to track changes in vitals such as blood pressure, heart rate, and stress markers. The result is alarming: almost immediately, Nestor experiences increased snoring, restless sleep, elevated blood pressure, and a feeling of systemic stress. Over time, he reports mental fog and irritability, confirming just how detrimental mouth breathing can be for the body and mind.

Upon switching back to nasal breathing, many of these issues improve or resolve. This stark difference forms the backbone of Nestor's argument that nasal breathing is not a minor preference but a foundational aspect of health. The data collected suggests that mouth breathing isn't just inconvenient or embarrassing; it can have wide-ranging negative impacts, from cardiovascular strain to cognitive dysfunction.

The experiment also exemplifies Nestor's willingness to subject himself to the methods he writes about, adding a vivid, personal dimension to the book. His direct experiences underscore the book's thesis that conscious, controlled nose breathing could be a powerful tool for preventing and reversing a variety of common ailments. Although critics might question the small sample size—Nestor himself—his trials parallel countless clinical and anecdotal cases that highlight the value of nasal respiration.

Breathing and the Nervous System

Nestor dedicates a significant portion of the book to exploring how the breath interfaces with the autonomic nervous system. He details the sympathetic (fight-or-flight) and parasympathetic (rest-and-digest) branches, showing how rapid, shallow breathing can perpetuate a stress response, while slow, deep breathing signals the body to relax. By consciously controlling the pace of breath, individuals can modulate stress hormones like cortisol and adrenaline, mitigating chronic tension and anxiety.

A highlight of this exploration is the role that specific techniques—such as the 5.5-second inhale and 5.5-second exhale method—play in balancing the autonomic system. Some studies suggest that breathing in a rhythm of about 5 to 6 breaths per minute entrains the heart and lungs, creating a state of "coherence." This means that heart rate variability (HRV) improves, stress decreases, and mental clarity heightens. Nestor references interviews with scientists who measure how a coherent breathing pattern resonates through the entire body, linking cardiac function, blood pressure, and brain states in a harmonious loop.

Additionally, Nestor underscores that many ancient rituals—from prayer chants to mantras—often fit this 5- to 6-second pacing, suggesting a long-standing, intuitive grasp of how breath can regulate the mind-body interface. When the book draws parallels between these diverse cultural practices and contemporary scientific findings, it highlights the unifying principle that slow, measured breathing is a primal yet profound tool for achieving inner equilibrium.

☯ CO₂ Tolerance Training and High Altitude Simulation

Another intriguing aspect of *Breath* is the exploration of "Intermittent Hypoxia Training" (IHT) and other techniques aimed at boosting CO_2 tolerance. High-altitude athletes have long known that training in low-oxygen environments can improve endurance and oxygen efficiency. Nestor discusses how guided breath holds and reduced-oxygen exercises simulate high-altitude conditions, prompting the body to become more adaptable in releasing oxygen to tissues.

Methods such as the Wim Hof Technique incorporate breath holds and cold exposure to stimulate the body's stress response in controlled doses, building physiological resilience. Nestor interviews experts who note that a steady increment of CO_2 tolerance can have myriad benefits, including enhanced athletic performance, improved mental focus, and even better immune function. By learning to remain calm in a state of air hunger—where the urge to breathe is strong—the body supposedly develops more efficient oxygen usage.

While these practices can be powerful, Nestor warns about their risks if done improperly. He reiterates the importance of guidance and safety, underscoring that extreme breath-holding or oxygen deprivation can be dangerous without proper supervision. Still, the main takeaway is that by challenging our respiratory limits in a measured way, we can trigger adaptive responses that fortify our cardiovascular and nervous systems. This resonates with the book's overarching theme: by reexamining centuries-old breath practices and coupling them with modern science, we can access a deeper well of health and human potential.

☯ The Link Between Breath and Metabolism

Nestor's research also touches on how breathing impacts metabolism and weight regulation. Drawing on scientific findings, he highlights how the rate and depth of respiration can influence the body's acid-base balance, hormones, and energy expenditure. Some theories posit that poor breathing habits may contribute to metabolic disorders by altering the body's ability to balance oxygen and carbon dioxide effectively, thereby affecting oxidative processes involved in energy production.

Moreover, the book cites studies suggesting that mindful breathing practices can help regulate appetite and stress-related eating. Stress often triggers shallow, rapid breathing, which in turn can cause the body to remain in a heightened sympathetic state, promoting fat storage and perpetuating cravings. By contrast, deliberately slowing the breath and shifting into a parasympathetic state can support better digestion and hormone regulation.

Though Nestor doesn't claim that breathing alone is a cure-all for obesity or metabolic syndrome, he proposes that a comprehensive health strategy, which includes optimized breathing, could help prevent and address these issues. By refining our respiratory patterns, we may not only improve oxygen efficiency but also gain better control over stress responses that drive unhealthy eating behaviors. Thus, breath emerges once again as a foundational layer of wellbeing, touching multiple dimensions—physical, psychological, and metabolic.

Sleep, Snoring, and Sleep Apnea

One of the pressing concerns Nestor addresses is the epidemic of disordered sleep in modern society, much of which is linked to snoring, sleep apnea, and other forms of disrupted breathing at night. He recounts stories of individuals who, despite appearing otherwise healthy, suffer from chronic fatigue and health complications due to nocturnal breathing problems. Often, these individuals are unaware of how frequently they stop breathing during sleep or how severely snoring affects oxygen flow.

Nestor illustrates how nose breathing can alleviate or even eliminate some of these issues. Nasal passages, compared to the mouth, naturally reduce the incidence of airway collapse by maintaining a certain level of muscular engagement. Additionally, nasal breathing fosters the proper balance of gases like nitric oxide. In the book's many case histories, switching from mouth breathing to nasal breathing at night significantly decreases snoring and the dangerous pauses in breath characteristic of sleep apnea.

He also covers practical interventions like mouth taping—a gentle adhesive placed on the lips before bed—to encourage nose breathing. While this may sound extreme, thousands of people have reported benefits, including more restful sleep and higher daytime energy levels. These anecdotes, paired with emerging clinical research, underline how crucial it is to address breathing quality in the quest for better sleep. Nestor suggests that focusing on correct nighttime respiration could be among the most cost-effective and transformative steps in tackling the public health crisis of sleep disorders.

Practical Exercises and Protocols

Throughout *Breath*, Nestor sprinkles in practical exercises designed to help readers reap the benefits of better breathing. Some of these are straightforward, like "box breathing" (inhale for four counts, hold for four, exhale for four, hold for four) or the 5.5-second inhale-exhale pattern. Others, like Buteyko breath holds or moderate CO_2 tolerance challenges, require more instruction and caution. By sharing detailed approaches, Nestor offers a toolkit that readers can experiment with to find what best suits their physiology and lifestyle.

Importantly, he underscores the value of consistency over intensity. Rather than sporadically practicing extreme breath holds, daily routines of slow, nasal breathing can produce significant cumulative benefits. For those grappling with specific ailments—like asthma or anxiety—he provides a snapshot of how professionals integrate breathing exercises into treatment plans. Moreover, he suggests that even elite athletes can refine their performance by training nasal-only breathing during moderate-intensity workouts, thereby gradually increasing CO_2 tolerance.

Nestor cautions that many of these exercises, especially those involving breath holds or hypoxia, should be approached conservatively and ideally under expert guidance. Nevertheless, the practical sections of the book serve as a bridge between theory and application, helping to demystify these breathing protocols. In essence, Nestor contends that breathing better isn't about perfection or competing with anyone else; it's about embracing a lifelong practice that can continually improve our health and wellbeing.

☯ Case Studies and Anecdotes

To illustrate the transformative potential of breathwork, Nestor cites numerous case studies. These range from high-profile athletes who adopt nose breathing to manage stress and optimize endurance, to everyday people who reverse chronic conditions like asthma or severe sleep apnea. A compelling example involves teenagers struggling with ADHD symptoms who see improvements in focus and emotional regulation after consistent practice of slow, rhythmic breathing.

Additionally, Nestor references historical figures like medieval monks, yogis, and indigenous tribes who employed specialized breathing techniques for vitality, healing, and spiritual insight. While these may seem far removed from modern life, they underscore the universality of breath as a human experience. Taken together, these stories aim to show that the benefits of breathing are not limited by geography, culture, or era.

By weaving personal anecdotes with broader scientific findings, Nestor grounds his overarching argument in relatable, human experiences. He acknowledges that individual results vary, but the sheer diversity of success stories strengthens the case that breath training has tangible, far-reaching impacts. This narrative approach keeps the book engaging and accessible, spurring readers to envision how a similar shift in their own breathing habits might lead to concrete improvements in health and well-being.

☯ Skepticism, Criticisms, and Limitations

No exploration of alternative or holistic health practices would be complete without addressing skepticism. Throughout *Breath*, Nestor acknowledges that while mounting evidence supports the efficacy of specific breathing techniques, not all methods have undergone large-scale, double-blind clinical trials. Breathing practices can be difficult to standardize, and placebo effects are not always accounted for in smaller studies. Furthermore, there is an ongoing debate within the medical community about the long-term impact of techniques like Buteyko or Wim Hof, particularly for individuals with serious conditions.

Nestor also underlines that breathing alone is not a panacea. Diet, exercise, genetics, and mental health interventions all play crucial roles in a person's well-being. He encourages a measured approach, urging readers to see breathwork as a foundational element that can work synergistically with other healthy habits. The intent is not to dismiss conventional medicine but to highlight breathing as an underutilized and cost-effective complement.

In acknowledging the limitations, Nestor fosters a sense of scientific curiosity rather than dogmatic acceptance. He presents breathing as an emerging frontier in medicine, one ripe for further research. By grounding the narrative in a blend of anecdotal success and scientific rationale, he bridges the gap between mainstream skepticism and the credible benefits reported by practitioners, leaving room for future studies to confirm or refine his insights.

☯ The Mind-Body Connection

Breath devotes significant attention to the intertwined nature of the mind and body, particularly how stress, anxiety, and emotional states can disrupt breathing patterns—and vice versa. Nestor discusses how, when faced with psychological stress, humans instinctively tighten the chest and revert to shallow breathing. Over time, these ingrained habits can become chronic, exacerbating conditions like panic disorder, generalized anxiety, and depression.

Conversely, targeted breathwork can retrain the stress response. Techniques like resonant breathing or slow diaphragmatic breathing engage the parasympathetic nervous system, dampening the physiological underpinnings of anxiety. For instance, focusing on lengthening the exhale is known to stimulate the vagus nerve, which slows heart rate and calms the body.

Nestor also touches on how mindfulness meditation has long recognized the value of breath awareness. By simply observing one's inhale and exhale, meditators can cultivate greater presence and reduce the intensity of ruminative thoughts. The synergy of meditation with carefully designed breath practices offers a powerful toolkit for self-regulation. Thus, in highlighting the mind-body connection, Nestor underscores breathing's versatility—not only can it enhance physical health, but it can also serve as a potent psychological anchor.

🌑 Cultural and Medical Rediscovery

A recurrent theme in the book is the idea of rediscovery. Nestor points out that the medical community is starting to appreciate what many indigenous traditions, Eastern philosophies, and even Western respiratory specialists have long known: the breath is a cornerstone of health. He cites how integrative medicine programs now incorporate yoga, mindfulness, and breathing retraining as adjunct therapies for conditions ranging from hypertension to chronic pain.

At the same time, businesses in the wellness industry are capitalizing on the surge of interest in breath-based therapies by offering retreats, workshops, and online courses. Nestor presents both the promise and the pitfalls of this trend. On the one hand, more people are learning to harness the power of the breath. On the other hand, commodification can lead to oversimplification, where nuanced practices are distilled into quick-fix marketing slogans.

Despite these concerns, the broadening acceptance of breathwork marks a cultural shift. As insurance companies begin to fund research into non-pharmaceutical interventions, and as more physicians refer patients to respiratory physiotherapists or yoga instructors, breathing is stepping into the mainstream spotlight. *Breath* captures this zeitgeist, presenting a compelling case that humanity is returning to a skill that was once deeply woven into daily life but gradually lost in the rush of modernity.

🌑 A Personal Journey and Call to Action

Nestor's personal journey—marked by sinus problems, skepticism, and transformative experiments—lends the book an intimate narrative that complements its scientific backbone. He intertwines his own story with that of the experts he meets, the patients he interviews, and the historical anecdotes he uncovers. This approach makes the text more than just a health manual; it becomes a quest to reclaim a lost art and a vital part of the human experience.

By the closing chapters, Nestor offers a nuanced perspective: breathing techniques are not magic bullets, yet they hold tremendous potential for improving daily life and possibly mitigating chronic diseases. He challenges readers to embark on their own experiments—simple steps like practicing nasal breathing during walks, trying a few breath-hold intervals, or consciously slowing the breath before bedtime. These small actions, he argues, can accumulate into significant improvements over time.

Ultimately, the book is a call to action for readers to re-evaluate how they breathe. The tone is hopeful: given how profoundly breath can shape our health, becoming more aware of it is a powerful, accessible way to take charge of one's well-being. In a world inundated with quick fixes, *Breath* presents a return to basics—encouraging us to tune into the most fundamental action of all: inhaling and exhaling.

James Nestor reiterates that breathing is a primal, universal function transcending age, culture, and health status. Yet, it's also a function often neglected or taken for granted, especially in Western societies focused on technology and convenience. The cumulative evidence—historical, anthropological, experimental, and clinical—points to an urgent need to revive conscious breathing as a central aspect of self-care.

For those who embrace the insights in *Breath*, the impacts can be wide-ranging: improved sleep, better management of respiratory and metabolic conditions, greater mental clarity, and reduced stress. Nestor's book suggests that the path to healing or enhancing many aspects of human physiology may involve something as simple—and yet as challenging—as changing the way we breathe. While more research is necessary to fully integrate breathwork into mainstream medicine, the momentum is palpable.

In a broader sense, *Breath: The New Science of a Lost Art* stands as a catalyst, igniting public conversation about how we can reconnect with our bodies' innate wisdom. By synthesizing cutting-edge science with age-old traditions, Nestor illustrates that the lost art of breathing is, in fact, an essential piece of human heritage waiting to be reclaimed. With its blend of compelling narrative, personal experimentation, and scientific inquiry, the book inspires readers to explore their own breath and, in doing so, rediscover a key to better health and a deeper sense of vitality.

James Nestor advocates for incorporating breathing techniques into everyday life rather than isolating them into separate sessions.

1. Morning Routine
   o Start the day with a few minutes of mindful, nasal breathing or slow, coherent breathing.
   o Some individuals enjoy a short Wim Hof or Tummo-style energizing practice to wake up the body.
2. Throughout the Workday
   o Schedule mini-breaks to do 2–3 minutes of slow breathing.
   o Practice nose breathing whenever possible, especially during phone calls, walking between tasks, or mild exercise.

3. Evening Wind-Down
   - As part of a pre-bed routine, focus on slow exhalations and gentle inhales.
   - If mouth-taping is appropriate, prepare accordingly to ensure a full night of nose breathing.

Nestor includes anecdotes and case studies of individuals who have transformed their health through consistent breathwork practice.

1. Asthmatics and Chronic Illness Sufferers

   - Many people dealing with asthma reported fewer attacks, reduced reliance on inhalers, and overall better respiratory function.
   - Some with persistent anxiety discovered that daily breathwork calmed their sympathetic drive and improved mood.

2. Athletic Improvements

   - Athletes note faster recovery times and increased endurance by training to tolerate higher CO_2.
   - Nose breathing during cardio can be challenging at first, but yields long-term performance benefits.

3. Anecdotal Yet Compelling Evidence

   - While not every story is part of a formal clinical trial, the cumulative personal accounts emphasize the broad scope of breathwork's impact.
   - Nestor balances these stories with scientific data, but he highlights that personal experimentation often speaks volumes.

In the final pages of his book, James Nestor reiterates that breathing techniques are not a quick fix but a lifelong practice that can enhance quality of life on multiple levels.

1. Recap of Key Techniques

   - Nose Breathing: Emphasize nasal breathing day and night.
   - Slow or Coherent Breathing: Five to six breaths per minute to calm mind and body.
   - Breath Retention: Incorporate controlled holds to increase CO_2 tolerance.
   - Buteyko Method: Gently reduce breathing volume and track the control pause.
   - Tummo/Wim Hof: Use short bursts of rapid breathing to energize and build stress resilience (with caution).

2. Holistic Health Improvements

   o Better sleep, reduced stress, enhanced athletic performance, improved respiratory function, and even spiritual growth can all stem from consistent breathwork.
   o Breath is a foundational pillar of health, intersecting with nutrition, movement, mental wellness, and more.

3. A Call to Self-Experimentation

   o Nestor encourages each reader to explore various techniques and see which ones resonate.
   o He highlights that no single approach is universally perfect; personalization is key.
   o Through experimentation and mindful daily practice, you can rediscover the "lost art" of breathing and unlock better health, tranquility, and vitality.

James Nestor's *Breath: The New Science of a Lost Art* underscores that proper breathing is essential yet often overlooked. By examining techniques from ancient traditions alongside modern scientific research, Nestor demonstrates that breathing is not just a reflexive process—it's a powerful tool. When harnessed correctly through nose breathing, controlled CO_2 levels, and mindful practice, the breath can profoundly impact physical health, emotional stability, and overall well-being.

Chapter 20: Enhancing Sensory Perception through Meditation

The human senses are our physiological capacities that allow us to perceive and interact with our environment. While the traditional framework, and mindset, to be accurate, often highlights just the five primary senses—vision, hearing, touch, taste, and smell—modern scientific understanding recognizes a much broader spectrum of sensory modalities.

Below, I provide a comprehensive overview of the human senses, including both the well-known and less commonly discussed ones, with explanations grounded in physiological mechanisms and their significance. And then I discuss how meditation can help unlock these subtle yet more complex senses we are all blessed with.

1. Vision (Sight)

- Description: Vision enables perception of light, color, shape, and movement through the eyes.
- Mechanism: Photoreceptors (rods and cones) in the retina detect light wavelengths, converting them into electrical signals processed by the visual cortex in the brain.
- Sub-aspects: Includes color perception, depth perception, and motion detection.
- Significance: Vision is critical for spatial awareness, object recognition, and navigation.

2. Audition (Hearing)

- Description: Hearing allows detection of sound waves, enabling perception of pitch, volume, and timbre.
- Mechanism: Sound waves vibrate the eardrum, which transmits vibrations through the ossicles to the cochlea, where hair cells convert them into neural signals for the auditory cortex.
- Sub-aspects: Includes localization of sound sources and speech recognition.
- Significance: Essential for communication and environmental awareness.

3. Somatosensation (Touch)

- Description: Somatosensation encompasses tactile sensations, including pressure, vibration, pain, and temperature.

- Mechanism: Mechanoreceptors, thermoreceptors, and nociceptors in the skin and other tissues detect physical stimuli, sending signals via the somatosensory cortex.

- Sub-aspects:
  - Tactile sensation: Detection of pressure, texture, and vibration.
  - Thermoception: Perception of temperature (hot or cold).
  - Nociception: Perception of pain, which protects against harm.
- Significance: Facilitates interaction with objects and environment to assist in everyday tasks and assess and enhance safety.

4. Gustation (Taste)

- Description: Taste enables perception of chemical compounds in food, identifying flavors such as sweet, sour, salty, bitter, and umami.
- Mechanism: Taste buds on the tongue and oral cavity contain chemoreceptors that detect specific molecules, sending signals to the gustatory cortex.
- Sub-aspects: Taste interacts closely with olfaction to create flavor perception.
- Significance: Guides dietary choices and aids in detecting spoiled or toxic substances.

5. Olfaction (Smell)

- Description: Smell allows detection of airborne chemical compounds (odorants).
- Mechanism: Olfactory receptors in the nasal cavity bind to odor molecules, transmitting signals to the olfactory bulb and cortex.
- Sub-aspects: Includes distinguishing thousands of distinct odors and contributing to memory and emotion.
- Significance: Influences taste perception and environmental awareness.

Much can be written and explored on those 5 senses alone. But here is where things get really interesting. The human sensory spectrum extends well beyond these traditional five senses to include proprioception, vestibular sense, interoception, and potentially others like chronoception.

6. Proprioception (Body Position Sense)

- Description: Proprioception is the sense of body position, movement, and orientation in space.
- Mechanism: Proprioceptors in muscles, tendons, and joints (e.g., muscle spindles, Golgi tendon organs) detect stretch and tension, relaying information to the brain.

- Significance: Essential for coordination, balance, and motor control without visual input.

7. Vestibular Sense (Balance and Spatial Orientation)

- Description: The vestibular sense governs balance, head position, and spatial orientation.
- Mechanism: The vestibular system in the inner ear, including the semicircular canals and otolith organs, detects head movement and gravity, sending signals to the cerebellum and brainstem.
- Significance: Maintains posture, stabilizes gaze, and prevents falls.

8. Interoception (Internal Sensation)

- Description: Interoception involves sensing internal bodily states, such as hunger, thirst, heartbeat, and the need to breathe.
- Mechanism: Receptors in internal organs (e.g., baroreceptors, chemoreceptors) monitor physiological conditions, with signals processed by the insular cortex and other brain regions.
- Sub-aspects: Includes visceral sensations like fullness, nausea, or organ-specific pain.
- Significance: Regulates homeostasis and informs emotional states.

9. Chronoception (Time Perception)

- Description: Chronoception is the sense of time, allowing perception of duration and temporal order.
- Mechanism: Involves complex brain processes, including the suprachiasmatic nucleus and cortical networks, though not tied to a specific sensory organ.
- Significance: Aids in coordinating activities and anticipating events.
- The suprachiasmatic nucleus (SCN) is a small, paired cluster of approximately 10,000–20,000 neurons located in the anterior hypothalamus of the brain, directly above the optic chiasm (the point where the optic nerves partially cross). It serves as the primary circadian pacemaker in mammals, including humans, coordinating the body's internal 24-hour rhythms—known as circadian rhythms—with external environmental cues, particularly the light-dark cycle.

Anatomy of the SCN

- **Location and Structure**: The SCN sits bilaterally (one on each side) along the midline third ventricle in the hypothalamus, making it part of the diencephalon. It measures less than 1 mm³ and is divided into two main subregions: the ventrolateral "core" (which receives direct sensory input) and the dorsomedial "shell" (which integrates and propagates signals).

Neurons in the SCN express specific neuropeptides, such as vasoactive intestinal peptide (VIP) in the core and arginine vasopressin (AVP) in the shell.

o **Blood Supply**: It receives blood from branches of the anterior cerebral and anterior communicating arteries.

Function of the SCN

o The SCN acts as the "master clock," generating and synchronizing circadian oscillations in gene expression, neuronal firing, hormone release, and behavior across the body. It regulates:

o **Sleep-Wake Cycle**: By influencing melatonin production in the pineal gland (via projections to the paraventricular nucleus of the hypothalamus), it promotes sleep at night and wakefulness during the day.

o **Other Rhythms:** Feeding, body temperature, metabolism, hormone levels (e.g., cortisol), and cognitive performance.

o **Entrainment Mechanism:** The SCN receives direct input from intrinsically photosensitive retinal ganglion cells via the retinohypothalamic tract (RHT), allowing it to "reset" daily based on light exposure. Additional inputs come from the intergeniculate leaflet (for non-photic cues like activity) and serotonergic pathways from the raphe nuclei. Outputs project to nearby hypothalamic areas (e.g., subparaventricular zone), thalamus, and limbic structures to coordinate peripheral clocks in organs like the liver and heart.

o At the molecular level, SCN rhythmicity arises from a transcription-translation feedback loop (TTFL) involving clock genes like CLOCK, BMAL1, PER, and CRY. These genes cycle over ~24 hours, with positive activators (CLOCK-BMAL1) promoting transcription and negative inhibitors (PER-CRY) suppressing it, modulated by phosphorylation and calcium signaling.

Clinical Relevance of the SCN

o Disruptions to the SCN—due to jet lag, shift work, aging, or lesions—can lead to circadian misalignment, contributing to sleep disorders (e.g., insomnia, delayed sleep phase syndrome), mood disorders (e.g., depression), metabolic issues (e.g., obesity), and neurodegenerative diseases (e.g., Alzheimer's). Therapies like bright light exposure or melatonin target SCN pathways to realign rhythms.

10. Other Potential Senses

o Magnetoception: While not well-established in humans, some evidence suggests weak sensitivity to magnetic fields, potentially mediated by cryptochromes in the eyes or brain. Its role is minimal compared to animals like birds.

- ○ Echolocation: Extremely limited in humans, though some visually impaired individuals develop rudimentary echolocation by interpreting sound reflections.
- ○ Chemosensory Sensations: Beyond taste and smell, humans may detect pheromones or other chemical signals via the vomeronasal organ (though its functionality in humans is debated).

Notes on Sensory Integration

- ○ Multisensory Integration: The brain combines inputs from multiple senses to create a cohesive perception of the environment. For example, vision and touch integrate for object manipulation, while olfaction and gustation combine for flavor.
- ○ Variability: Sensory acuity varies among individuals due to genetic, environmental, or neurological factors. Some conditions, like synesthesia, result in atypical sensory integration.

The human sensory spectrum extends beyond the traditional five senses to include proprioception, vestibular sense, interoception, and potentially others like chronoception. Each sense relies on specialized receptors and neural pathways to process environmental or internal stimuli, enabling survival, interaction, and adaptation. If you require further details on any specific sense or its neurological basis, please let me know. The human sensory system encompasses a wide array of mechanisms that enable perception of both external and internal stimuli, facilitating interaction with the environment and maintenance of physiological balance. Traditionally, five primary senses—sight, hearing, taste, smell, and touch—have been recognized since Aristotle's classification in *De Anima* (circa 350 BCE). However, contemporary neuroscientific and physiological research indicates that the total number of distinct senses extends far beyond this, ranging from 8 to 33 depending on definitional criteria. These criteria typically involve specialized sensory receptors that transduce specific stimuli (e.g., light, mechanical forces, chemicals) into neural signals processed by dedicated brain regions.

A sense is generally defined as a biological system comprising sensory cells responsive to a particular physical or chemical stimulus, distinct from broader perceptual processes like cognition. Sources vary in enumeration due to overlaps (e.g., submodalities within touch) and debates over internal (interoceptive) versus external (exteroceptive) senses. For instance, occupational therapy frameworks recognize eight core sensory systems, while broader classifications, such as those from the University of Utah's genetic research, propose up to 21 based on receptor types and signal transduction pathways. Other estimates reach 30 or more when including nuanced internal states like blood pressure regulation.

Below is a comprehensive overview of the human senses, categorized into exteroceptive (external environment), proprioceptive/vestibular (body position and movement), and interoceptive (internal body states). This list draws from established scientific consensus, prioritizing distinct receptor-based modalities while noting submodalities for clarity. It aims to represent the "full spectrum" without arbitrary inflation, focusing on well-substantiated examples.

Exteroceptive Senses (External Stimuli Detection)

These involve specialized organs interacting with the external world.

1. **Vision (Sight)**: Detection of light in the visible electromagnetic spectrum (approximately 370–730 nanometers) via photoreceptors (rods and cones) in the retina of the eyes. Enables perception of color, shape, motion, and depth through binocular disparity. The brain's visual cortex integrates this for image formation. Submodalities include sensitivity to brightness and contrast.
2. **Audition (Hearing)**: Perception of sound waves (vibrations in air or other media) through mechanoreceptors (hair cells) in the cochlea of the inner ear. Humans detect frequencies from about 20 Hz to 20 kHz. The auditory cortex processes pitch, volume, and spatial location.
3. **Olfaction (Smell)**: Chemical sensing of airborne molecules via olfactory receptors in the nasal epithelium. Approximately 400 receptor types allow discrimination of thousands of odors, influencing flavor perception and emotional responses via the olfactory bulb and limbic system.
4. **Gustation (Taste)**: Chemical detection of dissolved substances on the tongue and oral cavity via taste buds containing chemoreceptors sensitive to five basic qualities: sweet, sour, salty, bitter, and umami. Integrated with olfaction for a full flavor experience.
5. **Somatosensation (Touch and Related Submodalities)**: Mechanical and thermal detection through skin and body tissues via mechanoreceptors, thermoreceptors, and nociceptors. Encompasses:
    o Light touch and pressure (e.g., via Meissner corpuscles and Merkel cells).
    o Vibration and texture discrimination.
    o Temperature (thermoception: warm via TRPV channels, cold via TRPM8).
    o Pain (nociception: sharp or aching via free nerve endings responding to tissue damage or extremes).

Proprioceptive and Vestibular Senses (Body Position and Movement)

These provide spatial awareness without visual input.

6. **Proprioception (Body Position Awareness)**: Sensing the relative position of body parts and limbs via proprioceptors (muscle spindles and Golgi tendon organs) in muscles, tendons, and joints. Allows unconscious

coordination, such as touching one's nose with eyes closed. Also termed "kinaesthesia" in some contexts.

7. **Equilibrioception (Balance and Spatial Orientation)**: Detection of head position, linear acceleration, and angular rotation via the vestibular system in the inner ear (semicircular canals and otolith organs). Maintains posture and stabilizes gaze during movement; processed in the cerebellum and brainstem.

Interoceptive Senses (Internal Body States)

These monitor physiological conditions for homeostasis, often subconscious but perceivable as discomfort or urges.

8. **Interoception (Internal Awareness)**: Broad detection of visceral states via receptors in organs and tissues. Includes:
   o Hunger and satiety (via ghrelin/leptin-sensitive cells in the stomach and hypothalamus).
   o Thirst (via osmoreceptors in the hypothalamus detecting blood osmolarity).
   o Fullness in bladder/rectum (stretch receptors signaling urinary or bowel urgency).
   o Cardiocception (perception of heartbeat via baroreceptors in blood vessels).
   o Respiratory sensations (e.g., suffocation via chemoreceptors detecting CO_2 levels).
   o Nausea or gastrointestinal discomfort (via vagal nerve afferents).
9. **Nociception (Pain, Internal and External)**: Distinct from somatosensory pain, this includes visceral nociception for internal organ pain (e.g., appendicitis), mediated by polymodal nociceptors. Often overlaps with somatosensation but is considered separate for its role in alerting to internal threats.

Additional proposed senses, based on specialized receptors, extend the spectrum further but are debated for distinctness:

- Chronoception: Internal timing perception via suprachiasmatic nucleus, estimating time passage without external cues.
- Magnetoreception: Weak evidence in humans for sensing Earth's magnetic field, potentially aiding subconscious navigation (observed in brain activity studies).
- Osmoreception: Direct sensing of blood solute concentration for hydration balance.
- Baroreception: Blood pressure monitoring via carotid and aortic receptors, influencing autonomic responses.

This spectrum underscores the multisensory nature of human perception, where senses integrate (e.g., vision and proprioception for coordinated movement). Impairments in any one can affect daily function, as seen in conditions like sensory processing disorder. Research continues to refine this list, emphasizing cultural and individual variations in sensory prioritization.

Expanding Sensory Perception Beyond the Five Basic Senses and How to Achieve It Through Meditation

The human experience has long been framed by the five basic senses: sight, hearing, touch, taste, and smell. These senses serve as our primary interfaces with the physical world, allowing us to navigate environments, detect dangers, and enjoy pleasures. However, scientific research and philosophical inquiries reveal that human perception extends far beyond these traditional boundaries. Additional senses, such as proprioception (the awareness of body position) and interoception (the sense of internal bodily states), are now recognized by neuroscientists as integral to our perceptual toolkit. Furthermore, esoteric traditions speak of extrasensory perception (ESP), intuition, and psychic abilities that transcend physical limitations, offering glimpses into non-physical realities.

This essay explores the expansion of sensory perception beyond the five basic senses, drawing on both empirical science and contemplative practices. We will examine scientifically acknowledged additional senses, phenomena like synesthesia, and psychic faculties. Central to this discussion is meditation, a time-tested method that enhances awareness, quiets mental noise, and unlocks subtler perceptual abilities. Through structured meditation techniques, individuals can cultivate heightened intuition, emotional empathy, and even experiences of interconnectedness with the universe. By the end, readers will understand not only the theoretical foundations but also the practical steps to expand their own perceptual horizons.

The journey begins with acknowledging the limitations of our default sensory framework. Our senses are tuned for survival, filtering vast amounts of information to focus on what's immediately relevant. Yet, as species like bees perceive ultraviolet light or bats use echolocation, humans, too, possess untapped potentials. Meditation acts as a bridge, training the mind to perceive subtler stimuli and integrate them into conscious awareness.

Beyond the Five Senses - Scientific Perspectives

Human perception is not limited to the Aristotelian five senses. Modern science identifies at least eight core senses, including the vestibular system (balance and spatial orientation), proprioception (body position and movement), and interoception (internal signals like hunger or heartbeat). These "hidden" senses operate below conscious awareness but profoundly influence our daily lives. For instance, the vestibular sense helps us maintain equilibrium during movement, while interoception allows us to detect internal states like emotional arousal or fatigue.

Expanding further, researchers like Guy Murchie in the *Music of Spheres* and *The Seven Mysteries Of Life: An Exploration of Science and Philosophy* and other writings (all of which I recommend) proposed up to 32 senses, categorized into radiation, feeling, chemical, mental, and spiritual domains. These include sensitivity to radiation (e.g., perceiving electromagnetic fields), temperature sense (distinct neural pathways for heat detection), and electromagnetic sense (as in animals like electric eels or insects navigating via magnetic polarity). Humans may experience these subtly; for example, some individuals report sensitivity to Wi-Fi signals or atmospheric changes, potentially heightened in conditions like autism.

Another fascinating extension is **chronoception**, the sense of time's passage, which meditation can refine by altering subjective time perception. Studies show that mindfulness practices slow down perceived time, allowing practitioners to "stretch" moments and gain deeper insights into temporal flow.

Synesthesia represents a neurological bridge beyond isolated senses, where stimuli in one modality trigger experiences in another, such as seeing colors when hearing sounds. Affecting about 4% of the population, synesthesia involves increased "cross-talk" between brain regions, unmasking neural pathways present in all humans but typically dormant. Infant brains exhibit synesthetic traits, suggesting it's a primal state that differentiation suppresses. Cultural influences, like language, further shape perception; Russian speakers, with distinct words for light and dark blue, discriminate shades better than English speakers.

Sensory substitution technologies exemplify this expansion, where devices convert visual information into tactile sensations, allowing blind individuals to "see" via touch. This demonstrates perception's plasticity, hinting that with training—like meditation—we can rewire sensory processing.

In critical sectors like healthcare, understanding these extended senses improves diagnostics; for example, interoceptive awareness correlates with emotional regulation in therapy. Overall, science affirms that our perceptual limits are not fixed but expandable through awareness and practice.

Esoteric and Psychic Senses

Venturing into esoteric realms, perception beyond the physical includes psychic senses, often termed "clairs" (from the French for "clear"). These faculties allow interaction with subtle energies, transcending the vibrational range of traditional senses.

Clairvoyance, or clear seeing, involves perceiving visions, auras, or future events extrasensorily. It can manifest as mental images during quiet reflection. Clairaudience, clear hearing, entails receiving non-physical sounds, like inner guidance or spirit voices, often in the mind's ear. Clairsentience, clear feeling, senses others' emotions or energies, akin to empathy but more intuitive, useful for detecting unspoken tensions.

Claircognizance provides sudden "knowings" without logic, aiding decision-making. Less common are clairalience (smelling non-physical scents), clairgustance (tasting without stimuli), and clairstactility (feeling phantom sensations). Animal communication and remote viewing further extend this, enabling telepathic links or distant perceptions.

Intuition, often called the sixth sense, integrates these as subconscious deductions. Podcasts on higher mind faculties describe six such abilities: *perception, will, reason, memory, imagination, and intuition*, linking them to neuroscience for enhanced cognition.

Inner vision and collective consciousness offer profound expansions, blurring individual boundaries to sense universal interconnectedness. Spiritual senses like conscience or ecstasy emerge in deep states, fostering sublime love or cosmic awareness.

While skeptics view these as illusions, anecdotal evidence and practices like meditation suggest they represent untapped human potential.

☁ The Role of Meditation in Expanding Perception

Meditation serves as a gateway to expanded perception by clearing mental "static," allowing subtler stimuli to surface. Regular practice sharpens sense organs, enabling detection of subtle energies.

Mindfulness meditation promotes "beginner's mind," heightening sensory awareness through present-moment focus. Studies show multisensory experiences, combining audio, olfactory, and visual stimuli with biofeedback, increase parasympathetic activity, reducing anxiety and enhancing relaxation.

By observing thoughts as a sixth sense, practitioners gain meta-awareness, distinguishing mental activity from physical sensations. This fosters intuition, as quieted minds receive clearer insights.

Yoga and standing postures expand presence, using balance to cultivate curiosity and awareness beyond senses. Courses on developing intuition emphasize daily practices to strengthen ESP.

Ultimately, meditation rewires the brain, enhancing cross-sensory integration and opening doors to psychic faculties.

☁ Practical Meditation Techniques

To expand perception, begin with foundational practices and progress to advanced ones.

Technique 1: Five Senses Mindfulness (From Mindful.org)

Find a comfortable seat. Scan physical sensations: feet on floor, breath changes. Attend to sounds, distant and internal. Notice smells, tastes. Open eyes for sight: macro to micro views. Close eyes, observe thoughts as they arise. Practice daily for 10-15 minutes to heighten awareness.

Technique 2: Expanding Awareness Through Senses (30-Day Challenge)

Breathe deeply, ground with imagined light. Observe thoughts' location and energy. Expand hearing outward, then inward. Feel touch externally and internally. Connect with emotions via heart hand placement, breathing kindness. End with silence and intentions.

Technique 3: Sensory Diary and Exploration

For sight: Observe colors and movements while turning body. Sound: Take walks, listen mindfully. Taste: Sample foods slowly. Smell: Explore perfumes or nature. Touch: Feel objects with eyes closed. Journal experiences to uncover emotional links.

Advanced Technique: Psychic Sense Development

Meditate on clairs: Visualize for clairvoyance, listen inwardly for clairaudience. Journal insights, trust gut feelings. Practice remote viewing by focusing on distant targets.

Technique 4: Multisensory Mindfulness

Incorporate stimuli: Use essential oils and incense (smell), nature sounds (hearing), and heartbeat visualization (interoception). Measure HRV for feedback.

Technique 5: Inner Vision Meditation

Sit quietly, focus on breath. Cultivate empathy by visualizing others' perspectives. Extend to collective consciousness, sensing unity.

Consistency is key; start with 5 minutes daily, building to longer sessions. Track progress in a journal, noting new perceptions.

Expanding sensory perception enriches life, fostering deeper connections and insights. Through meditation, we transcend limitations, accessing scientific and esoteric realms alike. Embrace these practices for transformative growth.

Chapter 21: The Role of Meditation in Enhancing All Types of Human Intelligence

 Introduction to Human Intelligence and Meditation

Human intelligence is a complex, multidimensional construct that goes beyond conventional metrics like IQ, embracing diverse cognitive, emotional, and perceptual abilities. Obviously, volumes have been written on it, and there is just as vast a space of unknowns and yet to be explored and understood. I present this chapter to make you aware of these intelligences and that alone can help you be cognizant and mindful of them, and thus, be able to develop them in meaningful ways. I believe this introduction and overview can stimulate further exploration into this vital topic.

Howard Gardner's Theory of Multiple Intelligences, introduced in 1983 in *Frames of Mind: The Theory of Multiple Intelligences,* revolutionized this understanding by proposing that intelligence comprises distinct forms, each representing unique ways of processing information and interacting with the world. Initially outlining *seven intelligences*, Gardner later expanded to include Naturalistic intelligence and suggested existential (or spiritual) as a ninth. He followed with *Multiple Intelligences: The Theory in Practice* in 1993, and all of his works are thought—provoking and expand the understanding of intelligence in an enlightened way.

Emotional intelligence, championed by Daniel Goleman in the 1990s, complements this framework by emphasizing the recognition, understanding, and management of emotions in oneself and others. These intelligences are not fixed traits but can be nurtured through targeted practices.

Meditation, rooted in ancient traditions like Buddhism and Hinduism, involves techniques such as mindfulness, focused attention, and loving-kindness practices that cultivate awareness, reduce stress, and foster neuroplasticity—the brain's ability to reorganize itself. Modern neuroscience supports meditation's role in enhancing intelligence: functional MRI studies show increased gray matter density in regions like the prefrontal cortex (for executive function) and hippocampus (for memory), leading to improved cognitive performance across domains. Longitudinal research indicates that even short-term meditation (e.g., 8-week programs) yields trait-like changes, such as better attention regulation and emotional stability, which underpin multiple intelligences. This essay expands on nine intelligences from Gardner's model, plus emotional intelligence, providing detailed definitions, real-world examples, evidence-based benefits of meditation, and practical development strategies.

∀ **Linguistic Intelligence**

Linguistic intelligence refers to the adept use of language for expression, comprehension, and persuasion, encompassing skills like vocabulary building, rhetoric, and multilingual proficiency. Individuals with high linguistic intelligence, such as novelists like J.K. Rowling or orators like Martin Luther King Jr., excel in crafting narratives, debating ideas, and interpreting nuanced texts. This intelligence is crucial in professions involving communication, from journalism to law.

Meditation enhances linguistic intelligence by sharpening focus, accelerating word recognition, and neutralizing emotional biases in language processing. A study on novices found that mindfulness meditation speeds up responses to single words and balances valence ratings of emotional terms, suggesting improved semantic processing. It also promotes alpha brain waves, which facilitate relaxed states ideal for creative language acquisition, making it easier to learn new languages by reducing anxiety and enhancing retention. Further, meditation fosters self-awareness, sparking creativity in verbal expression, as seen in practices that encourage active engagement with material for deeper comprehension.

To develop it: Begin with mantra meditation, repeating a meaningful phrase (e.g., "clarity in words") for 15-20 minutes daily while focusing on breath. This builds phonetic sensitivity and internal verbal fluency. Transition to guided language meditations, visualizing words as vivid images, then journal post-session to expand ideas into essays or poems. Incorporate apps for language learning during mindful breaks. Consistent practice, as evidenced by studies on meditation's impact on cognitive improvements, leads to enhanced verbal creativity and comprehension over months.

∀ **Logical-Mathematical Intelligence**

Logical-mathematical intelligence involves deductive reasoning, pattern recognition, and quantitative analysis, enabling problem-solving in abstract domains. Exemplified by figures like Albert Einstein or Ada Lovelace, it drives innovation in fields such as mathematics, engineering, and computer science.

Meditation bolsters this intelligence by reducing mind-wandering, enhancing executive functions, and fostering intuitive insights. Research shows that mindfulness practices strengthen prefrontal cortex activity, improving attention allocation and logical reasoning, with practitioners exhibiting better performance on fluid intelligence tasks. Yoga and meditation have been linked to preserved brain organization in aging, maintaining cognitive sharpness for mathematical intuition. Additionally, meditation promotes "fact-free learning" by emphasizing stillness, which refines predictive processing and problem-solving without over-reliance on prior biases. Studies indicate it boosts overall IQ through hemispheric synchronization and memory enhancement.

Development method: Practice analytical meditation by contemplating a math theorem (e.g., Pythagoras) while anchoring on breath for 20 minutes, visualizing logical chains. Follow with puzzles like Sudoku. For advanced users, integrate self-reflection techniques, as highlighted in talks on meditation's role in mathematical intuition. Eight-week regimens yield measurable gains in reasoning, per cognitive studies.

∀ Visual-Spatial Intelligence

Visual-spatial intelligence entails mentally manipulating images, navigating spaces, and perceiving visual details, vital for artists like Pablo Picasso or architects like Frank Lloyd Wright.

Meditation develops this by expanding attentional focus and boosting visuospatial memory. A study on Buddhist deity meditation showed temporary enhancements in retaining visual images, suggesting activation of relevant brain pathways. Mindfulness improves mental rotation and spatial cognition, with effects independent of gender, through better attention depth. Long-term practitioners exhibit hippocampal changes linked to spatial abilities, and visualization meditations directly train imaginative mechanics. Research confirms meditation's role in sustained visual tasks and attention span.

To build it: Engage in visualization meditation, imagining rotating objects or landscapes for 20-25 minutes, noting details. Post-session, sketch or use 3D modeling tools. Techniques like mirror meditation enhance self-awareness in spatial contexts. Regular practice sharpens abilities, as per studies on short-term visual memory boosts.

∀ Musical Intelligence

Musical intelligence encompasses discerning pitch, rhythm, and timbre, allowing composition and performance, as seen in musicians like Beethoven or Adele.

Meditation fosters this by heightening auditory awareness and creativity. Vipassana practices build mindfulness and concentration, enabling deeper engagement with musical elements and enhancing performance. It connects practitioners to inner creativity, upgrading musical output by accessing subconscious sources. Musical training itself grows brain regions, but meditation amplifies this through mindful involvement, developing listening skills and mindfulness. Studies link meditation to reward and rhythm processing improvements.

Development approach: Use sound meditation, focusing on tones or rhythms for 15-20 minutes, then improvise music. This hones expression, supported by research on meditation's creative benefits.

Here are five extremely unusual practice approaches drawn from the methods of Miles Davis, John Coltrane, John McLaughlin, Chris Potter, and Yusef Lateef. Each musician's technique highlights a distinctive musical sense and intelligence to enhance musical abilities, often blending technical rigor with creative or philosophical innovation.

1. *Miles Davis: Minimal sketches for unpreconceived improvisation*

   Davis often provided his band with only vague, minimal musical sketches rather than full compositions or rehearsals, forcing musicians to approach sessions without expectations or habits. This method cultivated fresh, instinctive playing by emphasizing real-time discovery over preparation, as seen in recordings like *Kind of Blue*.

2. *John Coltrane: The "spider technique" for tempo mastery*

   Coltrane used a non-linear "spider" method to build speed and control, practicing exercises at tempos that jumped erratically (e.g., starting at 60 BPM, then 80, back to 70, up to 90, then down to 80). This avoided rote linear increases, simulating real performance variability and enhancing adaptability in fast passages.

3. *John McLaughlin: Manipulating beat cycles for odd rhythms*

   McLaughlin practiced by breaking down and reassembling 16-beat cycles to explore odd or alternating time signatures, creating syncopated patterns that felt natural in complex fusion contexts. This rhythmic experimentation drew from Indian influences, allowing him to internalize unconventional grooves through repetition and variation.

4. *Chris Potter: Transposing entire method books across all keys*

   As a young musician, Potter rigorously transposed comprehensive exercise books—like Charlie Parker's Omnibook—into all 12 keys, building encyclopedic facility and ear training. This exhaustive approach enabled him to fluidly navigate any tonality, turning technical drills into a foundation for hearing and executing complex ideas instantly.

5. *Yusef Lateef: Autophysiopsychic integration of body, mind, and spirit*

   Lateef coined "autophysiopsychic" practice to fuse physical technique with mental and spiritual elements, incorporating exotic scales from

African and Asian traditions while studying indigenous instruments like the sarewa flute. This holistic method treated music as self-expression from one's entire being, balancing scales with meditative reflection for deeper creativity.

∀ Bodily-Kinesthetic Intelligence

Bodily-kinesthetic intelligence is the skillful use of the body for expression or problem-solving, prominent in athletes like Serena Williams or dancers like Mikhail Baryshnikov.

Meditation enhances this by improving body awareness and emotional regulation, aiding precise movements. It strengthens prefrontal control, reducing reactivity for better coordination. Yoga integrates meditation to connect learners with kinesthetic self-discovery. Practices like journaling or "stop, listen, feel" build body intelligence (BQ), attuning to physical signals. Focused attention meditation increases precision in sensory experience.

To enhance: Walking meditation for 15-20 minutes, sensing movements, then yoga. Classroom exercises like brief meditations develop it.

∀ Interpersonal Intelligence

Interpersonal intelligence involves reading social cues, empathizing, and building relationships, essential for leaders and people in all walks of life.

Meditation cultivates this by boosting empathy and emotional regulation. Studies show positive links between mindfulness and EI, especially emotion management. Loving-kindness meditation enhances compassion and interpersonal skills. It promotes self-observation, disengaging automatic reactions for better interactions. Transcendental meditation increases EI scores.

Method: Metta meditation for 20 minutes, extending wishes, then mindful listening. This builds skills, per workplace studies.

∀ Intrapersonal Intelligence

Intrapersonal intelligence is self-knowledge, regulating emotions and motivations, key for introspective figures like journaling philosophers.

Meditation directly advances this through self-awareness and calm. It changes brain structures for better EI and self-assessment. Transcendental meditation boosts intrapersonal awareness and adaptability. Deep breathing enhances concentration and peace. Habits like meditation foster resilience.

Development: Vipassana for 15-20 minutes, noting sensations, then journal. This yields growth, as per studies.

∀ Naturalistic Intelligence

Naturalistic intelligence is identifying patterns in nature, categorizing flora/fauna.

Meditation supports this by fostering present-moment focus and inner peace, aiding environmental attunement. It balances mind-body-spirit for natural observation. Silence in meditation reveals innate intelligence. Transcendental practices enhance intellectual functions.

To develop: Outdoor meditation on elements for 20 minutes. This builds connection, supported by brain enhancement research.

∀ Existential/Spiritual Intelligence

Existential intelligence grapples with life's big questions, like meaning and death, seen in philosophers like Socrates.

Meditation sharpens this by activating beliefs and values, fostering transcendence. It develops SI through awareness and meaning-making. Practices enhance spiritual power and existential coping. SI is trainable, aiding mental health.

Method: Contemplative meditation on purpose for 25 minutes. This cultivates insights, per models of SI.

∀ Emotional Intelligence

Emotional intelligence (EQ) comprises self-awareness, regulation, motivation, empathy, and social skills. Meditation elevates EQ by building self-control and empathy, restructuring the brain. Mindfulness correlates with better regulation. It increases awareness of others' emotions. Transcendental meditation reduces stress, boosting scores.

To develop: Mindfulness of emotions for 20 minutes, labeling feelings. This enhances EQ, backed by deep-level awareness.

Meditation serves as a powerful, evidence-based tool for expanding these intelligences, promoting comprehensive personal development through dedicated practice.

Chapter 22: Neuroplasticity and 'Mind Magic'

The field of neuroscience is a fascinating, vast one. While great strides have been made in recent decades, obviously, so much is still not fully understood. I worked on one of the more famous robots in the 20th century – Dante II with the Field Robotics Lab at Carnegie-Mellon University in the 1990s and at that time motor skills were still quite rudimentary and cognitive skills very prescriptive and unadaptable in any broad sense. In the intervening decades, amazing strides in Artificial Intelligence and advanced reasoning and language models have been remarkable. All that said, it's impossible to discuss the advancement of our inner mastery without touching on neuroscience again as I have at some introductory level in previous chapters.

In this chapter, I'd like to go a little deeper and introduce the concept of Neuroplasticity – the brain's capacity to reorganize its structure, functions, and connections in response to intrinsic or extrinsic stimuli. **Intrinsic stimuli** originate from within an individual, driven by internal desires, values, or personal satisfaction. These are motivations tied to internal rewards, such as a sense of purpose, joy, or fulfillment.

Whereas **extrinsic stimuli** come from external sources, such as rewards, recognition, or consequences imposed by the environment or society. These are motivations driven by external outcomes, like money, status, or avoiding punishment.

Then, ultimately, to introduce methods that researchers and clinicians have found for tapping into and enhancing and implementing these concepts and ideas through meditation and breathing techniques, which I find interesting, exciting, and quite useful.

Introduction to Neuroplasticity

Neuroplasticity, also known as brain plasticity, refers to the brain's capacity to reorganize its structure, functions, and connections in response to intrinsic or extrinsic stimuli. This dynamic process allows the brain to adapt to new experiences, learn skills, recover from injuries, and even rewire itself in the face of disease or aging. Far from being a static organ, the brain exhibits plasticity throughout life, challenging the long-held belief that significant changes occur only during childhood. At the cellular level, neuroplasticity involves mechanisms such as the growth of new dendritic spines, remodeling of axonal pathways, modification of synaptic receptors, and even the generation of new neurons (neurogenesis) in regions like the hippocampus. These changes enhance neural communication efficiency, particularly in areas involved in learning, memory, and motor control.

The concept of "neurons that fire together, wire together," coined by neurobiologist Carla Shatz, encapsulates the essence of synaptic plasticity, where repeated activation of neural pathways strengthens connections, facilitating learning and memory formation. In children, the brain is highly malleable during critical developmental periods, easily absorbing languages or skills through sensory input that sculpts synaptic connections. As we age, however, plasticity diminishes; molecular "brakes" stabilize circuits to prevent constant rewiring, which aids reliability but hinders new learning. This shift underscores the balance between adaptability and stability in brain function.

Stanford University has been at the forefront of neuroplasticity research, leveraging interdisciplinary approaches in neuroscience, psychology, and medicine to uncover how the brain adapts—and maladapts—in various contexts. From studies on learning disabilities to addiction and aging, Stanford researchers have illuminated practical applications, offering hope for therapeutic interventions. I want to explore key Stanford studies, highlighting their contributions to our understanding of neuroplasticity.

🌐 Stanford's Foundations in Neuroplasticity Research

Carla Shatz, a pioneering Stanford neurobiologist and Sapp Family Provostial Professor, has shaped the field through her work on developmental plasticity and its persistence into adulthood. In a 2023 discussion, Shatz explained how childhood brains undergo rapid synaptic changes driven by experience, linking sensory inputs (e.g., hearing speech) to motor outputs (e.g., speaking). This process is vulnerable to instability, increasing risks like epilepsy, but it enables profound adaptability. As brains mature, plasticity molecules shift from accelerators to brakes, preserving learned knowledge—such as one's native language—while making novel learning more effortful.

Shatz's lab has explored ways to counteract age-related rigidity. In a 2015 study, undergraduate researcher Richie Sapp contributed to developing a "decoy drug" targeting the protein PirB, which inhibits new neural connections in adults. By blocking PirB in mice, the team enabled the formation of juvenile-like synapses, published in *Science Translational Medicine*. This work, motivated by Sapp's personal connection to neurodevelopmental disorders like his twin brother's hydrocephalus and autism, demonstrated that adult brains retain untapped plasticity potential, with implications for stroke recovery and learning enhancement. Sapp's research, supported by Stanford's Bio-X Undergraduate Fellowship, exemplifies how early training can yield high-impact discoveries.

Complementing Shatz's synaptic focus, the Stanford Cognitive & Systems Neuroscience Laboratory (SCSNL), led by Vinod Menon, investigates neuroplasticity in cognitive development, particularly math learning. A landmark 2015 study by Iuculano et al., published in *Nature Communications*, showed that intensive cognitive tutoring induces widespread neuroplasticity in children with mathematical learning disabilities. Using functional MRI (fMRI), the researchers observed remediation of brain dysfunction: tutoring normalized activity in the intraparietal sulcus (a key math-processing region) and enhanced connectivity across fronto-parietal networks. This plasticity not only improved math performance but also generalized to other cognitive domains, suggesting tutoring as a scalable intervention for learning disorders.

Another SCSNL study by Jolles et al. (2015) in *Brain Structure and Function* linked plasticity in left perisylvian white-matter tracts to individual differences in math learning. Diffusion tensor imaging revealed that adaptive changes in these tracts—bundles of myelinated axons—correlate with learning gains, highlighting white-matter remodeling as a substrate for skill acquisition. Evans et al. (2015) in the *Journal of Neuroscience* further demonstrated how baseline brain structural integrity and intrinsic functional connectivity predict six-year growth in children's numerical abilities, underscoring neuroplasticity's role in long-term developmental trajectories.

These studies collectively affirm Stanford's emphasis on experience-dependent plasticity, showing how targeted interventions can harness the brain's adaptability to remediate deficits.

⑥ Advanced Stanford Studies: From Myelination to Addiction and Beyond

Recent Stanford research has expanded neuroplasticity beyond synapses to include myelin plasticity—the dynamic regulation of myelin sheaths that insulate nerve fibers and speed signal transmission. Michelle Monje, a pediatric neuro-oncologist, and Rob Malenka, a psychiatry professor, have pioneered this area, revealing its maladaptive potential in disorders like addiction. In a 2024 study discussed in the Wu Tsai Neurosciences Institute podcast, Monje's team found that drugs like morphine and cocaine trigger myelin growth in the brain's reward circuitry, specifically the ventral tegmental area (VTA) and its projections to the nucleus accumbens. Unlike food rewards, which elicited no such changes, opioids and stimulants increased myelination, enhancing dopamine release synchrony and reinforcing drug-seeking behavior.

This "adaptive myelination" represents a new form of plasticity: neuronal activity drives oligodendrocytes (myelin-producing cells) to wrap axons more thickly, optimizing circuit efficiency for pathological learning. Blocking myelination in mice prevented preference formation for drugs, suggesting it as a therapeutic target. Malenka noted parallels to synaptic plasticity, where repeated drug exposure rewires reward pathways, but myelin adds a layer of timing precision crucial for coordinated signaling. While beneficial for motor learning, this mechanism maladapts in addiction, contributing to relapse vulnerability. The findings, building on Monje's 2020 work, imply that myelin plasticity governs not just healthy adaptation but also disorders like epilepsy, where excessive myelination worsens seizures.

Andrew Huberman, a Stanford neuroscientist and host of the Huberman Lab podcast, provides broader insights into enhancing neuroplasticity. His research emphasizes protocols to boost brain-derived neurotrophic factor (BDNF), a protein promoting neuron growth. Cardiovascular exercise elevates BDNF, facilitating structural changes in the hippocampus and motor cortex, while sleep—especially REM and deep stages—consolidates learning by reorganizing pathways. Huberman advocates techniques like spaced repetition and active recall to maximize synaptic strengthening in adults, who require deliberate effort unlike passive childhood exposure. He also explores psychedelics (e.g., psilocybin, ketamine), which surge BDNF and forge novel connections between brain regions, creating "critical periods" for emotional rewiring. This heightened plasticity shows promise for treating depression, PTSD, and addiction by disrupting maladaptive patterns, though clinical applications remain cautious due to ongoing research.

In aging and neurodegeneration, Shatz's lab targets molecular brakes to restore plasticity. Mouse models of Alzheimer's revealed excessive synapse loss as a primary memory impairer. By genetically removing a brake protein, researchers preserved synapses despite amyloid plaques, halting cognitive decline. This suggests therapies that modulate plasticity molecules could slow Alzheimer's progression, emphasizing early intervention to maintain synaptic integrity.

Stanford's Knight Initiative for Brain Resilience further integrates these themes, fostering collaborative research on healthy aging through plasticity. Though details are emerging, the initiative aims to blend startup innovation with academic rigor to develop interventions preserving cognitive vitality.

⬕ Implications and Future Directions

Stanford's neuroplasticity studies have profound implications for education, mental health, and medicine. In learning, SCSNL's tutoring models advocate for personalized interventions that leverage white-matter and functional plasticity to address disabilities, potentially transforming education for millions. For addiction, Monje and Malenka's myelin insights open doors to drugs blocking maladaptive myelination, reducing relapse without targeting synapses directly—a safer approach given addiction's complexity.

Aging research from Shatz and Huberman highlights lifestyle factors: exercise, sleep, and focused learning counteract plasticity decline, while psychedelics offer targeted boosts for therapy-resistant conditions. Ethically, reopening critical periods raises questions about unintended instability, like epilepsy risks, but controlled applications could revolutionize treatment.

Future Stanford efforts, including the Brain Stimulation Lab's work on neuropsychiatric disorders via non-invasive techniques, promise to translate plasticity principles into clinical tools. James Doty's 2024 book *Mind Magic*, rooted in Stanford neuroscience, explores attention's role in redirecting plasticity for goal manifestation, blending manifestation with evidence-based rewiring.

Stanford's research demystifies neuroplasticity as a lifelong, modifiable process. From Shatz's synaptic foundations to Monje's myelin breakthroughs, these studies not only advance science but also empower individuals to harness their brain's potential for resilience and recovery. As of September 2025, ongoing trials and initiatives signal a future where plasticity-targeted therapies could mitigate the burdens of learning deficits, addiction, and neurodegeneration, fostering healthier brains across the lifespan.

🜚 Mind Magic: The Neuroscience of Manifestation and How It Changes Everything by James R. Doty (2024)

James R. Doty, MD, a renowned neurosurgeon and clinical professor at Stanford University, draws on his extensive background in neuroscience, compassion research, and personal experiences to demystify the concept of manifestation in his 2024 book *Mind Magic*. As the director of Stanford's Center for Compassion and Altruism Research and Education, Doty blends cutting-edge science with practical wisdom, challenging the notion that manifestation is mere "magic" or pseudoscience. Instead, he presents it as a neurological process rooted in neuroplasticity—the brain's ability to rewire itself through focused attention and intention. Published in May 2024, the 304-page book offers a six-step program to help readers reclaim agency, overcome limiting beliefs, and achieve meaningful goals, ultimately fostering not just personal success but a kinder world. Doty's narrative is enriched with anecdotes from his life, including his own struggles with poverty and health issues, and stories from patients and historical figures, making the science accessible and relatable.

At its core, *Mind Magic* argues that in an era of constant distractions—smartphones, social media, and information overload—our ability to focus has atrophied, leading to feelings of helplessness and unfulfilled potential. Doty explains that manifestation isn't about wishing upon a star or attracting cosmic forces; it's about harnessing the brain's four key networks: the Default Mode Network (for mind-wandering and self-referential thinking), the Central Executive Network (for focused attention and decision-making), the Salience Network (for detecting important stimuli), and the Attention Network (for directing focus). These, along with the vagus nerve's role in shifting from stress (fight-or-flight) to calm (rest-and-digest), enable us to embed intentions into the subconscious, where they drive behavior and opportunity recognition. The book emphasizes self-efficacy—the belief in one's capacity to influence outcomes—as the foundation for this process, countering negativity bias and evolutionary adaptations that keep us stuck in survival mode.

☯ The Neuroscience Foundation: From Thought to Reality

Doty begins by grounding **manifestation** in biology. The brain consumes 20% of the body's energy, constantly filtering vast sensory input to prioritize what's deemed important. Without intentional direction, it defaults to habitual patterns, often negative ones shaped by childhood experiences or societal pressures. Neuroplasticity offers hope: repeated mental practices can forge new neural pathways, making desired behaviors automatic. For instance, **visualization** activates the same brain regions as real experiences, tricking the subconscious into pursuing goals as if they've already occurred. Doty cites research showing how mental rehearsal enhances performance in athletes and surgeons, illustrating that "the brain does not distinguish between an actual physical experience and one that is intensely imagined."

A pivotal concept is metacognition—thinking about one's thinking—which allows us to observe and interrupt unhelpful thought loops. Doty warns of the "shadow self," internalized fears and limiting beliefs (e.g., "I'm not worthy") that sabotage progress. These stem from evolutionary wiring for caution but can be rewired through self-compassion, which reduces cortisol and boosts dopamine, creating a fertile ground for change. The book differentiates hedonic well-being (fleeting pleasure from material gains) from eudaimonic well-being (deep fulfillment from purpose), urging readers to align desires with values that serve others. This not only sustains motivation but leverages social networks, as prosocial goals make us more magnetic to support and synchronicities—meaningful coincidences that arise from heightened awareness.

Doty's personal story anchors these ideas: As a child facing abuse and illness, he learned "mind magic" from a store owner who taught him compassion meditation, leading to his medical career and philanthropy. This narrative underscores the book's message: The same mind that creates obstacles holds the power to dissolve them. "The reality is that the same mind that creates the obstacles to the life you want is also the source of the intention that will make the life that you want real. This is the real secret."

☯ The Six-Step Manifestation Program

The heart of *Mind Magic* is a practical, step-by-step framework, designed for daily integration rather than one-off rituals. Each step builds on the last, incorporating neuroscience-backed exercises like meditation, journaling, and visualization.

1. **Reclaim Your Focus and Agency**: Start by rebuilding attention, eroded by modern distractions. Practice metacognition to notice distractions without judgment, then sit with discomfort to build resilience. A key exercise: Deep breathing to activate the vagus nerve, shifting to a calm state. Visualize a simple behavior (e.g., exercising) for five minutes daily,

then write it down and affirm it each morning. This fosters self-efficacy, essential for manifestation.

2. **Clarify Your True Desires**: Tune into your "inner compass" by reflecting on what brings eudaimonic joy. Use body scans to relax and explore emotions tied to goals—ask, "Does this serve a larger purpose?" Visualize success vividly, engaging senses and feelings. Doty stresses aligning with authenticity to avoid superficial pursuits, like chasing wealth without meaning.

3. **Remove Mental Obstacles Through Self-Compassion**: Identify limiting beliefs via journaling (e.g., "What fears hold me back?"). Counter them with kindness: Visualize a safe space, offer self-forgiveness, and reframe negatives (e.g., "I am capable" instead of "I always fail"). This heals the "shadow," reducing resistance and freeing energy for growth. "Self-compassion has the power to heal the parts of us that feel chronically unsafe and unloved."

4. **Embed Intentions in the Subconscious**: Once clear and unblocked, use multisensory visualization for 20 minutes daily. Imagine the goal as achieved, infusing it with emotion—joy, gratitude—to etch it into neural circuits. Write intentions as present-tense affirmations and review them. Doty shares Jim Carrey's story of visualizing a $10 million check, which manifested years later, to show repetition's power.

5. **Pursue Passionately with Higher Purpose**: Action is crucial; align goals with altruism to sustain drive. Reflect on how your success benefits others—volunteer or share generously to activate social engagement circuits. Start small, track progress, and persist through setbacks, viewing them as feedback. "The effect you have on others is the most valuable currency there is."

6. **Release Expectations and Embrace Synchronicity**: After effort, cultivate equanimity: Let go of attachment via gratitude practices and openness to detours. Meditate on impermanence to trust life's flow. This invites unexpected opportunities, as rigid control blocks them. Doty reminds: "Manifesting is subject to the same rules of life, physics, and reality as everything else."

Throughout, Doty includes guided meditations and troubleshooting for challenges like ADHD or systemic barriers (e.g., racism), advocating an additive approach rather than blame.

🜨 Broader Implications

Mind Magic extends beyond individual gain, arguing that collective manifestation—through compassion and shared purpose—can heal societal divides. Doty critiques "toxic positivity" and entitlement mindsets, emphasizing humility and realism: The universe doesn't conspire for you, but your trained mind can navigate it effectively. Quotes like "Between stimulus and response there is a space. In that space is our power to choose our response" (echoing Viktor Frankl) reinforce empowerment.

Ultimately, Doty's work is a call to action: By mastering "mind magic," we not only realize goals and dreams but contribute to a more compassionate world. This neuroscience-driven guide equips readers with tools to transform intention into reality, proving that true power lies within.

Breathing Techniques to Enhance Neuroplasticity: A Comprehensive Summary

☯ Introduction to Neuroplasticity and the Role of Breathing

Neuroplasticity refers to the brain's remarkable ability to reorganize itself by forming new neural connections throughout life. This process allows the brain to adapt to new experiences, recover from injuries, and improve cognitive functions such as memory, focus, and emotional regulation. While factors like exercise, learning, and sleep are well-known contributors to neuroplasticity, emerging research highlights the profound impact of breathing techniques. These practices, rooted in ancient traditions like yoga and modern neuroscience, influence the autonomic nervous system, brain oxygenation, and stress responses, creating an optimal environment for neural rewiring.

Breathing is more than a basic physiological function; it directly affects brain function through mechanisms such as vagus nerve stimulation and modulation of brain waves. Slow and controlled breathing can increase levels of brain-derived neurotrophic factor (BDNF), a protein essential for neuron growth and survival, thereby promoting neurogenesis in areas like the hippocampus. Additionally, these techniques reduce cortisol levels, mitigating chronic stress that otherwise hinders neuroplasticity. By activating the parasympathetic nervous system, breathing practices foster a state of calm that enhances the brain's adaptability. This summary explores key breathing techniques, their scientific underpinnings, benefits for neuroplasticity, and practical applications, drawing from recent studies and expert insights.

The connection between breath and brain plasticity is supported by systematic reviews showing that slow breathing enhances autonomic, cerebral, and psychological flexibility. For instance, practices that slow respiration to fewer than 10 breaths per minute improve heart rate variability (HRV), a marker of autonomic balance, which correlates with better emotional resilience and cognitive performance. As we delve deeper, it becomes clear that incorporating breathwork into daily routines can be a simple yet powerful tool for brain health.

🌑 Key Breathing Techniques and Their Mechanisms

Several breathing techniques have been studied for their ability to enhance neuroplasticity. These methods vary in complexity but share common goals: regulating oxygen flow, stimulating neural pathways, and reducing stress.

One foundational technique is **diaphragmatic breathing**, also known as belly breathing. This involves inhaling deeply through the nose, allowing the abdomen to expand while keeping the chest relatively still, followed by a slow exhale. This method increases oxygen delivery to the brain, supporting cellular metabolism and reducing oxidative stress. By engaging the diaphragm, it activates the vagus nerve, promoting parasympathetic dominance and lowering inflammation that could impair nerve regeneration. Studies indicate that regular diaphragmatic breathing can increase gray matter volume in brain regions responsible for memory and executive function, directly aiding neuroplasticity.

Another effective practice is **box breathing**, popularized in stress management protocols. It consists of inhaling for four seconds, holding the breath for four seconds, exhaling for four seconds, and holding again for four seconds. This rhythmic pattern helps synchronize brain waves, increasing alpha wave activity associated with relaxation and learning. Box breathing is particularly useful for improving focus and reducing anxiety, as it shifts the autonomic nervous system toward calm, creating a fertile ground for neural adaptations. Research from neuroscience labs suggests it enhances attentional control by building neural pathways for self-regulation.

The **4-7-8 breathing** technique, developed by Dr. Andrew Weil, involves inhaling for four seconds, holding for seven, and exhaling for eight. This extends the exhale phase, which boosts dopamine production and modulates the hypothalamic-pituitary-adrenal (HPA) axis to reduce stress reactivity. Prolonged exhalation promotes myelination—the insulation of neural pathways—optimizing communication between brain regions and supporting long-term plasticity. It's especially beneficial for emotional balance, as it increases awareness of unconscious stress patterns, allowing for rewiring of habitual responses.

Alternate nostril breathing (Nadi Shodhana in yoga) alternates inhalation and exhalation between nostrils, synchronizing the brain's hemispheres. This technique enhances neurointegration, improving problem-solving and creativity by fostering bilateral brain activity. It stimulates the vagus nerve and increases BDNF, linking directly to neurogenesis and resilience against stress.

More advanced methods include **physiological sighs** and **cyclic hyperventilation**. The physiological sigh—a double inhale followed by a long exhale—rapidly reduces stress by offloading carbon dioxide and shifting to parasympathetic states. Cyclic hyperventilation, involving 25 deep breaths, releases adrenaline for heightened alertness, which can prime the brain for focused learning and adaptation. Pranayama variants like Bhastrika (bellows breath) and Kapalabhati (breath of fire) energize the system, increasing oxygen intake and supporting cognitive vitality.

These techniques work through shared mechanisms: vagus nerve activation, which carries signals from body to brain influencing emotion; increased HRV for autonomic flexibility; and modulation of brain oscillations, such as alpha and theta waves, for better synchronization. Slow breathing, in particular, entrains hippocampal rhythms, potentially linking to memory enhancement and neuroplastic changes.

❂ Scientific Evidence and Benefits for Neuroplasticity

The scientific backing for breathing's role in neuroplasticity is robust, drawn from EEG, fMRI, and systematic reviews. A key review on slow breathing practices demonstrates enhancements in cerebral flexibility, with increased activity in prefrontal and parietal cortices, areas crucial for executive function and attention. These changes correlate with psychological benefits like reduced depression and improved vigor, suggesting breathwork fosters an adaptive brain state.

Neuroimaging shows that breathwork increases BDNF, promoting neural growth and connectivity. For example, deep breathing oxygenates the hippocampus, stimulating new neuron birth and modulating stress via the HPA axis. This is vital for combating age-related cognitive decline, as aerobic-like effects from breathwork trigger growth factors similar to exercise.

Benefits extend to mental health: breathwork reduces anxiety (effect size g = -0.32) and depressive symptoms (g = -0.40), creating space for positive neural rewiring. It improves focus by decreasing distractibility and enhances emotional resilience through better self-regulation. Long-term practitioners exhibit structural brain changes, such as increased gray matter in memory-related areas.

Respiratory training may directly enhance neuroplasticity by modulating neural oscillations and interoception—the awareness of internal states—which strengthens connections in the default mode network. Studies on yoga breathing, like Sudarshan Kriya, show significant symptom improvements in depression over eight weeks, linked to serotonergic system activation. Overall, these practices counter chronic stress, a major barrier to plasticity, by lowering cortisol and inflammation.

❂ Practical Applications

Incorporating breathing techniques into daily life is accessible and requires no equipment. Beginners can start with 5-10 minutes of diaphragmatic or box breathing, ideally in a quiet space, to build consistency. For focus enhancement, use cyclic hyperventilation before tasks; for stress relief, opt for physiological sighs during high-tension moments. Combining breathwork with mindfulness or movement amplifies effects, as seen in integrated practices that sync breath with bilateral exercises for hemisphere balance.

In therapeutic settings, breathwork is scalable for groups, aiding anxiety and depression management. It's particularly useful for aging populations to maintain cognitive fitness, complementing exercise by releasing growth factors. However, consult professionals if dealing with respiratory issues.

It is becoming more and more evident that breathing techniques offer a potent, evidence-based approach to enhancing neuroplasticity. By improving oxygenation, reducing stress, and stimulating neural growth, they empower individuals to rewire their brains for better health and performance. Regular practice not only boosts immediate well-being but fosters lasting adaptability in an ever-changing world. As research evolves, breathwork stands as a bridge between ancient **wisdom and modern neuroscience, unlocking the brain's full potential.**

Chapter 23: The Role of Ritual in Daily Life

A single lit candle can embody your intention. It holds the flame of your awareness, shedding light on the path from moment to moment.

Introduction and Historical Context

Zen Buddhism, with its roots stretching back through Chinese Chan to Indian Mahayana traditions, has gained worldwide recognition for its emphasis on meditation (zazen) and direct, experiential insight into the nature of reality. While Zen's philosophy is often understood in the West as primarily focused on silent meditation and mindfulness, ritual holds a significant place in Zen practice, providing structure, meaning, and community cohesion. These rituals, ranging from the seemingly simple act of bowing to the more elaborate tea ceremonies, are deeply intertwined with Zen's core teachings on non-duality, compassion, and awareness of the present moment.

Historically, Zen emerged in China as Chan Buddhism in the 6th century CE, attributed traditionally to the Indian monk Bodhidharma. Over the centuries, Chan evolved distinctive methods of practice that focused on direct insight, often through meditation and the use of gōng'àn (kōan in Japanese). As Chan spread to Japan and became Zen, it integrated Japanese cultural, aesthetic, and social elements. This fusion gave rise to specific forms of ritual, many of which remain in practice today. Modern-day Zen, while often streamlined in its Western manifestations, retains many of these traditional rituals because they offer valuable support for cultivating mindfulness, compassion, and the Zen ideal of "every-moment practice."

Zen rituals are not rote performances or dogmatic requirements. Instead, they function as anchors for attention—opportunities to engage the body, mind, and spirit with presence. By making mundane tasks into intentional, graceful acts, Zen practitioners learn to see how meditation can be extended beyond the zendo (meditation hall) into everyday routines. Over the following pages, we will explore how these rituals function, the meanings behind them, and the ways in which they shape daily life for Zen practitioners.

Defining Ritual in Zen Context

In many Western contexts, the term "ritual" carries associations of dogmatism or empty repetition. From a Zen perspective, however, ritual is seen as a cohesive and mindful activity that transcends mere formality. Zen teacher Shunryu Suzuki famously observed that the essence of Zen is found in "things as they are," free from conceptual overlays. Rituals, in this sense, are vehicles for seeing reality directly, as they encourage participants to be fully present in each action.

Zen rituals often include chanting, bowing, incense-offering, communal meals, tea ceremonies, and prostrations. Each action is deliberate, focused, and performed with the intent of awakening to the present moment. Though outwardly it can look like a series of prescribed motions, the inward experience is one of heightened awareness. The external structure of a ritual offers a container within which practitioners can drop into a deeper state of mindfulness.

One central aspect of Zen ritual is the principle of "form is emptiness, emptiness is form," drawn from the Prajñāpāramitā Heart Sūtra. When we engage in ritual, we acknowledge both its formal, structured aspects ("form") and the insight that these actions point beyond themselves to a fundamental emptiness or interdependence. The bowing, chanting, or tea serving are not "holy" in and of themselves. Rather, they become occasions to see the sacred in the ordinary. By diligently following these forms, practitioners gradually recognize that reality is fluid and interconnected, inseparable from our own nature. Thus, ritual in Zen, far from being mere symbolism, becomes a profound practice of realizing non-duality.

Zen Ritual and the Body-Mind Connection

One of the core teachings of Zen is that the body and mind are not two separate entities but manifestations of the same reality. This insight is especially apparent in the realm of ritual. Zen ceremonies and daily observances often emphasize the physical body—sitting, walking, bowing, pouring tea—in ways that cultivate an embodied awareness.

For instance, the ritual of bowing is a hallmark of many Zen communities. Practitioners bow when entering the zendo, when greeting teachers, and during services. The physical gesture of bowing helps cultivate humility and gratitude, grounding practitioners in the reality that they stand in connection with all beings. In dropping the head below the heart, one symbolically relinquishes ego-centered concerns and reaffirms an attitude of respect. While the practice might initially feel awkward or forced, over time, the consistent act of bowing helps integrate the Zen teachings into one's physical being, making the principle of humility a lived, rather than merely intellectual, experience.

Similarly, walking meditation (kinhin) is a structured ritual that draws attention to each step and the breath. Practitioners move slowly and deliberately around the meditation hall, synchronizing footfalls with a calm, steady breath. In this way, the simple act of walking becomes a powerful vehicle for mindfulness, bringing the body and mind into harmonious focus. This ritual underscores the fact that Zen meditation is not confined to sitting still but can be practiced in any activity—so long as the practitioner pays careful, caring attention.

Morning Rituals and Daily Life

Much of Zen practice revolves around incorporating rituals into daily life, starting first thing in the morning. In many Zen monasteries and communities, practitioners rise before dawn to engage in zazen (sitting meditation) or chanting. These early morning hours, often referred to as "the noble silence," set the tone for the day. Even lay practitioners who live outside the monastery may adopt a scaled-down version of these morning rituals at home.

Upon waking, a Zen practitioner might begin the day with a brief bow and a moment of gratitude. Some recite the Gatha of Atonement or the Four Bodhisattva Vows. These short verses remind practitioners of their intention to do no harm, to practice kindness, and to continue learning. The ritual of breakfast might then be approached as a continuation of mindfulness. Each spoonful of oatmeal or sip of tea is accompanied by awareness—awareness of the taste, the texture, the warmth, and the fact that countless beings and conditions made this meal possible.

Even mundane tasks such as brushing one's teeth, washing dishes, or dressing for work become mindful rituals in Zen practice. The key is to engage wholeheartedly, with no residue of the past and no anxious anticipation of the future. This complete absorption in the here-and-now gradually transforms routines that might otherwise be done on autopilot into activities that deepen one's appreciation for life. In this way, Zen ritual merges seamlessly with the demands of modern living, fostering a sense of calm and presence that carries into the rest of the day.

Chanting and Sacred Texts

Chanting occupies a special place in Zen communities and is often done in a call-and-response format or as a collective recitation. Common chants include the Heart Sūtra (Hannya Shingyō) and the Verse of the Kesa (the robe verse). The melodic repetition of these texts may seem mysterious to newcomers, especially if they are in Sino-Japanese or another liturgical language. Yet, the purpose of chanting is multifaceted.

First, chanting acts as a unifying force. When a group of practitioners chant in unison, a powerful collective energy arises. This shared vocal practice can create a sense of harmony and interconnection that transcends individual differences. Second, the repetitive nature of chanting serves as a mindfulness technique. Instead of letting the mind wander, one focuses on the sound, the rhythm, the breath, and the meaning (if understood) of the verses. Finally, chanting is a way of honoring the lineage and wisdom of Buddhist teachings. By reciting classical texts, practitioners connect with the centuries-old tradition of those who have walked the Zen path before them.

While chanting may appear more formal and ritualized than silent meditation, the essence remains the same: the cultivation of presence and insight. Just as zazen trains the mind to rest in the moment, chanting provides a vocal and communal means of doing so. Over time, practitioners often find that chanting resonates with them emotionally, opening the heart and reinforcing a sense of commitment to the path.

The Tea Ceremony (Chanoyu) as a Zen Ritual

Among the most well-known Zen-inspired rituals in Japanese culture is the tea ceremony (chanoyu or chadō). Although the tea ceremony is sometimes considered a separate art form, its roots are deeply interwoven with Zen philosophy. The formality of the tea room, the prescribed steps of preparing the matcha (powdered green tea), and the etiquette of serving and receiving tea all serve to cultivate a particular state of mind—one of awareness, humility, and respect.

The host, who performs the tea preparation, does so with precise, deliberate movements. Each gesture is intentional, whether wiping the tea bowl, whisking the tea, or folding the cloth. The guests, in turn, receive the tea with gratitude, bowing to acknowledge the host's care and the collective moment of sharing. Silent harmony infuses the ceremony, and the flick of the wrist or gentle placement of the tea bowl becomes a meditation in motion.

From a Zen perspective, the tea ceremony is a microcosm of life itself. The process demands that each participant be fully present, responsive to subtle cues, and respectful of the shared space. The ritual exemplifies the famous Zen saying, "When drinking tea, just drink tea." No part of the ceremony is rushed or done haphazardly. This meticulous attention to detail underscores the fundamental Zen teaching that enlightenment (satori) is not separate from ordinary activities but can be realized in the midst of them.

Sesshin and Intensive Ritual Practice

Another notable dimension of Zen ritual is the sesshin—an intensive meditation retreat that typically spans several days or even a week. The word sesshin literally means "to touch the heart-mind." During this period, practitioners devote themselves almost exclusively to zazen, kinhin (walking meditation), dharma talks, and silent meals. The daily schedule is rigorous and highly structured, often beginning well before dawn and ending late in the evening.

Within sesshin, every aspect of the schedule becomes ritualized. Even the cleaning of the zendo and the preparation of meals are done in a mindful, silent manner. Chores become "work practice" (samu), another extension of meditation. Bowing before and after tasks, handling utensils carefully, and offering silent gratitude before meals are all rituals that help transform seemingly mundane activities into opportunities for heightened awareness.

For many practitioners, sesshin is a transformative experience. The extended periods of silence and meditation can bring deep insights, emotional releases, and a sharpened sense of presence. Ritual acts, performed consistently day after day, serve as touchstones that ground the practitioner in the shared atmosphere of devotion. Over the course of a sesshin, participants often discover that the line between formal ritual and everyday movement blurs, revealing that any activity can be an expression of the Way when undertaken with full awareness.

Bowing, Prostrations, and Their Symbolism

Bowing and prostrations (touching the forearms, knees, and forehead to the ground) are common in Zen, though their specifics can vary among lineages and cultures. In many Zen centers, practitioners offer a series of three prostrations at the beginning or end of services, often dedicated to the Three Treasures: Buddha (the awakened nature in all beings), Dharma (the teachings), and Sangha (the community).

At face value, these bows and prostrations might appear subservient or even antiquated. However, in Zen, they are considered acts of reverence and humility rather than deference to a deity. They symbolically acknowledge that no one stands above or below another, and that all beings are interconnected in the shared pursuit of awakening. As the practitioner bows, they let go of self-centered thoughts and attitudes, affirming a willingness to learn from teachers, fellow practitioners, and life itself.

Furthermore, prostrations can be a potent exercise in cultivating gratitude. By lowering one's body to the earth, the practitioner recognizes the infinite conditions—ancestors, teachers, and the natural world—that have allowed for this moment of practice. This sense of gratitude permeates into daily interactions, helping to counterbalance the often isolating tendencies of modern individualism. In the end, the ritual of bowing is not about idolizing images or persons; it is about recognizing the inherent dignity and shared interdependence of all life.

Integrating Ritual into Modern Life

One of the ongoing questions for contemporary Zen practitioners—especially those not living in monastic settings—is how to integrate formal rituals into busy, modern schedules. Many find that setting aside brief moments during the day for ritualistic mindfulness can have a profound impact. This might involve lighting incense and reciting a short verse before starting work, or simply pausing to take three conscious breaths every hour.

Technology, often blamed for distraction, can be harnessed in the service of Zen rituals. For instance, a simple phone app can remind practitioners to stand, stretch, and take a mindful breath periodically. Some people use wearable devices that vibrate at set intervals, prompting them to check in with their posture or mental state. In this way, daily life—replete with emails, meetings, and errands—can be woven into the fabric of practice.

Moreover, many Zen centers offer shorter, more accessible rituals for lay practitioners, such as half-day retreats, online sittings, and chanting sessions via video conferencing. Even if one cannot attend a full sesshin or maintain an elaborate morning liturgy, these micro-rituals can help sustain a sense of connection and presence. Ultimately, the goal is not to add more stress to an already full schedule but to find meaningful ways to bring Zen awareness into the heart of one's everyday routine.

Ritual as a Bridge to Awakening

Zen, at its core, points to the immediate experience of reality as it is, unclouded by concepts, judgments, and ego attachments. Ritual, far from being an obstacle or an unnecessary formality, serves as a powerful bridge between lofty teachings and actual, embodied practice. From the rhythmic chanting in the zendo to the quiet intimacy of the tea ceremony, these structured, time-honored activities ground practitioners in the present moment, remind them of their interconnectedness with all beings, and encourage humility and gratitude.

In daily life, Zen rituals become touchstones that bring mindfulness to ordinary activities—waking, eating, working, and resting. Rather than confining spiritual practice to a meditation cushion, ritual helps permeate every corner of experience with awareness. Bowing ceases to be merely a ceremonial gesture and becomes a way to soften the ego. Chanting is not just about reciting ancient words but about harmonizing one's energy with a community. The tea ceremony is not a matter of etiquette alone but a poignant lesson in simplicity and presence. Through repeated engagement with these rituals, Zen practitioners learn that each moment contains the possibility of awakening.

In a world increasingly characterized by distraction and fragmentation, the role of Zen ritual in daily life is more relevant than ever. Whether in a monastery, a city apartment, or an online community, these practices serve as a reminder that awakening is not somewhere "out there"; it is available in the quiet wonder of pouring tea, the gentle bow to a fellow being, or the steady hum of breath during seated meditation. The forms may vary from culture to culture and from one lineage to another, but the essential purpose remains: to illuminate the sacredness of each moment and to live in a way that reflects our deepest understanding of interconnectedness and compassion. Through ritual, Zen teaches us that enlightenment is not a distant goal but a continuous unfolding available here and now, in the heart of our daily lives.

Chapter 24: 5 AM Club

The 5 AM Club by Robin Sharma is a self-help book presented as a fictional narrative, blending motivational insights with practical strategies for personal and professional success. The story follows an entrepreneur, an artist, and a tycoon who, under the guidance of a mysterious mentor called the Spellbinder, learn the transformative power of waking up at 5 AM and adopting a structured morning routine. Through their journey, Sharma introduces the 5 AM Club philosophy, emphasizing how early mornings can unlock creativity, productivity, and personal growth. Below is a 10-page summary of the key themes, concepts, and actionable advice from the book.

 ## The Power of Early Mornings

The book opens with the idea that waking up at 5 AM offers a unique opportunity to start the day with intention and focus, before the distractions of the world take over. Sharma argues that the early morning hours are a "Victory Hour" where one can cultivate habits that lead to extraordinary results. The narrative introduces the main characters—an entrepreneur struggling with her business, an artist facing creative blocks, and a billionaire mentor who embodies the principles of *The 5 AM Club*. The mentor explains that owning the morning sets the tone for the rest of the day, providing clarity and energy. Sharma emphasizes that early rising is not just about waking up early but about using that time purposefully to align with one's highest goals.

The 20/20/20 Formula

A cornerstone of *The 5 AM Club* is the 20/20/20 formula, a structured morning routine to maximize the Victory Hour (5:00–6:00 AM). The formula divides the hour into three 20-minute segments:

- **Move (20 minutes):** Engage in physical exercise to boost energy, release endorphins, and enhance mental clarity. This could include running, yoga, or strength training.
- **Reflect (20 minutes):** Spend time journaling, meditating, or planning to gain clarity on goals and values. Reflection fosters self-awareness and emotional resilience.
- **Grow (20 minutes):** Dedicate time to learning, such as reading, studying, or reviewing goals, to stimulate intellectual growth and personal development. This formula is designed to optimize physical, mental, and emotional states, setting a strong foundation for the day.

The Four Interior Empires

Sharma introduces the concept of the "Four Interior Empires:" Mindset, Heartset, Healthset, and Soulset—which represent the core areas of personal growth. *The 5 AM Club* routine is designed to nurture all four:

- **Mindset:** Cultivate positive thinking, focus, and mental discipline through reflection and learning.
- **Heartset:** Build emotional strength by processing feelings, practicing gratitude, and fostering optimism.
- **Healthset:** Prioritize physical health through exercise and nutrition to sustain energy and longevity.
- **Soulset:** Connect with one's purpose and inner peace through meditation and spiritual practices. Balancing these empires ensures holistic development, aligning one's inner world with external success.

 ### The Habit Installation Protocol

To make the 5 AM routine a lasting habit, Sharma outlines the Habit Installation Protocol, a 66-day process to ingrain new behaviors. This is based on the idea that habits require consistent effort to become automatic. The protocol consists of three phases:

- **Destruction (Days 1–22):** Break old patterns and push through initial discomfort as you adopt the new routine.
- **Installation (Days 23–44):** Build the habit through repetition, even when motivation wanes.
- **Integration (Days 45–66):** The habit becomes part of your identity, requiring less conscious effort. Sharma stresses the importance of persistence, noting that small, consistent actions lead to significant transformation over time.

 ### The Science of Early Rising

The book delves into the science behind waking up early, citing research on circadian rhythms, cortisol levels, and dopamine production. Sharma explains that early mornings align with the body's natural rhythms, as cortisol (the stress hormone that aids alertness) peaks shortly after waking. By rising at 5 AM, you capitalize on this natural boost, enhancing focus and productivity. Additionally, the quiet of the early morning minimizes distractions, allowing for deep work and creativity. The mentor in the story shares how successful people, from historical figures to modern leaders, have leveraged early mornings to achieve greatness.

The Twin Cycles of Elite Performance

Sharma introduces the Twin Cycles of Elite Performance: High Excellence Cycles (HEC) and Deep Recovery Cycles (DRC). The 5 AM routine is a key part of the HEC, where intense focus and productivity occur during the early morning. However, to sustain high performance, one must balance HEC with DRC—periods of rest and recovery. This includes practices like napping, spending time in nature, or disconnecting from technology. The book emphasizes that overworking without recovery leads to burnout, while strategic rest enhances creativity and resilience.

The Four Focuses of History Makers

The mentor teaches the characters the Four Focuses of History Makers, which are essential for achieving extraordinary results:

- o *Capitalization:* Invest in your personal growth and skills rather than relying solely on natural talent.
- o *Freedom from Distraction:* Eliminate distractions like social media and multitasking to maintain focus on high-value tasks.
- o *Personal Mastery Practice:* Continuously refine your inner world (mindset, heartset, healthset, soulset) to perform at your best.
- o *Day Stacking:* Build each day with small, consistent actions that compound over time to create massive results. These focuses encourage a disciplined, intentional approach to life and work.

The 10 Tactics of Lifelong Genius

Sharma provides 10 practical tactics to sustain *The 5 AM Club* lifestyle and achieve lifelong success:

1. *The Tight Bubble of Total Focus (TBTF):* Create an environment free of distractions to do deep work.
2. *The 90/90/1 Rule:* Spend the first 90 minutes of your workday on your most important project for 90 days.
3. *The 60/10 Method:* Work intensely for 60 minutes, then take a 10-minute break to recover.
4. *The Daily 5 Concept:* Accomplish five small but meaningful tasks each day to build momentum.
5. *The Second Wind Workout:* Schedule a second workout later in the day to boost energy.
6. *The 2 Massage Protocol:* Get two massages per week to reduce stress and enhance recovery.
7. *Traffic University:* Use commuting time to learn through audiobooks or podcasts.

8. *The Dream Team Technique:* Surround yourself with inspiring, high-performing people.
9. *The Weekly Design System*: Plan your week in advance to align with your goals.
10. *The 60-Minute Student:* Dedicate at least 60 minutes daily to learning and growth. These tactics provide a roadmap for sustained productivity and personal development.

 ## Overcoming Resistance and Excuses

The book addresses common barriers to adopting *The 5 AM Club*, such as fatigue, lack of motivation, or skepticism about its effectiveness. Sharma encourages readers to reframe resistance as an opportunity for growth. For example, feeling tired is a sign to improve sleep hygiene, not an excuse to skip the routine. The mentor advises the characters to start small, perhaps waking up at 6 AM and gradually moving to 5 AM, to ease into the habit. The narrative also highlights the importance of self-compassion, acknowledging that setbacks are part of the process but should not derail long-term commitment.

 ## The Ripple Effect and Legacy

The book concludes with the idea that *The 5 AM Club* is not just about personal success but about creating a ripple effect that inspires others. By mastering their mornings, the characters transform their lives—the entrepreneur revitalizes her business, the artist rediscovers his creativity, and the tycoon deepens his impact. Sharma emphasizes that small daily improvements lead to a legacy of excellence, influencing others to live with purpose and discipline. The book ends with a call to action: embrace *The 5 AM Club* to unlock your potential and contribute to a better world.

 ## Key Takeaways

- Waking up at 5 AM and following the 20/20/20 formula (Move, Reflect, Grow) sets the stage for a productive day.
- The Four Interior Empires (Mindset, Heartset, Healthset, Soulset) are critical for holistic growth.
- Building habits through the 66-day Habit Installation Protocol ensures lasting change.
- Balancing High Excellence Cycles with Deep Recovery Cycles prevents burnout.
- The 10 Tactics of Lifelong Genius provide practical tools for sustained success.
- Overcoming resistance and starting small are key to adopting *The 5 AM Club* lifestyle.

- Personal transformation creates a ripple effect, inspiring others and building a meaningful legacy.

This book distills an instant lifestyle change that rewards with immediate impact and lasting multiplicative results.

Chapter 25: Fasting Methods and Benefits

⑥ Introduction

Fasting, the deliberate abstinence from food and sometimes drink for a defined period, has been practiced for centuries across cultures for spiritual, health, and therapeutic reasons. From ancient religious rituals to modern wellness trends, fasting has evolved into a scientifically studied approach to improving metabolic health, longevity, and overall well-being. In recent years, particularly as of 2025, research has illuminated its potential to combat chronic diseases like diabetes, heart disease, and even age-related decline, while highlighting various methods tailored to different lifestyles and goals. This summary explores the primary methods of fasting, their implementation, and the evidence-based benefits, drawing from clinical studies, expert guidelines, and systematic reviews. While fasting offers promising advantages, it is not a one-size-fits-all solution and requires careful consideration of individual health factors. Over the following sections, we delve into practical methods, substantiated benefits, potential risks, and tips for safe practice, aiming to provide a thorough resource equivalent to a 10-page overview (approximately 4,000-5,000 words in standard formatting).

Fasting differs from starvation by being voluntary, time-bound, and nutritionally planned. During fasting windows, the body shifts from glucose-dependent energy to fat-burning (ketosis), triggering processes like autophagy—cellular "self-cleaning" that removes damaged components and promotes repair. Modern interest surged with intermittent fasting (IF), popularized by researchers like Dr. Valter Longo and Dr. Jason Fung, whose works emphasize its role in mimicking caloric restriction without constant deprivation. As of October 2025, ongoing trials, including those from MIT and Harvard, continue to refine our understanding, balancing benefits against emerging risks like potential cardiovascular concerns in specific protocols. This guide equips readers with the knowledge to explore fasting thoughtfully.

⑥ Methods of Fasting: Types and Implementation

Fasting methods vary in duration, frequency, and intensity, allowing customization based on experience level, health goals, and schedule. Below, we outline the most common approaches, including rules, timelines, and practical tips, synthesized from expert guides. Beginners should start with shorter fasts and consult a healthcare provider, especially if managing conditions like diabetes or pregnancy.

1. Time-Restricted Eating (TRE): Daily Windows

Time-restricted eating limits food intake to a specific daily window, aligning with natural circadian rhythms for simplicity and sustainability.

- **12-Hour Fast**: Fast for 12 hours overnight (e.g., dinner at 7 p.m., breakfast at 7 a.m.). This mimics natural overnight fasting and requires no calorie cuts during eating hours. Ideal for novices, it promotes fat utilization via ketone release, supporting mild weight loss without disruption. Preparation: Gradually shift meals earlier; track with apps like Zero.
- **16:8 Method (Leangains)**: Fast 16 hours, eat within 8 (e.g., noon to 8 p.m.). Women may begin with 14:10 to ease adaptation. Focus on nutrient-dense meals: proteins, veggies, healthy fats. Benefits include improved insulin sensitivity; a 2025 meta-analysis confirmed 3-8% body weight reduction over 8-12 weeks. Tip: Hydrate with water, black coffee, or tea; avoid artificial sweeteners to preserve ketosis.
- **18:6 or 20:4 (Warrior Diet)**: Extend to 18-20 hours fasting, with a 6-4 hour window for one large evening meal. Include raw fruits/veggies during fast if needed. This emulates ancestral patterns but risks nutrient gaps; supplement electrolytes to combat fatigue.

2. Periodic or Alternate-Day Fasting: Weekly Cycles

These involve full or partial fast days, spaced for recovery.

- **5:2 Diet**: Eat normally five days; restrict to 500-600 calories on two non-consecutive days (e.g., veggies, lean proteins). A 2025 review showed sustained weight loss (4-7% over six months) when paired with support groups. Implementation: Plan "fast" days mid-week; break with broth to ease digestion.
- **Alternate-Day Fasting (ADF)**: Fast every other day (0-500 calories) or fully abstain. Non-fast days allow ad libitum eating. Effective for rapid fat loss but challenging; studies indicate 5-10% weight drop in 3-12 weeks, though adherence wanes long-term. Safety: Monitor for irritability; start with modified versions.
- **Eat-Stop-Eat (24-Hour Fast)**: Complete 24-hour fasts 1-2 times weekly (e.g., dinner to dinner). Allows zero calories; resume normally after. Triggers autophagy peaks around 24 hours, aiding repair. Tip: Use for "reset" days; follow with light meals.

3. Extended Fasts: Multi-Day Protocols

For advanced users, these induce deeper metabolic shifts but demand supervision.

- **36-48 Hour Water Fast**: Consume only water, tea, or black coffee. Growth hormone surges 5-10x by 48 hours, enhancing fat metabolism and insulin reset. A 2025 Nature study on 8-day water fasts showed profound changes in glucose, IGF-1, and leptin, outperforming exercise for metabolic tweaks.
- **3-5 Day Fast**: Supervised water or broth fasts boost neurogenesis via BDNF. Valter Longo's 5-day Fasting Mimicking Diet (FMD)—low-calorie plant-based meals—mimics benefits without full abstinence, reducing inflammation and aging markers in trials. Preparation: One-week anti-inflammatory diet (no sugar, processed foods).
- **Fasting Mimicking Diet (FMD)**: 5 days of 800-1,100 calories (nuts, veggies, soups). Repeats monthly; clinical data from 2025 supports disease prevention, with 2-3% body fat loss per cycle.

Method	Duration/Frequency	Best For	Key Tip
12-Hour Fast	Daily, 12 hrs	Beginners	Align with sleep
16:8	Daily, 16 hrs fast	Weight management	Nutrient-dense windows
5:2	2 days/week, 500 cal	Flexibility	Non-consecutive days
ADF	Every other day	Rapid results	Modified calories
24-Hour	1-2x/week	Autophagy	Hydrate heavily
36-48 Hour	Occasional	Metabolic reset	Medical oversight
FMD	5 days/month	Longevity	Plant-based focus

Preparation for any method: Eliminate inflammatory foods a week prior, hydrate (2-3L water/day), and track progress. Breaking fasts: Start with bone broth or smoothies to avoid refeeding issues.

Benefits of Fasting: Evidence-Based Insights

Fasting's benefits span metabolic, cellular, and systemic levels, backed by randomized trials and meta-analyses up to 2025. While individual responses vary, population studies show consistent gains, often rivaling or exceeding traditional diets. We categorize them below, with scientific substantiation.

Metabolic and Weight Management Benefits

Fasting excels in calorie reduction without tracking, promoting sustainable loss.

- **Weight and Fat Loss**: Reduces intake by 200-500 calories/day, yielding 3-9% body weight drop in 3-24 weeks. A 2025 systematic review of RCTs confirmed IF's superiority for visceral fat reduction vs. continuous restriction. Harvard studies link 16:8 to half-pound weekly loss via ghrelin suppression.

- 🕯 **Blood Sugar and Insulin Control**: Lowers resistance by 20-31%, stabilizing glucose and reducing type 2 diabetes risk. Peterson's 2018 trial (cited 1,600+ times) showed pre-diabetics normalizing levels with early TRE; 2025 updates affirm this in diverse cohorts.
- 🕯 **Lipid Profile Improvement**: Decreases triglycerides (20-30%), LDL, and total cholesterol while raising HDL. ADF trials report heart-protective shifts, per Mayo Clinic reviews.

Cellular and Anti-Aging Effects

Fasting activates repair mechanisms, extending healthspan.

- 🕯 **Autophagy and Cellular Repair**: Post-13-16 hours, cells recycle damaged parts, reducing oxidative stress (linked to cancer/heart disease). MIT's 2024 mouse study showed enhanced stem cell regeneration, though human translation is emerging.
- 🕯 **Longevity and Aging Biomarkers**: Boosts sirtuins and gut microbiome diversity; animal models extend lifespan 10-30%. Longo's 5-day FMD trials (2025) slowed aging in humans via IGF-1 reduction.
- 🕯 **Growth Hormone Surge**: Increases HGH 5-10x, aiding muscle preservation and metabolism. 37.5-hour fasts triple concentrations, per endocrine studies.

Cardiovascular and Inflammatory Benefits

- **Blood Pressure Reduction**: Drops systolic by 4-7 mmHg; Peterson's work attributes this to fasting duration over weight loss alone. 2025 BBC reports link overnight extension to metabolic repair.
- **Anti-Inflammatory Effects**: Lowers C-reactive protein by 20-40%; combined with exercise, combats arthritis and neurodegeneration.

Neurological and Oncological Potential

- 🕯 **Brain Health**: Enhances BDNF for neuron growth, potentially preventing Alzheimer's/Parkinson's. Ketones provide efficient brain fuel; rodent studies show cognitive boosts.
- 🕯 **Cancer Support**: Slows tumor growth via reduced IGF-1; enhances chemo efficacy in preclinical data. A 2025 Nature article highlights IF's role in fending off cancer alongside cognition gains.
- 🕯 **Hunger and Energy Regulation**: Stabilizes ghrelin, reducing evening cravings; users report sustained energy post-adaptation.

Benefit Category	Key Outcomes	Supporting Evidence (2024-2025)
Metabolic	3-9% weight loss, insulin sensitivity ↑	Meta-analysis of RCTs
Cellular	Autophagy activation, longevity ↑	Longo FMD trials
Cardiovascular	BP ↓ 4-7 mmHg, lipids improved	Peterson RCTs
Neurological	BDNF ↑, cognition enhanced	Animal/human studies

These benefits accrue cumulatively; a 2025 Hopkins overview notes organ protection against chronic ills.

⑥ Risks, Considerations, and Safety Guidelines

Despite benefits, fasting isn't risk-free. Short-term side effects include hunger, fatigue, headaches, and mood swings, often resolving in 1-2 weeks. A 2024 MIT study revealed refeeding post-fast heightens intestinal cancer risk in mice, underscoring moderation. Observational 2025 data links 16:8 to 91% higher cardiovascular mortality vs. moderate TRE, though causation is unproven.

Contraindications: Avoid if pregnant, underweight, eating-disordered, or with gout/diabetes without supervision. Menstrual disruptions or bone loss risks exist for some women. Always: Hydrate, electrolyte-balance, and monitor via apps. Consult providers; integrate with balanced nutrition.

Fasting's methods—from gentle 12-hour TRE to potent FMD—offer versatile paths to metabolic harmony, weight control, and cellular vitality, substantiated by robust 2025 evidence. Benefits like reduced inflammation, enhanced longevity, and disease prevention position it as a powerful tool, yet safety demands personalization. Start small, listen to your body, and view fasting as a lifestyle ally, not a fad. For deeper dives, explore resources like *The Complete Guide to Fasting* or clinical trials at NIH. Embrace it mindfully for enduring health gains.

Chapter 26: Minimalism as a Path to Freedom

An uncluttered room mirrors an uncluttered mind: each object purposeful, each moment precious.

❋ Introduction and Historical Roots

Minimalism has become something of a buzzword in recent years, used to describe everything from interior design trends to smartphone apps that promise to streamline your schedule. At its core, however, minimalism is far more than a simple aesthetic or life-hack; it is a deliberate choice to strip away excess and focus on what truly matters. Beyond decluttering closets or scaling back commitments, minimalism has emerged as a genuine lifestyle philosophy—one that offers a path to freedom from the stresses and constraints of modern living. This freedom can manifest itself in multiple ways: freedom from material possessions, freedom from social pressures, freedom from mental clutter, and ultimately the freedom to live more authentically.

The roots of minimalism can be traced to several philosophical and religious traditions. The ancient Greek philosopher Diogenes famously lived in a large ceramic jar (or tub), owning almost nothing and openly questioning the values of a society that placed such high importance on wealth and belongings. He challenged Alexander the Great's power simply by asking the emperor not to block his sunlight. Similarly, early Christian ascetics sought spiritual purity by abandoning worldly possessions and living in solitude. In Buddhism, the Four Noble Truths and the practice of renunciation emphasize letting go of attachment in order to alleviate suffering and cultivate a peaceful mind.

From these philosophical and religious backgrounds, we can see that the desire to live more simply has existed throughout human history. Indeed, whenever societies have become overwhelmed by excess, there have been voices calling for a return to life's essentials. Minimalism, as we discuss it today, is a modern extension of these ancient calls for focus and restraint. By choosing minimalism, one engages in a deliberate questioning of cultural norms and personal priorities. It asks the individual to step away from the noise of consumerism and discover the calm center of a more intentional life.

Yet, minimalism is often misunderstood. Many believe it to be solely about rejecting possessions, living with bare white walls, or owning fewer than 100 objects. While reducing possessions is one aspect of the movement, minimalism's true power is in its capacity to liberate a person from the tyranny of "too much"— too much clutter, too many commitments, too much mental chatter. In essence, minimalism is about choosing clarity, consciousness, and purpose. It is about reorienting your life around the things, people, and experiences that align with your highest values.

❧ The Allure of Excess and the Rise of Modern Minimalism

To understand minimalism's appeal as a path to freedom, it is vital to examine its opposite: the culture of excess. In consumer-driven societies, we are continually bombarded with advertisements telling us that happiness lies just one purchase away. Over time, this messaging contributes to a collective notion that material acquisitions, status symbols, and endless productivity are the markers of success. We accumulate items, schedule activities, and chase achievements—often without pausing to consider whether any of these pursuits truly enrich our lives.

This relentless drive toward "more" can lead to cluttered homes, overburdened schedules, and high levels of stress and anxiety. We feel a constant sense of obligation to maintain or surpass certain standards set by advertising, social media, or even our peers. Ironically, the more we gather, the heavier our psychological and emotional burdens can become. Debt, disconnection from loved ones, and a pervasive sense of emptiness may result from placing too much value on endless consumption.

Against this backdrop, modern minimalism emerged as a countercultural response, urging individuals to reclaim agency in a world that sometimes seems to spin out of control. Popularized by figures like Leo Babauta (creator of the Zen Habits blog), Joshua Fields Millburn and Ryan Nicodemus (known as "The Minimalists"), and Marie Kondo (through her KonMari Method for decluttering), minimalism began to shift from a niche movement to a mainstream conversation. Through books, documentaries, and online platforms, they and others shared personal stories of how letting go of non-essentials led to greater peace, productivity, and happiness.

Crucially, these modern proponents do not solely focus on possessions. They incorporate discussions of emotional baggage, toxic relationships, digital overload, and the unseen stressors of everyday life. By attacking the problem on multiple fronts, modern minimalism positions itself not just as a cleaning exercise but as a lifestyle transformation. Minimalism becomes a filter through which one can pass every choice—be it about physical items, daily commitments, or social interactions—and in doing so, remove any element that does not serve genuine well-being.

❧ Core Principles of Minimalism

Before delving into how minimalism can offer freedom, it helps to articulate some of the key principles. While definitions may vary between teachers and practitioners, several themes consistently recur:

1. **Intentionality:** Perhaps the most crucial principle of minimalism is intentionality—making choices with a clear sense of purpose and alignment with personal values. This means questioning whether each item you own, each commitment on your calendar, and each relationship in your life contributes to your well-being or values.
2. **Simplicity:** Simplicity involves paring down to the essentials. This does not mean living in stark, joyless environments; rather, it is about creating space—physical, mental, and emotional—for what is truly important. When life is simpler, you reduce distractions, which can free up energy and attention for meaningful endeavors.
3. **Quality Over Quantity:** A minimalist might own fewer items, but each item is generally of higher quality, greater utility, or deeper personal significance. This principle extends beyond possessions to encompass experiences, relationships, and even hobbies.
4. **Mindfulness:** Minimalists strive to be present in their daily lives, acknowledging that mindless accumulation—of either objects or tasks—can overshadow what genuinely matters. Mindfulness also helps to cultivate gratitude for what one already has, diminishing the sense of lack that drives overconsumption.
5. **Sustainability and Social Responsibility:** Many minimalists link their reduced consumption habits to environmental and social considerations. Consuming less means a smaller carbon footprint, less waste, and potentially a more equitable distribution of resources.

These principles, when practiced consistently, create a framework that can guide an individual toward freedom—freedom from clutter, from needless spending, from relentless social demands, and from the inner turmoil that often accompanies an overly complicated life. By stripping away the superfluous, one can see more clearly the values and goals that are paramount.

🌸 Physical Minimalism and the Liberation of Space

One of the most recognizable aspects of minimalism is the process of simplifying one's living environment. In concrete terms, physical minimalism involves consciously evaluating each item in your home and deciding if it serves a useful or meaningful role in your life. This might mean tackling the overflowing closet that holds clothes you never wear, or going through kitchen cabinets jam-packed with gadgets you do not need. The process can be tedious, but the psychological and practical benefits are substantial.

First, a decluttered home often translates into a calmer state of mind. Messy surroundings can contribute to a feeling of chaos, making it harder to focus or relax. Conversely, a clean, orderly space offers room to breathe—both literally and metaphorically. The anxiety that often comes from a never-ending cycle of cleaning and organizing is reduced when you simply own fewer items.

Second, letting go of unused or unloved possessions can be surprisingly liberating. Often, we hold onto things out of guilt ("I spent so much money on this!") or out of fear ("What if I need this someday?"). By releasing these items, we release the negative emotional baggage they carry. We learn to trust our ability to adapt and thrive without the safety net of excess. This process fosters self-confidence and a newfound appreciation for what we do have.

Third, fewer possessions can lead to greater mobility and financial flexibility. For those who feel stifled by a houseful of stuff and the debt that often accompanies it, downsizing can open up new possibilities: traveling light, relocating more freely, or simply redirecting financial resources into experiences rather than objects. In this way, minimalism in the physical realm sets the stage for other freedoms—such as exploring new places or investing in personal development.

🦋 Emotional and Psychological Minimalism

While the decluttering of physical possessions is an important entry point, minimalism's real transformative power often lies in the emotional and psychological realms. We accumulate emotional baggage much like we collect trinkets, allowing past regrets, anxieties, and unhelpful self-talk to occupy space in our minds.

Minimalism can serve as a catalyst for mental clarity by encouraging the practice of conscious reflection and mindfulness. When you begin to question why you hold on to certain beliefs or resentments, you can start the process of letting them go. Here are a few pathways to emotional minimalism:

1. **Setting Healthy Boundaries:** Just as you might eliminate unnecessary objects from your home, you can also choose to release toxic relationships or social obligations that drain your energy. Minimizing emotional clutter means identifying people and situations that consistently cause stress or do not align with your values, and setting boundaries that preserve your mental well-being.
2. **Simplifying Goals and Priorities:** In a world that applauds multitasking and glorifies busyness, minimalism pushes back by suggesting you focus on fewer, deeply meaningful objectives. Rather than chasing every opportunity, minimalists strive to excel in a smaller number of pursuits that align with their passions and values.
3. **Practicing Mindfulness and Gratitude:** Simple daily habits—like a brief meditation session, journaling, or even a morning gratitude list—can drastically reduce the mental noise that clutters our minds. These practices help us appreciate the present moment and recognize how little we truly need to be content.

By actively decluttering your emotional life, you create room for genuine connections, productive passions, and a sense of inner calm. This newfound emotional space is a significant form of freedom, allowing you to respond to life's challenges more intentionally rather than reflexively.

🐾 Financial Freedom Through Minimalism

Another key dimension of minimalism is its impact on personal finances. The pressure to keep up with new trends—whether it's the latest phone upgrade, fashion label, or luxury vacation—can easily lead to debt and financial stress. Minimalism offers a stark alternative: spend intentionally on what truly matters to you and forgo the rest. In many cases, this shift can radically improve one's financial health.

Reduced Debt and Expenditures: By purchasing fewer items and resisting impulsive consumption, one can allocate more money toward savings, investments, or paying off existing debts. Financial freedom grows from a discipline of thoughtful spending, which is at the heart of minimalism.

Aligning Spending with Values: Minimalists often find that when they spend less on trivial purchases, they have more resources to direct toward experiences and causes that resonate deeply with their values—such as travel, education, personal growth, or philanthropic endeavors. This alignment can lead to greater life satisfaction and a sense of purpose.

Buffer Against Uncertainty: A frugal, minimalist approach to life also builds resilience. By living on less, you inherently develop a financial buffer that can help you navigate unexpected expenses or life changes (such as job loss, medical emergencies, or relocating). The freedom that comes from having a safety net cannot be overstated; it reduces anxiety and provides greater autonomy when making life decisions.

Financial freedom, fostered by mindful minimalism, translates into a broader sense of personal empowerment. Suddenly, taking a passion-based career break, going back to school, or launching a small business all become more feasible. This expansive sense of possibility is one of the most tangible ways in which minimalism offers a path to a freer life.

🐾 Minimalism and Relationships

While minimalism is often discussed in the context of personal belongings and finances, its influence on relationships—both with oneself and with others—can be equally liberating. A minimalist perspective calls for authenticity, honesty, and respect for personal boundaries, creating a supportive framework for healthier connections.

Quality of Connections Over Quantity: Much like the concept of "quality over quantity" for possessions, a minimalist approach to relationships emphasizes depth rather than breadth. Instead of spreading one's time and energy across a wide, shallow network of acquaintances, minimalists often focus on cultivating deeper bonds with a core group of people who align with their values and truly enrich their lives.

Emotional Transparency: By consciously removing distractions and emotional clutter, minimalists can engage more fully and authentically with loved ones. This can mean more focused conversations, more present family dinners, and a greater willingness to share vulnerabilities. Without the incessant drive to keep up appearances or juggle too many social obligations, people often discover that their relationships become more meaningful and supportive.

Respect for Individual Space and Growth: In a minimalist lifestyle, each person values their own mental and physical space. This is especially important in romantic partnerships or family dynamics, where setting clear boundaries and respecting each other's need for solitude can prevent conflict and resentment.

Ultimately, minimalism provides a lens through which to evaluate and nurture relationships, encouraging deliberate choices about whom we spend time with and how we spend it. By valuing depth, presence, and authenticity, minimalism frees us from superficial connections and opens the door to more genuine, fulfilling interactions.

❈ Overcoming Challenges and Misconceptions

Despite its appealing promise of freedom, adopting a minimalist lifestyle is not without challenges. Several misconceptions persist, which can deter individuals from fully embracing its benefits:

1. **Minimalism Is All or Nothing:** One of the biggest myths is that you must follow an extreme version of minimalism—owning fewer than 100 items, living in a tiny house, or otherwise adopting a spartan existence. In reality, minimalism is a personal journey that varies for each individual. One person may find happiness in drastically reducing possessions, while another may derive immense joy from a modest collection of books or art.
2. **Minimalism Is Boring or Sterile:** Another misconception equates minimalism with austere white walls and a lack of personality. However, the goal is not to strip away self-expression but to eliminate needless distractions. Many minimalists fill their spaces and schedules with things that bring genuine joy or serve a clear purpose.
3. **It's Just About Organizing:** Minimalism goes beyond a well-organized closet; it's rooted in a fundamental shift in values. Organization might be a first step, but the deeper challenge—and reward—lies in continuous reflection on what is and isn't essential.

4. **Fear of Missing Out (FOMO):** A common hurdle is the worry that by saying "no" to certain social events or possessions, one might miss out on something important. Overcoming this fear involves a mindset shift: understanding that each "no" makes space for a more meaningful "yes."

Additionally, minimalists often face social pressures. Friends or family may misunderstand, interpreting a decision to downsize or avoid certain purchases as a moral judgment on their own choices. Constructive communication and a willingness to explain your motivations can help ease these tensions. Ultimately, practicing minimalism is a personal choice, and each person must find their balance between simplicity and enjoyment in everyday life.

🐾 Practical Steps to Embrace Minimalism

For those intrigued by minimalism's promise of freedom, the question becomes: how to begin? Below are practical steps to help guide you on your journey:

1. **Start Small:** Instead of emptying your entire house, begin with a single drawer, closet, or category of items (such as books or kitchenware). Assess each item's purpose and how it fits into your life. If it no longer serves you, donate or recycle it responsibly.
2. **Use the "One In, One Out" Rule:** To prevent re-accumulation, commit to letting go of one item for every new item you bring into your home. This simple rule helps maintain a steady balance of possessions.
3. **Set Clear Intentions for Your Day:** Practice daily mindfulness by setting three key priorities in the morning. By focusing on what truly needs to be done, you minimize time spent on trivial tasks or distractions.
4. **Practice Digital Decluttering:** Our virtual spaces can become just as cluttered as our physical ones. Regularly clean out your email inbox, unsubscribe from unnecessary newsletters, and limit social media usage to predetermined times. This not only frees up mental bandwidth but also reduces the digital noise in your life.
5. **Reevaluate Commitments:** Look at your calendar and see which obligations are non-negotiable and which could be scaled back or eliminated. Focus on what aligns most with your values and long-term goals.
6. **Create a Capsule Wardrobe:** Reduce decision fatigue and streamline your morning routine by curating a smaller collection of versatile, high-quality clothing items. This also decreases the desire to shop for new clothes simply to keep up with trends.
7. **Reflect Regularly:** Minimalism is an ongoing process. Schedule periodic check-ins—perhaps monthly or seasonally—to reassess your possessions, commitments, and state of mind. Ask yourself if what you have and what you do still serves your current goals and values.

By incorporating these practical steps, you can begin to experience the benefits of minimalism incrementally. Over time, the changes accumulate, and you'll likely notice a growing sense of liberation—from both tangible clutter and intangible burdens.

Brenda Diamond

Chapter 27: Reconnecting with Nature

Standing in a grove of towering pines, you may feel small, yet also infinitely expanded, as though each breath is woven into the wind.

Introduction

Nature has played a pivotal role in human civilization since the dawn of history. Our ancestors depended on natural resources for sustenance, used landmarks for navigation, and developed cultural traditions around the rhythms of the earth. Yet in the modern age, as urban centers expand and technology increasingly mediates our everyday lives, many of us find ourselves more detached from the natural world than ever before. The hum of automobiles, the glow of screens, and the ubiquity of digital devices can obscure the call of the wind through the trees or the subtle magnificence of a starry sky. This growing gulf between humans and nature has prompted renewed interest in the concept of "reconnecting with nature."

Reconnecting with nature is more than just escaping the hustle and bustle of city life for occasional weekend excursions. It is a process of rediscovering our inherent bond with the earth—the air we breathe, the food and water that sustain us, and the symbiotic relationship we share with every living organism. Countless spiritual traditions and philosophies teach that understanding our place in nature can foster deep insights into our identities and values. From the concept of "Shinrin-yoku," or forest bathing, in Japanese culture to the American Transcendentalists like Ralph Waldo Emerson and Henry David Thoreau, connecting to nature is seen as a path to wellness, self-reflection, and creative inspiration.

In recent decades, a wave of scientific research has emerged to support these ideas, demonstrating the tangible benefits of interaction with the natural world— from boosted immune function and improved mental health to enhanced creativity and reduced stress levels. As a result, we have witnessed a resurgence of environmental movements, outdoor education programs, and policy initiatives aimed at restoring and protecting green spaces. However, bridging the gap between our modern lifestyles and the call of the wild can be challenging. City dwellers may find it impractical to visit forests regularly, while nature enthusiasts may still rely heavily on technology for their livelihoods. Despite these hurdles, opportunities abound for individuals and communities to forge deeper, more meaningful connections with the environment.

This paper explores various dimensions of reconnecting with nature, analyzing the psychological and physical benefits, examining cultural and philosophical perspectives, and providing practical strategies to integrate nature into our daily routines. Although the path to reconnection may be different for everyone, the ultimate goal remains the same: to nurture a healthier, more sustainable relationship with the earth—a relationship that can renew our sense of wonder, foster ecological stewardship, and help us find wholeness amid an increasingly fragmented modern world.

The Psychological Benefits of Connecting with Nature

One of the most compelling reasons to reconnect with nature lies in the numerous psychological benefits that come with regularly immersing ourselves in green spaces. Researchers have consistently found a correlation between contact with nature and improved mental health. For instance, studies suggest that individuals who spend time in natural environments often report lower levels of stress, anxiety, and depression compared to those who primarily remain indoors or in urban settings. The phenomenon is linked to multiple factors, including exposure to natural light, cleaner air, and visually calming landscapes, all of which can help regulate mood and induce feelings of calm.

A widely cited concept is "attention restoration theory," introduced by psychologists Stephen and Rachel Kaplan, which proposes that spending time in nature replenishes our capacity for directed attention. Modern life places heavy demands on our cognitive resources: constant notifications, busy schedules, and multitasking can leave us mentally exhausted. Green spaces, in contrast, provide a restorative environment where our minds can wander without becoming overstimulated. This restful state helps our cognitive processes recover, improving focus, creativity, and problem-solving abilities once we return to daily tasks.

Additionally, nature can foster mindfulness—a mental state characterized by present-moment awareness and acceptance. When walking through a forest trail or sitting by a flowing stream, the senses often become more attuned to subtle details: the texture of leaves underfoot, the fragrance of wildflowers, or the interplay of sunlight through branches. As we immerse ourselves in such sensory richness, we become more grounded in the here and now. This heightened awareness can serve as a natural antidote to rumination on past or future worries, thereby reducing anxiety and promoting emotional well-being.

Engaging with nature can also nourish a sense of awe and wonder—emotions that have been linked to increased life satisfaction, a broader perspective, and greater altruistic behavior. Whether witnessing the expansive grandeur of a mountain range or observing the intricate patterns in a spider's web, moments of awe can shift our focus away from self-centered concerns, encouraging us to recognize the interconnectedness of life. This sense of connection can alleviate feelings of isolation or meaninglessness, reminding us that we are part of something far larger than our individual selves.

Overall, the psychological benefits of connecting with nature are extensive and well-documented. However, to reap these benefits fully, we need to move beyond mere occasional encounters. Incorporating daily or weekly "nature breaks" into our routines—be it a quick walk in a local park or tending to a small garden—can cumulatively enhance mental well-being. By fostering this regular engagement, we not only reduce stress and sharpen our minds but also deepen our appreciation for the living world around us.

Physical Health Benefits of a Closer Relationship with the Outdoors

Beyond the psychological dimension, reconnecting with nature offers a wide array of physical health advantages. At the most basic level, outdoor activities often involve movement—walking, hiking, or even simply exploring a park. Increased physical activity can help manage weight, lower blood pressure, and reduce the risk of chronic diseases such as diabetes and heart conditions. While it is possible to exercise indoors, nature-based activities often feel less like a chore and more like an adventure, which can foster a more sustained commitment to a healthy lifestyle.

Furthermore, regular exposure to green spaces is correlated with improved immune function. Several studies have highlighted the health benefits of "forest bathing," where participants spend time in wooded areas, consciously engaging all of their senses. The air in forested environments frequently contains phytoncides—organic compounds released by plants—that have been linked to increased activity of natural killer (NK) cells in the human body. NK cells play a critical role in the immune system's defense against viruses and tumor cells, suggesting that spending time in the forest can yield tangible physiological benefits.

Sunlight is another crucial factor that contributes to well-being. While excessive sun exposure carries its own risks (notably skin damage), moderate amounts of sunlight are essential for vitamin D synthesis, which supports bone health and immune function. Spending time outdoors in natural light also helps regulate our circadian rhythms. In contrast, too much indoor living under artificial lighting can disrupt sleep cycles, contributing to fatigue, mood swings, and metabolic issues. By reconnecting with nature and soaking up a healthy dose of sunlight, we align our biological rhythms more closely with the day-night cycle, improving sleep quality and overall vitality.

Additionally, spending time in nature can positively impact respiratory health. Air in natural settings—especially coastal regions and forests—tends to be cleaner than air in densely populated urban areas, reducing exposure to pollutants that can aggravate asthma and other respiratory conditions. Even brief periods of breathing fresh, clean air can have a positive effect on respiratory function, promoting clearer lungs and less irritation.

It is also worth mentioning the indirect physical health benefits that come from nature's role in stress reduction. Chronic stress is associated with numerous health problems, including compromised immune function, cardiovascular disease, and gastrointestinal issues. When we use the outdoors as a space to decompress—whether by meditating in a garden, walking a dog in the park, or practicing yoga under the trees—we help mitigate the deleterious effects of prolonged stress. Over time, these preventative measures can contribute to better health outcomes and a stronger sense of well-being.

In essence, reconnecting with nature aligns with holistic health practices that consider both mind and body. By incorporating more green time into our daily lives, we can fortify our immune systems, enjoy better sleep, and remain physically active, all while reaping the emotional rewards of feeling at peace in the natural world.

Historical and Cultural Perspectives

Throughout history and across cultures, humans have viewed nature through myriad lenses, reflecting both our reliance on and reverence for the environment. From sacred groves in ancient Greece to the sinuous landscapes immortalized in Chinese brush paintings, nature has long been considered a source of spiritual insight and artistic inspiration. The integration of nature into religious practices, philosophical thought, and societal norms underscores just how deeply it shapes our collective consciousness.

In many indigenous cultures around the world, nature is not merely a resource but a living community of which humans are an integral part. The Earth, sky, water, animals, and plants are revered as kin, each possessing a spirit or essence that deserves respect. Activities like hunting, farming, and foraging are conducted with a keen sense of gratitude and reciprocity, ensuring that nature's gifts are not exploited to the point of depletion. This worldview is grounded in a recognition of interdependence—a concept that modern ecological science increasingly supports, as we learn more about the intricate interactions among species within an ecosystem.

Looking to the East, Taoism and Buddhism emphasize harmony with nature, encouraging adherents to observe natural processes as a way of understanding universal truths. Concepts like "wu wei" (non-action or effortless action) in Taoism encourage humans to align with the natural flow of life rather than struggling against it. Similarly, in Shinto, the indigenous spirituality of Japan, kami (divine spirits) inhabit elements of the natural world such as trees, rocks, and rivers, making the reverence for nature an intrinsic part of daily life.

In the Western world, the Romantic era in literature and art witnessed a profound shift in how nature was perceived, particularly during the late 18th and early 19th centuries. Writers like William Wordsworth, Samuel Taylor Coleridge, and Mary

Shelley explored themes of the sublime—a mixture of awe and terror—experienced when encountering the raw power of untamed landscapes. Across the Atlantic, American Transcendentalists such as Ralph Waldo Emerson and Henry David Thoreau championed self-reliance, introspection, and communion with nature as pathways to spiritual and moral growth. Thoreau's experiment in simple living at Walden Pond remains a seminal example of retreating to the natural world for reflection and personal development.

Modern culture, marked by rapid urbanization and industrialization, has in many ways drifted from these traditions. Yet, there is a growing movement to revive or adapt them. Ecospirituality, for example, borrows from ancient philosophies while blending contemporary environmental concerns. Spiritual retreats in nature, eco-therapy, and conservation groups dedicated to preserving sacred natural sites all represent ways that current societies are rediscovering ancestral wisdom regarding our relationship with nature.

Understanding these historical and cultural perspectives can deepen our motivation to reconnect with nature. By recognizing the rich tapestry of human-nature relationships, we can glean lessons on how to cultivate ecological respect and personal well-being. These cultural legacies serve as reminders that our connection to the natural world is not a modern fad, but a timeless component of the human experience.

The Science of Awe and Connection

In recent years, scientists have turned their attention to studying the intangible yet powerful emotion of awe—often triggered by encounters with vast, majestic, or complex aspects of nature. Awe is distinct from other positive emotions like joy or happiness in that it involves a feeling of "small self," where one's focus shifts away from individual preoccupations toward broader perspectives. This shift can lead to profound changes in cognition, emotion, and behavior.

Research suggests that awe experiences can enhance overall well-being by lowering stress levels, reducing inflammation, and promoting altruistic behavior. One plausible explanation for these effects is that the experience of awe temporarily disrupts habitual patterns of thought, pushing us to accommodate a new perspective. Whether it be standing at the edge of the Grand Canyon, gazing up at towering redwoods, or marveling at the celestial spectacle of the Milky Way, these moments challenge our conventional understanding of self and place. Such experiences can foster humility, curiosity, and a sense of profound interconnectedness—qualities that can transform not only our internal states but also how we engage with others and the environment.

From a neurological standpoint, awe appears to activate regions of the brain associated with emotion regulation and social cognition. Functional MRI scans have shown that the default mode network—often related to self-referential processing—can be dampened during states of awe, suggesting a temporary quieting of rumination and self-focus. This mental shift opens the door to greater empathy, creativity, and a heightened sense of belonging.

Awe is not reserved solely for grand, once-in-a-lifetime encounters. Micro-moments of awe can be cultivated in daily life by attuning ourselves to the intricacies of the natural world—such as the geometry of a flower petal, the patterns of a leaf, or the subtle interplay of shadow and light at sunrise. These small doses of wonder can accumulate, gradually shaping a more awe-oriented perspective that enhances emotional resilience.

By understanding the science behind awe, we can appreciate the profound impact that even brief nature-based experiences can have on our mental and emotional landscape. Seeking out and recognizing moments of wonder in nature—whether in vast wilderness settings or small urban green pockets—can thus be a key part of reconnecting. When we intentionally cultivate awe, we deepen our relationship with the world around us, tapping into a wellspring of inspiration, gratitude, and empathy that can inform how we live and interact with both people and the planet.

Overcoming Modern Barriers to Nature

While the benefits of reconnecting with nature are clear, modern lifestyles often present substantial barriers. Urbanization has placed more than half of the global population in cities, where access to natural spaces can be limited. Many city dwellers may see only small patches of grass and a few trees in their daily routine, while some have virtually no green space in their immediate environment. Besides spatial constraints, time is another major hurdle, as demanding work schedules and digital engagements can leave little room for leisurely strolls or day trips to the countryside.

Financial concerns can also impede frequent nature engagement. Although walking in a local park is usually free, more immersive experiences—like visiting national parks or going on wilderness retreats—often require travel expenses that may not be feasible for everyone. Furthermore, societal expectations and cultural norms that prioritize productivity and constant connectivity can make it difficult to set aside moments for introspection and unstructured time in nature.

Technology itself, while often seen as a culprit, can also be a tool for reconnection if used wisely. Smartphone apps can guide individuals on local hiking trails, identify birds and plants, or track one's daily step count, potentially making nature exploration more accessible and engaging. However, technology use becomes a hindrance when it substitutes for direct experiences—excessive reliance on virtual tours, nature documentaries, or social media can give a false sense of connection without any tangible time spent outdoors.

Additionally, issues of safety and accessibility can be barriers. For those living in neighborhoods with high crime rates, venturing into local parks might feel risky. Similarly, individuals with disabilities may find it challenging to access natural spaces that are not equipped with ramps, paved trails, or other necessary accommodations. Overcoming these barriers requires not only personal initiative but also community-based solutions—such as improving park infrastructure, ensuring safe public spaces, and offering nature programs tailored for diverse populations.

Ultimately, addressing these challenges demands a multi-faceted approach. On an individual level, setting priorities and scheduling "nature time" can help ensure that daily life does not overshadow our innate need for green spaces. On a societal level, policy changes that preserve and expand public parks, establish more green roofs and urban gardens, and promote environmental education in schools can help integrate nature into our collective consciousness. By recognizing and actively dismantling these barriers, we open the door for more inclusive and widespread opportunities to reconnect with the living world.

Practical Strategies for Daily Reconnection

1. *Micro-Doses of Nature*

   Even the busiest schedule can accommodate brief encounters with the natural world. A five-minute walk outside during a lunch break, a moment spent observing the sky, or a pause to admire a potted plant can help ground and refresh the mind. These small moments accumulate over time, fostering a habit of mindfulness and a renewed sense of connection.

2. *Urban Gardening and Houseplants*

   For city dwellers with limited access to green spaces, creating a small garden on a balcony or windowsill can be transformative. Tending to plants, watching them grow, and learning about their care encourages an ongoing relationship with nature. If space is extremely tight, even a few houseplants—such as succulents, herbs, or ferns—can brighten an indoor environment and purify the air.

3. *Nature Journaling*

   Keeping a journal to sketch or record observations about the natural world encourages close attention to detail. Whether noting changes in the seasons, writing about the local birdlife, or reflecting on how certain landscapes make you feel, journaling sharpens awareness and keeps you engaged with your surroundings.

4. *Mindful Walking and Listening*

   Incorporating nature into daily exercise routines, such as taking a mindful walk in a local park, allows you to combine physical movement with sensory exploration. By consciously tuning in to the sounds of birds, the rustle of leaves, or the rhythm of your footsteps, you transform what might have been a mundane activity into a ritual of presence.

5. *Weekend Excursions and Vacations*

   When possible, dedicate weekends or vacations to exploring national parks, beaches, or rural landscapes. Immersion in more expansive natural settings can offer a deeper reset for the mind and body. Activities like camping, hiking, and swimming in natural bodies of water can help re-establish the ancient connection our species has long had with the environment.

6. *Join Local Conservation Efforts*

   Engaging in community-based environmental initiatives—be it a neighborhood clean-up, a tree-planting event, or volunteering at a wildlife sanctuary—provides both hands-on experience with nature and a chance to meet like-minded individuals. Contributing to a collective effort fosters a sense of purpose and responsibility for the places we inhabit.

7. *Limit Screen Time*

   Setting boundaries around the use of electronic devices is crucial for freeing up mental space that can be devoted to the outdoors. Simple steps, like turning off unnecessary app notifications or designating device-free hours, can help break the cycle of digital addiction, opening up more opportunities to observe and engage with the living world outside our screens.

8. *Support Environmental Education*

   Encouraging children (and adults) to learn about local ecosystems, plant and animal species, and environmental challenges can deepen respect and curiosity. Whether through formal school programs or informal community workshops, education fosters a more informed and empathetic perspective on humanity's role in nature.

By integrating these practical strategies into daily life, we transform "reconnection with nature" from a lofty ideal into a sustained, meaningful practice. These changes can be tailored to individual circumstances, ensuring that no matter where we live or how packed our schedules are, we can still nurture our bond with the earth.

Ecological Stewardship and Sustainability

Reconnecting with nature is not solely an inward-looking exercise for personal growth; it also carries ethical and ecological implications. As we develop a closer bond with the natural world, we become more inclined to protect it. This shift in perspective can have far-reaching consequences, from how we consume resources to the policies we support.

On an individual level, awareness of our impact might encourage us to reduce waste, recycle more diligently, conserve water, and opt for renewable energy sources when possible. Practices like composting kitchen scraps or supporting local, organic farms can also help minimize our ecological footprint. When these behaviors become widespread, collective efforts can shape market demands and influence corporate practices toward more sustainable models.

On a community or global scale, reconnecting with nature can fuel grassroots movements and political advocacy. Public outcry over deforestation, pollution, or the loss of biodiversity often emerges from individuals who have personally experienced the value of healthy ecosystems. As more people grow attuned to nature's inherent worth and recognize our dependence on it, we are more likely to vote for leaders and policies that prioritize environmental preservation, climate action, and social equity in resource distribution.

Furthermore, ecological stewardship encompasses a sense of justice—recognizing that environmental degradation disproportionately affects vulnerable communities. Low-income neighborhoods often face higher exposure to pollution and reduced access to clean water and green spaces. Indigenous communities frequently battle for land rights and the protection of sacred natural sites. A deep connection with nature can expand our circle of compassion to include not just non-human species, but also marginalized human groups whose well-being is intricately tied to environmental health.

Ultimately, sustainability and stewardship arise naturally from understanding our place in the broader web of life. When we realize that the forests, rivers, and oceans are not separate entities but vital support systems, our choices become more conscientious. Reconnecting with nature can thus serve as a catalyst for genuine environmental ethics, bridging the gap between personal well-being and planetary health.

Final thoughts on re-connecting

In an era defined by technology, urbanization, and a frenetic pace of living, the call to reconnect with nature has never been more urgent or more compelling. The physical and psychological benefits of time spent outdoors are both numerous and scientifically substantiated, offering a potent antidote to the stresses and strains of modern life. Beyond individual health, however, lies a broader tapestry of cultural heritage, spiritual insight, and ethical responsibility woven through our relationships with the earth.

Reconnecting with nature does not demand grand, sweeping gestures; it thrives in the small, daily acts of noticing, caring, and engaging with the living world. It can be cultivated in a window-box garden or found in a forest trail. It can blossom during mindful walks in urban parks or flourish amid awe-inspiring mountaintops. In each case, the journey back to nature is ultimately a journey back to ourselves—a reminder that we are not merely inhabitants of this planet, but participants in a vast and intricate community of life.

By integrating accessible, practical strategies—such as nature journaling, mindful walking, weekend retreats, and community conservation efforts—into our routines, we enrich our lives and contribute to a collective ethos of stewardship. As we restore our bond with nature, we become more attuned to its fragility and more invested in its protection. In this way, reconnection with nature transcends self-improvement; it becomes an act of responsibility and love that resonates far beyond personal boundaries.

Our ancestors understood the vital importance of living in harmony with the earth, weaving respect and wonder for nature into their cultural and spiritual practices. In rediscovering this wisdom for the modern age, we have the opportunity to heal not only our own psyches but also the world we share. Each step we take on a dirt path, each seed we plant in the ground, and each breath of fresh air we savor can be a conscious act of renewal—a promise that the human story will continue to evolve alongside the unfolding story of nature itself.

In answering nature's invitation to reconnect, we reclaim a part of our humanity that has long been overshadowed by concrete and glass. We step out of our digital haze and open ourselves to wonder, awe, and humility—emotions that catalyze empathy, insight, and transformation. Through this reconnection, we learn that nature is not merely a backdrop to our lives, but a vital and nourishing presence. Ultimately, by forging a deeper bond with the earth, we nurture a sense of wholeness that resonates within us and ripples outward—strengthening our commitment to safeguard the planet for generations to come.

Chapter 28: Fostering Creativity in Quiet Spaces

In silence, creativity is like a hidden spring—turn a moment's attention inward,
and it flows from depths you didn't know existed.

∞ Introduction

In our modern world, creativity is one of the most sought-after capacities, fueling innovation, personal growth, and societal progress. Historically, creativity was perceived as a special gift reserved for a few extraordinary individuals, but research increasingly demonstrates that creativity resides in everyone. The challenge, then, is how to nurture and foster it in daily life. One key finding in the realm of creativity research is the importance of quiet spaces—both literal and metaphorical. Quiet spaces help calm our overstimulated minds and grant us the mental and emotional bandwidth necessary to connect ideas in novel ways.

Society's rapid pace, ever-present technology, and non-stop demands on attention can disrupt the creative process. While brainstorming sessions and collaborative group discussions can be valuable, equally important—yet often underemphasized—are the solitary moments of introspection and mindful solitude that can unleash creative impulses. Fostering creativity in quiet spaces involves more than just turning down the noise; it involves intentionally designing physical and psychological environments that encourage reflection, experimentation, and playful thinking.

This paper explores how quiet spaces support the creative process, the specific strategies that individuals and organizations can adopt to integrate such spaces into their routines, the importance of solitude in artistic and problem-solving endeavors, and how cultivating these environments can lead to greater well-being. By understanding the interplay between solitude and creativity, individuals can take deliberate steps to harness the power of silence, ultimately propelling themselves—and their respective organizations—toward higher levels of innovation and imaginative thinking.

∞ The Power of Quiet: An Overview

Quiet spaces provide a sanctuary for the mind, free from constant interruptions and external stimuli. Throughout history, numerous great thinkers, from writers and philosophers to scientists and musicians, have cherished moments of solitude. They recognized that the mental calmness found in these quiet intervals allowed them to explore ideas deeply and create breakthroughs in their fields.

One of the best-known examples is Albert Einstein, who enjoyed playing the violin alone to "think in music," as he would say. He found that these solitary musical interludes allowed him to approach his scientific work from fresh angles. Similarly, Henry David Thoreau's legendary experiment at Walden Pond exemplifies how introspection and time away from societal pressures can spark profound philosophical insights. Thoreau's solitude was more than just physical isolation; it was a psychological stance of being open to the flow of ideas, unfettered by the cacophony of everyday life.

Quiet spaces also operate on a neurological level. Research in cognitive psychology suggests that our brains benefit from breaks in stimulation. During these periods of low external input, the default mode network (DMN) becomes more active. This network is associated with internally focused thought, such as daydreaming, creative ideation, and reflection on past experiences. When we give ourselves time to tune out from the outside world, our minds have the opportunity to form unique connections, bridging seemingly unrelated concepts and forging innovative ideas.

Furthermore, quiet spaces alleviate the cognitive load brought on by multitasking. When we constantly switch our attention from one task to another, the brain works overtime, leaving little cognitive capacity for deeper, more creative thinking. By contrast, solitude allows individuals to focus on one line of thought without interruption. Paradoxically, giving the mind room to wander in a quiet environment can yield hyper-focused creative insights—a phenomenon sometimes referred to as "structured daydreaming." Thus, establishing these mental landscapes can help individuals achieve bursts of creativity that would be difficult in perpetually noisy or overstimulated settings.

∞ Designing Physical Spaces for Creative Solitude

Physical environments play a crucial role in nurturing creative thought. Our surroundings influence our mental states, often determining whether we can settle into the reflective, generative mode essential for creativity. Yet many workplaces and living spaces are designed for efficiency rather than creativity. Offices are commonly noisy, open-concept environments that encourage constant collaboration but provide minimal privacy. Homes can be similarly hectic, with televisions, mobile devices, and myriad other distractions readily available.

To counteract these external pressures, one of the most straightforward approaches is to intentionally carve out a designated "quiet room" or corner in a home, office, or other shared space. This area, ideally, would have minimal external stimuli—soft or natural lighting, muted color schemes, comfortable seating, and perhaps even elements of nature such as potted plants. Soundproofing or noise-cancelling features further enhance the tranquility of such spaces. The goal is to create an environment that visibly and audibly signals to its occupant, "This is a safe, quiet zone for deep thought."

Some organizations have also experimented with "quiet pods" or "silence booths," which can be installed in open office plans. These pods are small, enclosed spaces designed to reduce noise, limit visual distractions, and allow employees to retreat for a brief period of uninterrupted work or reflection. Initial feedback from businesses that adopt such pods suggests that employees value the opportunity to step away from the busyness of open-plan office life. They find it easier to think creatively, write, or even just rest their minds, returning to their tasks afterward feeling recharged.

If space and resources permit, incorporating natural elements into quiet spaces can be particularly beneficial. Studies show that plants and natural light can reduce stress and increase mental clarity. Views of nature or even natural imagery on walls (like landscape photographs or nature-themed artworks) can enhance a sense of calm. This peaceful foundation, in turn, supports the free flow of creative thought. Whether small or expansive, the physical space must serve as a deliberate invitation to pause, breathe, and think, free from the chaos of the outside world.

∞ The Role of Solitude in the Creative Process

Solitude is not merely about the absence of people or external stimuli. It is also about achieving a certain mental spaciousness that encourages original thinking. The creative process often involves four distinct stages: preparation, incubation, illumination, and verification. Quiet solitude can facilitate each of these stages in profound ways.

1. *Preparation:* During preparation, individuals gather information, learn techniques, and immerse themselves in a subject. While some parts of preparation may benefit from collaboration—e.g., brainstorming or expert consultations—quiet study ensures depth. When a person has the space to read widely, take notes, and reflect in solitude, they create a robust mental framework, laying the groundwork for future creative leaps.
2. *Incubation:* This stage is perhaps the most associated with solitude, as it involves a period of stepping away from conscious problem-solving. The brain continues to process the information unconsciously, making connections behind the scenes. Solitary activities—such as taking walks alone, meditating, journaling, or simply daydreaming—can all support the incubation process.
3. *Illumination:* Illumination or the "aha moment" can happen unexpectedly. However, it's more likely to occur when the mind is relaxed and open. While insight can strike during group collaborations, many epiphanies arise in moments of quiet reflection—perhaps while taking a shower, sitting in a secluded space, or even lying in bed before sleep.
4. *Verification:* During verification, the creative idea is tested, refined, and evaluated. Although collaboration and feedback from peers are often

invaluable at this stage, solitary time for self-reflection remains crucial. By stepping back from external opinions, creatives can assess the core of their ideas, ensuring that the work aligns with their personal vision and fully capitalizes on the spark of creativity.

The role of solitude in these stages, therefore, cannot be underestimated. It offers a haven for digesting information, exploring possibilities, and, ultimately, articulating ideas in their purest form. Through periods of intentional quietness, individuals can feed their curiosity and hone their creative instincts in ways that might never materialize in highly social or overstimulating environments.

∞ Mindfulness and the Art of Slowing Down

Amid the clamor of 21st-century life, mindfulness has emerged as a powerful practice for enhancing well-being and mental acuity. It focuses on bringing one's attention to the present moment, observing thoughts and feelings without judgment, and cultivating a sense of calm awareness. Such practices dovetail naturally with the pursuit of creativity, because they help cultivate the mental clarity and focus required to explore ideas deeply and openly.

Mindfulness can transform a space from simply being physically quiet to fostering genuine mental quiet. This is significant because even a quiet room can feel loud if our internal monologue is racing. Mindfulness practices—such as deep breathing exercises, guided meditations, or even mindful coloring—help still the chatter of the mind, making it easier for the default mode network to operate effectively.

Incorporating brief periods of mindful solitude into a daily routine can yield significant benefits. For instance, spending just 10 to 15 minutes each morning meditating before starting work can prime the brain for creative pursuits throughout the day. Over time, these short rituals help cultivate mental resilience, making it easier to shift between states of deep focus and open-ended creative exploration. They also help with stress management: if stress levels are high, creative thinking typically suffers because the mind becomes fixated on perceived threats or anxieties.

Moreover, slowing down via mindfulness techniques can counterbalance the constant push for productivity that many workplaces advocate. Interestingly, slowing down can actually improve productivity by fostering deeper insights and preventing burnout. For creative work, especially, "fast and frantic" methods are rarely the most fruitful. By approaching tasks with a calm, focused presence, individuals can unlock greater imaginative potential. In essence, mindfulness practices help ensure that quiet spaces are not just empty of noise, but are rich in mental clarity and receptivity to fresh ideas.

∞ Technology Management: From Distraction to Tool

Technology can be both an asset and a hindrance in cultivating quiet spaces for creativity. On one hand, tools such as digital whiteboards, design software, and brainstorming apps can provide valuable ways to visualize and organize emerging ideas. Online libraries and databases offer instant access to research materials that can spark new insights. Communication platforms, too, enable creatives to share ideas swiftly with peers, gather feedback, and refine concepts.

On the other hand, technology often brings relentless notifications, social media, and other interruptions that can disrupt deep focus and reflection. The ubiquitous smartphone pings can jar the mind out of a creative flow, fracturing ideas before they have time to solidify. For this reason, learning to manage technology use is essential for sustaining quiet, creative moments.

One pragmatic approach is to designate specific "technology-free" periods or zones within a day or environment. For instance, an organization might encourage employees to spend the first hour of their workday offline, dedicating that time to immersive tasks that benefit from solitude. Alternatively, individuals might create "phone-free" corners in their homes where devices are not allowed, permitting them to read, write, or simply think without digital interruptions.

When using technology in a quiet creative space, setting boundaries around notifications and digital clutter is crucial. Switching off push notifications, putting devices on airplane mode, or installing website blockers during a focus session can help maintain the tranquility necessary for the creative process. Additionally, curating digital workspaces by organizing files, using minimalistic design software interfaces, and keeping only relevant tabs open can help minimize the overwhelm that often stifles creativity.

Ultimately, technology should be harnessed as a tool to amplify creativity, rather than a constant conduit of distraction. Balancing digital usage with intentional "unplugged" time is key. By managing technology mindfully, one can integrate it seamlessly into quiet spaces without sacrificing the serenity that fosters creative thought.

∞ Fostering Team Creativity Through Individual Quiet Time

A common misconception is that creative breakthroughs in organizations primarily result from group brainstorming sessions. While collaborative creativity has its merits—enabling the cross-pollination of ideas and diverse perspectives—there is increasing evidence that individuals generate more creative ideas in solitude before bringing them to a group. Studies show that group brainstorming can sometimes lead to groupthink, social loafing, or the overshadowing of quieter voices.

By integrating structured quiet time into the collective creative process, teams can leverage the strengths of both solitude and collaboration. For instance, a manager could assign a problem-solving task but require each team member to spend at least 30 minutes thinking about the issue on their own before a group meeting. During this solitary time, individuals can explore unconventional angles without worrying about judgment or peer influence. They can jot down any ideas—no matter how outlandish—without fear of interruption.

Once the team reconvenes, members can share their individually nurtured ideas, which often prove more diverse and original than those generated in a purely collaborative setting. The group discussion then becomes an opportunity to refine, merge, and expand upon these distinct ideas. In this way, quiet time forms a critical cornerstone of the collective creativity process, serving as an incubator for fledgling concepts. When balanced properly, the synergy between solitary thinking and group collaboration can lead to creative breakthroughs that neither approach could have achieved alone.

Additionally, workplaces that champion quiet spaces and respect employees' need for reflection typically see benefits in morale and mental health. It sends a message that the organization values depth, focus, and thoughtful exploration over constant busyness. This cultural shift can yield a healthier environment where genuine creativity is encouraged as an integral part of daily work, rather than an occasional "innovation sprint."

∞ The Importance of Rituals and Habits

Fostering creativity in quiet spaces is not merely about setting aside time or building a soundproof room. It also involves developing habits and rituals that encourage the mind to transition smoothly into a creative mode. Rituals can serve as cues, signaling to the brain that it's time to enter a more introspective, imaginative state.

For example, many writers have daily rituals—like lighting a candle, making a cup of tea, or listening to a particular type of music—that mark the beginning of a writing session. These small, repeated behaviors help the mind shift into creative gear more readily. Similarly, visual artists might have a ritual of cleaning their workspace, sharpening pencils, or sketching freestyle doodles before working on a main piece.

Habits that support creativity in quiet spaces also extend to how one manages time. Adopting strategies such as time blocking can help ensure that reflective tasks don't get pushed aside by more urgent, but not necessarily more important, responsibilities. For instance, scheduling a "creative window" from 8:00 a.m. to 9:00 a.m. each day—during which emails and messages are turned off—can encourage a more disciplined approach to solitude and reflection. Over time, the regularity of these windows becomes ingrained, making it easier to slip into the creative process without prolonged mental resistance.

Developing these habits requires self-knowledge and experimentation. Some people find their creative peak in the quiet hours of the early morning, while others might prefer late-night sessions. By testing different times of day, locations, and pre-work rituals, individuals can discover the combination that most effectively nurtures their creative spark. Moreover, consistent practice in maintaining and protecting these routines can yield incremental but compounding improvements in overall creative output.

∞ Balancing Collaboration and Solitude

The modern narrative often highlights collaboration as the holy grail of innovation. Yet, many breakthroughs are the direct result of one individual's deep dive into an idea, problem, or craft. In truth, creativity is enriched by both solitary exploration and collective interaction. The key lies in finding the right balance— one that acknowledges the strengths each approach offers and mitigates their respective weaknesses.

Organizations and institutions that recognize this balance often provide various modes of working: open collaborative areas for team-based tasks and quiet zones or private rooms for focused individual work. The autonomy to choose between these environments empowers individuals to manage their creative processes effectively. Similarly, universities and public libraries that offer both bustling common areas and silent study rooms cater to the diverse working styles of students, fostering an inclusive atmosphere for creative and intellectual pursuits.

In personal contexts, balancing collaboration and solitude might involve scheduling coffee meetups or brainstorming calls for idea exchange, followed by stretches of solitary "lock-in" time to process and develop those ideas. The synergy between these modes of working can fuel deeper insights. Solitude aids in gestation of raw concepts; collaboration refines them through feedback and collective wisdom.

Another benefit of balancing collaboration and solitude is the prevention of creative burnout or stagnation. Overly isolating oneself can sometimes lead to echo chambers of thought, where ideas become repetitive or insular. Conversely, excessive group work can overwhelm more introspective individuals, leading to frustration or "analysis paralysis." A flexible framework—one that encourages the interplay between quiet contemplation and shared exploration—can unlock higher levels of creativity while maintaining sustained momentum.

Creativity is not a mysterious quality reserved for a chosen few; it is a fundamental human capacity that can be nurtured with the right conditions. Quiet spaces, both physical and mental, serve as powerful catalysts in this nurturing process by offering respite from constant stimulation and distraction. Through solitude, mindfulness, and deliberate habit formation, individuals can access deeper layers of thought and engage with ideas in more profound ways.

Organizations, educational institutions, and communities that prioritize creating and maintaining quiet environments will likely see tangible benefits—from more innovative problem-solving to greater overall well-being among their members. However, the path to fostering creativity in quiet spaces does not require radical transformations. Simple steps, such as designating a quiet zone at work or committing to daily "unplugged" intervals, can have an outsized impact on creative potential.

Looking ahead, further research could delve into the optimal ratio of collaboration to solitude, identifying best practices for different fields or personality types. Additionally, exploring the neurological underpinnings of how quiet spaces influence creativity can bolster the argument for designing environments more intentionally. Finally, emerging technology solutions—like virtual reality "quiet rooms" and AI-driven productivity tools—offer new frontiers for investigation, potentially blending the best of both technological innovation and uninterrupted creative focus.

In a world increasingly saturated with noise, notifications, and near-constant engagement, embracing the power of quiet spaces is both a practical strategy and a profound act of self-care. By fostering creativity in these silent sanctuaries, we honor the mind's intrinsic need for contemplation, imagination, and discovery. The reward is not just better ideas but a richer, more introspective, and ultimately more humane experience of life and work.

Chapter 29: Maintaining Relationships While Embracing Solitude

Solitude is not a wall but a bridge—when we return from our inner journeys, we reconnect with others more authentically.

℘ Introduction

The tension between solitude and social connection lies at the heart of the human experience. We are innately social beings who thrive on companionship, yet we also yearn for moments of quiet reflection to gather our thoughts and find inner balance. Relationships, whether romantic, platonic, or familial, provide us with a sense of belonging, support, and understanding. On the other hand, solitude offers unique opportunities for self-discovery, creativity, and personal growth. The interplay of these two dimensions can sometimes feel contradictory, especially in cultures that emphasize extroversion and constant interaction. However, learning to embrace solitude while maintaining healthy relationships is not only possible; it is essential for holistic well-being.

Contrary to popular belief, solitude does not necessarily mean isolation or loneliness. It can be a conscious choice to spend time alone, recharging and exploring inner landscapes. When approached intentionally, solitude becomes a powerful tool for self-awareness and emotional regulation, leading individuals to become more attuned to their own needs and better able to empathize with others. Yet the fear of being perceived as distant, aloof, or uncaring often prevents people from setting aside this vital space for themselves.

This document explores the concept of solitude, its significance in personal growth, and its impact on our relationships. It examines how one can maintain genuine, close connections while still carving out time to be alone. We will discuss strategies for balancing the two, such as setting healthy boundaries, engaging in meaningful communication, and learning to navigate emotional challenges that arise when personal needs collide with those of our loved ones. Ultimately, the goal is to show that cultivating solitude enriches relationships, allowing us to show up for others more compassionately and authentically. By the end, you will have practical insights and tools to harmonize solitude and social life in a way that strengthens both your relationships and your sense of self.

℘ Understanding the Concept of Solitude

Solitude, at its core, is a deliberate act of drawing inward, granting ourselves the autonomy to exist in quiet, unhurried moments. It stands in contrast to loneliness, which typically manifests as an unwelcome sense of isolation or lack of connection. While loneliness often stems from social deficits—feeling unloved or unseen—solitude is a voluntary, positive choice. It is a form of self-care that allows us to reflect on our thoughts, values, and aspirations without external influence or judgment. By distinguishing solitude from loneliness, we can better appreciate its value and purpose.

Historically, renowned thinkers, writers, and artists have praised solitude as a fertile ground for creativity and introspection. Philosophers such as Henry David Thoreau and Ralph Waldo Emerson championed the virtues of solitary living, explaining that stepping away from the collective noise of society frees the mind to explore new ideas and cultivate wisdom. Even in today's hyperconnected world, scientific research supports the notion that periods of solitude enhance creativity, problem-solving, and emotional resilience.

One reason solitude can be so transformative is that it encourages self-discovery. Without outside pressure, we gain the freedom to explore personal interests, question deeply held beliefs, and process complex emotions. In this quiet, contemplative space, we can more easily identify our own needs and desires. This heightened self-awareness supports healthier communication patterns and empathy toward others. After all, understanding ourselves is the first step to truly understanding another person.

Yet, we must also recognize the importance of balance. Excessive solitude can morph into isolation, hindering our capacity to build and maintain supportive relationships. The key is mindful management of alone time, ensuring it does not become an escape mechanism or a wall that shuts people out. By learning to embrace solitude in healthy doses, we set the stage for stronger, more meaningful interactions with friends, family members, and romantic partners.

℘ The Importance of Healthy Boundaries

A major factor in balancing solitude with relationships is the establishment of healthy personal boundaries. Boundaries define where one person ends and another begins, allowing for individual autonomy while still preserving emotional connections. They communicate personal needs and comfort levels, clarify roles within relationships, and safeguard mental and emotional well-being. When boundaries are unclear or absent, misunderstandings, stress, and resentment can easily take root.

Boundaries around solitude can be tricky, particularly when loved ones interpret a need for personal time as rejection. However, setting and communicating these boundaries can prevent problems down the line. For example, explaining to a partner that you need a quiet hour each day to read or reflect can ward off feelings of neglect, simply by offering clarity. Likewise, agreeing on weekly or monthly "personal days" can give everyone involved the space they need to pursue personal interests or indulge in self-care.

In setting these boundaries, assertive communication is key. Instead of making vague or passive statements, it helps to convey your needs in a direct but respectful manner. Phrases like, "I value our time together, but I also need some time to myself to recharge," reassure loved ones that your solitude is not about pushing them away. It's also vital to remain open to others' needs. While you request time alone, your partner, family member, or friend might need consistent check-ins or shared activities. A willingness to engage in dialogue about each person's needs fosters a spirit of mutual respect.

Healthy boundaries are especially important in an era of digital connectivity, where we are reachable at all hours via texts, emails, and social media. By deliberately carving out "no-contact" zones or by turning off notifications during certain hours, you grant yourself a window to retreat from external demands and reconnect with your inner self. This practice can rejuvenate your mind and deepen your capacity to be present when you do engage socially.

℘ Nurturing Emotional Security in Solitude and Relationships

Emotional security underpins both solitude and intimacy. We need to feel secure enough to spend time alone without worrying that our relationships will disintegrate in our absence. Conversely, we also need confidence in our bonds to feel comfortable inviting others into our mental and emotional space when we reconnect. This emotional security is closely tied to trust—both in ourselves and in those we care about.

One way to foster emotional security is through consistent positive reinforcement in relationships. Whether you are seeking some quiet time or are about to embark on a vacation alone, open communication reduces ambiguity. By reassuring loved ones of your unwavering commitment and emphasizing that solitude is an act of self-maintenance rather than withdrawal, you lay a foundation of trust. Over time, these patterns can dispel fears of abandonment or rejection.

On a personal level, building emotional security often involves self-acceptance. Solitude can reveal vulnerabilities or insecurities that we might otherwise mask in social settings. Recognizing these feelings and working through them can boost overall emotional well-being, making us more resilient in the face of relational challenges. Practices such as journaling, mindfulness meditation, or therapy offer structured ways to explore thoughts and emotions in solitude. When we learn to identify and process our own emotional triggers, we become better equipped to handle conflicts or misunderstandings with loved ones.

For the relationship side of the equation, it is important to create an environment where your friends, family, or partner can express their feelings openly, too. If someone worries about your need for alone time, encourage them to share their concerns. Make it a mutual effort: they can voice their fears or worries, and you can provide reassurance or propose compromise. This dialogue builds trust, nurtures emotional security, and prevents either side from feeling unheard. In doing so, solitude and companionship cease to be in opposition—they become complementary forces that reinforce each other in healthy, dynamic ways.

℘ Communication in the Age of Digital Distractions

Technology has revolutionized the way we connect, offering unprecedented convenience and immediacy. We can reach people around the globe within seconds and maintain contact through social media platforms and messaging apps. However, this digital revolution also creates new challenges for those trying to maintain relationships and, at the same time, embrace solitude.

The incessant notifications, pings, and messages can fracture our attention spans and make it difficult to truly disconnect. Even moments of solitude can be invaded by the sense of obligation to respond to messages promptly. One key to safeguarding solitude is to manage digital communication responsibly. For instance, scheduling dedicated times to check emails or social media can help prevent the constant bombardment of notifications. Silence or disable push alerts, and if possible, set your phone to "Do Not Disturb" mode during specific hours to preserve the sanctity of your alone time.

On the relational side, technology can be a double-edged sword. While it allows for easy touchpoints with loved ones, over-reliance on digital mediums can lead to surface-level interactions. Constantly texting or chatting online might give the illusion of closeness, but real emotional intimacy often requires deeper, face-to-face conversations or thoughtful phone or video calls. Balancing these modes of communication is vital. Prioritize quality interactions over frequency; a meaningful conversation once or twice a week can be far more nourishing than daily bursts of small talk that never scratch the surface.

Additionally, it's important to communicate your digital boundaries with friends and family. Let them know that while you value staying in touch, you also reserve certain times for offline existence. Convey that stepping away from screens is not a rejection of connection but a way to protect personal well-being. Healthy communication in the digital era hinges on mutual understanding, respect for each other's schedules and mental space, and the acknowledgment that alone time is not only permissible but essential for mental and emotional health.

℘ Overcoming Guilt and Fear Around Solitude

For many people, the biggest hurdles to embracing solitude are the feelings of guilt and fear. Guilt arises when we believe we're neglecting our loved ones or obligations by taking time for ourselves. Fear manifests as anxiety—worrying that others might judge our need for space, or worse, that we might lose important relationships if we don't constantly engage. These emotions can be amplified by cultural norms that equate sociability with success or psychological well-being, leading us to believe that we must be "on" all the time.

To navigate guilt, it can help to reframe solitude as self-care rather than selfishness. Just as you wouldn't feel guilty for sleeping at night to recharge your body, you shouldn't feel guilty for setting aside solitude to recharge your mind. When approached with intention, solitude is an investment in your mental health. This positive mindset shift helps alleviate the sensation that you're somehow letting others down.

As for fear, it often dissipates when we see evidence that healthy relationships can withstand and even flourish with appropriate alone time. Consider starting with small increments of solitude—a half-hour walk every day, a weekend afternoon dedicated to a solo hobby, or an hour of digital detox each evening. Communicate these plans to your friends and family and maintain open dialogue. Over time, as they accept and respect your boundaries, your fears of rejection should lessen. You'll gradually develop confidence in your ability to preserve and nurture relationships without sacrificing your personal space.

Another technique to overcome guilt and fear is practicing self-compassion. When negative emotions surface, gently remind yourself that human needs vary—while some individuals recharge in large groups, others find solace in quiet reflection. Recognizing that your need for solitude is valid, just like others' need for social engagement, will help you cultivate the self-esteem and assurance necessary to strike a harmonious balance between solitude and connectedness.

℘ Quality Over Quantity in Relationships

One critical insight for those looking to cultivate solitude while keeping relationships strong is the idea of prioritizing quality over quantity. It's easy to assume that close bonds demand frequent interaction and constant updates, yet the depth of connection often hinges on the richness of shared experiences, not their frequency. This is where solitude can actually enhance relationships: by granting yourself time to reflect and develop a deeper sense of self, you bring more authenticity and presence to your interactions.

Consider a scenario where someone consistently socializes without pause— jumping from one gathering to the next, never spending a moment alone. While this individual appears highly sociable, they might lack the space needed to process experiences or truly engage in deeper dialogue with those around them. In contrast, someone who dedicates part of each day or week to solitude might approach social events with renewed focus, fresh perspectives, and emotional availability. This concentrated energy can lead to more thoughtful conversation and shared growth.

Quality time in relationships also hinges on mindfulness and intentional engagement. When you do interact, strive to be fully present. Turn off your phone or reduce distractions to concentrate on the other person's words, expressions, and emotional cues. Ask open-ended questions that encourage meaningful exchange. Share your own experiences and insights gained from periods of introspection, inviting a deeper level of understanding.

Finally, it's important to remember that relationships have life stages. Some friendships or romantic partnerships naturally flourish during certain periods and then require more personal space as circumstances change. Learning to accept these ebbs and flows can alleviate the pressure to be perpetually "available." By leaning into solitude and placing emphasis on the significance of your shared moments, you maintain the essence of closeness without placing undue stress on the relationship or yourself.

℘ Building Emotional Intelligence to Support Balance

Emotional intelligence (EI) is the ability to recognize, understand, and manage our own emotions while also empathizing with the emotions of others. When striving to harmonize solitude and social interaction, EI becomes a powerful ally. It equips us with the self-awareness needed to discern when we need alone time and the empathy to articulate those needs in a compassionate way to the people who matter.

First, self-awareness involves understanding our triggers, energy levels, and emotional states. By paying attention to our internal signals—feelings of overwhelm, irritability, or disconnection—we can identify the ideal moment to step back and recharge. Additionally, self-awareness helps us notice when we're isolating ourselves to avoid unresolved issues, rather than engaging in healthy solitude. The more in tune we are with our internal world, the better we can calibrate our behavior to serve both personal well-being and relational harmony.

Second, self-regulation refers to our capacity to manage emotional impulses. With heightened EI, we learn to communicate our need for space calmly, without lashing out or waiting until we're overwhelmed. This disciplined approach fosters understanding instead of tension. For instance, rather than abruptly canceling social plans when feeling overstimulated, a person with strong EI might say, "I'm feeling a bit drained today. Can we reschedule for a time when I can be more fully present?"

Empathy is the third component that strengthens our relationships while we seek solitude. Truly understanding how our alone time may affect others—and acknowledging their feelings of concern or misunderstanding—creates a supportive environment for respectful dialogue. Empathy paves the way for compromise; if a friend is anxious about your absence, you can reassure them by scheduling a future meet-up or offering a quick check-in call on a mutually agreed-upon day.

Lastly, building social skills—such as active listening, conflict resolution, and open communication—completes the emotional intelligence package. These skills help sustain healthy relationships that recognize solitude as a vital component, ensuring that moments apart serve to refresh and fortify the connections we value.

℘ Strategies for Balancing Solitude and Social Life

Finding a healthy rhythm between solitude and togetherness requires intentional strategies that cater to individual personalities, relationships, and lifestyles. Below are several approaches that can help:

1. *Create a Structured Schedule:* Designate specific time blocks for solitude. Perhaps you allocate early mornings or late evenings as "quiet hours" where you meditate, journal, or engage in personal hobbies. This predictable routine reduces last-minute stress about finding alone time and demonstrates to others that you respect your commitments to both yourself and them.
2. *Use "Transition Moments" Wisely:* Small windows, like commuting or lunch breaks, can become mini-retreats for decompressing. Instead of scrolling through social media or texting, try taking a mindful walk, reading, or simply reflecting on the day. These bite-sized bits of solitude can prevent mental and emotional overload.
3. *Plan Social Interactions Around Shared Values:* It's not merely about the quantity of social events but the quality. Seek out opportunities that resonate with your interests and passions. Whether it's a cooking class with friends, a volunteer activity, or a hiking trip, you're more likely to feel fulfilled if your social experiences align with your authentic self—something you discover and refine during alone time.
4. *Leverage Technology Thoughtfully:* While technology can interrupt solitude, it can also make social life more manageable. Coordinate group outings with efficient communication tools and politely decline or reschedule when you sense your energy is depleted. Use apps to share calendars, so your loved ones can see your "busy" or "unavailable" blocks without feeling left in the dark.
5. *Establish Clear Boundaries and Expectations:* Make it known that you are not rejecting others by taking time for yourself. Regularly communicate your intentions—this fosters respect and reduces misunderstandings. Some people find it helpful to post a simple note on the door or send a group message saying, "I'll be offline for a bit, but I'll check in later."

By combining these strategies with self-compassion and emotional intelligence, you can smoothly navigate the tightrope between solitude and social engagement. The result is a more balanced life that honors both personal growth and meaningful connections.

In a world that often prizes busyness and constant engagement, it can feel counterintuitive to seek out moments of quiet reflection. Yet solitude is not only beneficial—it is vital for our mental, emotional, and even spiritual health. By carving out meaningful alone time, we deepen self-awareness, nurture creativity, and enhance our capacity to connect authentically with others. Rather than being antagonistic forces, solitude and relationships can fortify one another when approached with intention and respect.

Maintaining relationships while embracing solitude hinges on several key principles. First, understanding solitude as a positive, restorative choice—distinct from loneliness—removes much of the stigma that might prevent people from taking the necessary steps to reclaim their personal space. Second, establishing healthy boundaries and communicating needs effectively ensures that solitude does not inadvertently harm relationships. It becomes a shared understanding rather than a point of contention. Third, emotional intelligence allows us to remain attuned to our own needs and those of others, providing a framework for empathy, compromise, and mutual support.

Ultimately, the quality of your relationships is not measured by the frequency of contact, but by the depth of understanding and emotional presence each person brings to the table. Intentional, mindful interactions can flourish when each individual has had the time and mental clarity afforded by solitude. By overcoming guilt, fear, and cultural misconceptions, we can confidently claim the alone time we need while remaining firmly rooted in the love and camaraderie of those around us.

Solitude, when balanced with genuine connection, acts as a cornerstone of psychological resilience and relational well-being. Through thoughtful scheduling, clear communication, and mutual respect, you can maintain strong bonds without sacrificing your inner life. The harmonious interplay of solitude and togetherness offers a potent recipe for a fulfilling, enriched existence—one where you can stand firmly on your own feet and walk hand-in-hand with the people you cherish.

Chapter 30: Technological Boundaries and Digital Detox

Each beep of your phone can be an invitation to pause and reflect: Do I need to respond externally, or is it time to listen internally?

Introduction

In an era dominated by smartphones, wearable devices, and constant online connectivity, it can be difficult to separate our digital lives from our real lives. Technology has enriched our world with convenience, speed, and global reach—connecting us with people and information on an unprecedented scale. However, this digital revolution has also ushered in mental, emotional, and physical challenges, often rooted in our inability to disengage from our devices. Many people find themselves caught in a cycle of screen overuse, checking notifications habitually, and struggling to remain present in face-to-face interactions. As this phenomenon grows more widespread, individuals are increasingly seeking ways to establish healthier relationships with technology.

One valuable strategy is to set deliberate "technological boundaries" or rules and guidelines about the time, place, and manner in which we use our devices. Alongside these boundaries, a "digital detox" can serve as an opportunity to recalibrate, rest, and refocus on non-digital aspects of life. A digital detox does not require renouncing technology altogether; rather, it involves consciously stepping back from screen-based activities for a set period. In doing so, individuals can cultivate mindfulness, reduce stress, and create room for meaningful human connections. This paper explores the importance of establishing boundaries with technology, discusses the psychological and societal factors fueling digital dependency, offers strategies for a successful digital detox, and examines the long-term benefits of a healthier relationship with our devices.

The Necessity of Setting Technological Boundaries

 Living in a Hyperconnected World

The modern world is in a state of hyperconnectivity. From the moment we wake up to the moment we fall asleep, it is easy to remain tethered to our smartphones—checking social media feeds, scrolling through emails, or watching videos. The convenience of instantaneous communication has triggered an "always-on" culture, where work emails arrive at all hours, social media updates never pause, and the default expectation is to respond promptly. In such an environment, it's difficult to remember a time when long stretches of silence were the norm.

Although technology undoubtedly brings forth benefits—facilitating remote work, enabling international friendships, and providing quick access to news—its omnipresence also makes it challenging to create downtime for oneself. This can lead to stress, interruptions in daily life, and even addictive tendencies, as each "ping" or "ding" can prompt a dopamine-driven reward cycle. The path to regaining control over how we engage with technology begins with building protective structures around its use. These boundaries ensure that we remain active, discerning participants rather than passive consumers in the digital sphere.

Indicators of Digital Overload

Before individuals can effectively set boundaries, they must first recognize the signs of digital overload. These can be subtle or overt, but key indicators include:

1. **Compulsive Checking**: An uncontrollable urge to check one's phone, even in situations where it is inappropriate or unsafe (e.g., while driving).
2. **Social Withdrawal**: Preferring virtual communication to face-to-face interaction, or feeling anxious in situations where devices are not allowed.
3. **Sleep Disturbances**: Difficulty unwinding at night due to late-night scrolling or excessive exposure to blue light.
4. **Decreased Productivity**: Struggling to complete tasks without interruptions from online alerts or notifications.
5. **Emotional Distress**: Experiencing anxiety, irritability, or mood swings related to digital connections, such as comparing oneself to others on social media.

Recognizing these patterns is the crucial first step toward a healthier relationship with technology. Once identified, individuals can better tailor strategies for setting boundaries and reclaiming a sense of control.

The Psychological and Societal Impact of Digital Overuse

 *Mental Health Concerns*

Overuse of technology has been linked to an array of mental health concerns, including heightened stress, anxiety, and depression. The constant flood of information—news alerts, online debates, social media notifications—can overload our cognitive processes and exacerbate stress. Additionally, social media platforms encourage a culture of comparison. Users frequently view curated, idealized versions of others' lives, leading to feelings of inadequacy or low self-esteem. These negative emotions may compound over time, contributing to burnout and other mental health issues.

Another significant concern is the "fear of missing out" (FOMO), a phenomenon fueled by social media where individuals worry about being excluded from social events or missing important updates. This fear, in turn, drives perpetual engagement with digital platforms, resulting in a vicious cycle of dependency. Hence, boundaries are an essential safeguard to prevent technology from adversely impacting mental health.

⭐ *Societal Expectations and Pressures*

On a societal level, continuous connectivity has shifted norms around communication and availability. Prompt responses to work emails or text messages are often not just desired but expected, even if they arrive late at night or on weekends. For many, this infringes on personal time and fuels stress, as work-life boundaries become blurry. The societal pressure to always be reachable can make individuals feel guilty when they step away from their devices, contributing to a sense of obligation that perpetuates screen overuse.

Additionally, the omnipresence of technology influences interpersonal dynamics. Instead of sharing quality time, friends and family members may simultaneously scroll through their smartphones, focusing more on curated digital feeds than on genuine conversations. Over the long term, this can erode meaningful connections and undermine emotional well-being. By recognizing the impact of these social pressures, we can become more deliberate about crafting personal boundaries, resisting the impulse to be constantly available, and choosing genuine presence over virtual engagement.

Introducing the Digital Detox

☁ *Defining Digital Detox*

A digital detox can be understood as a conscious, temporary break from electronic devices and online services to reduce stress, restore balance, and promote healthier habits. This break can last for varying lengths of time—from a few hours per day to an entire weekend or even longer, depending on individual needs. The essence of a digital detox lies in creating space for offline activities, whether that involves reading a physical book, going for a walk in nature, engaging in face-to-face conversations, or exploring creative pursuits without digital interference.

It's important to note that a digital detox is not about rejecting technology outright. In many cases, technology is integral to work or personal obligations, and a complete removal might be neither feasible nor desirable. Instead, the detox encourages mindfulness about technology use, prompting users to reflect on their digital habits and reintroduce them selectively and purposefully.

☁ *Benefits of a Temporary Digital Break*

Engaging in a digital detox can yield several short-term and long-term benefits. Immediately, participants often experience reduced stress and anxiety due to the decreased burden of notifications and online comparisons. There is a heightened sense of mindfulness, as individuals become more attuned to their immediate surroundings rather than their smartphone screens.

Over time, a regular practice of digital detoxing can cultivate better self-awareness. Individuals learn to identify triggers for overuse (e.g., boredom, procrastination, social pressure) and develop proactive strategies to cope with them. They may also observe improvements in sleep quality, as avoiding late-night device usage fosters healthier circadian rhythms. Moreover, digital detoxes create space for real-life connections, hobbies, and creative pursuits. By "unplugging" more often, individuals often find renewed motivation and a sense of balance in their personal and professional lives.

Strategies for Establishing Technological Boundaries

Identify Your Core Values and Needs

Before setting boundaries, it is helpful to reflect on personal priorities and values. For instance, one might value spending uninterrupted time with family, cultivating a meditative or spiritual practice, or focusing on academic or work performance. Identifying these core values clarifies why we need to minimize distractions. Setting boundaries that align with these values ensures that the measures taken will feel meaningful and worthwhile.

For example, if someone values quality time with family, they might create a "phone-free dinner" rule or limit social media usage in the evening. If another individual values productivity at work, they might schedule email check-ins to specific intervals each day, thus reducing the temptation to respond to every ping in real-time. By connecting boundaries to personal values, individuals can avoid viewing them as restrictions; rather, they become paths to fulfilling what matters most.

Create Device-Free Zones and Times

One of the most tangible ways to maintain technological boundaries is through physical or temporal constraints. A "device-free zone" might be a designated space in the home—such as the dining table or the bedroom—where no electronic devices are permitted. This helps foster presence during mealtimes or rest periods. Similarly, setting "device-free times" can ensure uninterrupted blocks for work, reading, family interactions, or relaxation. An example might be implementing a "no-screens-after-9PM" rule, allowing the mind and body to wind down before bedtime.

These boundaries can also extend to professional contexts. For instance, an organization might establish a rule that emails should not be sent after a certain hour, respecting employees' personal time and helping minimize burnout. Clear guidelines around technology usage reduce ambiguity and free individuals from the guilt of disconnecting.

☁ Utilize App Limits and Digital Well-Being Tools

Many smartphones now come with built-in digital well-being features that monitor screen time and allow users to set time limits for specific apps. Similarly, numerous third-party tools can block distracting websites or social media platforms during certain hours. By harnessing these solutions, individuals can customize their usage to align with healthy boundaries. For example, someone might configure their phone to lock social media apps after one hour of daily use or turn off notifications from non-essential apps. Over time, these small, automated changes can have a substantial impact on reducing mindless scrolling and promoting healthier digital habits.

☁ Communicate Your Boundaries

Setting boundaries is more effective when they are communicated to friends, family, and coworkers. Explaining one's reasons—such as the desire to be more present, to reduce stress, or to focus on important tasks—can garner respect and support from others. When boundaries are clear, people are less likely to feel slighted by delayed responses or unavailable phone calls. In professional environments, respectfully asserting boundaries might involve specifying that emails sent after a certain hour will be addressed the next workday. Although some people may initially resist these limits, open communication ensures that your boundaries are understood rather than perceived as acts of negligence or disinterest.

Conducting a Successful Digital Detox

☁ Plan and Prepare

A digital detox that happens spontaneously can still be effective, but thorough preparation increases the likelihood of lasting benefits. This might involve:

- **Choosing a Timeframe**: Decide how long the detox will last and mark it on the calendar.
- **Informing Others**: Let colleagues, friends, and family know you will be "off the grid" for certain hours or days.

- **Setting Goals**: Outline what you hope to achieve, whether it's improved focus on a creative project, more quality time with loved ones, or simply stress relief.
- **Gathering Alternatives**: Stock up on reading material, plan outdoor activities, or arrange social events that don't rely on screens.

By setting these foundations, individuals can avoid emergencies or misunderstandings and maximize the benefits of their detox period.

Reflect and Track Your Experience

During the detox, it's helpful to keep a journal or take mental notes of the emotional and physical changes that unfold. Some may notice a spike in restlessness or anxiety at the beginning, which gradually subsides as the urge to check the phone diminishes. Others might observe an increased ability to focus, surging creativity, or a new appreciation for offline activities.

Reflecting on these observations consolidates learning and empowers individuals to identify triggers and opportunities for better habits. For instance, one might realize that social media usage spikes during periods of low mood or boredom, leading to self-awareness that can inform future boundaries.

Reintroduce Technology Mindfully

When concluding a digital detox, the key is intentional reintroduction. Instead of returning to old habits, consider implementing the strategies mentioned earlier—device-free zones, app limits, and designated tech-free periods. The detox period serves as a reset button, but lasting improvements hinge on whether individuals incorporate new behaviors into their daily routines. Mindful reintroduction could include checking social media at set times, turning off push notifications, or limiting streaming services to specific hours. The ultimate goal is not total abstinence but rather a healthier, more balanced relationship with technology.

The Role of Social Media in Digital Detox

Understanding Social Media's Pull

Social media platforms are designed to be engaging, with infinite scrolling, "likes," and content algorithms that deliver personalized posts to keep users hooked. By providing social validation and facilitating rapid communication, these platforms tap into fundamental human desires: the need for connection, self-expression, and acceptance. However, this design can also lead to detrimental effects, including time waste, comparison anxiety, and reduced self-esteem.

⑥ *Moderating Social Media Usage*

An effective digital detox often involves rethinking social media habits. For many, social media is the main conduit of screen overuse, and breaks from these platforms can be particularly restorative. Some practical tips for moderating social media usage include:

- **Unfollowing or Muting**: Curate your feed by removing accounts that trigger negative emotions, anxiety, or self-comparison.
- **Batch-Processing Posts**: Limit the times of day you check or post on social platforms.
- **Using Web Extensions**: Install browser extensions that block social media after a set duration.
- **Switching Off Notifications**: Turning off push notifications prevents the phone from dictating when you engage.

By incorporating these measures, individuals can remain connected with friends and family while safeguarding their mental health and personal time.

Boundaries in Various Contexts

⑥ *The Workplace*

In professional environments, the omnipresent nature of digital devices can blur the lines between work and personal life. Setting clear boundaries at work is essential for maintaining a sustainable routine. Some companies have begun adopting policies that discourage sending emails after hours or on weekends, recognizing that constant connectivity can contribute to employee burnout. On a personal level, workers can set specific times to check emails and messages, use focus apps to block distracting websites, and communicate with colleagues about expected response times.

⑥ *The Home and Family Life*

Families that seek deeper connections and healthier habits may decide to implement household rules around technology usage. For instance, parents can limit children's screen time, designate "no-phone" time during meals, or create a shared charging station in a common room where phones must be deposited at night. By modeling these behaviors, adults set an example for younger family members, fostering responsible tech use. Family digital detox weekends can also offer unique bonding opportunities, encouraging outdoor activities, board games, or communal projects without the distractions of notifications.

Social Circles and Relationships

In friendships and romantic partnerships, smartphones can be both a tool for connection and a source of conflict. Some couples or friend groups establish "tech-free" date nights or hangouts to enhance in-person engagement. If you feel that a relationship is suffering due to excessive digital engagement, honest communication about boundaries can help reset expectations. Balancing digital and in-person communication ensures that technology remains a supportive tool rather than a barrier to meaningful relationships.

Long-Term Benefits of Healthy Technological Boundaries

∀ *Improved Well-Being and Mental Health*

When individuals consistently enforce technological boundaries, they often report lower stress levels, more restful sleep, and a heightened sense of calm. By disconnecting from a barrage of digital stimuli, the mind gets a chance to rest and refocus, improving mental clarity and emotional resilience. Over time, this can reduce anxiety, promote better mood regulation, and even enhance one's sense of self-worth, as constant external validation or comparison loses its hold.

∀ *Enhanced Productivity and Focus*

Another significant advantage is the boost in productivity. Constant interruptions and multitasking can negatively impact our ability to concentrate. By scheduling technology usage, designating device-free times, and engaging in periodic digital detoxes, we create an environment conducive to deep work. Tasks can be completed more efficiently, and people often find themselves achieving higher-quality outcomes because they are better able to concentrate on the work at hand without distraction.

∀ *Stronger Interpersonal Connections*

True presence—free from digital interruptions—fosters more authentic conversations and connections. When individuals are not splitting their attention between the person in front of them and notifications on their phone, they can engage more deeply and empathetically. Over time, healthier technological boundaries can lead to more intimate, fulfilling relationships, both at home and within wider social circles.

∀ *Relapse into Old Patterns*

Just as with any habit change, there is a risk of reverting to old behaviors, such as mindless scrolling or over-reliance on devices, once the novelty of establishing boundaries wears off. It is critical to consistently assess and adjust one's habits. Periodic "check-ins" help detect slippages early, allowing for timely course correction. For example, if you realize you are gradually returning to excessive social media use, revisit app limits or take another short-term digital detox as a refresher.

∀ *Social or Professional Resistance*

Not everyone in an individual's social or professional circle may understand or support strict boundaries around technology. Coworkers might demand immediate responses; friends might feel ignored. In such cases, proactive communication is key. Explaining why these boundaries matter—emphasizing the benefits to mental health, work quality, and personal relationships—can help mitigate misunderstandings. Ultimately, standing firm in one's choices, while still being flexible about emergencies or critical tasks, ensures boundaries remain effective without entirely isolating the individual from important responsibilities.

∀ *Overzealous Restrictions*

An equally important consideration is finding balance in boundary-setting. In extreme cases, individuals may overcompensate by excessively limiting their digital access, risking difficulties in everyday tasks such as responding to work emails, staying informed, or maintaining necessary social connections. The goal is not total abstinence but balance. If restrictions start causing undue stress or inconvenience, it may be time to recalibrate and adopt a more moderate approach.

Establishing technological boundaries and engaging in periodic digital detoxes offers a powerful antidote to the relentless demands of a hyperconnected world. While technology continues to shape the global landscape, the choice to consciously moderate its use rests in our hands. By identifying core values, creating device-free zones, leveraging digital well-being tools, and communicating boundaries openly, individuals can reclaim control over their digital lives.

A healthy relationship with technology is one in which devices serve as helpful instruments rather than tyrannical masters. Through mindful usage, we can protect our mental health, strengthen real-life connections, and promote productivity. Digital detoxes, in particular, act as resets—providing valuable insights into our patterns, priorities, and triggers. Once we re-enter the digital realm, we can do so with clarity and intentionality, ensuring that our screens are instruments of empowerment rather than sources of stress.

As society continues to integrate technology more deeply into everyday life, setting these boundaries will only grow in importance. For individuals, families, and communities alike, embracing balanced tech habits can lead to more meaningful experiences, improved well-being, and a sustainable approach to the digital frontier. By choosing when and how to engage with our devices, we ultimately choose to invest in our overall quality of life.

Chapter 31: Solitude in the Modern World

In a society that idolizes busyness, choosing solitude is a radical step toward self-discovery and liberation.

Solitude in the Modern World

Introduction

Solitude has been a subject of philosophical, psychological, and literary fascination for centuries. From ancient hermits retreating into remote caves to spiritual seekers finding stillness in cloistered monasteries, the pursuit of solitude has been intertwined with quests for wisdom, self-knowledge, and transcendence. In the modern world, however, solitude has taken on new shapes and meanings. With unprecedented connectivity enabled by digital technologies, we live in an era where solitude can seem increasingly rare—and at times, ironically, increasingly necessary. Our hyper-connected lives can make quiet time alone a luxury that is either elusive or misunderstood.

But what does solitude in the modern world truly entail? Is solitude just another word for privacy, or does it encompass deeper experiences of self-reflection and creative contemplation? This essay aims to explore these questions by examining the role of solitude today, the benefits and potential drawbacks of seeking time away from constant contact, and the unique ways that solitude can help us cope with, understand, and flourish within the complexities of our digital age.

Defining Solitude: Past and Present

Before exploring solitude in the modern context, it is necessary to lay down some definitions. Solitude refers to a state of being alone, but this aloneness need not be synonymous with loneliness. In fact, many philosophers and psychologists make a clear distinction between solitude (a positive or neutral condition of being by oneself) and loneliness (a painful emotional experience of lacking meaningful connections).

Historically, solitude has often carried connotations of spiritual reflection, introspection, and creative incubation. Thinkers like Henry David Thoreau, who famously withdrew to Walden Pond, or hermits within various religious traditions, have shown that solitude can be sought deliberately for personal growth. Solitude has also been essential in art, literature, and scientific endeavors: authors, painters, and inventors alike have testified to the power of withdrawing from society to stimulate reflection, creativity, and self-discovery.

In the modern world, however, solitude is shaped by the cultural and technological milieu in which we find ourselves. Constant stimuli—from social media notifications to ceaseless advertisement streams—often threaten to overwhelm our senses and diminish our capacity to be alone. At the same time, the demands of work, family, and social relationships can leave little room for time spent in solitude. When we do manage to secure moments alone, we may feel pressured to fill these moments with digital distractions or interpret them as "unproductive" or even antisocial. Hence, the very meaning and practice of solitude must be continuously reevaluated in light of ever-changing social norms and technological realities.

The Cultural Context of Solitude

The modern world's emphasis on productivity and perpetual engagement has generated a cultural context in which solitude is often undervalued. From a young age, many children are encouraged to participate in extracurricular activities and social endeavors, while their quiet time or unstructured play is seen as idle or wasteful. As individuals grow older, the expectation to stay connected intensifies: people are inundated with social obligations, networking events, and an endless stream of digital communications that can make the idea of extended solitude feel like a fantasy.

Moreover, some fear that solitude might hinder professional growth or disrupt social ties. The ubiquitous presence of smartphones and social media platforms has only heightened these concerns: missing out on group chats, networking opportunities on LinkedIn, or even ephemeral Stories on platforms like Instagram can feed into FOMO (Fear Of Missing Out). This cultural conditioning can subtly reinforce the notion that solitude is synonymous with social isolation or personal stagnation.

However, these beliefs may be driven more by social constructs than by any universal truth about human well-being. Indeed, numerous studies in psychology and neuroscience suggest that solitude—deliberate and thoughtful time alone—can be profoundly beneficial for mental health, creativity, and emotional regulation. By understanding how cultural expectations shape our views on solitude, we can actively question whether those perspectives serve us—or whether they might be depriving us of a valuable aspect of human experience.

The Benefits of Solitude

One might wonder, in a culture that so often prizes sociability and constant availability, what is the value of solitude? Research in psychology and personal testimonies from artists, scholars, and contemplatives point toward various benefits.

Psychological Resilience and Self-Reflection

Spending time alone enables us to step back from the busyness of daily life and examine our thoughts, emotions, and behaviors more carefully. Without the noise and immediate feedback of external influences, we can listen more closely to our inner voices. In doing so, we gain clarity about our personal values, long-term objectives, and emotional states. This self-reflection can foster greater self-awareness, which is linked to improved emotional intelligence and stronger personal boundaries.

Moreover, solitude can be protective for our mental health. It allows space for decompressing from social stress or workplace anxiety. When we afford ourselves the time to process our experiences, we often find that problems which seemed overwhelming in the heat of daily interactions become more manageable.

Enhanced Creativity

Creativity thrives in solitude for many people. When working alone in a distraction-free environment, individuals can more easily enter a state of flow. Whether painting, writing, composing music, or solving complex problems, the unbroken attention that solitude affords can dramatically improve the creative process. Historically, myriad artists, from Vincent van Gogh to Virginia Woolf, have noted the importance of solitude to their work.

In the modern age, innovative thinkers and entrepreneurs alike have echoed these sentiments. Effective brainstorming, while it can benefit from group input, also demands periods of individual reflection. Solitude fosters an atmosphere where novel ideas can blossom without the immediate constraints or judgments of others.

Spiritual and Existential Exploration

Many of the world's spiritual traditions incorporate periods of solitude as a vital element of their practices. Meditation retreats, silent monastic orders, and hermitages are just a few examples. The purpose behind these practices is often to help practitioners develop deeper insight into the nature of the mind, reality, and existence itself. In solitude, questions about meaning, purpose, and interconnectedness can be approached without the distractions of routine social chatter.

For those less inclined toward formal religious or spiritual traditions, solitude can still offer an opportunity for existential exploration. The quietness of being alone may awaken a sense of awe or wonder about life. Though this can be unsettling for some, many find it profoundly enriching, as it touches on the core of what it means to be human.

Emotional Regulation and Stress Reduction

The modern world is saturated with stress-inducing stimuli: tight deadlines, global news of crises, social comparison on digital platforms, and more. In solitude, we can control our environment more effectively. By choosing when and how to engage with technology or social interactions, we protect ourselves from constant stimulation. This helps in regulating emotions and reducing stress, which, in turn, supports better overall health—physically and mentally.

The Pitfalls and Challenges of Solitude

Despite its many benefits, solitude is not without potential challenges. For individuals who experience social anxiety, depression, or other mental health concerns, extended periods of solitude can exacerbate feelings of isolation. Moreover, those who lack a social support network might find that solitude morphs into unwelcome loneliness, intensifying emotional pain.

From Solitude to Loneliness

For solitude to be healthy, it typically needs to be chosen or embraced rather than imposed by external circumstances. When people are forced into isolation—due to factors such as social marginalization, health conditions, or lack of mobility—they may experience genuine loneliness. Over time, loneliness has been correlated with a range of negative health outcomes, including increased inflammation, lowered immune response, and even a heightened risk of mortality.

Thus, while cultivating solitude can be beneficial, it must be done with a balanced perspective that recognizes the value of relationships and community. Healthy solitude, in essence, works best when coupled with supportive connections in one's life.

Misuse of Digital Tools

Some people believe they are enjoying solitude when they are, in fact, continuously distracted by digital tools. Scrolling through social media feeds, binge-watching television, or immersing oneself in endless podcasts might offer physical separation from others, but these activities do not necessarily foster genuine solitude. They can simply be another form of noise that stifles introspection. In the modern world, effectively cultivating solitude may require conscious efforts to engage in what Cal Newport calls "digital minimalism," i.e., deliberately limiting or structuring technology use to reduce mental clutter.

Social Stigma

Choosing to be alone can also generate social stigma. Friends and family might interpret a person's desire for solitude as rejection or aloofness. In professional environments, someone who seeks quiet time might appear less of a "team player." These reactions can discourage people from pursuing solitude, despite its benefits. Navigating these cultural and social pressures may require assertiveness and clear communication about one's need for personal space.

Technology, Social Media, and the Decline (or Transformation) of Solitude

Arguably, one of the most significant transformations in modern solitude has been driven by digital technology. Social media, messaging platforms, and video conferencing tools have revolutionized how we communicate, making it possible to maintain near-continuous contact with friends, acquaintances, and even strangers. While these technologies can improve the sense of community for those who are physically isolated, they also intensify the sense of being perpetually reachable.

The Illusion of Connection

Social media platforms can foster the illusion of closeness. One might assume that scrolling through a friend's pictures or reading brief status updates offers genuine insight into their life. However, passive consumption of curated online personas often lacks the empathy, depth, and reciprocity of real conversations. Over time, this discrepancy can leave individuals feeling more isolated, not less.

Additionally, when we rely on digital platforms to fill every quiet gap in our day— checking our phones in waiting rooms, in line at the store, or in bed before sleep— we deprive ourselves of micro-moments of solitude. These small windows of time once allowed for daydreaming or reflection, but are now often filled with digital noise.

The Pressure to Be Constantly Available

In many workplaces, especially post-pandemic where remote and hybrid work are common, the boundaries between "on" and "off" have blurred. Employees may feel obliged to monitor work emails or chat channels well beyond traditional office hours. The capacity for solitude is further eroded by the expectation of immediate response.

This pressure is not limited to the professional realm. Socially, individuals might feel obligated to respond instantaneously to text messages or invitations. Though these norms vary across cultures, the general trend is toward expecting rapid digital engagement. Resisting such norms in pursuit of uninterrupted solitude can require significant self-discipline and the ability to set firm boundaries.

Technology as a Facilitator of Solitude

Interestingly, technology can also foster solitude when used with intention. For instance, guided meditation apps can help users cultivate solitary mindfulness practices, while digital libraries grant immediate access to reading material that can enhance solitary learning. Similarly, some forms of social media can connect individuals with communities that value solitude—such as groups dedicated to quiet reading, mindful living, or nature retreats—offering resources and encouragement to maintain balanced solitude in an otherwise noisy world.

In other words, the same digital tools that can undermine solitude can also be harnessed to support it. The key is mindful usage and setting digital boundaries to ensure that technology is enhancing rather than eroding one's capacity for true alone time.

Solitude in Urban Environments

As our world becomes more urbanized, the question of finding solitude in crowded cities looms large. Noise pollution, crammed living spaces, constant movement, and ubiquitous advertising make city dwellers especially vulnerable to a loss of solitude. Yet, city life can also provide unique opportunities for solitude—sometimes unexpectedly.

Public Spaces and Anonymous Solitude

Cities are filled with public spaces—parks, libraries, museums—where individuals can blend into the crowd while still enjoying a private mental bubble. For some people, solitude does not require complete physical isolation; it can be a matter of immersing oneself in a place where no one demands your attention. Sitting in a café with a book, taking a quiet walk in a city park, or simply standing on a busy street corner lost in thought can yield a sense of separation from others, enabling introspection.

Architectural and Urban Design Solutions

Urban design can influence the availability and quality of solitude. Spaces that incorporate green areas, pedestrian zones, and smaller, more human-scale neighborhood layouts encourage quieter, more reflective experiences. For instance, urban planners who prioritize walkable neighborhoods, tranquil pocket parks, or communal gardens create a buffer from the frenetic pace that might otherwise dominate city life.

Moreover, innovative architectural designs can address the need for personal space, whether through communal living arrangements that balance shared amenities with private retreats or the integration of soundproofing measures to reduce ambient noise.

The Quest for Nature

Cities also offer gateways to larger natural environments—forests, mountains, or bodies of water—if only for a short retreat. Weekend getaways, hiking excursions, or secluded beach visits can offer meaningful respites from urban chaos. While not always a sustainable daily practice, these journeys into nature can be crucial for those who find deeper solitude and renewal in the wilderness.

Solitude as a Path to Self-Actualization

Modern psychology, following pioneers such as Abraham Maslow and Carl Rogers, emphasizes the importance of self-actualization: the process of realizing one's full potential and cultivating authenticity. Solitude can play a significant role in this journey.

Discovering Personal Values and Passions

When individuals step away from the influence of others—be it family, friends, or societal expectations—they can more clearly discern their true interests and values. In solitude, one can experiment, reflect, and make choices based on intrinsic motivations rather than external pressures. Over time, this leads to greater authenticity and personal fulfillment.

Strengthening Self-Reliance

Spending time alone helps cultivate self-reliance. Even mundane activities like cooking for oneself, traveling alone, or undertaking personal projects without outside assistance can bolster confidence in one's abilities. These small successes can translate into a stronger sense of agency in other areas of life, including relationships, career decisions, and personal projects.

Building Emotional Maturity

Emotional maturity requires understanding and managing one's inner world. In solitude, there is less distraction, making it possible to notice subtle emotional currents that might be drowned out during social interactions. As individuals become more familiar with their emotions, they can learn healthier coping mechanisms and develop greater empathy for others. This self-knowledge also reduces the risk of projecting unresolved issues onto friends, partners, or co-workers.

Practical Strategies for Cultivating Solitude

Given the many pressures of modern life, how can one realistically incorporate solitude into daily or weekly routines?

Scheduling Solitude

Planning solitude proactively ensures that it does not get squeezed out by competing demands. Individuals might start by setting aside a specific time—perhaps half an hour each morning for quiet reading, journaling, or meditation. Alternatively, a weekly "retreat" to a local park, museum, or library can become a cherished ritual.

Creating Technology Boundaries

Because digital connectivity is one of the primary barriers to solitude, it is often essential to set firm boundaries with technology. This can involve turning off notifications during certain hours, implementing social media "fasts," or establishing phone-free zones in one's home. Devices can also be used more consciously: for instance, dedicating a tablet solely to reading and turning off internet access while doing so can limit the temptation to check notifications.

Engaging in Solitude-Friendly Activities

Not all activities are equally conducive to solitude. Some, like painting, writing, contemplative walking, gardening, or certain sports (e.g., distance running, cycling, or swimming) naturally lend themselves to solitary reflection. Choosing an activity that one finds genuinely enjoyable increases the likelihood of sustaining the habit of solitude over time.

Learning to Communicate One's Needs

Since solitude can be misconstrued as antisocial, it is often helpful to explain to friends, family, or colleagues why you are seeking this time alone. Emphasizing that solitude helps you recharge, reflect, and ultimately be more present in relationships can mitigate misunderstandings. Clear communication about boundaries—such as not replying to messages after a certain time—can also reduce the social friction that arises when you begin to prioritize alone time.

Balancing Solitude and Connection

While celebrating the virtues of solitude, it is essential to acknowledge that human beings are inherently social creatures. A balanced life usually involves a healthy interplay between solitude and connection.

Healthy Interdependence

Rather than perceiving solitude and social life as competing forces, one can see them as complementary. Solitude allows for deeper self-understanding and personal growth, which can enrich one's relationships. Meanwhile, social interactions provide emotional support, shared experiences, and the joys of companionship.

In recognizing this interdependence, an individual can mindfully shape relationships that respect personal boundaries and value alone time. For instance, couples or roommates might agree on "quiet hours" or personal retreats, while also scheduling quality time together.

Social Solitude

In certain contexts, a sense of solitude can be maintained even in the presence of others, especially if there is a shared understanding of quiet and independence. Silent retreats, co-working spaces that prioritize minimal chatter, or reading clubs where people gather but focus on individual reading can provide a social dimension without disrupting solitude.

The Future of Solitude

As technology continues to evolve, the relationship between solitude and connectivity will remain in flux. Advances in virtual reality, artificial intelligence, and immersive communication platforms might further erode traditional boundaries, making uninterrupted alone time more difficult to preserve. However, these same technologies might also usher in creative solutions, such as personalized "quiet rooms" using noise-canceling materials, or digital detox programs that become widely recognized and socially supported.

Climate change and global population growth may also impact our ability to find physical spaces for solitude. Crowding, environmental crises, and resource scarcity could spur reevaluations of urban planning and resource distribution, possibly making communal efforts toward preserving spaces of quiet reflection even more critical.

Ultimately, the value of solitude will likely remain a constant in human life. As we move further into the 21st century, cultivating the capacity for solitude could prove to be an essential skill—a form of mental and emotional literacy that enables individuals to navigate a rapidly changing social and technological landscape.

Solitude in the modern world is both a challenge and an opportunity. Cultural expectations often pressure individuals to remain perpetually connected, while new technologies serve as both facilitators and obstacles to being alone. Yet, the benefits of solitude are manifold: enhanced creativity, emotional resilience, spiritual and existential exploration, and self-actualization, to name just a few.

To fully harness the power of solitude, one must navigate social stigma, carefully manage digital devices, and intentionally carve out time for reflection. In doing so, solitude can become a source of balance and clarity, enabling individuals to better engage with the fast-paced, noisy realities of modern life. Far from being a relic of the past, solitude emerges as a vital practice for those seeking to live more thoughtful, healthy, and meaningful lives in an era of constant distraction.

In recognizing the timeless value of solitude—and by challenging the cultural biases that dismiss it—modern individuals have the opportunity to reclaim a much-needed space for introspection and growth. Whether found in a crowded city park, a quiet room at home, or a remote cabin in nature, solitude remains a refuge where the mind can wander, creativity can flourish, and the self can come into sharper focus. By weaving deliberate solitude into the fabric of our daily routines, we preserve a touch of stillness and depth in a world that, more than ever, seems hungry for constant motion.

And finally, to clear the way when constant obligations intercede, one must simply master the "Art of Saying 'No'.

 The Art of Saying "No"

High achievers often emphasize that true success comes not just from pursuing opportunities, but from ruthlessly prioritizing by declining the rest. This "art of no" protects time, energy, and focus for what truly matters. Below, I've compiled key insights and direct quotes from Elon Musk (via close accounts) and other high achievers such as Steve Jobs and prominent figures like Warren Buffett. These are drawn from interviews, talks, and writings where they've addressed the topic.

While Musk hasn't shared a direct public quote on saying "no," his ex-wife Justine Musk (in a TEDx talk) attributes his extraordinary success to mastering this skill: "Behind every no is a deeper yes." She explains that Musk guards his time by rejecting distractions and non-essential activities, allowing full dedication to ventures like Tesla and SpaceX. This intentional "no" reshapes boundaries and self-worth, a lesson she learned from him.

Justine Musk highlights how Musk's selective focus on ambitious goals stems from saying "no" often, enabling him to channel energy into transformative projects.

Steve Jobs has repeatedly emphasized that *"Focus is about saying no and you have to say no."* Sometimes expanding to *"People think focus means saying yes to the thing you've got to focus on. But that's not what it means at all. It means saying no to the hundred other good ideas that there are."* Jobs viewed "no" as the ultimate tool for innovation at Apple, arguing that simplicity and breakthroughs require rejecting even appealing distractions to hone in on the essential.

Warren Buffett would often emphasize that *"The difference between successful people and really successful people is that really successful people say no to almost everything."* Buffett stresses that protecting your calendar is key to compound growth—by declining most requests, you create space for high-impact work. This habit separates the merely accomplished from the legendary.

Richard Branson (Founder of Virgin Group) *"If somebody offers you an amazing opportunity but you are not sure you can do it, say yes—then learn how to do it later. But learn to say no to everything else that doesn't light you up."*

Seth Godin (Author, marketer) *"Instead of wondering when your next vacation is, maybe you should set up a life you don't need to escape from."* (Tied to saying no to unfulfilling commitments.) Godin promotes "no" as essential for crafting a remarkable, intentional life.

Brené Brown (Researcher, author on vulnerability) *"Choosing to say no is choosing yourself—it's an act of courage that builds boundaries and resilience."* Brown frames "no" as a boundary-setting practice for emotional well-being and authenticity.

Since this is a topic an chapter dedicated to a particular idea, there is a tendency to want to elaborate. You needn't be rude and certainly establishing one's moral and personal character, goals and priorities is key to saying yes to the right things, and no to the distractions. So, here elaboration is simply "No" or more politely "No, thank you" is a complete sentence.

Chapter 32: Creating Healthy Relationships with Internalization

Internalization is the process of adopting external ideas, beliefs, values, or behaviors as part of an individual's or group's own internal framework. It involves integrating external influences—such as societal norms, cultural values, or learned behaviors—into one's personal identity, worldview, or decision-making process, often unconsciously or through socialization.

A child may internalize their parents' moral values, like honesty, by adopting them as their own guiding principles.

Internalization, the process of adopting external ideas, beliefs, values, or behaviors into one's own framework, plays a significant role in shaping personal identity, relationships, and mental well-being. While internalization can foster growth and social cohesion, an unhealthy relationship with it can lead to self-doubt, loss of individuality, or rigid adherence to external expectations. Cultivating a healthy relationship with internalization involves self-awareness, critical reflection, and intentional choices to ensure the values and behaviors you adopt align with your authentic self and promote well-being. Below, we explore strategies to create a healthy relationship with internalization in personal and social contexts.

Understanding Internalization in Relationships

Internalization occurs naturally in relationships as individuals absorb values, norms, or behaviors from family, friends, partners, or society. For example:

- *Family Influence:* A person might internalize their parents' emphasis on kindness, shaping how they interact with others.
- *Cultural Norms:* Societal expectations, such as gender roles or professional ambitions, can influence one's self-perception and behavior.
- *Romantic Relationships:* Partners may adopt each other's habits, values, or communication styles over time.

While internalization can strengthen bonds and create shared values, it can become problematic when it leads to:

- Loss of individuality, where one suppresses personal desires to conform to others' expectations.
- Internalized negativity, such as adopting harmful stereotypes or self-critical beliefs from external sources.

- o Codependency, where one's sense of self becomes overly reliant on a partner's or group's approval.

A healthy relationship with internalization balances external influences with personal authenticity, ensuring that adopted values align with one's core beliefs and contribute to personal growth.

Strategies for Healthy Internalization

1. Cultivate Self-Awareness

Self-awareness is the foundation of a healthy relationship with internalization. By understanding your own values, emotions, and motivations, you can critically evaluate which external influences are worth adopting.

- o *Practice Reflection:* Regularly journal or meditate to explore your beliefs and identify which ones stem from external sources versus your authentic self. Ask: "Is this belief mine, or was it shaped by my environment?"
- o *Identify Triggers:* Notice when you feel pressured to conform (e.g., in social settings or relationships). Reflect on whether adopting those behaviors aligns with your values.
- o *Example:* If you feel compelled to prioritize career success over personal hobbies due to societal pressure, assess whether this aligns with your definition of fulfillment.

2. Engage in Critical Thinking

Not all external influences are beneficial. Critically evaluate the ideas, norms, or behaviors you encounter before internalizing them.

- o *Question Sources:* Consider the credibility and intent behind external messages. For instance, are media-driven beauty standards realistic or manipulative?
- o *Seek Diverse Perspectives:* Expose yourself to varied viewpoints to avoid internalizing a narrow set of beliefs. Engage in conversations with people from different backgrounds to broaden your understanding.
- o *Example:* If a friend group emphasizes material wealth, evaluate whether this aligns with your values or if it's a superficial norm you can reject.

3. Set Boundaries

Healthy internalization requires boundaries to protect your individuality and mental health.

- *Limit Toxic Influences:* Distance yourself from relationships or environments that pressure you to adopt harmful beliefs, such as self-criticism or perfectionism.
- *Communicate Needs:* In relationships, express your values and boundaries clearly. For example, if a partner expects you to adopt their lifestyle, discuss how you can maintain your individuality while growing together.
- *Example:* If a family member pushes traditional career expectations, politely assert your interest in a different path while appreciating their perspective.

4. Align Internalized Values with Authenticity

Ensure that the values or behaviors you internalize resonate with your true self.

- **Reflect on Core Values**: Identify 3–5 core values (e.g., honesty, creativity, compassion) that define you. Use these as a filter for deciding which external influences to adopt.
- **Practice Intentional Adoption**: Consciously choose to internalize behaviors that enhance your life. For instance, adopting a partner's habit of daily gratitude can strengthen your relationship and well-being if it feels authentic.
- **Example**: If you admire a friend's discipline in maintaining a healthy lifestyle, adopt similar habits only if they align with your goals and feel sustainable.

5. Foster Growth-Oriented Relationships

Surround yourself with people who encourage mutual growth rather than conformity.

- **Seek Supportive Connections**: Build relationships with individuals who respect your individuality and inspire positive growth. For example, a partner who encourages your passions rather than demanding you adopt theirs fosters healthy internalization.
- **Model Positive Behaviors**: Be a source of positive influence for others. By demonstrating authenticity and self-awareness, you create a reciprocal environment where healthy internalization thrives.
- **Example**: In a romantic relationship, both partners can internalize each other's strengths (e.g., one's optimism, the other's resilience) to grow individually and as a couple.

6. Monitor Mental Health Impacts

Unhealthy internalization can lead to anxiety, low self-esteem, or identity conflicts. Regularly check in with your mental health to ensure internalization serves you positively.

- o *Recognize Red Flags:* Signs of unhealthy internalization include feeling inauthentic, overly self-critical, or disconnected from your goals. Seek therapy or counseling if these persist.
- o *Practice Self-Compassion:* Forgive yourself for internalizing harmful beliefs in the past. Focus on replacing them with affirming, growth-oriented values.
- o *Example:* If you've internalized societal pressure to "have it all" (career, family, perfection), work with a therapist to reframe your priorities around personal fulfillment.

Internalization in Specific Contexts

Romantic Relationships

In healthy romantic relationships, internalization can strengthen bonds through shared values or habits. However, it's crucial to:

- o Maintain individuality by pursuing personal interests alongside shared ones.
- o Avoid codependency by ensuring your self-worth isn't tied to your partner's approval.
- o Example: Adopting a partner's habit of open communication can improve the relationship, but sacrificing your hobbies to mirror theirs may erode your identity.

Social and Cultural Contexts

Society and culture heavily influence internalization, often unconsciously. To navigate this:

- o Challenge stereotypes or norms that conflict with your values, such as rigid gender roles or consumerism.
- o Embrace cultural values that resonate, like community or respect, while rejecting those that feel oppressive.
- o Example: Internalizing a cultural emphasis on family can be enriching, but rejecting pressure to conform to outdated traditions preserves authenticity.

Professional Settings

In the workplace, internalization of professional norms (e.g., punctuality, collaboration) can drive success, but:

- o Avoid over-identifying with corporate culture at the expense of personal values.

- Seek workplaces that align with your ethics to ensure internalized behaviors feel authentic.
- Example: Adopting a company's focus on innovation can inspire creativity, but internalizing a toxic "hustle culture" may lead to burnout.

Long-Term Benefits of Healthy Internalization

A healthy relationship with internalization fosters:

- **Authenticity**: You live in alignment with your true self, integrating external influences that enhance rather than suppress your identity.
- **Resilience**: By critically choosing what to internalize, you build confidence to navigate societal pressures or challenging relationships.
- **Stronger Connections**: Internalizing positive traits from others (e.g., empathy, discipline) strengthens relationships while maintaining mutual respect.
- **Personal Growth**: You evolve by adopting values and behaviors that align with your goals, leading to a more fulfilling life.

Creating a healthy relationship with internalization requires balancing external influences with self-awareness, critical thinking, and authenticity. By reflecting on your values, setting boundaries, and choosing growth-oriented relationships, you can internalize beliefs and behaviors that enhance your well-being and relationships. Regularly reassess what you've internalized to ensure it serves your authentic self, and seek support from trusted individuals or professionals if you struggle to maintain this balance. With intentional practice, internalization becomes a tool for personal growth rather than a source of conflict or conformity.

Chapter 33: Integrating Zen principles into one's Christian walk

I included this chapter as a Christian for several reasons. First and foremost, I maintain quite simply that Christianity and Zen Buddhism are not at all antithetical. That is to say, one can be a Christian and hold Zen practices to be very insightful and beneficial that do not directly oppose the teachings of Christ and His Church.

Mr. Ravi Zacharias unravels this most succinctly. Mr. Zacharias, an expert on comparative religions, and a prominent Christian apologist, argued that Christianity and Zen Buddhism are not competing religions on equal footing because only Christianity provides coherent and comprehensive answers to what he considered the four fundamental questions of life: origin, meaning, morality, and destiny.

∞ **Christianity's Answers to the Four Existential Questions:**

1. *Origin:* Zacharias asserted that Christianity offers a clear explanation of human existence through a purposeful intelligent design by a personal God, grounding the universe in a divine act of creation.
2. *Meaning:* He believed Christianity provides a robust framework for life's purpose, rooted in a relationship with God and the teachings of Jesus Christ, offering a transcendent source of significance.
3. *Morality:* Christianity, according to Zacharias, establishes an objective moral framework based on God's nature, providing a consistent standard for right and wrong.
4. *Destiny:* He emphasized Christianity's promise of eternal life through salvation in Jesus Christ, addressing humanity's ultimate fate with hope and assurance.

Zen Buddhism's Perspective: Zacharias contrasted this with Zen Buddhism, which he described as nontheistic and focused on personal enlightenment through meditation and detachment. He argued that Zen Buddhism lacks a definitive explanation for:

- *Origin:* It does not posit a purposeful intelligent design, often viewing existence as cyclical or illusory.
- *Meaning:* Its emphasis on transcending desire and achieving nirvana lacks a relational or ultimate purpose tied to a divine being.
- *Morality:* Zacharias saw its moral framework as subjective, based on individual enlightenment rather than an objective standard.

- *Destiny:* Zen Buddhism's concept of nirvana, a state of liberation from suffering, was seen as less concrete or personal compared to Christianity's promise of eternal life.

Non-Competing Nature: Zacharias did not view Christianity and Zen Buddhism as competing in the sense of offering equally valid paths to truth. He argued that Zen Buddhism's nontheistic and relativistic framework fails to provide coherent answers to the four questions, as its answers are often vague or self-referential. In contrast, he believed Christianity's Judeo-Christian worldview offers a unified, logical, and experientially satisfying response that aligns with human longing for transcendence and absolute truth.

For example, in his book *The Lotus and the Cross*, Zacharias staged a dialogue between Jesus and Buddha to highlight the irreconcilable differences between their teachings, emphasizing Christianity's unique claim to exclusivity through Christ's divinity.

While Zacharias respected Zen Buddhism's emphasis on introspection, he maintained that its rejection of a personal God and absolute truth makes it philosophically and practically inadequate compared to Christianity. He argued that all religions, including Zen Buddhism, are exclusivistic in some form, but Christianity's exclusivity is grounded in a coherent worldview that withstands scrutiny. Critics might note that Zacharias's view assumes the necessity of a theistic framework, potentially undervaluing Zen Buddhism's experiential approach to addressing suffering and existence.

Zacharias saw Christianity as uniquely capable of answering life's four mysteries with coherence and truth, positioning it not as a competitor to Zen Buddhism but as a fundamentally distinct and superior worldview.

This account explores Scriptures, and the life, teachings, and significance of Jesus Christ as presented in the Bible, with a focus on the fallen nature of humanity and the saving grace offered through Christ. Drawing from the canonical Gospels (Matthew, Mark, Luke, and John) and other New Testament writings, this account integrates key events, teachings, and theological themes, supported by scripture citations. Ravi's narrative is structured chronologically, covering Christ's birth, ministry, death, resurrection, and enduring impact, while emphasizing the biblical perspective on human sinfulness and redemption.

I want to include a note on blasphemy here. I am well aware as John Calvin who used to preach the Holy Scripture from start to finish throughout the year, starting with Genesis on the first day of the year and finishing with Revelation. He was known to say, "The preacher is to invent nothing of his own but declare only what has been revealed and recorded in Holy Scripture," and that if preaching strayed for even a few moments without referring to the Holy text that the possibility of blasphemy increases immensely. I include this section for non-Christians so that they may be inspired to explore the Word and for Christians who may struggle with deeper reflection and meaning of the Bible to perhaps help break through a block that is there.

∞ The Fallen Nature of Man

The Bible teaches that humanity is inherently sinful, a condition stemming from the disobedience of Adam and Eve in the Garden of Eden. This original sin corrupted human nature, separating humanity from God's holiness. As Romans 3:23 states, *"For all have sinned and fall short of the glory of God." This fallen state manifests in humanity's propensity to prioritize self-interest over God's will, leading to moral and spiritual brokenness* (Genesis 3:6-7; Romans 5:12).

The consequences of this fall are profound: spiritual death, alienation from God, and an inability to achieve righteousness through human effort alone (Ephesians 2:1-3). The Old Testament Law, given through Moses, revealed God's standards but also highlighted humanity's inability to fulfill them perfectly (Galatians 3:24). This sets the stage for the necessity of a savior, who would bridge the gap between a holy God and sinful humanity.

∞ Key Teachings

Jesus' teachings, often delivered through parables, emphasized the Kingdom of God, repentance, faith, and love. The Sermon on the Mount (Matthew 5-7) encapsulates many of His core teachings:

- The Beatitudes: Jesus outlined the characteristics of those blessed in God's Kingdom, such as the meek, the merciful, and the peacemakers (Matthew 5:3-12). These teachings inverted worldly values, prioritizing spiritual humility over pride.
- Love and Forgiveness: Jesus taught radical love, instructing His followers to "love your enemies and pray for those who persecute you" (Matthew 5:44). He emphasized forgiveness, as seen in the Lord's Prayer: "Forgive us our debts, as we also have forgiven our debtors" (Matthew 6:12).
- The Golden Rule: He summarized ethical living in Matthew 7:12: "So whatever you wish that others would do to you, do also to them, for this is the Law and the Prophets."
- Repentance and Faith: Jesus called for repentance, declaring, "The time is fulfilled, and the kingdom of God is at hand; repent and believe in the gospel" (Mark 1:15). Faith in God was central to His message, as seen in His interactions with individuals like the centurion (Matthew 8:5-13).

Jesus also taught through parables, such as the Parable of the Prodigal Son (Luke 15:11-32), which illustrates God's grace toward repentant sinners, and the Parable of the Good Samaritan (Luke 10:25-37), which redefines neighborly love across social boundaries.

∞ Theological Significance of Christ's Saving Grace

The New Testament emphasizes that salvation is by grace through faith in Christ alone, not through human works. Ephesians 2:8-9 states, "For by grace you have been saved through faith. And this is not your own doing; it is the gift of God, not a result of works, so that no one may boast." Jesus' sacrifice provides justification, where sinners are declared righteous before God (Romans 5:1), and sanctification, a process of becoming more like Christ (1 Thessalonians 5:23).

The fallen nature of humanity, marked by sin and rebellion, finds its remedy in Christ's redemptive work. As Romans 5:19 explains, "For as by the one man's disobedience the many were made sinners, so by the one man's obedience the many will be made righteous." Believers are called to repent, trust in Christ, and live transformed lives, empowered by the Holy Spirit (Acts 2:38; Galatians 5:22-23).

∞ Christ's Teachings on Living a Godly Life

Jesus' teachings provide a blueprint for Christian living, addressing the heart's condition and practical ethics:

- *Faith and Trust in God:* Jesus emphasized reliance on God, teaching His disciples to seek God's kingdom first (Matthew 6:33) and to trust in God's provision (Matthew 6:25-34).
- *Humility and Service:* He modeled servant leadership, washing His disciples' feet and saying, "Whoever would be great among you must be your servant" (John 13:14-15; Matthew 20:26).
- *Prayer and Communion with God:* Jesus frequently prayed and taught His disciples to do the same, as seen in the Lord's Prayer (Matthew 6:9-13).
- *Endurance in Persecution:* He prepared His followers for opposition, saying, "If the world hates you, know that it has hated me before it hated you" (John 15:18).

∞ Integrating Zen principles of mindfulness into a Christian walk

Integrating Zen principles of mindfulness into a Christian walk can enhance spiritual growth by fostering a deeper awareness of God's presence, cultivating inner peace, and aligning daily actions with Christ's teachings. While Zen Buddhism and Christianity are distinct traditions with different theological foundations, the practice of mindfulness—rooted in focused attention, intentionality, and presence—can complement Christian disciplines like prayer, meditation, and service. Below, I explore how Zen-inspired mindfulness can be practically applied to a Christian's daily life, supported by biblical principles and scripture citations, while maintaining fidelity to Christian theology.

∞ **Understanding Mindfulness in a Christian Context**

Zen mindfulness emphasizes living fully in the present moment, observing thoughts and actions without judgment, and cultivating a state of attentive awareness. For Christians, this can be understood as aligning one's heart and mind with God's will, being fully present to His presence, and living intentionally in response to His grace. Psalm 46:10, "Be still, and know that I am God," resonates with this call to quiet the mind and focus on God's sovereignty. Similarly, Jesus' teaching to "seek first the kingdom of God and his righteousness" (Matthew 6:33) encourages a focused, intentional approach to life.

Mindfulness, in this context, is not about emptying the mind or detaching from reality, as some Zen practices might emphasize, but about filling the mind with God's truth and being attentive to His guidance. It involves cultivating a heart attuned to the Holy Spirit, enabling Christians to live out their faith with greater clarity and purpose.

∞ **Six Practical Applications of Mindfulness in a Christian Walk**

1. Mindful Prayer and Meditation

Zen mindfulness encourages sustained attention to the present moment, which can deepen Christian practices of prayer and meditation on Scripture. By approaching prayer with full presence, Christians can move beyond rote recitation to a heartfelt communion with God.

- o *Application:* Set aside dedicated time each day for prayer, focusing on God's presence rather than rushing through words. For example, practice lectio divina, a mindful reading of Scripture where you slowly read a passage (e.g., Psalm 23), reflect on its meaning, pray in response, and rest in God's presence. As you read, notice each word and let it resonate, as Colossians 3:16 urges, *"Let the word of Christ dwell in you richly."*
- o *Daily Practice:* Begin your morning with a short prayer, such as, *"Lord, help me to be present with You today"* (inspired by Psalm 139:23-24). Throughout the day, pause briefly before prayers to center your thoughts, breathing deeply and focusing on God's nearness.
- o *Benefit:* This fosters a deeper connection with God, reducing distractions and aligning with Jesus' call to *"pray without ceasing"* (1 Thessalonians 5:17).

2. Living Intentionally in the Present

- o *Zen teaches non-attachment:* to past regrets or future anxieties, which echoes Jesus' words in Matthew 6:34: *"Do not be anxious about tomorrow, for tomorrow will be anxious for itself. Sufficient for the day is its own trouble.*" Mindfulness helps Christians focus on the present moment as a gift from God, trusting Him for the future. Also the Bible warns of earthly attachments.

- ○ *Application:* Practice single-tasking in daily activities, such as eating, working, or spending time with family, giving full attention to the task at hand. For example, when eating, thank God for His provision (Psalm 145:15-16) and savor the meal without distractions like phones or multitasking.
- ○ *Daily Practice:* At the start of each day, commit your plans to God (Proverbs 16:3) and ask for awareness of His presence in routine moments. If anxieties arise, pause, breathe, and recall Philippians 4:6-7: "*Do not be anxious about anything, but in everything by prayer and supplication with thanksgiving let your requests be made known to God.*"
- ○ *Benefit:* This reduces worry, deepens gratitude, and helps Christians live out their faith moment by moment, trusting God's provision.

3. Cultivating Compassion and Love

Zen mindfulness emphasizes compassion and non-judgmental awareness, which aligns with Christ's command to "love your neighbor as yourself" (Mark 12:31). By being mindful of others' needs and emotions, Christians can embody Christ's love more fully.

- ○ *Application:* Practice mindful listening in conversations, giving full attention to others without planning your response or judging their words. Reflect on Jesus' example of compassion, such as His interaction with the woman at the well (John 4:7-26), where He listened and responded with grace.
- ○ *Daily Practice:* Before interacting with others, pray for a heart of love and patience (1 Corinthians 13:4-7). If conflicts arise, pause to breathe and ask, "How can I reflect Christ's love here?" This mirrors the Good Samaritan's mindful care for a stranger (Luke 10:25-37).
- ○ *Benefit:* Mindful compassion strengthens relationships and witnesses to Christ's transformative love, fulfilling Galatians 5:22-23's call to bear the fruit of the Spirit.

4. Awareness of Sin and Repentance

Zen mindfulness involves observing one's thoughts and actions without immediate reaction, which can help Christians recognize sinful patterns and turn to God in repentance. Romans 12:2 calls believers to "be transformed by the renewal of your mind," which mindfulness can facilitate by fostering self-awareness.

o *Application:* Set aside time for self-examination, reflecting on your thoughts and actions in light of God's Word. For example, use Psalm 51:10, *"Create in me a clean heart, O God,"* as a prayer to guide mindful reflection on areas needing repentance.

o *Daily Practice:* At the end of each day, practice a brief examen, a Christian adaptation of mindfulness where you review your day, noting moments of alignment with or deviation from God's will. Confess sins and seek God's forgiveness, trusting in 1 John 1:9: *"If we confess our sins, he is faithful and just to forgive us our sins."*

o *Benefit:* This cultivates humility and reliance on God's grace, addressing the fallen nature of humanity through ongoing repentance and renewal.

5. Mindful Service and Work

Zen emphasizes doing tasks with full attention and intention, which can enhance a Christian's approach to work and service as acts of worship. Colossians 3:23-24 instructs, "Whatever you do, work heartily, as for the Lord and not for men."

o *Application:* Approach daily tasks—whether mundane chores or professional duties—with mindfulness, dedicating them to God. For example, when washing dishes or completing a work project, focus on the task and pray, *"Lord, I offer this to You"* (1 Corinthians 10:31).

o *Daily Practice:* Begin work with a short prayer for focus and excellence, and take brief pauses during tasks to re-center your purpose on glorifying God. If distractions arise, gently redirect your attention to the task and God's presence.

o *Benefit:* This transforms routine activities into spiritual disciplines, fostering a sense of purpose and countering the fallen tendency toward laziness or self-centeredness.

6. Sabbath Rest and Contemplation

Zen's emphasis on stillness and simplicity can enhance the Christian practice of Sabbath rest, a time to cease striving and trust God. Exodus 20:8-11 commands keeping the Sabbath holy, and mindfulness can help Christians enter this rest with intentionality.

o *Application:* Dedicate a day or time each week for restful contemplation, free from distractions. Use this time to reflect on God's goodness, read Scripture, or simply sit in His presence, as Psalm 23:1-3 describes God leading us to "green pastures" and "still waters."

o *Daily Practice:* During Sabbath moments, practice mindful breathing, inhaling with a prayer like "Lord, You are my peace" and exhaling distractions. Avoid digital devices to focus on God's creation and Word.

- *Benefit:* This restores the soul, combats the fallen nature's drive for constant busyness, and deepens trust in God's provision.

∞ Theological Considerations

While Zen mindfulness offers practical tools, Christians must anchor these practices in biblical truth to avoid syncretism. Zen's goal of detachment or enlightenment differs from Christianity's aim of communion with God and transformation through Christ. Mindfulness should not lead to self-reliance but to dependence on the Holy Spirit, who empowers believers to live out their faith (Galatians 5:16). Additionally, Christians should guard against emptying the mind without filling it with God's Word, as Matthew 12:43-45 warns of the dangers of an "empty house."

By grounding mindfulness in Scripture, Christians can use it to enhance their walk, focusing on God's glory rather than self. For example, Philippians 4:8 encourages focusing on *"whatever is true, noble, right, pure, lovely, admirable,"* aligning mindful thought with godly virtues.

Applying Zen-inspired mindfulness to a Christian walk involves practicing intentional presence, prayer, and compassion, all rooted in biblical principles. By being fully present in prayer, work, relationships, and rest, Christians can deepen their awareness of God's grace, resist the fallen nature's pull toward distraction or sin, and live out Christ's teachings with greater fidelity. As Psalm 119:15 says, "I will meditate on your precepts and fix my eyes on your ways." Mindfulness, when centered on Christ, becomes a powerful tool for spiritual growth, enabling believers to walk humbly, love deeply, and trust fully in God's saving grace through Jesus.

This approach not only enhances personal devotion but also strengthens the Christian witness in a world craving peace and purpose. By integrating mindfulness with faith, Christians can embody Jesus' call to "abide in me, and I in you" (John 15:4), living each moment for His glory.

And the life of Christ and His ministry is full of Zen dualities:

- † Many called him "Teacher" though He had no formal degree.
- † Many called Him "Healer" though he had no medical background.
- † He had no army, but Kings feared Him.
- † He's never lived in a Castle, though many call Him "Lord"
- † He's conquered no nations, but many call Him "King"
- † His kingdom is not of this world, but yet He lives today in the hearts of believers
- † He offers no material wealth, yet He is a treasure to millions
- † He offers no earthly power, but has brought strength to millions

✝ He's never left any written record, yet countless volumes have been written about Him

✝ It is in His suffering that we find Salvation

∞ The Trinity

The Christian doctrine of the Trinity—Father, Son, and Holy Spirit as three distinct persons in one indivisible God—embodies a profound paradox that echoes the enigmatic koans of Zen Buddhism. At its core, the Trinity defies linear logic, presenting a unity that transcends duality without dissolving into mere oneness or multiplicity. Just as Zen invites practitioners to confront the limitations of rational thought through riddles that point beyond words, the Trinity challenges believers to embrace a mystery where distinction and unity coexist eternally. This zen-like quality fosters a contemplative surrender, where the mind's grasp yields to an intuitive apprehension of divine reality, much like the sudden enlightenment (satori) in Zen that arises from grappling with the ungraspable.

In this trinitarian framework, the interplay of persons reflects a dynamic harmony akin to Zen's emphasis on interdependence and emptiness (sunyata). The Father begets the Son, and the Spirit proceeds from both, forming a relational essence that mirrors the Zen insight into the interconnectedness of all phenomena, where individual forms arise from and return to a boundless whole. This invites a meditative awareness, encouraging Christians to experience God's presence not as a static concept but as a living flow, transcending ego-bound perceptions. Thus, the Trinity's zen-like properties cultivate a path of humble wonder, dissolving rigid boundaries between creator and creation in a dance of eternal becoming.

∞ The Holy Spirit

The Christian concept of the Holy Spirit embodies zen-like qualities through its ethereal, pervasive presence that transcends physical form, much like the subtle essence of enlightenment in Zen Buddhism. Described in scripture as a wind or breath (pneuma in Greek, ruach in Hebrew), the Holy Spirit moves unpredictably and invisibly, guiding believers toward truth and inner peace without coercion or overt intervention. This mirrors Zen's emphasis on mindfulness and the flow of existence, where the Spirit fosters a state of spiritual awakening akin to satori— sudden insight into divine reality. By indwelling within individuals, it cultivates a harmonious unity with God and creation, promoting simplicity, detachment from worldly distractions, and a profound sense of interconnectedness that echoes the Zen pursuit of oneness with the universe.

Furthermore, the Holy Spirit's role as comforter and advocate parallels Zen's meditative practices that quiet the mind and alleviate suffering through presence and acceptance. It empowers transformation not through rigid doctrines but via gentle conviction and inspiration, resembling wu wei, or effortless action, where divine will unfolds naturally in the believer's life. This leads to fruits such as love, joy, and self-control, fostering an inner tranquility that aligns with Zen's goal of equanimity amid life's impermanence. Ultimately, the Holy Spirit invites a contemplative surrender, encouraging Christians to "be still and know" God, much like Zen's call to sit in zazen and observe the true nature of being without striving.

Chapter 34: Blossoms in the Void - Solitude Every Day

Where others see emptiness, you now see potential. Solitude, like a silent garden, awaits your mindful tending. May peace, resilience, and the gentle light of Zen guide your path.

May this guide inspire you to step confidently into the quiet corners of life and discover the beauty that emerges in solitude.

A monk asked the master, "In the bustling market, with voices clashing and feet trampling, how can one find solitude?"

The master replied, "See the lotus in the muddy pond. It rises untouched, its roots in the mire, its petals open to the sky. Walk through the crowd as the lotus sits in the water—present, yet apart."

The monk pondered and said, "But the crowd presses close, their words cling like dust. How do I remain untouched?"

The master smiled, "The wind carries a thousand sounds, yet the mountain stands still. Let your heart be the mountain, your breath the wind. Each step is yours alone, though a thousand walk beside you."

The monk sat in the market, eyes soft, breath steady. The crowd roared, yet he heard only silence.

In a world that thrives on constant connectivity and external stimulation, finding solitude in everyday life is both a challenge and a necessity. This chapter explores practical ways to weave solitude into the fabric of daily routines, drawing on the principles and practices outlined in previous chapters. By embracing solitude intentionally, we cultivate inner peace, self-awareness, and a deeper connection to our authentic selves, even amidst the demands of modern life.

Solitude as a Daily Practice

Solitude is not reserved for retreats or moments of extreme isolation; it can be integrated into the rhythm of everyday life. Building on the foundations of mindfulness (Chapter 8), minimalism (Chapter 25), and intentional living (Chapter 15), solitude becomes a deliberate act of carving out space for reflection and presence. Start with small, manageable moments—five minutes of silent morning tea, a brief walk without devices, or a pause to breathe deeply during a busy day. These micro-moments of solitude align with the practice of zazen (Chapter 18) and foster stillness amid chaos.

To make solitude a habit, consider *The Role of Ritual* (Chapter 23) and *The 5 AM Club* (Chapter 24) as a framework. Rising early offers a quiet window before the world awakens, allowing time for meditation, journaling, or simply sitting with one's thoughts. This aligns with Emerson's principle of self-reliance (Chapter 14), encouraging individuals to trust their inner voice. For those unable to commit to early mornings, solitude can be found in the margins of the day—during a commute, a lunch break, or before bed.

Creating Space for Solitude

Physical and mental space are essential for solitude. Drawing from minimalism (Chapter 10), declutter your environment to reduce distractions. A simple, tidy space invites calm and focus. Similarly, establishing technological boundaries (Chapter 24) is critical. Set specific times to unplug from devices, perhaps designating evenings as screen-free or using apps to limit notifications. This digital detox creates room for introspection and aligns with the practice of reconnecting with nature (Chapter 20), where a walk in a park or a moment gazing at the sky can restore inner quiet.

Rituals (Chapter 22) also anchor solitude in daily life. A morning ritual of lighting a candle and sitting in silence, or an evening practice of writing three things you're grateful for, can ground you in the present. These rituals don't require hours; even a few minutes can shift your mindset toward intentional solitude.

Meditation and Breathing

Meditation (zazen) and breathing (breath-work) are vital to exploration and advancement in this development of mindfulness, self-control, inner knowledge, and wisdom. So much so, I've dedicated 5 chapters to it (Chapters 18, 19, 20, 21, and 22).

Balancing Solitude and Connection

One of the greatest challenges of solitude is maintaining relationships while honoring personal space (Chapter 28). Communicate your need for solitude to loved ones, framing it as a practice that enhances your presence in relationships rather than a withdrawal. For example, schedule "solitude hours" where you retreat to read, meditate, or create, and balance this with quality time spent with others. This harmony reflects the Zen principle of balance (Chapter 7), ensuring solitude complements rather than competes with connection.

In the workplace, solitude can be trickier but not impossible. Use breaks to step away from colleagues for a brief mindfulness exercise or a quiet moment in a stairwell. These pauses recharge your focus and align with fostering creativity in quiet spaces (Chapter 23), as solitude often sparks innovative ideas.

Overcoming Resistance to Solitude

Resistance to solitude often stems from discomfort with emotional vulnerability (Chapter 6) or fear of facing inner shadows (Chapter 8). To ease this, practice self-compassion (Chapter 5) by approaching solitude with curiosity rather than judgment. If sitting alone feels daunting, start with guided meditations (Chapter 18) or journaling prompts to gently explore your thoughts. Non-attachment (Chapter 10) also helps by releasing expectations of what solitude "should" feel like, allowing you to embrace it as it unfolds.

In the modern world (Chapter 29), external noise can drown out inner peace. Counter this by cultivating a healthy relationship with internalization (Chapter 31). Instead of viewing solitude as isolation, see it as an opportunity to reconnect with your core values and purpose. This shift transforms solitude into a source of strength, as seen in the lives of historical figures like Thoreau or Merton and others (Chapter 31), who found wisdom in quiet retreat.

Solitude in Action: Practical Examples

To illustrate, consider a typical day: Rise at 5 am (Chapter 24). Begin with a 10-minute meditation upon waking, focusing on breath (Chapter 19). During your commute, forgo podcasts or social media for silent observation of your surroundings. At lunch, step outside for a brief walk, noticing the sounds and sensations of nature. In the evening, dedicate 15 minutes to journaling or sketching, reflecting on your day without judgment. These small acts, woven into daily life, create a tapestry of solitude that nurtures the soul.

For those with demanding schedules, adaptability is key. If a full meditation session isn't feasible, practice a single mindful breath between meetings. If a nature walk isn't possible, gaze out a window and imagine the wind on your face. These micro-practices, rooted in Zen principles (Chapter 1), make solitude accessible to all.

Solitude in everyday life is not about escaping the world but about finding space within it to reconnect with yourself. By integrating the practices of mindfulness, minimalism, and intentional living, you can cultivate moments of stillness that enrich your days. Like the blossoms in the void (Chapter 33), solitude blooms in the quiet spaces of the heart, offering clarity, creativity, and peace. As you move forward, let solitude be your companion, a gentle reminder that in stillness, you are never truly alone.

Amid the clamor of the marketplace, a monk sat still. A merchant asked, "How do you find peace here?"

The monk smiled, "The noise is outside; solitude is within."

Beginning.

Now.

About the Author

Carl Conti is a trailblazing embedded computer systems designer whose career has shaped cutting-edge technology across defense, academia, robotics and transportation. In the 1980s, as a key engineer at McDonnell Douglas Astronautics, he pioneered a Motorola 68000 single-board computer for a critical defense contract—outpacing Apple's own innovations. His expertise then fueled groundbreaking academic projects at MIT's Draper Lab and Carnegie-Mellon's Field Robotics Center, where he designed five essential boards for the Dante II robot, enabling its historic exploration of Antarctica's Mt. Erebus alongside NASA and JPL. Transitioning to rail transit, Conti engineered fail-safe, mission-critical systems, later founding SIL4 Systems Inc. and authoring a definitive book on safety-critical design. A global perspective, honed through extensive travels in China and Japan in his 20s, deepened his fascination with Zen Buddhism, infusing his work with disciplined creativity and profound insight.

www.ingramcontent.com/pod-product-compliance
Lightning Source LLC
Chambersburg PA
CBHW041110120626

46547CB00019B/2655